Religion on the Edge

De-Centering and Re-Centering the Sociology of Religion

EDITED BY
COURTNEY BENDER, WENDY CADGE,
PEGGY LEVITT, AND DAVID SMILDE

OXFORD
UNIVERSITY PRESS

OXFORD
UNIVERSITY PRESS

Oxford University Press is a department of the University of Oxford.
It furthers the University's objective of excellence in research, scholarship,
and education by publishing worldwide.

Oxford   New York
Auckland   Cape Town   Dar es Salaam   Hong Kong   Karachi
Kuala Lumpur   Madrid   Melbourne   Mexico City   Nairobi
New Delhi   Shanghai   Taipei   Toronto

With offices in
Argentina   Austria   Brazil   Chile   Czech Republic   France   Greece
Guatemala   Hungary   Italy   Japan   Poland   Portugal   Singapore
South Korea   Switzerland   Thailand   Turkey   Ukraine   Vietnam

Oxford is a registered trademark of Oxford University Press
in the UK and certain other countries.

Published in the United States of America by
Oxford University Press
198 Madison Avenue, New York, NY 10016

Library of Congress Cataloging-in-Publication Data
Religion on the edge : de-centering and re-centering the sociology of religion / edited by
Courtney Bender ... [et al.].
p. cm.
(pbk. : alk. paper)—ISBN 978-0-19-993864-3 (hardcover : alk. paper)—
ISBN 978-0-19-993862-9
1. Religion and sociology.   I. Bender, Courtney.
BL60.R36 2013
306.6—dc23
2012012103

ISBN 978-0-19-993862-9
ISBN 978-0-19-993864-3

1 3 5 7 9 8 6 4 2
Printed in the United States of America
on acid-free paper

Religion on the Edge

CONTENTS

ACKNOWLEDGMENTS

The idea for this volume was hatched in a series of conversations between the editors, over email, in the gardens of the Museum of Modern Art during the 2007 meetings of the American Sociological Association, and over dinners and coffees at Princeton, Columbia, and Brandeis. Conversations on their own rarely result in edited volumes, however, and with that in mind we are happy to thank the many institutions and individuals whose investments of intellect, time, and money helped make this book—and the conversations that have circulated around it—take shape in this form.

Our primary and enduring thanks go to Robert Wuthnow and the Princeton University Center for the Study of Religion, where, in October 2008, over twenty-five early-career sociologists gathered to discuss the issues at the core of this volume. Our meeting did not have a volume as a goal (indeed, we were eager to engage in a range of discussions that might prompt a variety of different goals—both textual and social, scholarly and institutional). Likewise, it did not include at the time any who had achieved the ranks of full professor: it was a lively meeting of younger scholars, and we were quite grateful to Bob Wuthnow for his trust and enthusiasm in making it possible.

The participants at the Princeton meeting included, in addition to the volume's contributors, Richard Wood, Nazli Kibria, Prema Kurien, Elaine Howard Ecklund, Nathan Wright, Rachel Rinaldo, Alison Denton Jones, John Evans, Ruth Braunstein, Phillip Connor, Eric B. Johnson, Alicia Juskewycz, Carol Ann MacGregor, Rebekah Massengill, Cecilia Menjívar, Steve Offutt, Jen'nan Ghazal Read, Amy Reynolds, Allison Youatt Schnable, and Liza Steele. Together, our conversations and arguments about the position of the study of religion within sociology were brisk and lively. We gratefully acknowledge each of the participants at this conference for their strong investment in the issues that we brought collectively to the table and for the wealth of experiences and intellectual insights they shared. We also gratefully acknowledge their enthusiasm and support for a variety of projects including, as it turns out, this edited volume—one of several tangible outcomes of that weekend's meetings. In addition to Bob Wuthnow's making possible this gathering, Center for the Study of Religion staff Jennifer Legath, Anita Kline, and Barbara Bermel tracked numerous details and made everything go smoothly.

As we began to consider what a volume would look like, Mark Chaves, then president of the Society for the Scientific Study of Religion, generously made space in the SSSR's annual program for an author's workshop and conference, where several of the contributors of this volume were joined by Michael Young to present drafts of chapters in progress. Mark's support furthered progress on the volume.

Simultaneously, the Social Science Research Council (SSRC) supported David Smilde and Matthew May's research into recent developments in the literature in the sociology of religion, which resulted in the 2010 working paper cited in this volume, and which helped us collectively to gain a stronger sense of where our concerns about the trajectories of the disciplines were correct or misguided—and which raised some surprising new issues for us to consider. Jonathan VanAntwerpen at the SSRC deserves particular thanks for supporting this initiative and for soliciting a range of excellent interlocutors in an online discussion of Smilde and May's research on *The Immanent Frame* (blogs. ssrc.org/tif). Generous and pointed interchanges on The Immanent Frame by John Evans, Penny Edgell, Michelle Dillon, John Torpey, Bryan S. Turner, Slavica Jakelic, Rhys Williams, Stephen Poulson, Grace Yukich, and Ruth Braunstein expanded the conversations of our conference and took them in new directions—while making it clear to us that there really are stakes in this game that we play. We likewise are deeply grateful for the invitation by Marie Cornwall, editor of the *Journal for the Scientific Study of Religion*, for the invitation to craft an article for the fiftieth-anniversary issue of the journal, and to the reviewers who offered generous comments.

As the idea of the volume turned into an actual manuscript, we were grateful for the guiding eye and enthusiasm of Theo Calderara at Oxford University Press, and to the intelligent and critical advice of several anonymous reviewers, whose perspicuous comments strengthened the volume. We thank Casey Clevenger, PhD candidate in Sociology at Brandeis University, for her assistance with manuscript preparation, and the Theodore and Jane Norman Fund for Faculty Research and Creative Projects for support of her work. We thank Matthew May for compiling the index.

This book was a fully collaborative effort and we have ordered our names alphabetically to indicate equal authorship.

ABOUT THE CONTRIBUTORS

Ateş Altınordu is an Assistant Professor in the Faculty of Arts and Social Sciences at Sabancı University, Istanbul. He received his PhD in Sociology from Yale University in May 2010. Altınordu's work focuses on religious politics, secularism, and political parties. His doctoral dissertation investigated the rise and political incorporation of religious parties, based on a comparative analysis of German political Catholicism (1848–1914) and Turkish political Islam (1970–2008). Altınordu's recent publications include "After Secularization?" (with Philip S. Gorski, *Annual Review of Sociology*, 2008) and "The Politicization of Religion: Political Catholicism and Political Islam in Comparative Perspective" (*Politics and Society*, 2010).

Courtney Bender, Associate Professor of Religion at Columbia University, is author of *Heaven's Kitchen: Living Religion at God's Love We Deliver* and *The New Metaphysicals: Spirituality and the American Religious Imagination*, and coeditor of *After Pluralism: Reimagining Models of Interreligious Engagement* (with Pamela Klassen) and *What Matters? Ethnographies of Value in a Not So Secular Age* (with Ann Taves). She currently chairs the Social Science Research Council's program on New Directions in the Study of Prayer.

Wendy Cadge is an Associate Professor of Sociology at Brandeis University. She teaches and writes about religion in the contemporary United States, especially as related to health care, immigration, and sexuality. She is the author of *Heartwood: The First Generation of Theravada Buddhism in America* (2005) and *Paging God: Religion in the Halls of Medicine* (2012). She has written many articles, including recent ones on intercessory prayer, physicians' experiences of religion and spirituality, hospital chaplains, and the prayers people write in hospital prayer books.

Kelly H. Chong is Associate Professor of Sociology at the University of Kansas. She is the author of the book *Deliverance and Submission: Evangelical*

Women and the Negotiation of Patriarchy in South Korea (2008), a recipient of two Distinguished Book Awards. She is the co-editor of a special issue of *Journal for the Scientific Study of Religion* (2013), "Comparing Religions: Theory and Empirical Analysis." She has also authored numerous journal articles, including "Negotiating Patriarchy: South Korean Evangelical Women and the Politics of Gender" (*Gender & Society*, 2006: Best Research Paper Prizes, Religion and Asian/American Studies Sections, ASA, 2008). She has written a number of book chapters, mostly recently in *Ritual Practice in Charismatic Christianity* (2011). Her current research is on the subject of intermarriage focusing on Asian Americans, and its relation to the construction of Asian American ethnic-racial identities and masculinities/ femininities within the global context.

Jacqueline Maria Hagan is the Robert G. Parr Distinguished Term Professor of Sociology at the University of North Carolina at Chapel Hill. Her central research area is international migration. She is author of *Deciding to be Legal* (1994) and *Migration Miracle* (2008), which has won several distinguished book awards. Her current research project, "Skills of the Unskilled," focuses on the role of skill acquisition and transferability in the economic mobility pathways of Mexican migrants.

Peggy Levitt is a Professor of Sociology at Wellesley College and the Co-Director of the Transnational Studies Initiative at Harvard University, and was recently Visiting International Fellow at the Vrije University in Amsterdam. Her books include *God Needs No Passport: Immigrants and the Changing American Religious Landscape* (2007), *The Transnational Studies Reader* (2007), *The Changing Face of Home: The Transnational Lives of the Second Generation* (2002), and *The Transnational Villagers* (2001). She has also edited special volumes of *International Migration Review, Global Networks, Mobilities,* and the *Journal of Ethnic and Migration Studies*. A film based on her work, *Art Across Borders,* came out in 2009.

Paul Lichterman is Professor of Sociology and Religion at the University of Southern California. A cultural sociologist and ethnographer, he has studied a variety of political and religious associations and is the author of *Elusive Togetherness: Church Groups Trying to Bridge America's Divisions* (2005) and *The Search for Political Community* (1996), and coeditor of *The Civic Life of American Religion* (2009). By asking how people practice active citizenship in an unequal and culturally diverse society, Lichterman's research has led him to study and theorize the public roles of religion. He has won Best Article awards twice from the American Sociological Association's Culture section; his book *Elusive Togetherness* won the Distinguished Book Award from the Society for the Scientific Study of Religion and the Distinguished Scholarship Award from the Pacific Sociological Association.

Dawne Moon is an Assistant Professor of Sociology at Marquette University and was previously an Assistant Professor of Sociology at the University of California, Berkeley. She studies how people define "us" and "them," and the concrete effects of these definitions, in a variety of situations, including Protestant debates about homosexuality (*God, Sex and Politics: Homosexuality and Everyday Theologies*, 2004) and American Jewish disagreements over Middle East politics. She is currently extending her research to Palestinians who have participated in dialogue efforts with Jews, exploring the tensions between identity and material conditions as bases for political organizing.

Michal Pagis is a postdoctoral fellow at the Buber Society of Fellows, the Hebrew University of Jerusalem. She received her PhD (2008) from the Department of Sociology, University of Chicago. Her research utilizes ethnographic methods to shed light on the complex ways social worlds construct and affect selfhood, emotions, and embodied experience. She is currently completing a book, based on three years of ethnographic research, entitled *Reembodying the Self: Vipassana Meditation and the Microsociology of Experience*. Her other projects include an ethnography of the culture of life coaching in Israel, where she studies new merges between emotional life and the economy, and an ethnographic research project that tracks the place of language, objects, and social interaction in constructing experiences of pain. She has published articles on the social dimensions of meditation, on embodied knowledge, and on the role of the body in self-reflexivity.

David Smilde is Associate Professor of Sociology at the University of Georgia, Senior Fellow at the Washington Office on Latin America, and Editor-in-Chief of the journal *Qualitative Sociology*. He is author of *Reason to Believe: Cultural Agency in Latin American Evangelicalism* (2007; winner of the 2008 Book Award of the Sociology of Religion section of the American Sociological Association, and finalist for the American Anthropological Association's Clifford Geertz Book Award in the Anthropology of Religion); "A Qualitative Comparative Analysis of Conversion to Venezuelan Evangelicalism: How Networks Matter" (*American Journal of Sociology*, November 2005); and "Public Rituals and Political Position among Venezuelan Evangelicals" (*Practicing the Faith: Ritual in Charismatic Christianity*, 2011). His recently published edited volume *Venezuela's Bolivarian Democracy: Participation, Politics and Culture under Chávez* (2011) includes a chapter called "Christianity and Politics in Venezuela's Bolivarian Democracy: Catholics, Evangelicals and Political Polarization."

Manuel A. Vásquez is Professor of Religion at the University of Florida, Gainesville. His area of expertise is the intersection of religion, immigration, and globalization in the Americas. Vásquez is the author of *More than Belief: A Materialist Theory of Religion* (2011) and *The Brazilian Popular Church and the*

Crisis of Modernity (1998). He also coauthored *Living "Illegal": The Human Face of Unauthorized Immigration* (2011) and *Globalizing the Sacred: Religion Across the Americas* (2003). In addition, he has coedited a number of volumes, including *A Place to Be: Brazilian, Guatemalan, and Mexican Immigrants in Florida's New Destinations* (2009), *Latin American Religions: Histories and Documents in Context* (2008), and *Immigrant Faiths: Transforming Religious Life in America* (2005).

Geneviève Zubrzycki is Associate Professor of Sociology at the University of Michigan. She studies national identity and religion, collective memory, and the role of symbols in national mythology. Her first book, *The Crosses of Auschwitz: Nationalism and Religion in Post-Communist Poland* (2006), received several distinctions. She is currently completing a historical ethnography of the genesis and transformation of French Canadian/Québécois national identity from the mid-nineteenth century to the present, paying specific attention to the 1960s' Quiet Revolution but extending her analysis to recent debates on secularism and immigration.

Religion on the Edge

Introduction

Religion on the Edge: De-centering and Re-centering

COURTNEY BENDER, WENDY CADGE, PEGGY LEVITT, AND
DAVID SMILDE

This volume highlights a growing body of research that de-centers taken-for-granted categories in the sociology of religion and, by doing so, re-centers some of its central tenets. This work takes shape along the edges of the sociology of religion, where it intersects with other disciplines, and takes sociologists away from their traditional focus on the US context, Christianity, voluntaristic organizational forms (e.g., the congregation), and investment in presenting religion as a positive force in American life. In contrast, the work this volume highlights draws our attention to religion in non-US contexts, to non-Christian religions, to the variety of settings and structures that produce and shape religion, and critically engages religion's social role and effects. As we argue, these are not just new arenas or approaches. While they do, in fact, expand interest in religion well beyond our sociological subfield and engage in and draw upon interdisciplinary conversations, they do not just leave the center intact. Taken together, the works we highlight critically challenge central ideas and concepts that have long held currency in sociological studies of religion. We intend this volume to further enliven ongoing conversations about the goals of our collective enterprise and the methods and theories best suited for their achievement.

In this spirit, our introduction is structured as a discussion of four of the central empirical and analytic tendencies in the sociology of religion in the US and as an account of what is going on at the edges where this core is being challenged. These four main elements are, to some degree, mutually constitutive. They developed together during years of internal debates about method and theory, and in response and rejoinder to the broader discipline's (often limited and misleading) understanding of religion. They support each other, forming a lingua franca, that shape our shared frameworks for engaging the central questions that concern us.

This introduction highlights the issues we believe to be at stake by posing a set of questions and providing a set of examples where the next generation of research might begin. What is revealed about the self, pluralism, or modernity when we look outside the United States or outside Christian settings where the center and the edges meet? What do we learn about how and where the religious is actually at work and what its role is when we unpack the assumptions about it embedded in these much used categories? What kinds of methods help bring to light these lacunae, and how do the insights they yield help us to re-center the sociology of religion? Discussing and describing the four "edges" in the abstract only allows us to sketch roughly what is at stake in any empirical context. With this in mind, the chapters of this volume present clear and cogent examples of (and, we hope, models for) how to rethink or de-center the central issues in sociological studies of religion and, by so doing, re-center them.

Provincializing the United States

In the last three decades, over 70 percent of all US journal articles on religion have focused on religious dynamics in the United States (Smilde and May 2010). This, in itself, is not necessarily a cause for concern. However, the effects of this parochial focus become problematic when the theorizing that develops out of the American model and context is used to analyze religion in other national contexts or claims to identify general properties of religious identity, beliefs, and processes.

For example, the American measure of religious strength operationalized as regular participation in a voluntary association such as a church service is embedded in surveys of religion around the globe (Norris and Inglehart 2004; Gill 2008). Little attention is paid to other kinds of formal and informal religious participation and identification, or to the widely varying relationships between religion, economics, law, and politics or the impact of gender or life-course stage on religious participation. This universalizing of American norms is striking and disturbing, considering the varying on-the-ground definitions of religious behavior and belonging and the various legal, political, and cultural processes that shape those differences. Universalizing the particular social valences and political norms that shape the United States at the level of method makes meaningful comparative analysis difficult, and similarly masks differences that feed into misunderstandings of religious and non-religious social phenomena.

Work by contributors to this volume make clear just how important it is to consider the ways in which US history and national approaches to ethnic and religious diversity management shape sociological understandings of what religion is (and is not) and where scholars can go to "find" it. They build on work by postcolonial scholars such as Dipesh Chakrabarty (2000) and anthropologist

Talal Asad (1993), who have long called for scholars to "provincialize Europe" not in the sense of shifting their attention from Europe to "elsewhere," but in calling attention to the ways that European and American self-understandings are generalized as universal theories. These universal theories tend to "other" non-Western religious experience and even obfuscate the actual lived practice of religion in the West.

Chakrabarty, in particular, argues that the development of European secular history as a natural, a-theoretical time (without its own history of development) has made all other concepts of history, including religious histories, appear secondary or derivative. Likewise, he continues, the force of secular history continues insofar as it embeds an assumption that "the human is ontologically singular, that gods and spirits are in the end 'social facts,' that the social somehow exists prior to them" (p. 16). As Chakrabarty notes, however (and as the term "provincializing" suggests), the purpose of critique is not to reject "European" theories and replace them with others, or to "fill out" our theoretical armature to include alternative points of view in ways that fail to look the shaping power of these dominant theories in the face. While a proliferation of theoretical views may result, the immediate focus of "provincializing" Europe is to suture the particular historical conditions of its theoretical projects back to those theories, so that scholars will be able to evaluate them in the same ways that they evaluate other nonuniversalizable theories. "European thought," he writes, "is at once both indispensable and inadequate in helping us to think through the experiences of political modernity.... [Hence] provincializing Europe becomes the task of exploring how this thought—which is now everybody's heritage and which affect us all—may be renewed from and for the margins" (p. 16).

Building on our observation of how particular religious concepts are embedded in sociological approaches to religion, we can ask how particular understandings of the relationship between religious strength and religious participation have become "global" or how and when such concepts become meaningful in particular social and political contexts. This will mean, for example, paying careful attention to the ways that the post-Maoist Chinese state's religious policies, which are shaped within a particular international political and diplomatic setting, drive differential rates of growth among different Buddhist and Christian groups (Sun 2010). It could also mean taking a hard look at how "personal empowerment" and the role of religion in achieving it means different things depending on how we understand religious belonging and participation. As Kelly H. Chong (2008) shows, for example, Christian concepts of submission and independence mean particular things for evangelical women living in South Korea. Similarly, David Smilde's (2007) research with evangelicals in Latin America demonstrates the value of understanding men's pragmatic reasons for converting to evangelicalism as a central component of their religious experiences. His work suggests that the kinds of religious practices that get labeled "instrumental" depends on the social and cultural context. It thereby shows the reified distinction between "religious" and "secular" motives that most sociologists of religion work with to be an emic construct disguised as an etic one.

Provincializing the United States, therefore, in no way means abandoning research on American issues or topics. It does mean recognizing the consequences of the uncritical, wholesale export of our theoretical debates and frames. And it means recognizing and appropriating resources produced by researchers working on non-US contexts to grapple with the theoretical challenges we face.

Moreover, it goes one step further by excavating how aspects of "national" religious life are transnational because they evolve in conversation with people and organizations across the world. Religious bodies, objects, and ideas leave from and travel to particular national contexts, but they do so through transnational networks, organizations, or movements. Some circulate within the context of traveling faiths that move to spread the word, while others do so within the context of migrant religions that circulate as people move and are moved, voluntarily or otherwise.[1] Empirically tracing the international, transnational, and "globalizing" processes through which religions circulate, which cross, complicate, and sometimes reassert national boundaries, allows us to ask how and in what ways actors and structures work, in concert or in opposition, to shape the object we call "religion." It reveals the interconnected architectures of religious life and the interconnected arenas where the knowledge is produced that we use to understand them.

Thinking outside the nation-state box allows us to see how things like religious authority, authenticity, and piety get negotiated across borders (see, e.g., Vásquez and Marquardt 2003; Stepick, Rey, and Mahler 2009; Yang and Ebaugh 2001; Ebaugh and Chafetz 2002; Kurien 2007; Hagan 2008; Chen 2008; Levitt 2007, Levitt, Luckens, and Barnett 2011). These dense circuits of power and influence allow some things to travel easily while blocking others and explain why some things are appropriated while others are ignored (Levitt and Merry 2009).

Finally, provincializing the United States brings to light how religious groups are caught up in modern projects where being "religious" or "ethnic" or "national" has a particular valence and power and affects how resources and visibility are allocated. It brings into sharper focus how models of and theories about the religious, as well as regimes of ethnic and religious diversity management, travel and change when religious bodies and organizations move (Levitt 2009). Just as we need better theories and methods to capture religion in motion, so we need to look at how words and concepts, and the power underlying their creation, change as they are imported and exported across space. We hope the contributions to this volume offer some, albeit very partial, response to Talal Asad's perspicuous questions about how "religion" as a developed theoretical concept that moves within and through "history" is powerfully mobilized, or powerfully acted upon, in secular worlds such as our own.

Beyond Christo-Centrism

The processes and questions that arise in studies that provincialize the United States bring to light the frequent sociological gloss wherein "religion" means "Christianity" and, more specifically, a narrow range of Protestant forms. This critique of sociological theorizing of religion is almost as old as the discipline itself. Mary Douglas (1966, in *Purity and Danger*) called attention to the troubling ways in which classical theories of religion tended to cast Catholicism into the realm of "magic" while lifting up Protestantism. Weber's comparative world religions projects (e.g., Weber 1958) developed broad frameworks and methods that sociologists could use to compare religions on their own terms—actively seeking to move "beyond" Christo-centric theories of religion. While his work was ultimately criticized for similar reasons, (see Turner 1994), Weber's broader questions about how to characterize religions comparatively and what epistemological, practical, and psychological frames to use to do so, are not ones that generally concern most American sociologists of religion. Indeed, for most scholars in the field, the default category reflects a broadly shared conception of American religion directly linked to Protestant American theological conceptions.

Religion, in this paradigmatic form, is above all a moral order, a framework that guides action (Parsons and Shils 1951; Berger 1967; Geertz 1973; Smith 2003; Taylor 2007) and consistently influences behavior. Working within the framework of secularization, wherein religion is easily identified (and distinguished from other things—such as politics, economics, etc.), religion emerges as a category that is primarily about belief, identity, and worldview orientations and, likewise, that harbors interests that are always oriented toward otherworldly desires or ends. Beliefs and practices spread through individual conversion; the religious actor with the greatest agency is the entrepreneurial evangelizer (Finke and Stark 1988, 1992).

By now, a trenchant and widely noted critique of the theological underpinnings of this view, and its connection to social scientific theories of secularization, is well known. Talal Asad's (1993) critique of Geertz's "Religion as a Cultural System" is that it is "essentially a view that has a specific Christian history" (p. 42). This history evolves in the context of Enlightenment and post-Enlightenment era jostling between secular and religious authorities competing over the meaning of religion, philosophy, and law and the proper domains of church and state authority. The resulting compromises and compacts affected official public discourse not only in European countries but also in their colonies. But this public discourse about Christianity should not be confused with "Christianity" itself. Indeed, Asad's essay proceeds, in its genealogical and theoretical fashion, by engaging with the very different "Christian" concepts and articulations linking practice, power, and meaning that can be found in the writings of St. Augustine and others. His description of the development of a particular "universal" or generalized view of "religion as meaning" from within a specific historical milieu and his identification of alternative ways of articulating Christian or "religious" understandings of such relationships challenge scholars to consider how our own concepts of the human subject and its links to "religion" are also informed by overarching historical narratives. Asad prompts us not toward critique of existing theories so much as toward raising the question of why "we" view some kinds of "religion" to be normal or natural now, and toward considering the multiple practices and processes, religious or otherwise, that coordinate and create those forms. Further, he urges us to ask why it is that we are, at any moment, preoccupied with some kinds of questions about religion rather than others. Why did midcentury sociologists find issues of anomie and social fragmentation so central? And why are many contemporary theorists today preoccupied by the question of religion's origins or location within the human condition (Smith 2003; Bellah 2011; Taylor 2007; Boyer 2001)?

Asad's critique has not gone unchallenged: in the two decades since he first wrote it numerous scholars including Geertz himself weighed in on whether the criticism is adequate or useful—or if perhaps Asad missed the nuances of Geertz's larger project. While sociologists have been slow to enter the fray, we do note that those who sympathize with the idea of a stable, universal human subject have started to engage with philosophy and psychology to reassert an intellectually grounded argument for this position. At the same time, sociological scholarship on religious practice and embodiment (influenced by Bourdieu 1990) and religious habituation and power continue to challenge what Paul Lichterman (this volume) calls the "default religious actor"—on the grounds that such concepts do not provide useful or sustainable tools for analyzing religion.

The scope of these arguments about what "religion" is and what "religious" actors experience is poised to expand exponentially, as more sociologists study religious phenomena in other parts of the world and become aware of how earlier intellectual struggles about the meaning of "religion" continue to shape our work. In our view, these inquiries expose the limits of earlier portraits of religion that focus only on issues of meaning and belief. Studies of Islam, particularly its multiple interactions with and expressions in "the West," underscore just how much sociological theorizing is based on clear distinctions between the public and private, or the political and the religious, and call into question the usefulness of these distinctions (Asad 2003; Moaddel 2005; Arjomand

1993). Research on Hinduism also drives home the limits of understanding religion as a set of consistent and coherent beliefs or "worldviews" that are articulated in texts or in self-evident theological traditions, thereby challenging another set of ingrained distinctions between orthodox and popular religion, sacred and profane practice, and even religion and culture (Kurien 2007; Levitt 2007). Research on Buddhism calls attention to the central role of networks of reciprocity and commitment over ethical discourse in particular contexts (Silber 1995) and highlights the limits of making clear distinctions between religion and philosophy. Research on Judaism emphasizes the value of understanding spatial and ritual acts as constitutive of, rather than expressive of, religious commitments and political-religious identities (Smith 1982; Goldschmidt 2006). Research into metaphysical religion shows how a loose set of practices and beliefs articulated in multicentered institutional spaces can nevertheless be viable, durable, and widespread (Bender 2010). Recent research on Christianity drives home the internal diversity of practice and meaning within the category of "Christianity"—particularly among Catholics (Carroll 2007; Orsi 2005).

These examples make abundantly clear that identifying religion with meaning systems and issues of ultimate concern severely limits sociological investigation into a wider range of ways that modern people conceptualize, experience, and engage religion. The interest in studying "practice" that has developed in recent years is one way to move forward. But what we propose goes several steps further. We call for a broader reframing in which questions of meaning and belief, worldview, and the like are raised in conversation with other theoretical frameworks.

This dialogue could fruitfully begin by identifying the theological visions of religion that undergird numerous "theories of religion." Moving beyond a particular kind of Christo-centrism does not mean that "different religions are different" and that they must be approached with different tools. Re-essentializing the "differences" in religious "traditions" is the last thing we hope to accomplish. For example, arguing that Judaism is about practice and Christianity is about belief (and so on) reinforces a highly undertheorized and empirically untenable approach. As with deprovincializing the United States, moving beyond Christo-centrism means holding up our own theoretical and epistemological understandings of religion to scrutiny and allowing a broader set of observations, theories, and concepts of religious interaction to reshape the various tools and understandings we bring to a variety of religious phenomena, Christian or otherwise.

Such intellectual moves would also prompt us to closely assess the various paradigmatic patterns that particular religious or social movement groups employ. For example, we might ask: How do contemporary evangelical proselytizing programs compare with the missionizing strategies their own faith traditions used earlier and with those employed by other groups? In what ways do these distinct groups engage or develop approaches to religious meaning or belief, and how do these concepts matter in their abilities to do their work? We might also ask why so many modern "secular" subjects claim to be "spiritual not religious" and inquire into the spaces and sites where such identities are produced (Bender 2010)? How should we describe and talk about the religious lives of people who are not active religious participants? Work in the sociology of culture that treats culture as a context, as discourses and assumptions embedded in institutions, or as repertoires of meanings that are marshaled to deal with specific dilemmas and purposes can help scholars move beyond these Christo-centric assumptions.

Religion Outside of Congregations

Analyzing religion and religious practice outside of congregations (or other voluntary membership organizations) is a third "edge" being reconsidered in recent and ongoing research. Sociologists have largely operated with a view that the congregation is the locus of religious expression and religious authority. It is the linking or mediating structure between religious identity and belief and public and private expressions of religion, as well as the central place of religious learning. This congregational focus is not confined to the voluminous literature of congregational ethnographies and large-scale surveys on congregational life (Chaves 2004, Chaves and Anderson 2008). The centrality of congregations is reasserted in survey research on religion that (as we have noted) emphasizes voluntary participation as a key indicator of religious identity (Finke and Stark 1992), in studies of new immigrant religiosity in the United States that focus directly on congregation building (Ebaugh and Chafetz 2000), in evaluations of the production of religious cultures in the United States (Ammerman 2007), and in studies of American religion's interface with social and political movements (Lichterman 2005 Wood 2002; Stout 2011).

There is, undoubtedly, an enormous amount of religious activity that happens in voluntary religious groups and congregations. However, the overall effect of scholarly efforts to understand congregational life has led, at times, to a view that religious life can be understood through congregations. Given that the American congregational form is primarily and historically a Protestant form that emphasizes voluntary participation and identification, a sociological focus on religion as produced and experienced in congregations further sediments the Christo- and US-centricness of perspectives in the discipline (Cadge 2008).

As with the other edges identified in this volume, we argue for looking "beyond" the congregation as a way to open up sociological approaches to the organization, scope, and development of religion in society. That is, moving beyond the congregation does not mean merely calling attention to noncongregational religious life and production, especially if this means (as it all too frequently has) identifying the kinds of religious actions that take place outside of congregations as "ordinary" or "everyday life" religion that complements, or resists or somehow goes on "despite" or "in addition to," congregational and voluntary organizational religion (see McGuire 2008). While valuable in its own right, we nonetheless note that much literature on the "everyday" has done little to dislodge or unsettle the broadly held view that places congregational life and experience at the center of sociological focus.

Current research that investigates how religious life is enacted in the workplace, in the schoolyard, on the bus, in government, and in health care organizations does more than show that religious people take their religious lives with them into various "secular" places. It shows how religious concepts and ideas are often produced (as well as reproduced) in arenas where individuals with sometimes very similar and sometimes very different religious beliefs and practices cooperate or come into conflict as they try to live together. Wendy Cadge and colleagues (2012, 2009) argue that religion is alive, well, and negotiated in a range of diverse ways in the allegedly secular, scientific halls of research hospitals as evidenced by studies of prayer, pediatric physicians, hospital chaplains, and hospital chapels. Michael Lindsay (2007) has shown how evangelical networks permeate the upper reaches of the American political, educational, and media elite, influencing who works together, on what issues, and in what ways. Other scholars have shown how progressive activists use religious discourses and practices as important resources in their work (Hondageneu-Sotelo 2008; Wood 2002; Hart 2001; Nepstad Erickson 2008; Smith 1996; Lichterman 2005, 2008).

These works, particularly those that engage the issue of religious networks, might identify congregations as one of a number of institutional settings—religious and nonreligious—where religious life is rooted and takes shape (Chaves 2004; Young 2006). Studies that embed congregations within a broader range of social settings and institutions would help contextualize the oft exaggerated role they are expected to play (that is often seen as the "norm"). Sociological research on new immigrant religions reflects this emphasis and point to its limits. While much of the first wave of scholarly work on immigrant religions emphasized the shaping power of congregational "isomorphism" for new immigrants (Warner 1993 Cadge and Ecklund 2007), more recent work, including several chapters in this volume, questions the degree to which isomorphism actually results in the kinds of changes that have been predicted.

Opening up the questions of how and where religion is practiced and produced calls attention, more clearly, to a broader range of social institutions that identify and organize religion in any social or national context. Focusing on the voluntary characteristics of congregations implies that religious groups are likewise able to voluntarily pursue their own ends. But scholarship that embeds congregations in networks or that identifies the range of ways religion is practiced outside them bring into focus the role of courts, legislature, regulatory bodies, and other "secular" institutions in shaping religion (Sullivan 2009; Sullivan, Yelle, and Taussig-Rubbo 2011). Immigration (Jaworsky et al, 2012, diplomacy and refugee resettlement programs (Moore 2011, Nawyn 2006), land use and zoning regulations (McNally 2010), national political conflict (Smilde and Pagan 2011), and national regulatory boards (Cadge 2012) are just some of the arenas where the scope of the religious is negotiated and determined both formally, through related court cases, and informally, in daily interactions with a variety of nonreligious organizations.

Indeed, we call for scholarship to go even further by analyzing the ways that various secular and religious organizations have shaped and continue to shape how researchers and the public at large take "religions" and "groups" as self-evident and naturally existing actors in social life. Most studies of pluralism, for example, take the distinctions between religious traditions for granted and also assume these boundaries are salient for people "on the ground." A promising step forward is research that brings to light the internal incoherence of religious groups, the "unusual" cross-religious coalitions and partnerships that arise between allegedly "strange bedfellows," and how religious boundaries are actually created and deployed. A recently edited volume by Courtney Bender and Pamela Klassen (2010) takes as its point of departure the question of how the boundaries of religions are formed, differently, within various state formations. Viewing even the distinctions among religions as produced through sociologically identifiable interactions and structures (ones that can also be compared across different historical and national contexts) generates a set of scholarly research questions that can produce a stronger conceptualization of religion's place within modern societies.

In short, moving beyond congregations and other self-evidently religious organizations ultimately leads to stronger engagement with the "secular" or "postsecular" turn in recent theorization of religion. These approaches ask not only how the environment outside of religious institutions—both in the context of other secular institutions and outside of organizations altogether—"acts upon" religion or how religion "responds to" it but also how the very object of religion, along with its identities, authorities, powers, and constraints, is shaped through these dynamic interactions. These approaches draw attention, in turn, to how sociological narratives of religious pluralism and the "new religious diversity" are used by various public groups, politicians, commentators, and scholars to focus their anxieties about the future of modern democratic engagements, personal liberties, and minority rights. In other words, we can begin to explore how discussions of pluralism's possibilities and perils are themselves part of strategies for managing and adjudicating religious difference.

Critical Engagements of Religion

The final edge we identify and highlight in the chapters to follow is the one being pushed against by scholars who have moved beyond the dyad of religion as opiate versus religion as empowerment. For many generations, sociologists studying religion faced such questions from their disciplinary peers. As a quintessentially secular discipline—one that articulated its own subject, "modern society," as one characterized as secular—it is not surprising that many sociologists have considered religion (in its modern social forms) to be largely a sideline issue. Religion, as an issue of private life in modernity, was interesting and important only when it unfettered itself from its private, individual settings to enter the public fray. The field's strong materialist and rationalist slants, coupled with the predominant view of religion as meaning and ritual that held less and less sway over other spheres of social life, further reinforced the view of religion as a kind of false consciousness. Sociologists of religion faced uphill battles in justifying the value of studying religion beyond its negative roles in disempowerment, inequality, and irrationality.

Sociologists of religion responded by portraying religion as overwhelmingly positive. As Smilde and May (2010) note, religion was almost as likely to be described in negative as positive terms in the 1970s, but by the beginning of the twenty-first century it was five times more likely to be described in positive terms than negative terms. This trend became more complicated after 2001, as both positive and negative descriptions increased. This is, in part, a sign of the times: the 2001 attacks in Washington, DC and in New York; religious-ethnic conflicts in the former Yugoslavia, Nigeria, South Asia, and Southeast Asia; sex scandals in the Catholic Church; and the high profile of evangelical Protestantism during the unpopular second Bush administration created a context in which critique ran rampant.

But critical and negative research in this period did not return to a materialist view that religion was an opiate, false consciousness, or a driver of violence. Rather, much of it included nuanced assessments of both the positive and negative social consequences of particular religious practices. Michael Emerson and Christian Smith (2000), for example, argue that evangelicalism is an important site for interracial encounters, although they also show its limits and counterproductive effects (see also Marti 2004). David Smilde shows how the same Evangelical narratives that help substance abusers overcome their problem also can lead to cruel isolation of persistent users (Smilde 2007). Dawne Moon's (2004) work on religion and sexuality also shows the complex ways in which Christianity both encourages and inhibits acceptance of homosexuality. Paul Lichterman (2005) shows how some Evangelical cultural models can facilitate the formation of effective social capital while others prevent it. This kind of more nuanced, measured work makes way for more meaningful conversations within and between social science disciplines.

We think this is an important trend, not just because it demonstrates a diplomatic even-handedness, but also because it opens up the field for alternative interests and conceptualizations. The long line of sociological research on the relationship between religion, "spirituality," and medical and mental health (see Ellison and Levin 1998), for example, accepted the classical vision of religion as a private concern. As such, and as a matter of interior, personal devotion, scholars identified the positive value of attending services, private devotional practices, and "feelings" of spiritual well-being. But such formulations still bear the weight of responding to accusations of false consciousness by focusing on an empowered subject. Religious studies scholars Robert Orsi (1998) and R. Marie Griffith (1997), as well as anthropologists Saba Mahmood (2005) and Carolyn Rouse (2004), raise cogent criticisms of the failure of the "liberal subject" to capture the complex social realities that people face. They also argue that such an empowered subject is frequently constructed through a negative comparison of women, minorities, and religious others, who apparently "lack" the modern capacities to be free. We need to question whether religious practice can be adequately understood within the conceptual framework of an acting, empowered subject versus a passive, disempowered subject.

The "cultural turn" in sociology afforded scholars a different position from which to argue for the value of understanding and studying religion, though in ways that were often posed as positive. In contributing to and drawing upon cultural approaches, which place issues of memory, ritual, discourse, and practice in the foreground, sociologists studying religion began paying attention once again to the religious aspects of public and social movement protests and other political and public acts that empowered citizens (Billing 1990). Religion, articulated as identity, social organizations, discourses, and ritual, began to take a more central place in narratives about the role of civil or political identities in the United States. However, much of this research focused on how religion shaped public citizens' actions; it was a means to the end of better understanding how religion shaped Americans' abilities to invest in and engage in civil life, democratic processes, and activities (Wood 2002; Stout 2011; Lichterman 2005; Verba, Brady, and Schlozman 1995). The theoretical baseline is that religion has an independent autonomous impact on social reality. Indeed, Smilde and May (2010) showed that while in the late 1970s it was most common for articles on religion to describe it as a dependent variable, by the turn of the century articles on religion were twice as likely to treat it as an independent variable .

Much of this recent work is subtle, offering new orientations that demand a thorough reconsideration of sociological frames. More work is needed, however, in this vein. For example, work on Buddhism by Wendy Cadge (2005), Michal Pagis (2010), and Ilana Silber (1995) productively questions the usefulness of theories that circle around the issue of structure versus agency in favor of more relational approaches that are embedded within and refracted quite differently in various Buddhist "traditions." Research by Jen'nan Ghazal Read (2004) and Rachel Rinaldo (2008) turn common views about the relationship between religion, social capital, and female empowerment on their head. These works broaden the contexts of empowerment and critically take up the question of what constitutes empowerment and for whom. This, in turn, raises additional concerns about why certain pathways to empowerment through religion are heralded while others are denigrated as either not "empowering" or not "religious."

This work also calls into question how we conceptualize religious versus social structures and practices. While earlier sociologists of religion felt compelled to treat religion as a coherent and bounded entity, recent scholarship no longer questions whether "religion" can "act" or "affect" certain things or is acted upon. Rather, the question, across a range of institutional settings, is about the intersections of religious and other processes. It is about the habits, discourses, and practices that shape social understandings of those things as religious, quasi-religious, or secular. It charts a path that focuses less on the objects than on the social processes that make them (Bender 2012; Lichterman, this volume). This opens up scholarship to the ways that the very questions of domination and resistance, and visions of religion as a cultural "tool" within other struggles for agency, are differently marked within various religious contexts.

In sum, in a postsecular era, sociologists of religion no longer need to reassure the world and themselves that religion is real and is not simply an opiate of the masses. A more confident position will allow us to critically engage religion, the way it functions, what it does for people, what people do with it, and its social impacts be they positive or negative. We recommend what religious studies scholar and historian Robert Orsi (2005, 4) calls a "tragic" register in the study of religious life. Writing of the powers that circulate within twentieth-century American Catholicism, where saints, the Virgin Mary, and supplicants—including children, women, and persons with disabilities—simultaneously live out resistance and submission, Orsi notes that the story he tells "rarely is a simple matter of either resistance or submission, but rather of negotiating compromises that are often tragic in their inevitability. Culture is a hard taskmaster, and saints and humans must find their way as best they can."

Embedding the Long-Standing Critiques in a Research Program: A Roadmap to Our Volume

Astute readers of this introduction will recognize that many of the theoretical critiques we identify have circulated widely and historically within the discipline—as well as without. Calls for "deprovincializing" European- and US-centric models of religion arguably began with the comparative work of Max Weber (1958), and much of the sociological work that takes shape around this critique takes a broadly Weberian cast (Gorski and Altınordu 2008; Gorski et al. 2012). Sociologists working in the United States and Europe have contributed important works on religion outside these borders; we can cite as examples the work of Robert Bellah (1957) and Jose Casanova (1994) as writing (though in very different ways) against the frameworks that implicitly assert the position that take religion in the United States as the norm. In a separate but related vein, numerous sociologists of religion have identified the problematic connection of religion to belief, beginning, certainly, with Durkheim, whose *Elementary Forms of Religious Life* (1995) confounds any easy gloss on the primacy of belief or the necessity for religion to have force. Mary Douglas (1966) and Robert Wuthnow (1987) have both challenged the belief-centered emphasis within the sociology of religion literature. Wuthnow (1993), in particular, outlines a range of empirically developed approaches for understanding "meaning" that do not demand or hinge on internalized belief structures or psychologies.

Sociologists of religion have similarly long been critical of the effects of the discipline's emphasis on congregations and other self-evidently voluntary communities as the appropriate sites where religion resides. Critical work has sought to call attention to the range of structures, religious and otherwise, that shape religious experience and congregational life. While such studies have often been framed around notions of "secularization" (Herberg 1955) or "popular religion" (Schneider and Dornbusch 1958), these studies all point in various ways to the limits of conceptualizing religion primarily along the lines of voluntary communities. And, while we need not note that sociological studies that critique the positive framing of religion are as old as the discipline itself (Marx 1972), we do note that, from the outset scholars, have been pushing back against the false dichotomy of religion as empowering versus disempowering.

Our volume seeks to build upon this developing and expanding body of work, with an eye toward not only de-centering but also re-centering the field. As our critical mass deepens and broadens, we will not just unsettle long-established categories and hierarchies, but reorder and redefine them in new ways. The selections in this volume challenge us to rethink the basic outlines of our subjects and the central theoretical tools we use to understand them. They move us beyond a focus on religion as a deeply held set of beliefs that determine behavior or as a set of practices carried out within congregations, toward an understanding of religion as discourses and practices enacted in religious and "nonreligious" spaces, ranging from the local and the everyday to the national and global.

While all of the chapters combine theoretical insights with empirical material, we have nevertheless grouped them into two broad sections. The first includes contributions that lean more toward the theoretical by directly challenging the assumptions about religion embedded in key sociological concepts and then showing what we learn about these categories and about religion by unpacking them in ways that touch on one or more of our edges. The second section includes chapters that exemplify the kind of decentering and re-centering we propose. They include case studies and methodological models for future research.

The first section begins with Manuel Vásquez, who clearly shows how taken-for-granted assumptions about modernity are embedded in our under-standings of religion and what we learn about religion and modernity by bringing those taken-for-granted assumptions to the fore. Ongoing work in the sociology of religion must proceed, as he and other authors in this volume argue, with an acute awareness that its categories are enacted and deployed in the context of everyday social life, not in laboratories outside it.

David Smilde also critically engages the social role of religion by showing in his chapter how the classic question of "why religion persists" reinforces the desire of sociologists of religion to delineate an autonomous category of reli-gion. Building on feminist, postcolonial, and pragmatist critiques of cultural autonomy, Smilde is able to pose broader questions about religion and its social role. Using tools from the sociology of culture, as well as recent cultural theory, he suggests some robust and inclusive concepts of religious culture that do not rest on structuralist assumptions.

The next chapters take on long-held assumptions by directly challenging con-cepts evident in discussion of one or more of our edges. Ateş Altınordu does this by comparing theoretical assumptions and methodological approaches in comparative historical approaches to sociology and the sociology of religion. Michal Pagis asks us to reconsider the sociological "self" because "contemporary theories of the religious self commonly rest on a definition of self or person-hood as an internalized structure of values and beliefs." Like Smilde, she argues that content and "cultures" are constitutive elements of religious practices of self-formation and need to be understood in the cultural contexts in which they are created. Paul Lichterman challenges the actor-centered sociological models that Vásquez suggests are partially constitutive of the "modern" and secular social actor. Courtney Bender's chapter highlights how religion rears its head in a range of contexts, beyond congregations, by questioning how notions of reli-gious autonomy are connected, in particular, to notions of American secular pol-ity and doctrine. Finally, Peggy Levitt's contribution provides a bridge between the more theoretically focused pieces in the first section and the empirical cases and methodological models that follow in section two. She offers a road map for studying religion in motion, which takes fluidity and movement as its starting point, but also pays attention to what is rooted and blocked.

The chapters in the second section of the volume make central the four edges by looking empirically more than theoretically. Dawne Moon's chapter begins the section by speaking to religion outside of congregations and the importance of critically engaging its social role in cases of reconciliation. Wendy Cadge brings forth analytic insights by exploring how religious pluralism is negotiated outside of congregations in the space of secular hospital chapels in the United States. Geneviève Zubrzycki's chapter continues the emphasis on religion outside of congregations by shifting attention from the United States to Canada and exploring how historical factors shape how diversity is negotiated in the present. Kelly H. Chong examines evangelicalism, women, and gender politics in South Korea, exploring how power operates in this religious milieu. Finally, Jacqueline Hagan's chapter concludes the volume by drawing attention to a transnational aspect of religion through the US sanctuary movement, a faith-based movement for social justice for immigrants that places religious ideologies and religious actors at the forefront of immigration debates.

Although these chapters enter these conversations through different doors, each offers a clear way to address how religion insinuates itself in multiple aspects of social life and demonstrates how unpacking well-worn sociological categories helps us see "the religious" in new ways. What connects these contributions is the belief that epistemological critique and investigation are not ends in themselves, but rather necessary steps toward understanding not only religious activity and meaning better but also the basic building blocks of social experience.

Notes

1.   The authors thank Diana Wong for pointing out this useful distinction.

References

Ammerman, Nancy. 2007. *Pillars of Faith: American Congregations and Their Partners*. Berkeley, CA: University of California Press.

Arjomand, Said, ed. 1993. *The Political Dimensions of Religion*. Albany: State University of New York Press.

Asad, Talal. 1993. "The Construction of Religion as an Anthropological Category." Pp. 27–54 in *Genealogies of Religion: Discipline and Reasons of Power in Christianity and Islam*. Baltimore: Johns Hopkins University Press.

———. 2003. *Formations of the Secular: Christianity, Islam, Modernity*. Stanford, CA: Stanford University Press.

Bellah, Robert. 1957. *Tokugawa Religion*. New York: Free Press.

———. 2011. *Religion in Human Evolution*. Cambridge, MA: Harvard University Press.

Bender, Courtney. 2010. *The New Metaphysicals: Spirituality and the American Religious Imagination*. Chicago: University of Chicago Press.

———. 2012. "Practicing Religion." Pp. 273–95 in *The Cambridge Companion to Religious Studies*, edited by Robert Orsi. Cambridge: Cambridge University Press.

Bender, Courtney, and Pamela Klassen, eds. 2010. *After Pluralism: Reimagining Models of Religious Engagement*. New York: Columbia University Press.

Berger, Peter. 1967. *The Sacred Canopy: Elements of a Sociological Theory of Religion.* Garden City, NY: Doubleday.

Bourdieu, Pierre. 1990. *The Logic of Practice.* Stanford, CA: Stanford University Press.

Boyer, Pascal. 2001. *Religion Explained: The Evolutionary Origins of Religious Thought.* New York: Basic Books.

Cadge, Wendy. 2005. *Heartwood: The First Generation of Theravada Buddhism in America.* Chicago: University of Chicago Press.

———. 2008. "De Facto Congregationalism and the Religious Organizations of Post-1965 Immigrants to the United States: A Revised Approach." *Journal of the American Academy of Religion* 76(2): 344–374.

———. 2009. "Saying Your Prayers, Constructing Your Religions: Medical Studies of Intercessory Prayer." *Journal of Religion* 89: 299–327.

———. 2012. *Paging God: Religion in the Halls of Medicine.* Chicago: University of Chicago Press.

Cadge, Wendy and Elaine Ecklund. 2007. "Immigration and Religion" *Annual Review of Sociology.* 33:359–379.

Carroll, Michael P. 2007. *American Catholics in the Protestant Imagination: Rethinking the Academic Study of Religion.* Baltimore: Johns Hopkins University Press.

Casanova, Jose. 1994. *Public Religions in the Modern World.* Chicago: University of Chicago Press.

Chakrabarty, Dipesh. 2000. *Provincializing Europe: Postcolonial Thought and Historical Difference.* Princeton, NJ: Princeton University Press.

Chaves, Mark. 2004. *Congregations in America.* Cambridge; MA: Harvard University Press.

Chaves, Mark and Shawna Anderson. 2008. "Continuity and Change in American Congregations: Introducing the Second Wave of the National Congregations Survey." *Sociology of Religion* 69 (4): 415–440.

Chen, Carolyn. 2008. *Getting Saved in America: Taiwanese Immigration and Religious Experience.* Princeton, NJ: Princeton University Press.

Chong, Kelly. 2008. *Deliverance and Submission: Evangelical Women and the Negotiation of Patriarchy in South Korea.* Cambridge: Harvard University Press.

Douglas, Mary. 1966. *Purity and Danger.* New York: Routledge.

Durkheim, Emile. 1995. *The Elementary Forms of Religious Life.* New York: Free Press.

Ebaugh, Helen Rose, and Janet Chafetz. 2000. *Religion and the New Immigrants.* Walnut Creek, CA: AltaMira Press.

Ebaugh, Helen Rose, and Janet Chafetz. 2002. *Religion Across Borders: Transnational Immigrant Networks.* Walnut Creek, CA: AltaMira Press.

Ellison, Christopher, and Jeffrey S. Levin. 1998. "The Religion-Health Connection: Evidence, Theory and Future Directions." *Health Education and Behavior* 25: 700–721.

Emerson, Michael, and Christian Smith. 2000. *Divided by Faith: Evangelical Religion and the Problem of Race in America.* Oxford: Oxford University Press.

Finke, Roger, and Rodney Stark. 1988. "Religious Economies and Sacred Canopies: Religious Mobilization in American Cities, 1906." *American Sociological Review* 53: 41–49.

———. 1992. *The Churching of America, 1776–1990: Winners and Losers in Our Religious Economy.* New Brunswick, NJ: Rutgers University Press.

Geertz, Clifford. 1973. "Religion as a Cultural System." Pp. 87–125 in *The Interpretation of Cultures.* New York: Basic Books.

Gill, Anthony. 2008. *The Political Origins of Religious Liberty.* New York: Cambridge.

Goldschmidt, Henry. 2006. *Race and Religion Among the Chosen Peoples of Crown Heights.* New Brunswick, NJ: Rutgers University Press.

Gorski, Philip S., and Ateş Altınordu. 2008. "After Secularization?" *Annual Review of Sociology* 34: 55–85.

Gorski, Philip S., John Torpey, David Kyuman Kim, and Jonathan VanAntwerpen, eds. 2012. *The Post-Secular in Question.* New York: NYU Press.

Griffith, R. Marie. 1997. *God's Daughters: Evangelical Women and the Power of Submission.* Berkeley, CA: University of California Press.

Hagan, Jacqueline. 2008. *Migration Miracle: Faith, Hope and Meaning on the Undocumented Journey.* Cambridge, MA: Harvard University Press.

Hart, Stephen. 2001. *Cultural Dilemmas of Progressive Politics: Styles of Engagement Among Grassroots Activists.* Chicago: University of Chicago Press.

Herberg, Will. 1955. *Protestant Catholic Jew.* Chicago: University of Chicago Press.

Hondagneu-Sotelo, Pierrette. 2008. *God's Heart Has No Borders: How Religious Activists Are Working for Immigrant Rights.* Berkeley: University of California Press.

Jaworsky, Nadya, Peggy Levitt, Wendy Cadge, Jessica Hejtmanek, and Sara Curran. 2012. "New Perspectives on Immigrant Contexts of Reception: The Cultural Armature of Cities." *Nordic Journal of Immigration Research.* 2(1): 78–88.

Kurien, Prema. 2007. *A Place at the Multicultural Table: The Development of American Hinduism.* New Brunswick, NJ: Rutgers University Press.

Levitt, Peggy. 2007. *God Needs No Passport: Immigrants and the Changing American Religious Landscape.* New York: New Press.

Levitt, Peggy. 2009. "Constructing Religious Life Transnationally: Lessons from the U.S. Experience." In ed. Paul Bramadat and Matthias Koenig *International Migration and the Governance of Religious Diversity.* Montreal: McGill-Queens University Press.

Levitt, Peggy and Sally Merry. 2009. "Vernacularization on the ground: Local uses of global women's rights in Peru, China, India and the United States." *Global Networks* 9 (4): 441–461.

Levitt, Peggy, Kristen Luckens, and Melissa Barnett. 2011. "Beyond Home and Return: Negotiating Religious Identity across Time and Space through the Prism of the American Experience." *Mobilities* 6(4): 467-482.

Lichterman, Paul. 2005. *Elusive Togetherness: Church Groups Trying to Bridge America's Divisions.* Princeton, NJ: Princeton University Press.

———. 2008. "Religion and the Construction of Civic Identity." *American Sociological Review* 73 (1): 83–104.

Lindsay, Michael. 2007. *Faith in the Halls of Power: How Evangelicals Joined the American Elite.* New York: Oxford University Press.

Mahmood, Saba. 2005. *The Politics of Piety.* Princeton, NJ: Princeton University Press.

Marti, Gerardo. 2004. *A Mosaic of Believers: Diversity and Innovation in a Multiethnic Church.* Indianapolis: Indiana University Press.

Martin, David. 2002. *Christian Language and Its Mutations: Essays in Sociological Understanding.* Aldershot: Ashgate.

Marx, Karl. 1972. *The Marx-Engels Reader,* edited by Robert Tucker. New York: W. W. Norton.

McGuire, Meredith. 2008. *Lived Religion: Faith and Religion in Everyday Life.* New York: Oxford University Press.

McNally, Michael. 2010. "Native American Religious Freedom Beyond the First Amendment." Pp. 225–251 in *After Pluralism: Reimagining Religious Engagement,* edited by Courtney Bender and Pamela Klassen. New York: Coumbia University Press.

Moaddel, Mansoor. 2005. *Islamic Modernism, Nationalism and Fundamentalism: Episode and Discourse.* Chicago: University of Chicago Press.

Moon, Dawne. 2004. *God, Sex, and Politics: Homosexuality and Everyday Theologies.* Chicago: University of Chicago Press.

Moore, Rick. 2011. "Genres of Religious Freedom: Creating Discourses on Religion at the State Department." Pp. 223–53 in *History, Time, and Memory: Ideas for the Sociology of Religion.* Barbara Denison and John Simpson, eds. Leiden and Boston: Brill.

Nawyn, Stephanie. 2006. "Faith, Ethnicity and Culture in Refugee Resettlement." *American Behavioral Scientist* 49: 1509–1529.

Nepstad Erickson, Sharon. 2008. *Religion and War Resistance in the Plowshares Movement.* New York: Cambridge University Press.

Norris, Pippa, and Ronald Inglehart. 2004. *Sacred and Secular: Religion and Politics Worldwide.* New York: Cambridge University Press.

Orsi, Robert A. 1998. *Thank You, St. Jude: Women's Devotion to the Patron Saint of Hopeless Causes.* New Haven, CT: Yale University Press.

————. 2005. *Between Heaven and Earth: The Religious Worlds People Make and the Scholars Who Study Them.* Princeton, NJ: Princeton University Press.

Pagis, Michal. 2010. "Producing Intersubjectivity in Silence: An Ethnography of Meditation Practices." *Ethnography* 11(2): 309–28.

Parsons, Talcott, and Edward A. Shils, eds. 1951. *Toward a General Theory of Action.* Cambridge, MA: Harvard University Press.

Read, Jen'nan Ghazal. 2004. *Culture, Class, and Work Among Arab-American Women.* New York: LFB Scholarly Publishing.

Rinaldo, Rachel. 2008. "Muslim Women, Middle Class Habitus, and Modernity in Indonesia." *Contemporary Islam* 2: 23–39.

Rouse, Carolyn. 2004. *Engaged Surrender: African American Women and Islam.* Berkeley: University of California Press.

Schneider, Louis, and Sanford Dornbusch. 1958. *Popular Religion: Inspirational Books in America.* Chicago: University of Chicago Press.

Silber, Ilana F. 1995. *Virtuosity, Charisma, and Social Order: A Comparative Sociological Study of Monasticism in Theravada Buddhism and Medieval Catholicism.* Cambridge: Cambridge University Press.

Smilde, David. 2007. *Reason to Believe: Cultural Agency in Latin American Evangelicalism.* Berkeley: University of California Press.

Smilde, David, and Matthew May. 2010. "The Emerging Strong Program in the Sociology of Religion: A Critical Engagement." Social Science Research Council Working Paper.

Smilde, David, and Coraly Pagan. 2011. "Christianity and Politics in Venezuela's Bolivarian Democracy: Catholics, Evangelicals and Political Polarization." Pp. 315–339 in *Venezuela's Bolivarian Democracy: Participation, Politics and Culture under Chávez,* edited by David Smilde and Daniel Hellinger. Durham, NC: Duke University Press.

Smith, Christian. 1996. *Disruptive Religion: The Force of Faith in Social Movement Activism.* New York: Routledge.

————. 2003. *Moral, Believing Animals: Human Personhood and Culture.* New York: Oxford University Press.

Smith, Jonathan Z. 1982. *Imagining Religion: from Babylon to Jonestown.* Chicago: University of Chicago Press.

Stepick, Alex, Terry Rey, and Sarah Mahler. 2009. *Churches and Charity in the Immigrant City.* New Brunswick, NJ: Rutgers University Press.

Stout, Jeffrey. 2011. *Blessed Are the Organized.* Princeton, NJ: Princeton University Press.

Sullivan, Winnifred F. 2009. *Prison Religion: Faith-based Reform and the Constitution.* Princeton, NJ: Princeton University Press.

Sullivan, Winnifred Fallers, Robert A. Yelle, and Mateo Taussig-Rubbo, eds. 2011. *After Secular Law.* Stanford, CA: Stanford University Press.

Sun, Yanfei. 2010. "Religions in Sociopolitical Context: The Reconfiguration of Religious Ecology in Post-Mao China." Ph.D. Dissertation. University of Chicago Department of Sociology.

Taylor, Charles. 2007. *A Secular Age.* Cambridge, MA: Harvard University Press.

Turner, Bryan. 1994. *Orientalism, Postmodernism and Globalism.* New York: Routledge.

Vásquez, Manuel, and Marie Marquardt. 2003. *Globalizing the Sacred: Religion Across the Americas.* New Brunswick, NJ: Rutgers University Press.

Verba, Sidney, Henry Brady, and Kay Scholzman.1995. *Voice and Equality: Civic Voluntarism in American Politics.* Cambridge, MA: Harvard University Press.

Warner, R. Stephen. 1993. "Work in Progress Toward a New Paradigm for the Sociological Study of Religion in the United States." *American Journal of Sociology* 98: 1044–1093.

Weber, Max. 1958. "The Social Psychology of World Religions." Pp. 267–301 in *From Max Weber,* edited by H. H. Gerth and C. Wright Mills. New York: Oxford University Press.

Wood, Richard L. 2002. *Faith in Action: Religion, Race, and Democratic Organizing in America.* Chicago: University of Chicago Press.

Wuthnow, Robert. 1987. *Meaning and Moral Order.* Berkeley: University of California Press.

————. 1993. *Communities of Discourse: Ideology and Social Structure in the Reformation, the Enlightenment, and European Socialism.* Cambridge, MA: Harvard University Press.

Yang, Fenggang, and Helen Rose Ebaugh. 2001. "Transformations in New Immigrant Religions and Their Global Implications." *American Sociological Review* 66(2): 269–288.

Young, Michael. 2006. *Bearing Witness Against the Sin: The Evangelical Birth of the American Social Movement.* Chicago: University of Chicago Press.

PART ONE

RETHINKING CATEGORIES: THEORETICAL APPROACHES

1

Grappling with the Legacy of Modernity: Implications for the Sociology of Religion

MANUEL A. VÁSQUEZ

Reflecting on sociology's epistemology, Pierre Bourdieu writes:

> Each discipline (as a field) is defined by a particular nomos, a prin-
> ciple of vision and division, a principle of construction of objective
> reality irreducible to that of another discipline—in accordance with
> Saussure's formula, "the point of view creates the object" (the arbi-
> trariness of the "disciplinary eye" as a constitutive principle is seen
> in the fact that it is most often expressed in the form of tautologies,
> with, for example, in sociology, "explaining the social by the social," in
> other words explaining social things sociologically). (2004, 51)

In this chapter, I will examine the implications of this epistemological commitment of explaining the social by the social, which sociology inherited from
modernity's Copernican turn—that is, from modernity's displacement of faith
and revelation as the sources of authority and their replacement with rationality
and empirical observation. Sociology's close imbrication with modernity's critical thrust has been enormously fruitful, allowing the discipline to historicize
and contextualize phenomena that have presented as doxa, as naturally given.
Nevertheless, this relationship also has an underside. To emerge as an autonomous scientific discipline, one totally committed to an immanentist view of
human action, sociology constructed religion as its epistemological "Other" in
time and space. While this process of othering allowed sociology to develop its
own methodologies and grounds for legitimation, it made religion its repressed
underside, a perennial problem whose existence always had to be explained.
This "epistemological unconscious," as Bourdieu puts it, helps explain why
sociology of religion became so wedded to the secularization paradigm, the

claim that modernization would bring religion's retrenchment from the public sphere, becoming increasingly privatized or rationalized, reduced to either a feckless personal spirituality or a diffuse and abstract civil religion or a religion of humanity. As such, the adoption of a modernist vision has often blinded sociology to religion's enduring vitality and creativity.

Moreover, despite the claim to explain the social by the social, sociology also borrowed from modernity the notion of an autonomous, rational, and self-transparent subject capable of grasping and eventually mastering the laws of society. This modernist idea of an unencumbered and unified self lies behind many of the assumptions about religion that the contributors to this volume seek to challenge. After excavating the modernist biases that have vitiated the social sciences' approach to religion, I conclude the chapter by presenting a more embedded, relational, embodied, and polyvalent under-standing of subjectivity that can help reorient the sociology of religion along more fruitful lines.

Modernity, Sociology, and the Denial of Religion's Coevalness

To constitute itself as an autonomous field of inquiry, sociology had to con-struct a viewpoint different from that of biology, which sought to explain social behavior as the emergent result of cellular processes, and from psychol-ogy, for which society was the aggregation of the psychic life and dyadic rela-tions of individuals. This can clearly be seen in Durkheim's vigorous efforts to affirm the reality of collective representations as social facts that not only precede and outlive the individual but also constrain his or her activities and relationships. A collective representation "is not simply an aspect of the condition of a neural element at the particular moment that it occurs, since it persists after that condition has passed..." (Durkheim 1972, 72). Rather, "collective ways of acting and thinking have a reality outside the individuals who, at any moment in time, conform to it. These are things which exist in their own right. The individual finds them already formed, and he cannot act as if they did not exist or were different from how they are" (Durkheim 1972, 71).

More important, however, explaining the social by the social meant that sociology had to adopt a thoroughly humanistic perspective that wrested agency away from the clutches of supernatural beings and forces and focused on the historical praxis of men and women. In other words, sociology had to differentiate itself from theology. It is thus not surprising that sociology took up the critical thrust of the Enlightenment, which sought to make "man the measure of all things" and to critique forms of authority not grounded on human reason, such as dogma and revelation. With sociology, a humanistic universalism replaced theological absolutism.

The critique of theology as a precondition for the emergence of an autonomous science of sociology is evident in August Comte's complaint that "the theories of Social science are still, even in the minds of the best thinkers, completely implicated with the theological-metaphysical philosophy; and are even supposed to be, by a fatal separation from all other science, condemned to remain so involved for ever" (1855, 399). To break the nascent social science's involvement with the theological-metaphysical, we must recognize "fundamental laws of continuous development, representing the existing evolution as of the gradual series of former transformation, by simply extending to social phenomena the spirit that governs the treatment of all other natural phenomena" (p. 432). Comte, thus, postulated the "law of the three stages" of development of humanity, which traced the evolution from the theological, in which a young naive humanity faced with an unruly world falls under the tutelage of the gods, through the metaphysical, with the elevation of rationality as our highest and universal faculty, to the positive age, when humanity grasps the underlying laws that determine the operations of the cosmos, including "social physics." This social physics, in turn, would be the basis for the construction of a society governed by the rational principles of order and progress.

To appreciate truly the consequences of sociology's quest to set itself apart from theology and religion, it is helpful to refer to postcolonial and postmodern critiques of modernity, because sociology's ambivalent relationship with theology and religion mirrors modernity's tensions with the *ancien régime*. Foucault, for example, argues that the rise of the stable, transparent, sovereign, and rational subjectivity at the heart of modernity was made possible by the construction of madness as the constitutive Other, which could be the target of disciplinary and panoptical discourses and practices: "What is originative is the caesura that establishes the distance between reason and non-reason; reason's subjugation of non-reason, wresting from it its truth as madness, crime, or disease..." (Foucault 1965, ix).

Descartes, modernity's seminal thinker, offers a poignant illustration of this process of othering. In holding at arm's length the demons and nightmares that threaten to undermine his search for ultimate foundations in the disembedded and transparent cogito, "the Cartesian formula of doubt is certainly the great exorcism of madness. Descartes closes his eyes and plugs up his ears the better to see the true brightness of essential daylight; thus he is secure against the dazzlement of the madman who, opening his eyes, sees only the night, and not seeing at all, believes what he sees when he imagines" (Foucault 1965, 94). This separation from madness, a separation that is not merely philosophical but that dovetails with the rise of a network of practices of exclusion and institutions of confinement, is essential for the consolidation of the human sciences. "[M]adness was shown, but on the other side of bars; if present, it was at a distance, under the eyes of reason that no longer felt any relation to it that would not compromise itself by too close a resemblance. Madness had become a thing to look at" (1965, 66). In his work on the birth of the prison, Foucault characterized the systematic application of surveillance and disciplinary techniques as a process of "normalization," which simultaneously "compares, differentiates, hierarchizes, homogenizes, and excludes" (1977, 183).

In the same way that Western modernity defined itself as enlightened civilization in opposition to the irrationality of the Dark Ages, it also stabilized itself against the civilizational Other, the colonial Other upon which it projected all its anxieties and desires. Orientalism, which Edward Said describes as an institutionally based "style of thought based upon an ontological and epistemological distinction between 'the Orient' and (most of the time) 'the Occident'" (1978, 2), is a particularly egregious example of this otherization. "Orientalism," according to Said, "depends for its strategy on [a] flexible positional superiority, which puts the Westerner in a whole series of possible relationships with the Orient without ever losing him the relative upper hand" (Said 1978, 7). From this positional superiority, the Orient is represented as "irrational, depraved (fallen), childlike, 'different'; [while] the European is rational, virtuous, mature, 'normal'" (p. 40).

Just as psychology and psychiatry played a key role in the segregation of reason from madness, so did anthropology contribute to the subjectivation of the Western scholar with his sovereign gaze and the objectivation of the exotic Oriental informant behind the veil. Anthropology came to identify its object of study, the non-Western Other, as the primitive, those societies that are not contemporaneous with us, but rather provide a window into the origins of humanity, into earlier stages of human development that we have already superseded. Anthropology "promoted a scheme in terms of which not only past cultures, but living societies were irrevocably placed on a temporal slope, a stream of Time—some upstream, others downstream (Fabian 1983, 17). It did this through a variety of "distancing devices" that denied coevalness, that is, that gave expression to "a persistent and systematic tendency to place the referent(s) of anthropology in a Time other than the present of the producer of anthropological discourse" (Fabian 1983, 31).

Since sociology's task was to study "hot" societies, contemporary societies driven by Western modernization, we might think that the discipline was able to escape the otherizing, Orientalist gaze that has contaminated anthropology and drove it to a profound period of crisis and self-reflection through the encounter with postmodernism and poststructuralism in the 1990s. However, sociology carried its own forms of epistemic violence. Just as Western modernity stabilized itself as a relatively unified and hegemonic "subject" against an exotic gendered and raced Oriental other through a denial of coevalness, so did sociology posit religion as its primitive, traditional, supernatural, enchanted, and sentimental other, against which it would have a "positional superiority." In turn, this positional superiority allowed sociology to "normalize" religion, to extract true, universal knowledge about the evolution of humanity.

This foundational process of otherization explains why the fathers of the discipline—Durkheim, Marx, Weber, and Simmel—not only were deeply interested in religion but also made the sociology of religion the epistemological point of departure for their theories of society. For them, religion was the "womb of civilization," the source of our elementary collective representations, ideologies, and this-worldly or other-worldly dispositions. Durkheim went as far as saying that "the first systems of representation with which men have pictured to themselves the world and themselves were of religious origin. There is no religion that is not a cosmology at the same time that it is a speculation on divine things" (1965, 21). Thus, our "categories of the understanding: ideas of time, space, class, number, cause, substance, personality, etc...are born in religion and of religion: they are the products of religious thought" (p. 22).

Along the same line, Marx considers religion as "the general theory of this world, its encyclopedic compendium, its logic in popular form, its spiritual *point d'honneur*, its enthusiasm, its moral sanction, its solemn complement, its general basis of consolation and justification" (1978 53–54). But if the founding fathers of sociology saw religion as central in human history, how is it that we ended up with the secularization paradigm and the need to explain why religion has not yet disappeared from the public sphere? In partaking in the Enlightenment's humanism, particularly its emphasis on the efficacy of human praxis and its privileging of time, of progress as a way to break with the heteronomous authority of divinely sanctioned tradition, sociology denies religion's coevalness. For the founding fathers, religion was important only because it revealed the origin of our conceptions, a mode of thought that, while foundational, has been overcome by a new humanistic, naturalistic, scientific thinking. Thus, they approached religion with great ambivalence, granting it the power to shape worldviews and ethos, but also theorizing it as an anachronism, as a phenomenon bound to disappear or, at a minimum, to be drastically transformed—privatized or rationalized—by the juggernaut of modernity.

Borrowing from Fabian, we can say that in order to constitute sociology as an autonomous discipline, the founding fathers had to enact a persistent and systematic tendency to place religion in "a Time other than the present of the producer of [sociological] discourse." This spatiotemporal distancing from religion involved first the evacuation of religion from the public sphere, which now fell under the purview of sociology and political science. Out of this evacuation emerged "religion as a new historical object; anchored in personal experience, expressible as belief-statements, dependent on private institutions, and practiced in one's spare time. This construction of religion ensures that it is

part of what is *inessential* to our common politics, economy, science, and morality" (Asad 1993, 207). Despite its critique of the secularization paradigm's dis-
missal of religion, such a construction of religion continues to inform the New
Paradigm, which construes religion as primarily about individual choices.

Secondly, the denial of coevalness operated through a variety of conceptual
devices enshrined in sociology's foundational analytical dualisms. Whether it
was the distinction between societies characterized by mechanical and organic
solidarity, or between *Gemeinschaft* and *Gesellschaft,* or between traditional
and charismatic authority and mean–ends bureaucratic authority, vital religion was always strongly associated with the first term of the duality, with the
asynchronous term in the conceptual pair. For example, Durkheim argued that
in groups characterized by mechanical solidarity, religion was the essence of
sociality, the powerful collective effervescence that bound everyone together.
This super-glue becomes diffuse and episodic as society becomes more differentiated, social roles become increasingly specialized, and as solidarity is built
on organic interdependence. The same assumption underlies Tönnies's claim
that "the guild is a religious community, and such is the town itself," such that
"art and religion exert influence and receive recognition as the meaning of daily
life in the functions of the town as standard and rule of thoughts and actions,
order and law" (1988, 63–64). In contrast, society is characterized by a "cosmopolitan life" legislated through the articulation of rational individual wills
in the public sphere. Along the same lines, Weber attributed to religion great
power in agrarian societies: "As a general rule the peasantry remained primarily involved with weather magic and animistic magic or ritualism . . ." (1963, 82).
This total enchantment of the world leads toward a mysticism standing in sharp
contrast with the "rational ethical religion" of the urban middle classes (1963,
97), which contributed to, but was eventually overtaken by, the *zweckrational-
ität* of modern capitalism. As the examples of Durkheim, Tönnies, and Weber
show, sociology's discourse on religion "was from the beginning—that is to say,
inherently, if also ironically—a discourse of secularization; at the same time, it
was clearly a discourse of othering" (Masuzawa 2005, 20).

Compounding the tendency to see religion in mythical terms, as a reality
that existed in the past, a formidable force that defined everything at the dawn
of humanity, but that is increasingly irrelevant in the present, sociology operated with quasi-teleological schemes that explained the movement from one
term of the foundational analytical dualism to the other. Thus, we have the
grand narratives of inexorable social differentiation, rationalization, and disenchantment. These narratives, which have often been presented as iron-clad
laws of social physics, have no doubt been very helpful in identifying *longue-du-
rée* trends. Nevertheless, they have militated against more context-sensitive
analyses of social phenomena at various, overlapping spatial and temporal
scales. These grand narratives of religion's fall from Eden have made it difficult

for sociology to study in specific historical and cultural contexts the multiple and changing relationships that religion and modernity sustain. These relationships are not always and automatically defined by opposition. Rather, as Talal Asad argues, the religious and secular have never been "essentially fixed categories" (2003, 25). They have been contested categories, and the social sciences have played a central role in this contestation by obscuring through the scholastic vision the contingent and shifting nature of these categories.

It is not surprising, thus, that the persistence of religion amidst (or despite) modernity has always been a problem. By denying religion's coevalness, by setting it as the archaic, irrational, and a temporal Other, sociology has, in its quest to become a science, rendered itself unable to understand fully the durable social vigor of religion.

Modernity, Christo-Centrism, and Domesticated Religion

Despite setting religion apart as its Other, sociology incorporated in secular form understandings of the self that were constructed by Christianity, particularly by Protestantism. According to Charles Taylor, beginning with the Reformation, there was a shift away from a premodern "porous self" that was closely connected and heavily dependent on society and nature, a self that found its identity as part of the feudal sociopolitical order and the spiritual order of the Catholic Church, toward modernity's "buffered self." Taylor explains, "As a bounded self I can see the boundary as buffer, such that things beyond don't need to 'get to me,' to use the contemporary expression. This self can see itself as invulnerable, as master of the meanings of things for it" (2007, 38). Modernity's buffered self is characterized by "its insistence on personal devotion and discipline, increase[ing] the distance, the disindentification, even the hostility to the older forms of collective ritual and belonging" (Taylor 2007, 156).

With the Reformation, the individual stands before his or her god as an indissoluble unit, free from the extraneous constraints of tradition and the Catholic Church's teaching and able to discern religious truth directly from the scriptures and to choose voluntarily Jesus Christ as his or her personal savior. Modernity also relies on this unencumbered self, only that now he or she seeks emancipation, mastery of himself or herself, as well as of society and nature, through the light of reason, which reveals the universality of human rights. While as part and parcel of modernity, sociology undermines religious sources of legitimation, the discipline also "liberates and reappropriates the image of the subject, which had previously been imprisoned in religious objectivations, or in the conflation of the subject and nature. It transfers the subject from God to man" (Touraine 1995, 230). Bourdieu puts it well when he states that:

> The social sciences, having been initially built up, often at the cost of indisputably scientistic distortions, against the religious view of the world, found themselves constituted as the central bastion on the side of the Enlightenment—with, in particular, the sociology of religion, the heart of Durkheim's undertaking and of the resistance it aroused— in the political and religious struggle for the vision of "humanity" and its destiny (1997, 132).

In taking the side of the Enlightenment, sociology imports the Cartesian-Kantian notion of a stable and unified self with an unchanging core grounded on supra-historical a priori of pure reason, practical reason (ethics), and aesthetic judgment. This self whose essence is unaffected by the contingencies of history and society can then assume a "sovereign gaze," a "scholastic point of view" that "presupposes a single, fixed point of view—and therefore the adoption of the posture of a motionless spectator installed at a point (of view)—and also the use of a frame that cuts out, encloses and abstracts the spectacle with a rigorous, immobile boundary" (Bourdieu 1997, 22–23; see also Bourdieu 1998, 127–140).[1] This is the vision that Paul Lichterman identifies in his chapter in this volume as the "default model" of the religious actor, a model that assumes that "religious people carry a core religious self" regardless of the setting and the socio-historical conditions that have made possible the emergence of a relatively stable subjectivity. Such a point of view militates against sociology's task of explaining the social by the social, thwarting the embedding of the self in the sociological and cultural processes that constitute it. Smilde, for his part, argues that this incomplete contextualization of the modern self is closely connected with the sharp distinction between the religious and the secular, with the failure to embed religion in everyday life as an ambivalent and shifting field among other fields of activity, and with the desire to "delineate a strong, autonomous category of religion." (Smilde, chapter 2, this volume).

Sociology's construction of an autonomous category of religion has specific characteristics. First, it sets Christianity as the paradigmatic form of modern religion, seeing other religions as either inferior, immature, or incomplete forms. This vision is particularly evident in the European exceptionalism that is behind the Weberian thesis that there is an elective affinity between the spirit of modern Western capitalism and the Protestant ethic. Only Christianity's this-worldly asceticism, as expressed in Puritanism, could serve as the psycho-cognitive basis for the methodical, thoroughly rational pursuit of wealth. Other religions proved either too mystical or other-worldly in their approach and locus of salvation. While the drive to acquisition was present among "the

Hindu, Chinese, or Muslim merchant, trader, artisan, or coolie," among these types "evolved no 'capitalist spirit,' in the sense that is distinctive of ascetic Protestantism." In Weber's words:

> Only ascetic Protestantism completely eliminated magic and the supernatural quest for salvation, of which the highest form was intellectualist, contemplative illumination. It alone created the religious motivations for seeking salvation primarily through immersion in one's worldly vocation (*Beruf*). This Protestant stress upon the methodically rationalized fulfillment of one's vocational responsibility was diametrically opposite to Hinduism's strongly traditionalistic concept of vocations. For the various popular religions of Asia, in contrast to ascetic Protestantism, the world remained a great enchanted garden.... (1963, 269–270)

As the authors in this volume show, the elevation of Christianity as sociology's paradigmatic modern religion, which left animism, animatism, and totemism to anthropology as primitive or elementary religious forms, and confined "Asian religions" to the Orientalist's library, as part of premodern, exotic societies, persists in the still dominant empirical focus on Christian beliefs, practices, and forms of organization.

Second, sociology's appropriation of the Reformation's buffered self with its scholastic attitude does not just lead to "Christo-centrism" in the study of religion. Since the Christianity that sociology posits as the paradigm of modern religion is what Robert Orsi calls a "domesticated Christianity," one that exists within the "limits of reason alone" (in Kant's words), sociology and the rest of academia have tended to focus on religion as "it positively contributes to believers' autonomy and agency and to the general social well-being." For the American academia:

> It was inconceivable that "religion" would be anything but good religion in this social and intellectual setting, "good" meaning acceptable in belief and practice to...domesticated modern civic Protestantism. Proponents of the academic study of religion claim a place in university culture by asserting that the study of "religion"—meaning the denominationally neutral version of Christianity recast as an ethical system— was good and even necessary for American democracy. Outside the walls of the academy, the winds of religious "madness" howled (in the view of those inside)—fire-baptized people, ghost dancers, frenzied preachers and gullible masses, Mormons and Roman Catholics" (Orsi 2005, 186).

Third, modernity bequeaths sociology not just a conception of religion as normatively good, a moral glue that holds people together, allowing for the social

body to function smoothly, as the Durkheim-Parsonian research program running through Peter Berger (1967) and Robert Bellah (1970) up to Christian
Smith (2003) demonstrates. Protestant-inflected modernity also brings into
sociology's epistemology a view of religion as a deeply held set of beliefs that
orient and shape the behavior of individuals and groups. While the Reformation
was a diverse movement, its overall effect was the increasing "excarnation, the
transfer of religious life out of the body forms of rituals, worship, practice, so
it come more and more to reside 'in the head' (Taylor 2007, 603). Rather than
religious images, relics, or artifacts, which could be easily manipulated by the
Catholic hierarchy, the "truth of Christianity was to be conveyed through the
Word of God, contained in the words of the scripture, preached from the pulpit, or read from the Bible" (McDannell 1995, 13). Moreover, the Reformation
reinforced a view of ritual as superstitious, mindlessly repetitive behavior, dis-
counting its efficacy and performative creativity. Ritual then became a pejora-
tive term "to describe the disreputable practices of somebody else: What I do
is ordained by God and is 'true religion': what you do is 'mere ritual,' at best
useless, at worst profoundly evil" (Muir 1997, 7).

I have argued elsewhere that the Protestant excarnation of Christianity has
contributed to a strong "textualism" in the discipline of religious studies, resulting in the privileging of belief, doctrine, text, and symbol over practice, ritual,
material culture, and power (Vásquez 2010). In religious studies, textualism
has meant not just the privileging of the great sacred texts written by religious
elites in the study of religion, but also a taken-for-granted approach to religious
practices and institutions as if they were only texts, expressions of symbolic
systems that the scholar must understand empathetically or decode through
"thick description." This mentalistic and excessively symbolicist approach fails
to capture the multiple ways in which religion, society, and nature interact.

Sociology has not bought into this textualism to the same degree as religious studies, thanks to Durkheim's strong focus on ritual and the practices
of sacralization of spaces and material objects, such as totems. After all,
Durkheim described the social effervescence produced in and through religious ritual in materialist terms: "to consecrate something, it is put in contact
with a source of religious energy, just as to-day a body is put into contact with
a source of heat or electricity to warm or electrize it" (Durkheim 1965, 467).
Nevertheless, Durkheim's materialism, his focus on superheated or electrified
religious bodies, artifacts, and spaces, is overpowered by his social Kantianism,
the association of social facts with collective representations that serve as a
prioris of perception and action. Thus, in the end, the sacred's material "maneu-
vers," Durkheim tells us, "are only the external envelop under which the mental operations are hidden." He continues: "It is sometimes said that inferior
religions are materialistic. Such an expression is inexact. All religions, even
the crudest, are in a sense spiritualistic; for the powers they put in play are

before all spiritual, and also their principal object is to act upon the moral life" (Durkheim 1965, 467).

Durkheim's ultimately idealist turn, and in particular his view of religion as being essentially "mental operations" acting upon "moral life," was picked up and magnified by Parsons in his synthesis with Weberian's *verstehende Soziologie*. And, despite its undeniable benefits in challenging positivism in the social sciences, the "linguistic turn," particularly Paul Ricoeur's suggestion that the metaphor of the text *may* be a useful model to understand human action,[2] has also unintendedly exacerbated textualist tendencies within sociology, tendencies to "identify thought, cognition, rationality, knowledge, and interpretation as linguistic processes" (Pagis, this volume). The result has been a persistent Protestant-inflected understanding of religion as a belief system or a set of collective representations or "core values" that regulate social action that are translated into structured practice. As Pagis argues in her chapter, the assertion that beliefs, values, and worldviews not only are distinct from rituals and institutions but also precede and determine material and external religious expressions has been an obstacle to re-embed fully the notion of the subject that sociology inherited from modernity, to develop a fully relational theory of self and religion in line with the call to explain the social by the social. Even the New Paradigm, which has challenged many of the modernist assumptions about religion in secularization theory (particularly the denial of coevalness) by stressing the ongoing flexibility and generativity of religion, continues to rely unreflectively on modernity's notion of the encumbered, buffered self.[3] This is evident in the New Paradigm's emphasis on methodological individualism, voluntarism, instrumental calculation, and bounded notions of identity and religious affiliation.

Sociology of Religion and the Re-Embedded Self

What would it take for the sociology of religion to confront and negotiate the ambivalent legacy of modernity? In order to de-center and re-center the sociological study of religion, we would have to go beyond the Protestant-based stress on text, belief, the buffered self, voluntarism, and bounded and territorialized notions of identity, which reproduces modernity's unencumbered subject. Notwithstanding powerful critiques of the secularization paradigm, this unencumbered subject dies hard. Stark and Finke, for example, state that "within the limits of their information and understanding, restricted by available options, guided by their preferences and tastes, humans attempt to make rational choices" (2000, 38). They recognize that "culture in general, and socialization in particular, will have a substantial impact on preference and tastes." However, they observe that there is "substantial variation across individuals in

their preferences and tastes" and that a "great deal of variation is so idiosyn-
cratic that people have no idea how they came to like certain things. As the old
adage says, 'there's no accounting for tastes'" (2000, 38). The failure to study
rigorously where tastes and preferences come from is a form of "genesis amnesia" that has been crucial for the rise and persistence of the unencumbered
subject, who assumes the scholastic vision with its practices of distancing and
denial of coevalness. Recent work about evangelical Protestants in Venezuela
by David Smilde shows that religious preferences, "tastes," and conversion
trajectories are strongly conditioned by the environment and the immediate
social networks in which individuals are embedded. Smilde also articulates an
alternative form of practical "imaginative rationality" that is context sensitive,
mediated by socially constructed narrative and tropes, as well as value laden.
He argues that "[c]onversion to Evangelicalism depends on structural contexts
that facilitate exposure to a particular meaning system or do not hinder cultural innovation" (Smilde 2007, 14).

Going beyond modernity's unencumbered subject would also mean the rel-
ativization of the strong focus on congregations, which are understood as the
form of religious organization that naturally follows from the voluntarism of
the unencumbered subject. In its zeal to counter the European-based secularization paradigm, the New Paradigm has elevated the trinity of the individual, the congregation, and the religious market, which has been central
in US religious history, into a new model to understand the global reality of
religion, in effect normalizing at large the mythology of American exceptionalism. Therefore, a radical critique of sociology of religion will also have to
challenge what migration scholars Andreas Wimmer and Nina Glick Schiller
(2003) have called "methodological nationalism": the tendency to view the
nation-state as the taken-for-granted unit of analysis, the container in which
all significant social action takes place. Because of widespread transnational
processes, "[t]he lives of increasing numbers of individuals can no longer
be understood by looking only at what goes on within national boundaries.
Our analytical lens must necessarily broaden and deepen because migrants
are often embedded in multi-layered, multi-sited transnational social fields,
encompassing those who move and those who stay behind" (Levitt and Glick
Schiller 2004, 1003). This critique will have to re-embed the subject in networks and fields through which myriad religious "artifacts" are produced,
circulated, contested, and consumed, artifacts ranging from missionaries,
itinerant pastors, pilgrims, and religious tourists to texts, relics, icons, theo-
dicies, (video) taped sermons, and money. These networks and fields may be
sustained by a variety of media, including transnational familial/kinship/
village ties, global popular culture, and mass media and computer-mediated
communications, which operate at multiple scales, from the personal, to the
local and national, to the transnational and global (Vásquez 2008).

Studying religion on the edge entails a view of individual and collective identities as shifting, but always relatively stabilized, emergent realities at the intersection of social, cultural, religious, neurosomatic, and ecological networks. Because the task is to map out and study the varied, multiscalar interplay of these networks—sometimes marked by clearly discernible causal chains and hierarchies, but at other times determined by nonlinear logics—a reinvigorated sociology of religion must engage a multiplicity of disciplines, ranging from anthropology, religious studies, and cultural studies to geography, evolutionary psychology, and the neurosciences. The specific contribution of sociology would be to foreground social dynamics as the point of entry and explanatory purchase in interaction with other processes.

Sociology already has the resources for the rehistoricized and rematerialized study of religion. A good example here is the notion of habitus. As Talal Asad (1993) has noted, Marcel Mauss originally meant the notion of habitus and the accompanying concept of "techniques of the body" to serve as tools to understand society through a "triple viewpoint, that of the 'total man,'" which focuses on "indissolubly mixed together" and "physio-psycho-sociological assemblages of actions" (Mauss 1979, 120). Mauss saw the habitus as the inculturated "art of using the human body" to construct self and society. According to him, the habitus is a coherent set of "acquired abilities" and embodied "faculties," which "do not vary just with individuals and their imitations; they vary especially between societies, educations, properties and fashions, prestiges. In them, we should see the techniques and work of collective and individual practical reason rather than, in the ordinary way, merely the soul and its repetitive faculties" (Mauss 1979, 101).

More recently, Bourdieu (1977, 1990) has enriched the notions of habitus and embodied practical reason through the concepts of social fields and multiple forms of capital. The habitus then becomes "incorporated and objectified history" and "political mythology realized, *em-bodied,* turned into a permanent disposition, a durable way of standing, speaking, walking, and thereby of feeling and thinking," as individuals mark their interrelated trajectories across overlapping fields where they deploy various forms of capital (Bourdieu 1990, 69–70). In turn, the habitus provides the social, psychological, and somatic preconditions for the generation of diverse yet relatively stable and regularized (religious) choices and practices. Thus, a focus on habitus within overlapping fields of power rather than the unencumbered subject opens up the enquiry "into the ways in which embodied practices...form a precondition for varieties of religious experience. The ability to enter into communion with God becomes a function of untaught bodies. 'Consciousness' becomes a dependent concept" (Asad 1993, 76–77).

A good example of how the notion of an embodied habitus moves us beyond modernity's buffered self is the Hindu notion of *rasa.* For second-generation

Hindus in diaspora, constructing ethno-religious identity is not simply, or even primarily, about demonstrating intellectual mastery of the complex metaphysics of the great sacred texts, such as the Vedas or the Upanishads. Rather, it is all about *rasa*, the incorporation of a particular way of carrying oneself, an embodied aesthetic or poetics of life, a kind of naturalized *joie de vivre*, a proper sensitivity and disposition to taste reality in all its gustatory, visual, olfactory, tactile, and kinetic intensities (Schwartz 2004). In diaspora, this inculcation is heavily kinesthetic. It takes place through the engagement in rituals like *pujas* or *darshans*, where the devotee exchanges energies, "radiance," in the form of recognition, respect, reverence, and blessings with a god, holy person, or image. Or the incorporation of *rasa* as a habitus may take place through the performance of what Narayanan (2003) calls "embodied cosmologies," the performance of shared narratives connected with national and ethnic identities through dance and theater. In the staging of the *Ramayana* or the *Mahabharata*, for instance, the movements of the actors are as important as the lines they utter. Or, rather, there is no dichotomy between form and content, for the content is lived through the enactment. In fact, the success of a performance of these epics—their authenticity, depth, nuance, and intensity—depends on the seamless coordination of form and content through the in-skilled bodies of the performers, whose movements, emotions, and ways of enacting "Hinduness" are recognized and experienced as authentic and authoritative by the spectators without the need to be able to articulate verbally what is going on.

The engraining of *rasa* in diaspora as kinesthetic learning is, in turn, influencing the politics of the Hindu diaspora, including the negotiation of multiculturalism and religious pluralism in the context of reception and the increasing visibility of the transnational Hindutva movement, which has attempted to naturalize certain embodied cosmologies as doxa, as the essence of being Hindu (Kurien 2007). Thus, the example of *rasa* dramatically illustrates how unsatisfactory the modernist notion of self that still dominates the sociology of religion is to capture the richness and the simultaneous embeddedness of religious practices in multiples scales, from the body to transnational fields of cultural production and consumption, which Peggy Levitt describes in her chapter.

While Bourdieu's notions of the habitus and fields are important steps toward a relational sociology of religion, we need a more robust understanding of the body's physicality, one that foregrounds the interaction between the social, the neurophysiological, and the ecological in the construction of selfhood. Despite Bourdieu's effort to bring the body back into sociology, in his appropriation of the notion of habitus, the biological angle of Mauss's triple viewpoint loses some of its sharpness. This is where emerging research in cultural neuro-phenomenology, especially on the relations of mutual determination among structured and structuring social, historical, and cultural contexts, the flexible architecture of the human brain, the sensory-motor apparatus, and ecological networks, can complement the move away from the disembodied, disembedded, sovereign, and fully transparent Cartesian subject that has haunted modernity, including sociology (Depraz, Varela, and Vermersch 2003; Laughlin and Throop 2006). Armed with a thicker, fully networked understanding of agency, we will gain new vistas into the complexities of religious experiences and practices.

Philosopher Shaun Gallagher, for example, points to how "movement and the registration of that movement in a developing proprioceptive system (that is, a system that registers its own self-movement) contributes to the self-organizing development of neuronal structures responsible not only for motor action, but for the way we come to be conscious of ourselves, to communicate with others, and to live in the surrounding world" (2005, 1). More specifically, he cites the recent discovery of "mirror neurons," which are activated both by the subject's own movement and by watching the motor activities of others. Thus, the operation of mirror neurons demonstrates how the brain, the body, and the (social) environment are tightly connected (Gallagher 2005, 220–223). In religion, research on Buddhist monks who have acquired the technologies of the body, the embodied skills and propensities to engage in deep meditation through a highly disciplined life, shows that there are tight relations of reciprocal determination among environments mediated by practices and narratives, the monastic embodied habitus, and the neurocognitive process. As Lutz, Dunne, and Davidson (2007) explain, "The cortical brain regions associated with attention, interoceptive, and sensory processing were found to be thicker for a group of mid-range [meditation] practitioners than for matched controls" (p. 523).

In sum, as Pagis demonstrates in her chapter through her exploration of Vipassana meditation in Theravada Buddhism, Muslim fasting, and Christian prayer, the emergence of a fully relational and contextualized sociology of religion requires the de-centering of modernity's buffered self and a recovery of the "importance of collective practice, the relation to the body, and the engagement with material objects."

A Call for Sustained Epistemological Work

In this chapter, I tried to shed light into the epistemological unconscious of sociology, seeking to objectify the objectifying practices and discourses that the discipline deployed against religion in order to carve its distinctive analytical terrain. Here I follow Pierre Bourdieu's call for full reflexivity. The sociologist's task is to break "the enchanted circle of collective denial. By working toward the 'return of the repressed,' by trying to know and make known what the world of knowledge does not want to know, especially about itself ... [s/]he breaks ranks" with the doxa of his or her own discipline (Bourdieu 1997, 5). Therefore, a rigorous social science "neutralizes" its own "effects of naturalization," whereby the discipline's amnesia "of a given that gives itself with all the appearance of nature and asks to be taken at face value, taken for granted" (1997, 182).

I have shown how sociology from its inception naturalized religion as its spatial and temporal Other while simultaneously borrowing the notion of an excarnated, buffered self from a secularized Protestantism that sociology saw as the only type of religion that could be reconciled with modernity. This ambivalence has made the enduring vitality and multifariousness of religion a perennial problem in the discipline. Despite recent efforts to overcome the grand teleologies of the past in favor of a more textured study of the practices and affiliations of individuals as they sort through deregulated religious markets, sociology still continues to rely on the modernist notion of the unencumbered subject. Only a full-fledged critique of this subjectivity and its thorough re-embedding in history, society, and nature will allow us to take seriously the multiple ways in which religious practices have potency and efficacy and to analyze religion's entwining with other realms of human activity. This critique of and re-embedding of the subject must start with the sociologist himself or herself. Holding the temptation to deny coevalness in check or, rather, turning the strategies of distancing into useful but fallible heuristic tools in our analytical arsenal is only possible if sociologists surrender the vision from nowhere or from the end of history and immerse themselves fully in time and space, rendering themselves contemporaneous with (religious) people they study: "To practise reflexivity means questioning the privilege of a knowing 'subject' arbitrarily excluded from the effort of objectification" (Bourdieu 1997, 119).

In contrast to religious studies (my area of training) and anthropology, sociology has not undergone a sustained and systematic examination of its epistemological bases.[4]

In the case of anthropology, the undeniable links between the rise of the discipline, the colonial enterprise, and modern capitalism, together with the dramatic rearticulation of the local as a result of globalization's dialectic of time-space compression and distanciation, have led to powerful critiques of the anthropological gaze. Here, one can readily think of Appadurai (1996), Clifford and Marcus (1986), Fabian (1983), Marcus and Fischer (1999), and Rosaldo (1993). Similarly, in the field of religious studies, Chidester (1996), Fitzgerald (2000), Masuzawa (2005), McCutcheon (1997), and Wiebe (1999) have demonstrated the constructed and contingent nature of the category of religion and its implication in various forms of Orientalism, colonialism, and the subjectivation of indigenous populations. Moreover, their genealogical analyses of categories like world religions, the sacred, the holy, and *homo religiosus* have challenged the *sui generis* tradition within religious studies, the assumption that religion is an autonomous and irreducible reality whose universal, transhistorical, and transcultural essence can be recovered by a "trained hermeneut" (McCutcheon 1997, 67).

It is true that some of these deconstructionist and postcolonial critiques have taken matters to an extreme, generating unproductive and self-indulgent conversations that have very little to do with the challenges of studying specific religious discourses, practices, institutions, and landscapes as they are constituted and contested "on the ground." Nevertheless, these critiques have facilitated a fuller awareness of the inherent tensions and contradictions in anthropology and religious studies, clearing spaces for the emergence of approaches that are simultaneously more humble (in the sense of eschewing grand, ahistorical, and decontextualized concepts and generalizations) and more robust (in terms of rigor, attention to difference, hybridity, multiple determination, and multiscalar embeddedness). Epistemological critiques have accompanied and re-enforced ethnographic, practice-oriented, spatial, and nonreductively materialist turns in religious studies (Vásquez 2010). These turns have enabled a revitalization of religious studies beyond the dominant Eliadean history of religions approach and its search for transhistorical archetypes. A case in point here is the "materialist phenomenology" of the lived religion school of Robert Orsi (2005), Leigh Schmidt (1997), Thomas Tweed (2006), and others.

I would like to suggest that sociology, and particularly sociology of religion, can benefit greatly from a thorough examination of its epistemological bases. Such a sustained examination will allow us to move beyond the unproductive aporias that heretofore have shaped the field, enabling us to reengage creatively the founding fathers and texts, to retrieve from them tools that continue to be useful, and to enter into conversations with new domains of knowledge.

Notes

1. Protestant Christianity pushed back against the hyperrationality of the Kantian self, stressing the affective side of religious piety (as in Schleiermacher's Romantic reaction). However, Protestant Christianity left unchallenged the notion of a stable and unified self, only that its core was not reason but *sola fides*, a deeply felt faith, lodged in the heart and untarnished by superficial practices and institutions that had the potential to be superstitious and corrupt.
2. See Ricoeur (1979) and more generally Rabinow and Sullivan (1979).
3. See Stark and Finke (2000) for a critique of the secularization theory from the perspective of the New Paradigm. Secularization theorists have responded to many of these critiques by relativizing and nuancing the theory (Berger, 1997; Casanova 1994; Norris and Englehart 2004). Overall, these exchanges have undoubtedly enriched the sociology of religion and contributed to what I call a robust methodological pluralism (Vásquez 2007).

4.   An important exception is Actor-Network Theory (ANT). Bruno Latour and other Actor-Network theorists challenge sociology for essentializing the social, for hypostasizing it as an ontological force that determines the behavior of individuals. In contrast, affirming that "[t]here is nowhere to hide beyond the performativity of webs" (Law 2009: 154), Actor-Network Theory (ANT) posits that "the social" is the relatively stabilized and durable outcome of shifting and heterogeneous assemblages of human and non-human "actants," ranging from human beings and non-human animals to plants, machines, objects, and tropes. Furthermore, ANT critiques the "modernist settlement" for operating with "the illusion...that the more we grew, the separate objectivity and subjectivity would become, thus creating a future radically different from our past" (Latour 1999: 214). "Why not let the 'outside world' invade the scene, break the glassware, spill the bubbling liquid, and turn the mind into a brain, into a neuronal machine sitting inside a Darwinian animal struggling for life?" (9) ANT's focus on "material-semiotic relationality" resonates with my call for a non-reductive materialist approach to religions as phenomena generated by emplaced, embodied, and networked practices. See Latour (1999, 2005) and Law and Hassard (1999).

References

Appadurai, Arjun. 1996. *Modernity at Large: Cultural Dimensions of Globalization.* Minneapolis: University of Minnesota Press.
Asad, Talal. 1993. *Genealogies of Religion.* Baltimore: Johns Hopkins University Press.
———. 2003. *Formations of the Secular: Christianity, Islam, Modernity.* Stanford, CA: Stanford University Press.
Bellah, Robert. 1970. "Civil Religion in America." In *Beyond Belief: Essays on Religion in a Post-Traditional World.* Berkeley: University of California Press.
Berger, Peter. 1967. *The Sacred Canopy: Elements of a Sociological Theory of Religion.* Garden City, NY: Doubleday.
———. 1997. "Epistemological Modesty: An Interview with Peter Berger." *Christian Century* 114: 972–978.
Bourdieu, Pierre. 1977. *Outline of a Theory of Practice.* Cambridge: Cambridge University Press.
———. 1990. *The Logic of Practice.* Stanford, CA: Stanford University Press.
———. 1997. *Pascalian Meditations.* Stanford, CA: Stanford University Press.
———. 1998. *Practical Reason: On the Theory of Action.* Stanford, CA: Stanford University Press.
———. 2004. *Science of Science and Reflexivity.* Chicago: University of Chicago Press.
Casanova, José. 1994. *Public Religions in the Modern World.* Chicago: University of Chicago Press.
Chidester, David. 1996. *Savage Systems: Colonialism and Comparative Religion in Southern Africa.* Charlottesville, VA: University of Virginia Press.
Clifford, James and George Marcus, eds. 1986. *Writing Culture: The Poetics and Politics of Ethnography.* Berkeley: University of California Press.
Comte, Auguste. 1855. *The Positive Philosophy of Auguste Comte.* New York: Calvin Blanchard.
Depraz, Natalie, Francisco Varela, and Pierre Vermersch. 2003. *On Becoming Aware: A Pragmatics of Experience.* Amsterdam: John Benjamins Publishing Company.
Durkheim, Emile. 1965. *The Elementary Forms of Religious Life.* New York: Free Press.
———. 1972. *Selected Writings.* Cambridge: Cambridge University Press.
Eliade, Mircea. 1959. *The Sacred and the Profane.* New York: Harcourt Brace Jovanovich.
Fabian, Johannes. 1983. *Time and the Other: How Anthropology Makes Its Object.* New York: Columbia University Press.
Fitzgerald, Timothy. 2000. *The Ideology of Religious Studies.* New York: Oxford University Press.
Foucault, Michel. 1965. *Madness and Civilization.* New York: Random Books.

————. 1977. *Discipline and Punish: The Birth of the Prison*. New York: Vintage.

Gallagher, Shaun. 2005. *How the Body Shapes the Mind*. Oxford: Oxford University Press.

Kurien, Prema. 2007. *A Place at the Multicultural Table: The Development of an American Hinduism*. New Brunswick, NJ: Rutgers University Press.

Latour, Bruno. 1999. *Pandora's Hope: Essays on the Reality of Science Studies*. Cambridge, MA: Harvard University Press.

————. 2005. *Reassembling the Social: An Introduction to Actor Network Theory*. Oxford: Oxford University Press.

Laughlin, Charles, and Jason Throop. 2006. "Cultural Neurophenomenology: Integrating Experience, Culture, and Reality through Fisher Information." *Culture and Psychology* 12(3): 305–337.

Law, John. 2009. "Actor-Network Theory and Material Semiotics." Pp. 141–158 in *The New Blackwell Companion to Social Theory*, edited by Bryan S. Turner. Malden, MA: Wiley-Blackwell.

Law, John and John Hassard, eds. 1999. *Actor Network Theory and After*. Oxford: Blackwell.

Levitt, Peggy, and Nina Glick Schiller. 2004. "Conceptualizing Simultaneity: A Transnational Social Field Perspective on Society." *International Migration Review* 38(3): 1002–1039.

Lutz, Antoine, John Dunne, and Richard Davidson. 2007. "Meditation and the Neuroscience of Consciousness: An Introduction." Pp. 499–551 in *The Cambridge Handbook of Consciousness*, edited by Philip Zelazo, Morris Moscovitch, and Evan Thompson. Cambridge: Cambridge University Press.

Marcus, George and Michael Fischer. 1999. *Anthropology as Cultural Critique: An Experimental Moment in the Human Sciences*. Chicago: University of Chicago Press.

Marx, Karl. 1978. "Contribution to the Critique of Hegel's Philosophy of Right: Introduction." Pp. 53–65 in *The Marx-Engels Reader*, edited by Robert Tucker. New York: W. W. Norton and Company.

Masuzawa, Tomoko. 2005. *The Invention of World Religions: Or How European Universalism Was Preserved in the Language of Pluralism*. Chicago: University of Chicago Press.

Mauss, Marcel. 1979. "Body Techniques." Pp. 95–123 in *Sociology and Psychology: Essays*, edited and translated by B. Brewster. London: Routledge and Kegan Paul.

McCutcheon, Russell. 1997. *Manufacturing Religion: The Discourse on sui generis Religion and the Politics of Nostalgia*. New York: Oxford University Press.

McDannell, Colleen. 1995. *Material Christianity: Religion and Popular Culture in America*. New Haven, CT: Yale University Press.

Muir, Edward. 1997. *Ritual in Early Modern Europe*. Cambridge: Cambridge University Press.

Narayanan, Vasudha. 2003. "Embodied Cosmologies: Sights of Piety, Sites of Power." *Journal of the American Academy of Religion* 71(3): 495–520.

Norris, Pippa, and Ronald Englehart. 2004. *Sacred and Secular: Religion and Politics Worldwide*. Cambridge: Cambridge University Press.

Orsi, Robert. 2005. *Between Heaven and Earth: The Religious Worlds People Make and the Scholars Who Study Them*. Princeton, NJ: Princeton University Press.

Rabinow, Paul, and William Sullivan. 1979. *Interpretive Social Science: A Reader*. Berkeley: University of California Press.

Ricoeur, Paul. 1979. "The Model of the Text: Meaningful Action Considered as a Text." Pp. 73–101 in *Interpretive Social Science: A Reader*, edited by Paul Rabinow and William Sullivan. Berkeley: University of California Press.

Rosaldo, Renato. 1993. *Culture and Truth: The Remaking of Social Analysis*. Boston: Beacon.

Said, Edward. 1978. *Orientalism*. New York: Vintage Books.

Schwartz, Susan. 2004. *Rasa: Performing the Divine in India*. New York: Columbia University Press.

Schmidt, Leigh. 1997. "Practices of Exchange: From Market Culture to Gift Economy in the Interpretation of American Religion." Pp. 69–91 in *Lived Religion in America: Toward a History of Practice*, edited by David Hall. Princeton, NJ: Princeton University Press.

Smilde, David. 2007. *Reason to Believe: Cultural Agency in Latin American Evangelicalism*. Berkeley: University of California.

Smith, Christian. 2003. *Moral Believing Animals: Human Personhood and Culture*. Oxford: Oxford University Press.

Stark, Rodney, and Roger Finke. 2000. *Acts of Faith: Explaining the Human Side*. Berkeley: University of California Press.

Taylor, Charles. 2007. *A Secular Age*. Cambridge: Harvard University Press.

Tönnies, Ferdinand. 1988. *Community and Society*. New York: Transaction Publisher.

Touraine, Alain. 1995. *Critique of Modernity*. Oxford: Blackwell.

Tweed, Thomas. 2006. *Crossing and Dwelling: A Theory of Religion*. Cambridge, MA: Harvard University Press.

Vásquez, Manuel A. 2007. Review of *Sacred and Secular: Religion and Politics Worldwide* (by Pippa Norris and Ronald Inglehart). *Sociology of Religion* 68(1): 111–112.

———. 2008. "Studying Religion in Motion: A Networks Approach." *Method and Theory in the Study of Religion* 20(2): 151–184.

———. 2010. *More than Belief: A Materialist Theory of Religion*. New York: Oxford University Press.

Weber, Max. 1958. *The Protestant Ethic and the Spirit of Capitalism*. New York: Scribner's.

———. 1963. *The Sociology of Religion*. Boston: Beacon.

Wiebe, Donald. 1999. *The Politics of Religious Studies*. London: Macmillan.

Wimmer, Andreas, and Nina Glick Schiller. 2003. "Methodological Nationalism, the Social Sciences and the Study of Migration: An Essay in Historical Epistemology." *International Migration Review* 37(3): 576–561.

2

Beyond the Strong Program in the Sociology of Religion

DAVID SMILDE

Alberto converted to Evangelical Protestantism in Caracas, Venezuela, after years of alcohol and drug abuse that began during his adolescence. During this period, he suffered from three separate motorcycle accidents, spent time in jail for street robbery, and even stole from his mother to support his drug consumption. A particularly low point for him that led to his reflection on a need for change happened when he took his toddler-aged daughter to a park outside of Caracas where creeks run across the road, perfect for him to wash his motorcycle and let her play. On the way he bought two half-pints of rum, which he drank during the course of the afternoon. Late afternoon it started to rain and Alberto and his daughter took refuge in a local restaurant. They ordered some hot soup and Alberto continued to drink beer. When the rain stopped, he put his daughter on the motorcycle to head home, not noticing, in his impaired state, how much the creek had risen. In rural Venezuela, small roads do not generally have bridges over creeks and small rivers, but rather reinforced cement basins over which the water flows and through which vehicles can drive. As Alberto drove through the swollen creek he went too deep and the motorcycle stalled. The current pushed over the motorcycle and Alberto and his daughter tumbled into the water. When Alberto came up, he saw his daughter being carried down the stream and had to jump, dive, and swim to catch her: "I grabbed her and hugged her and she was terrified; it was terrifying for her. I hugged her and let the river carry my motorcycle away. I lost the motorcycle."

Alberto was mainly affected by having almost lost his daughter because of drinking too much. But losing a motorcycle is also a life-changing setback for someone of his socioeconomic status. Indeed, working as a motorized messenger, it was not only Alberto's means of transportation but also his livelihood. The experience led him to want to change and he started frequenting Evangelical churches and street services. He describes not a dramatic conversion, but a slow process as he visited services occasionally and read a Bible he had been given. He eventually found a church where he felt comfortable, went through indoctrination classes and baptism, and was able to overcome his substance abuse. He explained to me what his religious practice does for him in the following terms:

> Jesus Christ said, "When you have the Holy Spirit, you will have freedom, understanding and wisdom." . . . I would read the Bible and then I noticed that when I would go to a place where people were drinking rum or whatever, the Holy Spirit would push me back and say, "What are you doing here? You're losing your way. All this is fleeting." So inside me I always have that fear of God—because before I was always involved in drinking, dancing, women. So it's something unexplainable because you—or really it's God that separates you from the bad. . . .

Whether this is an accurate recollection of Alberto's conversion process is beside the point. What is important for our purposes here is what this reveals about how he thinks about his religious practice. Alberto sees his religious participation as a way to keep on the straight and narrow and improve his life. For Alberto, if you are in contact with God, he keeps you from doing bad, which, in his case, is substance abuse and its consequences. This type of pragmatic religious practice—frequently and inaccurately referred to as "instrumental"—can be found anywhere. But in the global South—where needs are more urgent and dangers more present—it is arguably the dominant form of religious practice. Religious practices are oriented toward addressing concrete dilemmas in the here and now, and they are evaluated by their success in doing so. Nevertheless, understanding them presents a problem for sociological perspectives that conceptualize religious culture as an autonomous, moral order not significantly impacted by the practical concerns of life.

In this chapter, I will look at the issue of cultural autonomy as it relates to our portrayals of religion. First, I will look at the recent move toward a more robust view of religion and culture. Then I will look at some of the critiques of the idea of cultural autonomy that have taken place over the last several decades. Finally, I will review some alternatives for understanding the causal impact of religious culture.

Toward a Thicker View of Religious Culture

In a recent review of five sociological journals over the past thirty years, Matthew May and I (2010) found a steady growth of articles that portray religion as an independent rather than dependent variable. In fact, the situation

inverts. While in the late 1970s it was more common for religion to be portrayed as a dependent variable, by 2007 articles were more than twice as likely
to portray religion as an independent variable. Based on these findings and on
our reading of theoretical movements in the field, we argue there is an emerging "strong program" in the sociology of religion in which religion is increasingly portrayed as causal rather than caused.

The idea of a "strong program" comes not so much from within the sociological study of religion as from recent trends in the sociological study of
culture.[1] Jeffrey Alexander (2003) uses the idea of a "strong program" to
describe the agenda of cultural sociology, in the process criticizing the "weak
program" of the sociology of culture. The latter uses noncultural factors such
as self-interest or social structure to explain culture, while the former uses
culture to explain things like interests, social institutions, or social networks. The "strong program" of "cultural sociology" highlights the autonomy
and independence of culture. The strong program is based on the dualistic
idea that cultural structures can be analytically separated from nonsymbolic
structures. Then one can use the tools of cultural analysis to reveal the internal coherence and meaning of culture. Culture is not infinitely malleable and
can be causal, not just caused.

Within the sociology of religion proper, Christian Smith has made a similar indictment. He argues that despite its successes in the 1980s and 1990s,
the sociology of religion and culture never developed a convincing portrait of
human motivation, with the result that unconstructed rational action became
the default conceptualization (Smith 2003, 45). Smith believes that people certainly can be selfish and self-centered but that "homo economicus" should not
be our baseline portrayal of human personhood (pp. 31–32). "Humans are not
at bottom calculating, consuming animals, they are moral, believing animals"
(p.114). Smith follows Charles Taylor in portraying human action as having
two levels. The first-order level of desires, inclinations, and choices is moderated by an independent second-order level of beliefs and norms, in other words,
human morality. These beliefs and norms, in turn, are shaped by "moral orders."
Human beings cannot live without these moral orders—belief systems about
themselves and the worlds they live in. These moral orders are nonpractical
and nonempirical. They do not respond to interests but rather determine our
interests, desires, and less fundamental beliefs. Thus, while portraits of cultural toolkits and repertoires and the different social phenomena that impact
them are useful, they beg some of the most important questions.

> The idea of cultural tools nicely highlights the potential of strate-
> gies of action to be put to use to achieve various purposes. What the
> image tends to obscure, however, is the essential narrative constitu-
> tion and ordering of culture. Tools are mere practical instruments for

manipulating the physical world. Cultures, however, are epics, dramas, parables, legends, allegories. The meanings and motivations of culture are matters not finally of practical accomplishment, but emplotted moral significance. (Smith 2003, 80)

What Alexander's and Smith's portraits have in common is the search for a thicker view of culture as relatively autonomous and therefore holding the potential to be causal rather than just caused. In the case of Alexander, this is articulated in classic structuralist fashion through the "cultural arbitrary"— the idea that the meaning of cultural symbols comes from their relationship to each other rather than any relationship to an external world. The case of Smith is a little less clear since he explicitly denies the dualism characteristic of structuralist portraits of culture. Yet as we can see in the previous passage, his consistent distinction between cultural and practical matters connotes a persisting Durkheimian dualism.

The Critique of Cultural Autonomy

In this chapter, I do not seek to minimize the significant contributions of Jeffrey Alexander and Christian Smith to cultural sociology and the sociology of religion. Those contributions, however, should be read in the context of the particular disciplinary history of American sociology, which, in the post-Parsons era, tended to regard "structural" factors (in the materialist sense of the means of social reproduction) or "rational" interests (in the sense of material self-interest) as somehow more real and therefore as preferred explanatory factors. In this sense, Alexander's and Smith's moves away from a thin portrait of culture as the handmaiden of naked, unconstructed rationality are certainly welcome. However, sociologists of religion need to be aware that the idea of cultural autonomy has received important critiques from perspectives and disciplines that do not share sociology's disciplinary history. In this section, I will group these critiques into those having to do with the "politics of representation" and those having to do with basic conceptual issues in the study of culture. However, the distinction is only for expository purposes, as many of the points made by feminist, postcolonial, poststructural authors point to basic conceptual issues and many of the conceptual critiques point to political implications.

Politics of Representation

Christian Smith and Jeffrey Alexander focus on trying to create a nonreductive portrait of culture through the classic ideas of relatively autonomous symbolic structures or moral orders. However, they do not address the important politi-cal issues that have motivated myriad critiques of this position. In this section, I will look at the contributions of feminist theory, postcolonial scholarship, and postmodern ethnography before returning to some of the classics in sociologi-cal theory.

In the 1970s, feminist social scientists forwarded important criticisms of the idea of cultural autonomy. Anthropologists Michele Rosaldo and Louise Lamphere (1974) argued, in their now-classic *Women, Culture and Society*, that most cultures at most times map the culture/nature binary on to the male/ female binary. In effect, the men who sit around the fire creating myth, nar-rative, and collective identities are the same ones who say these beliefs are authorless, disinterested, and autonomous. They are also in the position to por-tray the beliefs and practices of women—themselves busy with the tasks of social reproduction—as intuitive, affective, and emotional at best and anoma-lous, erratic, and self-interested at worst. In her classic research on gender and moral reasoning, Carol Gilligan took on theories of moral development that resulted in portraits of women's moral reasoning as stunted and immature. Her experiments with moral development showed that while males tended to define the self by separation from others and evaluated moral situations with relation to abstract ideals, females tended to define the self through connection with others and evaluated moral situations by thinking through how varying paths of action would affect particular others (Gilligan 1982, 35). Gilligan portrayed these not as "essences" of male or female gender, but rather as diverging answers to basic contradictions of human experience that tended to be exhibited more or less by males and females. "These disparate visions in their tension reflect the paradoxical truths of human experience—that we know ourselves as sepa-rate only insofar as we live in connection with others, and that we experience relationship only insofar as we differentiate other from self" (Gilligan 1982, 63). Finally, in her feminist standpoint theory, Dorothy Smith critiques "the governing mode" of knowledge creation, which "lifts actors out of the immedi-ate, local, and particular place in which we are in the body" and presents the concepts it creates as abstract, objective, and disinterested (Smith 1990, 18).

For our purposes here, what can be taken from Rosaldo and Lamphere, Gilligan, and Smith is the claim that an image of culture as autonomous and disengaged from particular lives in the world most corresponds to the experi-ence of people in dominant social positions. The underside of such a view is that people in nondominant positions who tend to use meaning in an interested, engaged, and contextualized way are often portrayed as anomalous, deceptive, or lacking in integrity. This was also one of the key motivating ideas of post-structuralists such as Jacque Derrida and Michel Foucault.

Postcolonial scholars, for their part, have argued that the idea of religious autonomy is a historical artifact of the particular history of Western modernity.

Talal Asad, for example, argues that the concept of religion as a symbolization of the general order of existence, autonomous from science, politics, and economics, was central to the constitution of a new kind of legal and moral subject in European modernity. When taken as a social scientific construct, it occludes more than it illuminates (Asad 1993; Chakrabarty 2000).

> The separation of religion from science, common sense, aesthetics, politics, and so on, allows [Geertz] to defend it against charges of irrationality. If religion has a distinctive perspective (its own truth, as Durkheim would have said) and performs an indispensable function, it does not in essence compete with others and cannot, therefore, be accused of generating false consciousness. Yet in a way this defense is equivocal.... This kind of phenomenological approach doesn't make it easy to examine whether, and if so to what extent and in what ways, religious experience relates to something in the real world that believers inhabit.... Religious symbols are treated, in circular fashion, as the precondition for religious experience (which, like any experience, must, by definition, be genuine), rather than as one condition for engaging with life. (Asad 1993, 50–51)

Cordoning off religion into an autonomous sphere protects it from debunking but simultaneously abstracts it from life and relevancy. Understanding how people can get things done with religion becomes a problem rather than a base assumption. Dipesh Chakrabarty has argued that the concept of an autonomous Christianity abstracted from the struggles and politics of everyday social life means that the Christians of the Bengali province he studies are portrayed as instrumentalist, vacillating, and insincere (Chakrabarty 2000). In this view, notions of autonomous religious culture become part of the colonial gaze and "othering" of non-European peoples as Westerners impose their own views of legitimate religiosity onto cultures that may have an entirely different way of thinking about it.

Parallel to the work of postcolonial scholars, postmodern critics of ethnography such as James Clifford (1988) argue that "ethnographic authority" is created precisely by imposing a system on unruly experience, a discrete, bounded "other world." The ethnographic observer translates experience into textual writing. The actual ambiguities and diversity of situations constituting the research experience drop out, and the dialogical situation is banished from the final text. Finally, transnational feminist scholars have built upon these ideas, criticizing the "death by culture" that third-world women are subjected to when they are portrayed as determined by culture. Such portrayals misrepresent their situation, as well as their rationalities and agency (Narayan 1997).

None of these critiques should be foreign to sociology insofar as some of its canonical authors have made similar points.[2] Max Weber long ago portrayed the structural coherence of religious thought as itself a medium through which religious elites dominated their followers (Weber 1968). Whatever sincere religious motives might motivate them, the systematization of religious ideas and inevitable naturalization of them as true and autonomous also shored up the power of religious elites as the approved interpreters and disinterested guardians of the truth. Thus, when scholars portray culture as autonomous, systematized, and unmotivated by practical concerns, they are portraying the world in such a way that tends to empower those in socially dominant positions of cultural creation. Pierre Bourdieu has called this the "scholastic fallacy." He sees intellectuals as having a structural position in which they have an "interest in disinterestedness"—portraying the realm of ideas as autonomous ipso facto portrays the work of intellectuals as autonomous and provides them with symbolic capital (Bourdieu 1998; see Gartman 2007). Beyond academia, however, everyday people need to be engaged with the practical concerns of life and do so not through disinterested cultural logic, but through a practical cultural sense (Gartman 2007, 394–395). Indeed, the starting point of Bourdieu's (1987) practice theory was the idea that overly systematized versions of social structure represent the perspective of the academic onlooker rather than the temporality and corporality of the actor.

None of these important motivations and arguments is ever mentioned by Alexander or Smith in their focus on shoring up the autonomy of culture. When Alexander gives his history of the "cultural turn," he runs straight from hermeneutics through the structuralist revolution to symbolic anthropology, obviating poststructuralism, deconstructionism, feminist theory, and postcolonialism (Alexander 2003, 6; Alexander and Smith 2010, 13).

Substantive Theoretical Critiques

The aforementioned critiques are motivated by the politics of representation, the sense that certain forms of scholarly analysis misrepresent the experiences, behaviors, and sentiments of nondominant social sectors. However, they also point to a number of basic theoretical dilemmas caused by structuralist portraits of cultural autonomy. These are big issues about which a lot has been written. But for the purposes of this chapter, I will restrict myself to brief reviews of the problems of agency, causation, and boundaries.

Agency

One of the classic problems with structuralist portrayals of the autonomy of culture is, as Asad suggested, the difficulty of then reconnecting it with the rest of social reality, most particularly with the agency of social actors (see also Lizardo 2010). Pragmatist theorists have especially focused on this problem. Eugene Halton (1995) has critiqued the base supposition of the cultural arbitrary, the idea that cultural symbols have no necessary connection with any external, nonsymbolic reality, and therefore cannot be reduced to it. Similar to Asad, Halton argues that while this indeed succeeds in portraying an irreducible structure we can call culture, in the process it disengages culture from life. It becomes difficult to understand how culture can be involved in action, desire, or bodily existence of any kind and how it can ever change, much less how it was created in the first place. "The human creature, who, above all others both is open to and needs meaning, is denied the social capacity to germinate and body forth genuinely new feelings, perceptions, and ideas not reducible to, though growing out of, prior social norms" (p. 92). Several other scholars working from a pragmatist perspective have also called for an emphasis on creativity in culture rather than a simple focus on cultural autonomy, continuity, and reproduction (see Joas 1997, and Emirbayer and Mische 1998).

Causation

Another persistent conundrum faced by structuralist accounts is the conceptualization of causation. "Strong" approaches to culture tend to work with the notion of constant causation (Ragin 1987). If you view culture as a structure that works behind the backs of actors to frame their engagement with the world, you need to assume that it is always effective. However, it is increasingly evident that such portraits are inadequate. Mark Chaves has recently reviewed a host of examples that show that if sometimes culture has a given effect, at other times it will have the contrary effect, and at still other times it will have no effect at all. Chaves (2010, 5) sees this as a facet of the "congruence fallacy":

> Religiosity, for example, seems related to positive health outcomes in the United States but not in Europe. Another example: Evangelical Protestant pregnant teenagers are less likely than mainline Protestants to abort (controlling of other things), but Catholics are not—and girls in religious schools are more likely to abort than girls in public schools. After reviewing the literature on the connections between religion and prejudice and religion and deviance, Perrin concluded that "religiosity effects are not as significant as common wisdom and social scientific theory might suggest." And decades of psychological research looking for behavior consequences of intrinsic religiosity has yielded the conclusion that intrinsically religious people do not act in more pro-social ways than anyone else, but they think they do, or should or would, so

their behavioral self-reports often are different from those of other people even when their behavior is not.

Clearly religion can have causal effects. But these effects are inconsistent and sometimes absent altogether. Chaves suggests that we need to start with the presupposition of incongruence and seek to explain cases of congruence (i.e., when and how religion has causal effects).

Boundaries

A final issue afflicting strong views of culture is the problem of boundaries. Since the time of the "culture and personality" research program of Ruth Benedict (2005 [1934]) and others, figuring out exactly where one "cultural logic" ends and another begins has been a central problem (Fabian 1991). The general tendency has been to focus on the nation-state as a natural unit of analysis (and within this a focus on nations that have a degree of cultural homogeneity and uniqueness like Japan or France). Jeffrey Alexander generally focuses on the cultural binaries of something called "the United States" (Alexander 2003; Smith 2005). Another solution is to focus on cultural linguistic groups (Huntington 1998). The problem of boundaries is different from the problem of consensus—Alexander and others don't assume consensus and indeed often focus on conflicts over meaning. Rather, the problem is that if you assume that cultural structures constrain actors behind their backs, you need to be able to define what group of people is subject to these constraints.

This is also an issue of representation. It is often the need to find a community that corresponds to a cultural logic or moral order that leads to glosses such as "Russians," "New Yorkers," or "Muslims" that occlude internal variation and marginalize nondominant voices. Olivier Roy (2004), for example, has made the disassembling of the "Muslim other" the central analytic task of his recent work. In doing so, he usefully portrays the Middle East as a collage of different religious, ethnic, and national groups competing for power, rather than a uniform Islamist collectivity rising up against the West.

Explaining the Persistence of the Strong Program

Alexander marvels that it has taken sociologists so long to embrace "the cultural turn." In my view, it seems remarkable that a strong program focusing on the autonomy of culture has made such a comeback within the sociology of culture and religion, despite the decades of multifaceted, comprehensive critiques of the idea. Wherein lies the attractiveness of this perspective? I think it is simplistic to suggest a patriarchal, colonialist, or logocentric will to power.

Rather, there are a couple of understandable reasons for the enduring appeal of such a portrait.

First, at least since Immanuel Kant and arguably before, the ideas that human beings give form to the world rather than simply being determined by it, and that they can follow rules of their own making, have been enduring foundations of the idea of human freedom (Levine 1995). And for scholars who see the concept of human freedom as a cornerstone of human dignity and morality, the irreducibility of culture and its causal power on human behavior are important images.

Second, within the sociology of religion, the autonomy of at least some religion is a necessary condition of the reality of the supernatural and is thus a logical analytic goal for many people of faith. Indeed, as many have argued, the carving off of a domain of social reality as "religious," autonomous, and separate from other "secular" domains was precisely a mechanism by which the early modern church was able to maintain a space for religious authority vis-à-vis encroaching secular authority (Asad 1993; Hall 2009). Likewise, Courtney Bender (2010) has recently argued that the residual categorization of religious experience as ineffable, precultural, inexplicable experience extends from attempts of early twentieth scholars to carve off a domain of human experience not susceptible to scientific analysis. We should not be surprised, then, that this is an enduring interest within the scientific study of religion.

Finally, and perhaps most important, the idea of a phenomenon's autonomous reality provides a time-honored foundation of legitimacy for a discipline's professional activity. If there is a domain of knowledge dealing with X, it is most obviously in the interests of specialists in that domain to underline and drive home the reality and importance of X. Ferdinand de Saussure's (1972) *Course in General Linguistics* has become the seminal text in linguistics precisely because it succeeds in portraying language as an irreducible formal system of signs with a coherent structure beyond the messy details and disorder of actual speech. Emile Durkheim (1982) sought to create a foundation for sociology in turn-of-the-century France by arguing that society was a reality *sui generis* that needed a new discipline to study it. Talcott Parsons (1937) sought to do the same in the US context through his thesis that scholars from different disciplines and countries had simultaneously and independently converged on the "voluntaristic theory of action" in which the values and norms were irreducible.

These are all legitimate reasons for emphasizing cultural autonomy (although the last moves me the least), but we need to weigh these gains against the problems pointed out by the critiques described previously. In what follows, I will review some alternative tools for the study of religion—tools that suggest we can have a robust concept of culture without the added baggage.

Alternatives for Understanding Cultural Power

Alexander and C. Smith conceptualize the power of culture in the classic way: as an autonomous structure that guides action.[3] As we have seen previously, this path carries with it some well-identified analytic and representational problems. In this section, I will lay out some alternative directions. First, I will look at the conceptualization of culture as an "objective" reality as it is analyzed in the "weak program." Then I will look at some tools for understanding the subjective strength of culture without relying on structural definitions of culture.

The Strength of Weak Programs

David Gartman (2007) has argued that Alexander misrepresents the work of Pierre Bourdieu as not allowing for the relative autonomy of culture. Gartman argues that a proper understanding of the concepts of habitus and field show that the "weak program" of Pierre Bourdieu is actually much "stronger" than Alexander has portrayed it. The same point can be made about the strength of the "weak program" of the sociology of culture. In Alexander's 2003 articulation of the "strong program" of *cultural sociology,* he uses the "weak program" of the *sociology of culture* as a foil, giving the impression that in the latter perspective culture is always a dependent variable and has no concept of cultural causality. He admits that cultural sociology and the sociology of culture share a vocabulary, but argues that they are divided by structural antinomies (2003, 12): the very idea of the "sociology of culture" suggests "that culture is something to be explained by something else entirely separated from the domain of meaning itself." In contrast, in "cultural sociology" Alexander sees cultural meaning working unconsciously behind people's backs "as feelings of the heart" and "fearful instincts of the gut" (2003, 3). It is this unconscious meaning that gives shape to the way people interact with social structures, and this explains culture's causal power.

But these antinomies only exist for those who insist on seeing the world in terms of binary opposites, for they are patently untrue. As in the case of Bourdieu, while Alexander's criticism validly points to some analytic tendencies, it glosses over some of the most important features of the sociology of culture—features that are not beset by the problems of structuralism described earlier.

Of course, there are many things that can be described as the "sociology of culture," but the subdisciplinary movement represented by Wendy Griswold, Ann Swidler, Robert Wuthnow, and others has as its centerpiece what could be called an objectivist view of culture. "Objectivist" here is used not in the epistemological sense, but rather in an empirical-substantive sense. The basic point is to move from a focus on culture as present in subjectivities to a focus on culture as present in extrasubjective "cultural objects." Wuthnow says culture should be understood "not as some subjective or idealized world view that is to be distinguished from behavior but as a form of behavior itself and as the tangible results of that behavior" (1987, 15). Griswold speaks of "cultural objects" defined as "shared significance embodied in form" (1987a, 5). Among the implications of this view of culture is the portrait of causality. Ann Swidler (1995) has persuasively argued that the power of culture is best conceived as working "from the outside in" rather than "from in the inside out." Swidler gives the example of the ritual of gift giving, which is widely disparaged by people but can have a far-reaching impact on their behavior. As well, some deeply held beliefs can have little or no impact on behavior depending on context. For example, sociologists have frequently shown that impoverished populations with high rates of pregnancy out of wedlock have the same or more conservative values regarding premarital sex as the larger population. This does not mean that these cultural objects are not subjectively meaningful. Rather, it suggests that cultural power does not depend on subjective assent. The larger point in the sociology of culture is the same as that made by Chaves earlier—the causal power of culture should be considered a problem for investigation, not an assumption, nor a criterion for case selection.

The sociology of culture foregrounds the question of "why this culture now?" In a recent reassessment of the "strong program," Alexander concedes that this question provides a challenge for the strong program, but says, "traditional sociology would answer this question with reference to material resources, to informational control, to networks, or to interests or manipulative elites." He argues that the strong program has "avoided the easy choice of referring the triumph of one meaning system or another back to something that seems more concrete, insisting instead that there can be cultural factors behind cultural outcomes" (Alexander and Smith 2010, 21). Whether this is true of "traditional sociology" is up for debate, but it certainly does not distinguish cultural sociology from the sociology of culture. Griswold, for example, in her study of revivals of renaissance theater sees them as the "products of human actors operating in concrete social, institutional, *and cultural settings*" (Griswold 1986, 2, italics mine). The point here is that while a particular cultural object can be distinguished from its context, "culture" can also be one of the causal factors involved in "which culture when." And Wuthnow's institutional model of cultural explanation explains the success of a particular cultural object like religious discourses, political ideologies, or theater productions through the "transformative power" of "tropological elements" such as "social horizons, discursive fields, and figural actions" among other possibilities (Wuthnow 1987 14–15). Courtney Bender (2010) uses Wuthnow's approach in her ethnography of American mystics using a classic sociology of culture approach that focuses on practices that are inscribed in bodies, times, spaces, and discourses and embedded in institutions precisely to demonstrate the continuity involved in a form of religious practice that is generally portrayed as ineffable, discontinuous, and without a history. The point is that rather than assume that culture *has to be* a causal variable, we need to assume that it *can be, but is not necessarily,* a causal variable.

Before moving on, let us take a look at how this perspective avoids the problems of boundaries, causality, and coherence besetting strong approaches. First, the focus on extrasubjective cultural objects means that there is not necessarily any given community of people associated with them. Socialist meta-narratives, glossolalia, and bluegrass music do not necessarily correspond to a particular community—although they certainly can—in the same way that a deep binary cultural structure or moral order would seem to. They can be ignored by people close by or picked up by those far away. The image of cultural objects helps us think beyond bounded spaces and bounded actors and, instead, of a space with multiple competing cultural objects. Overcoming the problem of boundaries also helps with the political issues of representation as described earlier.

Second, the sociology of culture facilitates a move away from the idea of "constant association" (the idea that all elements of social action are always present across contexts) toward an assumption of conjunctural causality (the idea that at different moments different causal factors may dominate or recede into the background) (Ragin 1987). The difference can be seen by comparing two of Wendy Griswold's studies. Her study of nineteenth-century American novels (Griswold 1981) showed that a certain type of western became prominent in the nineteenth century not because of an "American character" reflected in literature, but because of copyright laws that meant Americans had to write something different from their European counterparts. Here an economic-legal structure clearly had causal predominance over culture. Yet in her study of the reception of the novels of George Lamming (Griswold 1987b), she shows how reviewers in the West Indies, Great Britain, and the United States saw quite different themes depending on the debates and discourses of their own national context. In other words, different national cultures determined how the text was received.

Alexander has recently said that adherents to the strong program do not reject a multidimensional view of social life, but rather choose to emphasize explanations that are "all about culture" even if they are not "just about culture." Sociology of culture, in contrast, truly embraces multidimensional explanations, deriving portraits of causality from the empirical phenomena studied. To put it bluntly, sometimes culture matters; sometimes it does not.

Finally, a focus on extrasubjective cultural objects leads directly to the idea that culture normally contains a repertoire of schemas, symbols, and discourses that are not brought together into any sort of coherent framework and that could be described as "cultural logic" or "moral order." It thereby helps avoid the scholastic fallacy. Coherence and order can certainly happen. Max Weber thought religions achieved a degree of rationalization in specific circumstances, such as when religious intellectualism becomes part of the religious practice of the laity, for example, with the Calvinist peasants of Holland (Weber 1968, 507). In any given context in which intellectuals gain an important role in defining culture, we can expect a degree of coherence and consistency. And there are certain cultural traditions that value consistency and clarity of ideas—such as Protestant Christianity. But in most circumstances, the repertoire of culture meanings and practices will not be rationalized, but rather will contain numerous, mutually contradictory meanings that are marshaled for dealing with specific situations.

With these last two points, then, I agree with Mark Chaves (2010) when he says that we simply need to change our presuppositions. Our working presupposition needs to be that in most cases and most situations, culture is not coherent and consistent, and that in most situations, its engagement in actual social behavior is inconsistent and not predetermined.

Realist Alternatives to Autonomous Cultural Structures

In the previous section, I suggested that objectivist understandings of the functioning of culture can help us avoid the scholastic fallacy that is at the root of the issues of representation at the same time that they help us skirt the issue of boundaries and facilitates a conjunctural view of causality. The problem of agency created by portrayals of culture as a structurally defined code requires going beyond the autonomy of culture. The problem of agency described by Halton previously is complex, and an adequate treatment is beyond the scope of this chapter (for an excellent review see Emirbayer and Mische 1998). Here we can affirm that when the causal power of culture is based on a notion of autonomy, it is difficult to understand how culture can be engaged in everyday life except as an unconscious, behind-the-back structure of influence. It can have an impact, but not be impacted in turn. As many authors have pointed out, once a cultural structure is separated from social structure, the causal arrow can only go one way (Archer 1982; Asad 1993; Lizardo 2010). In addition to the explanatory conundrums this leads to, it also brackets the causes of culture and portrays it as an essentially meaningless primordial, unmoved mover. The question then becomes, how can we have a concept of culture and religion that is not reductionist, that understands their ability to exercise causal power in any given context, but that is not abstracted from the agency of everyday life? Put more simply, how can we understand culture being causal yet also caused?

The classic alternative to portraits of culture as an arbitrary structure, of course, is a portrait of culture based on some form of realism. There are multiple variants of realism, but what they have in common is the suggestion that at least in part, the vitality of cultural beliefs and practices is explained by the underlying reality that they refer to (Abend 2008). Put differently, realism moves beyond the arbitrary character of culture and sees culture as a means of engaging the world just like science or common sense and thereby can explain both the causal power and the causation of cultural beliefs. Naïve realism would simply suggest that cultural beliefs and practices are effective to the degree that they accurately portray an underlying reality. This position, of course, does not get us far given the incompatible truth claims of equally vibrant religious meaning systems. But other forms of realism have emerged; here I will look at two: critical realism and embodied realism. These two forms of realism have in common the belief that there is a real world and the assumption that some concepts are better than others in helping people engage it. The difference is that critical realism is somewhat stronger in thinking that concepts are better insofar as they are closer to reality. Embodied realism, in contrast, assumes that the concepts that "work" can just as well be "useful fictions" that mobilize people precisely by distorting reality.

Critical Realism

Critical realism is an alternative to the idea of arbitrary cultural structures currently being developed by a group of scholars including Christian Smith and Douglas Porpora. It is a complex philosophical view based on the work of philosopher of science Roy Bhaskar, whose key assumption is that reality exists with its own objective structures and dynamics, independent of human consciousness of it (Smith 2010, 105). Human beings can obtain a "truthful, though fallible" and never complete knowledge of this reality. While this knowledge is fallible, it is not all equally fallible. Critical realism has mainly been used to think about the methodological bases of social science. However, it has also been used to conceptualize religious experience. Douglas Porpora (2006), for example, uses it to move beyond the classic position of "methodological atheism"—the idea that no part of a religious experience can be explained by the object of that experience—articulated long ago by Peter Berger and affirm instead a stance called "methodological agnosticism." Porpora argues that reified notions of what is experience, what is natural, and what science consists of have been overcome in the postmodern era and suggests that there is no prima facie reason to exclude experience of the supernatural from scientific explanation. Thus, methodological agnosticism neither asserts nor precludes supernatural realities. This position allows "the supernatural explanation to compete freely against naturalistic rivals so that it becomes an empirical matter in any given case which kind of explanation is best" (Porpora 2006, 58). On this perspective, then, what could account for the persistence and vitality of a specific set of beliefs is that they might actually be true; they might actually conceptualize the supernatural with a relative degree of accuracy. Put differently, our cultural concepts, just as much as our scientific concepts, can be more or less true, and this could explain their persuasiveness.

Perhaps I misunderstand, but critical realism strikes me as a moderated version of naïve realism – like the Apostle Paul's "seeing through a glass darkly." Concepts are effective to the degree that they resemble reality, however incompletely (for now). In the wrong hands, it seems likely to result in religious chauvinism and intolerance. Perhaps its attractiveness depends on whether one views our contemporary world more threatened by humanist denials of religious truth or the conflict generated by incompatible religious truth claims (for the latter possibility see Hall 2009). Indeed, within the intellectual history of critical realism, there has been considerable conflict over whether the notion of a "real world" can be extended from the physical to the social world.[4]

Embodied Realism

However, critical realism is not the only version of reconstructed realism available. Margaret Somers has laid out what she calls "relational pragmatic realism"—also in the context of debates on social science methodology. In this view, scientific concepts gain salience not because they are unmediated representations of the world but because the phenomenon as described is causally, practically, and relationally significant (Somers 1998, 743). If the concept helps us with our purposes, we tend to believe in it. This is somewhat different from critical realism insofar as the relationship between concepts and reality is less direct. The pragmatist input is to suggest that the fact that concepts work for us does not necessarily mean that they approximate the objective characteristics of reality. They could just as well work for us because they distort it in such a way that they facilitate action with respect to it or resonate with our relational context.

Cognitive linguist George Lakoff has also developed a pragmatist form of realism he once called "experientialist" and now calls "embodied." In Lakoff's view, metaphors should not be defined in contrast to rationality but rather as a form of "imaginative rationality" as they are used in action (Lakoff and Johnson 1980, 193). Metaphors are "concepts we live by." Whether in science, common sense, poetry, or religion, metaphors unite reason and imagination in the thought process and are confirmed or disconfirmed in practice. The distinction between "literal" and "figurative" meanings should be seen as a continuum rather than as a qualitative difference.

> Our conceptual system emerges from our constant successful functioning in our physical and cultural environment. Our categories of

experience and the dimensions out of which they are constructed not only have emerged from our experience but are constantly being tested through ongoing successful functioning by all members of our culture. (p. 180)

The pragmatist basis of this perspective comes from the classic Peircian notion that thought is an activity that consists of belief, which leads to action, which when it leads to unexpected or undesired results leads to doubt, which leads to inquiry, which leads to new beliefs. Thought is an activity, a means of acting in the world. Belief is not something that happens to us behind our backs. It is not something that is nonempirical. It is a moment in our thought process followed by action, doubt, and inquiry (Peirce 1887).

Thus, for example, in my research on Evangelicals in Caracas (Smilde 2007), some men who had been unable to overcome their substance abuse problem through straightforward willpower were able to when they became Evangelical. Evangelical meanings and practices redefined this struggle in supernatural terms. Every individual needs to maintain contact with Jesus Christ by dominating the body and thereby allowing himself to be controlled by the Holy Spirit. When he consumes alcohol, he breaks that contact and is susceptible to being controlled instead by the Devil. When participating in Evangelical services and hanging around with other Evangelicals kept the person away from drink, this Evangelical theory was validated in the minds of my respondents, and it most emphatically was not working behind their backs. The fact that the causality is quite different from how a secularized social scientist would describe it is irrelevant; the theory predicted certain results would follow certain actions and it was confirmed.

This pragmatist view skirts naïve realism because while it suspects there is a real world out there and builds in the notion that some concepts work better than others, the criteria for evaluating whether those concepts "work" also come from within the cultural context. The relational element highlights the importance of communities in defining truth criteria and plausibility. To quote Mayer Zald's (1995) paraphrase of the "turtles all the way down" response to the problem of infinite regress, no foundationalism is possible because "it's communities all the way down." In my research on Venezuelan Evangelicals, I get at this by complementing the concept of "imaginative rationality" with the concept of "relational imagination." What can be imagined, and whether particular imaginings are supported or discouraged, depends on an individual's location in relational context (Smilde 2007).

The same considerations go into Andreas Glaeser's (2011) recent development of "hermeneutic institutionalism" based on a "sociology of understanding" rather than a "sociology of knowledge." Glaeser uses the term *understanding* to get away from the objectivist sense of "pieces" of knowledge that exist independently of activity. As a gerund, "understanding" highlights not "knowledge" but "knowing, an ongoing process of orientation in the world" (Glaeser 2011, xxvii). Understandings are used to orient action and can have varying degrees of certainty, from "hunches" to "hypotheses" to "knowledge," or from implicit background assumption to "pangs of doubt" to "error" (p. xxviii). As orientations to action, our understandings are subject to validation. They can be directly corroborated or contradicted by events in the world. However, Glaeser avoids naïve realism by saying there are two other forms of validation. "Recognition" entails checking our understandings through interaction with other human beings. "Resonance" refers to our understandings "holding up...against what else we believe, know, or take for real against our desires as well as against our values" (p. 25). Glaeser refers to different ways of organizing and prioritizing these different forms of validation, as well as groupings of understandings that affect corroboration, recognition, and resonance as "meta-understandings" (pp. 26–28).

Let us be clear about what embodied realism can and cannot do. It cannot prove the existence of God. It cannot provide us with unmediated moral truth. And it cannot assure us of the desirability of any particular belief or practice. It cannot do any of these things because it does not make the assumption that people judge their beliefs on any abstract rationalist unconstructed theory of truth. Rather, for beliefs and the practices to be compelling, they simply need to, on average, provide the results they promise. People may convert because they have been told that when they become Evangelical Jesus Christ will act to rid them of their substance abuse problem. When their substance abuse problem is overcome, it strengthens beliefs in Jesus Christ's agency, even if social scientists would identify a process having to do with narrative control of self, social networks, and group ritual. What matters is that it is true within the Evangelical meaning system, not in the "objective" terms of social science. Furthermore, meaning systems are cultivated, maintained, and protected from disconfirming evidence by communities—or more broadly by relational contexts. Thus, in contrast to critical realism, embodied realism does not challenge the distinction between theology and science. Meaning systems and forms of religious practice that seem entirely unconvincing in scientific terms—such as rain dances, UFO cults, and doomsday predictions—can be entirely convincing to members of particular communities or networks. And conversely, theories that unequivocally convince scientists, such as evolution, can be entirely unconvincing to particular religious communities.

However, embodied realism can help us in several ways. First, it de-essentializes the proper or natural domain of religious practice. There is no reason to consider individual or collective identity, morality, or the afterlife as the natural or even normal domains of religion. Religious practices are simply practices that have reference to a supernatural domain and can be oriented toward any human interests. Conversely, since these interests are all constructed through cultural meanings, there is no need to portray certain interests as unconstructed "rational" self-interests. When a poor Venezuelan becomes Pentecostal in order to overcome his substance abuse problem and sidestep situations of violence, it is not an instrumental use of religion for non-religious interests, because part of the narrative he is adopting is that God is the creator and wants human beings to live in a safe and productive fashion.

It can also help us understand agency. Religion can, but does not necessarily or even most frequently, function through unconscious motivations or cultural categories. Since beliefs are not necessarily nonempirical, people can consciously think and act through religion rather than simply being acted upon by it or simply acting upon it, because beliefs are no longer nonempirical. Nor do we need the image of human beings combining their cultural frameworks with strategic interests, as in Alexander's dualism. Strategic interests arise from within cultural frameworks. Determinism is not a necessary result, because innovation and improvisation are always implied in the way structure gets put into motion. The idea that practice would be determined by culture is as unrealistic as the idea that the outcome of the World Cup would be determined by the rules of the game of soccer.

Finally, embodied realism provides an alternative portrait of religion as embodied practice. The "lived religion" school of religious studies has turned away from texts, theologies, religious institutions, and elites in order to focus on the way religion is actually practiced in everyday life, in "nonreligious" spaces. The goal is not so much to dismiss the former as to contextualize them as part of what is more basic: the actual practices that constitute religion: "The study of lived religion is not about practice rather than ideas, but about ideas, gestures, and imaginings, as media of engagement with the world" (Orsi 2003). Embodied realism based on metaphor theory provides some theoretical substance for understanding just how this engagement takes place.

To end this section, I should pause to address the apparent contradiction between the "objectivist" portrait of culture provided in the previous section and the look at realist views of "subjective" religious concepts in this section. The basic issue in both sections is to show ways that cultural power can be demonstrated beyond classic portraits of it consisting of an autonomous structure that affects actors behind their backs. The argument in the previous section is that we can portray culture as extrasubjective and causal, without having to recur to concepts of culture as an autonomous and arbitrary cultural structure. Meaning can be embodied in forms such as a piece of music, a poem, a ritual, or an ideology, none of which need to be part of a larger cultural structure or moral order. That argument is not antisubjective—saying a cultural object is extrasubjective does not mean it is not subjectively meaningful to people. It simply means that it has an existence beyond any given person's subjectivity and therefore whether and how it has causal impact on people is an object of research, not an assumption. The argument in this section also moves beyond the idea of an arbitrary cultural structure in order to think about cultural subjectivities in ways that allow us to understand agency. Rather than being portrayed as involuntary and deeply held beliefs doing their work behind the backs of actors, in critical and embodied realism, beliefs are media of interaction with the world. People can "try them on," assent to them when they work, and discard them when they do not. It does not imply that cultural is "subjective" in the sense of depending on individual experience. As noted earlier, which cultural concept is corroborated when depends on relational context.

Toward a "Broad Program" in the Sociology of Religion

The contemporary push beyond the reduced concept of culture often used in sociology and toward a more robust cultural concept in the sociology of religion can only be applauded. However, the emphasis on cultural autonomy has long-detected baggage that sociologists of religion need to keep in their sights. In effect, feminist, postcolonial, poststructural, and postmodern theorists have argued that concepts of cultural autonomy occlude the social, historical, and political process of cultural creation and obfuscate the experiences, sentiments, and cultural constructions of nondominant social strata. And approaches focusing on cultural autonomy have also been criticized repeatedly for their difficulties in facing the problems of agency, boundaries, and causality. Thus, rather than trying to reconstruct our understanding of religious culture by returning to concepts from mid-twentieth-century social science, we need to build upon the critiques and advances in the study of culture in the last decades of the twentieth century.

In a recent edited volume on cultural sociology, Hall, Grindstaff, and Lo (2010) call for a "broad program" that incorporates but moves beyond the narrow concerns of the strong program to include a breadth of phenomena, conceptual tools, and analytic intentions. A key element of their call is a move beyond the "Eurocentric biases" of sociological theorizations through increasing attention to globalizations at both the macro and micro levels conceptualized on their own terms. I think the sociology of religion would also do well to think in terms of a "broad program" and that focusing beyond the United States and more particularly on the global South will facilitate such a move. To be sure, the relative autonomy and causal power of religion will always be present as an analytic interest among those who seek to demonstrate human freedom from structural determination. However, a sociology of religion that pays more attention to global phenomena and to answering the pressing questions of our world will have to use conceptual tools other than a "strong" version of religious culture.

Such a broad program would entail four main moves. First, it will have to move beyond an exclusive focus on religious culture as an autonomous structure that works behind people's backs. Sociologists of religion need to also look at religion in terms of discourses, rituals, material culture, and everyday religious practices. As Paul Lichterman's chapter in this volume argues, a move beyond Christo-centric presuppositions will facilitate this. Second, the sociology of religion needs to move beyond a view of religious culture as autonomous and separate from everyday life to a view of religion as a medium of agency. For most people in most places, religion is not a sphere apart, focusing on morality, identity, and the afterlife. Rather, it is a means with which people engage the world and has no natural domain of action. Especially in the global South, religious practices oriented toward life concerns such as staying safe, sober, and faithful and putting food on the table are not instrumental misuses of religion. Rather, these basic, existential needs are experienced as religious given a God who wants it "to go well with thee...."

Third, the sociology of religion needs to go beyond the scholastic fallacy, that is, portrayals of religion as a rationalized cultural system or moral order to a focus on religion as lived practice in all of its contradictions. Actual religious practice involves a repertoire of beliefs and practices that may be mutually contradictory but are put into practice as needed (see Smilde 2004, 2007). This move is motivated by not only the conceptual conundrums but also the issues of representation to which the scholastic fallacy leads. Not only postcolonial but also feminist scholars have pointed out that oversystematization leads to misrepresentation of the experiences of people in nondominant social positions.

Finally, the sociology of religion needs to move beyond the assumption of constant association motivated by the desire to demonstrate the causal efficacy of religion. The sociology of religion should seek to work with an assumption of conjunctural causality, which is the same as saying it needs to assume multidimensional explanation in which sometimes religion will be causal and other times will be caused.

Acknowledgment

I would like to thank John R. Hall, Omar Lizardo, Isaac Reed, and my fellow editors for their comments on this chapter. It also benefitted from presentation at 2009 meetings of the Society for the Scientific Study of Religion.

Notes

1.   Within the sociological study of culture, this debate has taken place more clearly than it has in the sociology of religion, and much of what I discuss in this chapter will focus on the sociological study of culture in general, of which the sociology of religion is a subset.

2. For evidence of this see also Isaac Reed's *Interpretation and Social Knowledge* (2011).
3. This is not entirely fair to Christian Smith, as he explicitly rejects structuralism in his text. However, he frequently speaks in the dualist terms that semiotic structuralism leads to and does not provide an alternative understanding for where the causal power of culture comes from. Later we will see some of his more recent work on "critical realism," which could fulfill that role but which has not yet, to my knowledge, been reconciled with his 2003 statement.
4. Special thanks to Isaac Reed for pointing this out to me.

References

Abend, Gabriel. 2008. "Two Main Problems in the Sociology of Morality." *Theory and Society* 37(2): 87–125.

———. 2003. *The Meanings of Social Life: A Cultural Sociology*. New York: Oxford University Press.

Alexander, Jeffrey C., and Philip Smith. "The Strong Program: Origins, Achievements, and Prospects." Pp. 13–24 in *Handbook of Cultural Sociology*, edited by John R. Hall, Laura Grindstaff, and Ming-Cheng Lo. New York: Routledge.

Archer, Margaret S. 1982. "Morphogenesis Versus Structuration: On Combining Structure and Action." *British Journal of Sociology* 33: 455–483.

Asad, Talal. 1993. *Genealogies of Religion: Discipline and Reasons of Power in Christianity and Islam*. Baltimore: Johns Hopkins University Press.

Bender, Courtney. 2010. *The New Metaphysicals Spirituality and the American Religious Imagination*. Chicago: University of Chicago Press.

Benedict, Ruth. 2005 [1934]. *Patterns of Culture*. New York: Mariner Books.

Bourdieu, Pierre. 1977. *Outline of a Theory of Practice*. Cambridge: Cambridge University Press.

———. 1987. *Distinction: A Social Critique of the Judgment of Taste*. Cambridge, MA: Harvard University Press.

———. 1998. *Practical Reason: On the Theory of Action*. Stanford, CA: Stanford University Press.

Chakrabarty, Dipesh. 2000. *Provincializing Europe: Postcolonial Thought and Historical Difference*. Princeton, NJ: Princeton University Press.

Chaves, Mark. 2010. "SSSR Presidential Address—Rain Dances in the Dry Season: Overcoming the Religious Congruence Fallacy." *Journal for the Scientific Study of Religion* 49: 1–14.

Clifford, James. 1988. *The Predicament of Culture: Twentieth-Century Ethnography, Literature, and Art*. Cambridge, MA: Harvard University Press.

Culler, Jonathan D. 1983. *On Deconstruction: Theory and Criticism after Structuralism*. Ithaca, NY: Cornell University Press.

De Saussure, Ferdinand. 1972. *Course on General Linguistics*. Peru: Open Court Publishers.

Durkheim, Emile. 1982. *Rules of Sociological Method*, edited by Steven Lukes and translated by W. D. Halls. New York: Free Press.

Edgell, Penny. 2006. *Religion and Family in a Changing Society*. Princeton, NJ: Princeton University Press.

Eliasoph, Nina, and Paul Lichterman. 2003. "Culture in Interaction." *American Journal of Sociology* 108(4): 735–794.

Emirbayer, Mustafa, and Ann Mische. 1998. "What Is Agency?" *American Journal of Sociology* 103: 962–1023.

Fabian, Johannes. 1991. *Time and the Work of Anthropology: Critical Essays 1971–1981*. New York: Routledge.

Gamson, William. 1995. "Constructing Social Protest." Pp. 85–106 in *Social Movements and Culture*, edited by Hank Johnston and Bert Klandermans. Minneapolis: University of Minnesota Press.

Gartman, David. 2007. "The Strength of Weak Programs in Cultural Sociology: A Critique of Alexander's Critique of Bourdieu." *Theory and Society* 36(5): 381–413.

Gilligan, Carol. 1982. *In a Different Voice: Psychological Theory and Women's Development.* Cambridge, MA: Harvard University Press.

Glaeser, Andreas. 2011. *Political Epistemics: The Secret Police, the Opposition, and the End of East German Socialism.* Chicago: University of Chicago Press.

Griswold, Wendy. 1981. "American Character and the American Novel: An Expansion of Reflection Theory in the Sociology of Literature." *American Journal of Sociology* 86(4): 740–765.

———. 1986. *Renaissance Revivals: City Comedy and Revenge Tragedy in the London Theater, 1576– 1980.* Chicago: University of Chicago Press.

———. 1987a. "A Methodological Framework for the Sociology of Culture." *Sociological Methodology* 17: 1–35.

———. 1987b. "The Fabrication of Meaning: Literary Interpretation in the United States, Great Britain, and the West Indies." *American Journal of Sociology* 92(5): 1077–1117.

Hall, John R. 2009. *Apocalypse: From Antiquity to the Empire of Modernity.* Malden, MA: Polity Press.

Hall, John R., Laura Grindstaff, and Ming-Cheng Lo. 2010. "Introduction: Culture, Lifeworlds, and Globalization." In Pp. 1–10 *Handbook of Cultural Sociology.* New York: Routledge.

Halton, Eugene. 1995. *Bereft of Reason: On the Decline of Social Thought and Prospects for Its Renewal.* Chicago: University of Chicago Press.

Huntington, Samuel J. 1998. *The Clash of Civilizations and the Remaking of World Order.* New York: Simon and Schuster.

Jauss, Hans. 1982. *Toward and Aesthetic of Reception.* Minneapolis: University of Minnesota Press.

Joas, Hans. 1997. *The Creativity of Action.* Chicago: University of Chicago Press.

Kane, Anne. 1992. "Cultural Analysis in Historical Sociology: The Analytic and Concrete Forms of the Autonomy of Culture." *Sociological Theory* 9(1): 53–69.

Lakoff, George. 1993. "The Contemporary Theory of Metaphor." Pp. 202–251 in *Metaphor and Thought*, edited by Andrew Ortony. New York: Cambridge University Press.

Lakoff, George, and Mark Johnson. 1980. *Metaphors We Live By.* Chicago: University of Chicago Press.

Levine, Donald N. 1995. *Visions of the Sociological Tradition.* Chicago: University of Chicago Press.

Lizardo, Omar. 2010. "Beyond the Antinomies of Structure: Levi-Strauss, Giddens, Bourdieu and Sewell." *Theory and Society* 39: 651–688.

Narayan, Uma. 1997. *Dislocating Cultures: Identities, Traditions and Third World Feminisms.* New York: Routledge.

Orsi, Robert. 2003. "Is the Study of Lived Religion Irrelevant to the World We Live In? Special Presidential Plenary Address, Society for the Scientific Study of Religion, Salt Lake City, November 2, 2002." *Journal for the Scientific Study of Religion* 42(2): 169–174.

———. 2005. *Between Heaven and Earth: The Religious Worlds People Make and the Scholars Who Study Them.* Princeton, NJ: Princeton University Press.

Parsons, Talcott. 1937. *The Structure of Social Action.* Vol. I. New York: Free Press.

Peirce, Charles S. 1877. "The Fixation of Belief." *Popular Science Monthly* 12 (November): 1–15.

Peterson, Richard. 1999. *The Fabrication of Meaning: Literary Interpretation in the United States, Great Britain, and the West Indies.* Chicago: University of Chicago Press.

Porpora, Douglas. 2006. "Methodological Atheism, Methodological Agnosticism and Religious Experience." *Journal for the Theory of Social Behavior* 36(1): 57–75.

Ragin, Charles. 1987. *The Comparative Method: Moving Beyond Qualitative and Quantitative Strategies.* Berkeley: University of California Press.

Reed, Isaac. 2011. *Interpretation and Social Knowledge: On the Use of Theory in the Human Sciences.* Chicago: University of Chicago Press.

Rosaldo, Michelle Zimbalist. 1974. "Women, Culture, and Society: A Theoretical Overview." Pp. 17–42 in *Women, Culture and Society*, edited by Michelle Zimbalist Rosaldo and Louise Lamphere. Stanford, CA: Stanford University Press.

Roy, Olivier. 2004. *Globalized Islam: The Search for a New Ummah*. New York: Columbia University Press.

Smilde, David. 2004. "Contradiction Without Paradox: Evangelical Political Culture in the 1998 Venezuelan Elections." *Latin American Politics and Society* 46(1): 75–102.

———. 2005. "A Qualitative Comparative Analysis of Conversion to Venezuelan Evangelicalism: How Networks Matter." *American Journal of Sociology* 111(3): 757–796.

———. 2007. *Reason to Believe: Cultural Agency in Latin American Evangelicalism*. Berkeley: University of California Press.

Smilde, David, and Matthew May. 2010. "The Emerging Strong Program in the Sociology of Religion." *Social Science Research Council Working Papers*. Social Science Research Council, New York, NY.

Smith, Christian. 2003. *Moral Believing Animals: Human Personhood and Culture*. Oxford: Oxford University Press.

———. 2010. *What Is a Person?: Rethinking Humanity, Social Life, and the Moral Good from the Person Up*. Chicago: University of Chicago Press.

Smith, Dorothy E. 1990. *The Conceptual Practices of Power: A Feminist Sociology of Knowledge*. Boston: Northeastern University Press.

Smith, Philip. 2005. *Why War? The Cultural Logic of Iraq, the Gulf War, and Suez*. Chicago: University of Chicago Press.

Somers, Margaret. 1998. "'We're No Angels': Realism, Rational Choice, and Relationality in Social Sciences." *American Journal of Sociology* 104(3): 722–784.

Swidler, Ann. 1995: "Cultural Power and Social Movements." Pp. 25–40 in *Social Movements and Culture*. Edited by Hank Johnston and Bert Klandermans. Minneapolis: University of Minnesota Press.

Taylor, Charles. 1992. *Sources of the Self: The Making of the Modern Identity*. Cambridge, MA: Harvard University Press.

Walker Bynum, Caroline. 1987. *Holy Feast and Holy Fast: The Religious Significance of Food to Medieval Women*. Berkeley: University of California Press.

Weber, Max. 1968. *Economy and Society*. Berkeley: University of California Press.

Wilde, Melissa. 2007. *Vatican II: A Sociological Analysis of Religion Change*. Princeton, NJ: Princeton University Press.

Wuthnow, Robert. 1987. *Meaning and Moral Order: Explorations in Cultural Analysis*. Berkeley: University of California Press.

———. 1993. *Communities of Discourse: Ideology and Social Structure in the Reformation, the Enlightenment, and European Socialism*. Cambridge, MA: Harvard University Press.

Zald, M. N. 1995. "Progress and Cumulation in the Human Sciences After the Fall." *Sociological Forum* 10(3): 455–479.

3

Toward a Comparative-Historical Sociology of Religious Politics: The Case for Cross-Religious and Cross-Regional Comparisons

ATEŞ ALTINORDU

The sociology of religion has had a complex and somewhat puzzling relationship with comparative-historical sociology. Max Weber's sociology of religion had a decidedly comparative and historical orientation. His writings on religion, along with those of Durkheim, laid the theoretical foundations of the field, and it is still hard to imagine an undergraduate course or a graduate field exam on the sociology of religion that does not take Weber's works as a starting point. It is particularly surprising, then, that a vast majority of recent work in the American sociology of religion is characterized by a presentist and noncomparative outlook, with most studies focusing on contemporary American congregations.

This chapter will argue that comparative-historical approaches promise to make distinctive contributions to all four fronts in the project of de-centering and re-centering the sociology of religion presented by the editors in the introduction to this volume: provincializing the Unites States (and the "West" in general); paying attention to religion outside of congregations; overcoming the Christo-centric assumptions of existing conceptual frameworks; and reaching a balanced, critical perspective on the positive and negative influences of religion on normative ends such as recognition, justice, equality, and democracy. Through a detailed review of some recent studies, I will contend that an innovative strand of cross-religious and cross-regional comparative work is especially conducive to the furthering of this agenda.

The chapter begins with a discussion of the past and potential future contributions of comparative-historical research to the four avenues previously mentioned. The second section briefly takes stock of some of the recent literature at the intersection of comparative-historical sociology and the sociology of religion and discusses how "the religious factor" is pinned down in these works. The third and final section highlights cross-religious and cross-regional historical comparisons as a promising avenue of research for the new sociology of religion and discusses in detail three studies on religious parties to demonstrate the advantages of this research agenda.

De-centering and Re-centering Through Comparative-Historical Analysis

Comparative-historical sociology is one of the few subfields in the discipline that centrally focuses on non-American cases. The close study of these cases in itself helps scholars to think of the United States as a particular case among others. However, the provincialization of the United States is more explicitly furthered in studies that systematically compare it with other cases. Studies of this kind on religion (e.g., Casanova 1994; Davie 2002; Berger, Davie, and Fokas 2008; Kuru 2009) help explore what precisely sets the American religious landscape apart from others and what characteristics it shares with other contexts. The contours of the often mentioned "American exceptionalism" in religion can in fact only be determined by systematic in-depth comparisons of this kind.

Speaking in concrete terms, general hypotheses that seem to hold when observed in the US context can be revealed to be problematic when examined in a comparative perspective. A good example is the central argument of the proponents of the religious economies model that religious pluralism leads to religious vitality (Finke and Stark 1988). This theory, which sets out from the American experience (Casanova 2006, 8–9), is unable to explain important cases such as Ireland, Poland, Italy, and Austria, where the religious market is largely dominated by the Catholic Church but religious participation is relatively strong compared to the rest of Europe (Chaves and Gorski 2001).

It would be equally problematic, however, to limit this expansion of the comparative perspective to Europe and the United States. The debates between the classical secularization theorists and the adherents of the religious economies model, perhaps the most salient discussion of the previous half century within the sociology of religion, precisely had this effect. While there are many comparative-historical studies on religion that focus on non-Western cases, only a handful of them study Western and non-Western cases in comparative perspective. As a result, the study of non-Western cases often remains at the margins of the theoretical core in the sociology of religion, seen not as expanding our understanding of religion, secularization, or secularism as such, but as advancing knowledge on specific areas of the world. The more radical double move of defamiliarizing the familiar and familiarizing the unfamiliar can only be accomplished by cross-regional studies that explicitly and systematically place Western and non-Western cases in comparative perspective.

Secondly, comparative-historical research offers distinctive tools for overcoming the limits of "Christo-centrism." As Talal Asad and others have argued, modern concepts pertaining to religion, including the very definition of "religion" as a distinct sphere, have been constructed largely on the basis of the historical experience of Western Christianity (Asad 1993; Masuzawa 2005; Keane 2007). The Protestant mode of religiosity in particular has had a formative influence on the common conceptual apparatus used by sociologists of religion, with implications ranging from the way individual religiosity is imagined to the way religious vitality is measured, resulting in a "pastoral" bias in the field (Gorski and Altınordu 2008, 61–62). Within the discipline of sociology, comparative-historical sociologists can be given epistemological credit for advocating the genealogical investigation of analytical concepts and for problematizing the transposability of theoretical frameworks across time and space (Somers 1996, 1998; Mahoney and Rueschemeyer 2003, 9). Thus, we can expect comparative-historical sociologists of religion to do the same within the sub-discipline. Cross-religious comparative analysts in particular promise to generate reflexivity against the universalization and naturalization of categories that have been derived from specific contexts—in this case from the historical experience of Western Christianity.

The neglect or misrecognition of alternative modes of religious subjectivity, belief, ritual, authority, and organization is, however, only one side of the coin. A reverse problem occurs when structural similarities among different religious traditions (e.g., in their social activism, organizational forms, or engagement with politics) are obscured by unexamined assumptions of radical difference. Ironically, the incommensurability of the Christian and Islamic traditions is asserted both by critical anthropologists of Islamic subjectivity (Mahmood 2005) and by the representatives of a simplistic but influential version of religious-civilizational analysis (Huntington 1996) who depart from nearly opposite normative-political positions. Against this propensity to posit radical incommensurability, detailed and systematic comparative-historical studies facilitate a more nuanced approach.

The back-and-forth between the drive to compare, theorize, and generalize, on the one hand, and the deep attention to historical context and specificity on the other hand marks the difficult but productive endeavor of historically contextualized comparisons. Historical comparisons thus assume neither identity nor incommensurability. Cross-religious studies in this tradition pay attention to doctrinal, organizational, and historical differences but are open to the exploration of structural similarities across cases that belong to different religious traditions. These studies thus help overcome Christo-centric tendencies in both directions: the tendency to study other religions through categories that impose Western-Christian assumptions on the one hand, and the tendency to view non-Christian religions through an othering perspective and assume that their study requires radically different explanatory tools on the other.

Comparative-historical sociology since the 1970s has been characterized by a central concern with politics (Gorski 2005, 175). It is not surprising, then, that most works on religion within this tradition have focused on interactions between the religious and the political fields, as will be discussed in the next section. These studies move the focus in the sociology of religion outside the institutional context of congregations. Religious parties, for example, are venues where religious identities are reconstructed and religious activists are transformed into new kinds of religious-political actors. Barring simplistic accounts that view religious parties as the direct extension of religious authority and community in the political realm (e.g., Lepsius 1966), studies of religious politics reveal the limits of a congregational perspective. It is precisely through the interactions outside of the walls of formal religious institutions that religion becomes politically efficacious. Religious identities, discourses, and actors are in turn deeply transformed in the course of these interactions.

Finally, a comparative-historical perspective leaves little doubt that taking religion as a socially benevolent or harmful force in general is not a tenable position. To take another example from the field of religion and politics, comparative-historical sociologists of religion are widely familiar with cases where Catholic clergy and organizations widely collaborated with totalitarian regimes and military dictatorships, such as in Vichy France and in the first decades of the Franco dictatorship in Spain (Conway 1997, 47–77), and with other cases where they played a key role in resistance against authoritarianism and in transitions to democracy, such as in Spain in the 1970s and Poland in the 1980s (Casanova 1993). Comparative-historical perspectives thus help dispel pro- or antireligion sentiments that underlie a considerable portion of research in the sociology of religion and lead us toward more relevant critical questions, such as: What forms of religious politics are compatible or incompatible with democratic politics (Stepan 2001)? Under what conditions does religion become a vital force in the public spheres of modern societies (Casanova 1994)?

Comparative-Historical Studies on Religion

In an essay published in 2005, Philip Gorski investigated the causes of the "growing estrangement between historical sociology and the sociology of religion" (p. 189) that began in the late 1960s and early 1970s, in the very period when historical sociology entered its golden age and historical sociologists published seminal works on social revolutions, the rise of the nation-states, and the development of welfare states. The relative neglect of religion on the part of historical sociology, Gorski observed, resulted from theoretical perspectives and research questions influenced by materialist strands of Marxism. On the part of the sociology of religion, comparative-historical approaches were held back through the persistence of positivist assumptions that led to a teleological preoccupation with the future of religion at the cost of attention to patterns of historical change and causal mechanisms underlying these changes.

Since the mid-1990s, Gorski and others contributed to the development of a sophisticated literature that has enriched comparative-historical sociology by exploring the role of religion in major historical processes and has challenged the presentism that dominates much of the sociology of religion. Comparative-historical studies in sociology, political science, and history have explored the role of religious actors, organizations, and doctrines in the development of modern political institutions, such as in state formation (Gorski 2003a), the rise of absolutism (Fulbrook 1984), welfare states (Kahl 2005, 2009), national social movements (Young 2002, 2007), and long-distance advocacy networks (Stamatov 2010). Others focused on the historical interplay between religion and nationalism (Gorski 2000b; Zubrzycki 2006), investigated the role of religion in social movements (Smith 1996), analyzed the rise of confessional parties in late-nineteenth- and early-twentieth-century Europe (Kalyvas 1996), and developed comparative-historical perspectives on secularization (Gorski 2000a, 2003b) that avoid the teleological assumptions of classical secularization theorists and the ahistorical theories of the supply-siders alike.[1]

These studies are historical not only in the location of the cases in the past but also in their sensitivity to the historically variant nature of causal contexts and in their awareness of the limits of the transposability of analytical concepts across time. Furthermore, most of these scholars utilize systematic comparisons to formulate their research puzzles and to demonstrate the validity of their proposed explanations. These works made a major contribution not only to the sociology of religion but also to comparative-historical sociology, as they brought religion into major fields of research in comparative-historical social science, which had previously neglected the religious factor.[2]

But what do scholars precisely mean when they talk about "the religious factor"? What is the role of religious doctrine in determining social and political outcomes? What is the weight of the organizational aspects of religion? In other words, how exactly does religion exercise causal efficacy in history? The answers to these questions vary according to the researchers' theoretical orientation and the object of explanation in question, of course, but a close examination of the ways in which the religious factor comes into play will contribute to our understanding of these recurring issues in the sociology of religion.

In his study of the religious origins of long-distance advocacy networks, Peter Stamatov (2010) argues that neither the general values of Christianity nor the basic doctrinal differences across the confessions account for the development of transnational advocacy networks: many Christian groups did not mobilize in defense of indigenous populations, while those that did mobilize included both Catholic orders and Protestant groups. The decisive factors were rather these groups' activist disposition and their organizational autonomy from political and ecclesiastical authority.

While similar practices of religious groups with different doctrines lead Stamatov to discount doctrinal particularities as a central explanatory factor, the divergent political attitudes and actions of religious movements with similar doctrines leads Mary Fulbrook (1984) to a similar conclusion in *Piety and Politics*. While sharing a precisionist religious orientation, Puritans in England helped subvert efforts to institute absolutist rule, Pietists in Württemberg were opposed to absolutism but remained passive in the course of the constitutional struggles, and Pietists in Brandenburg-Prussia positively contributed to the establishment of the absolutist state. Based on this comparative perspective, Fulbrook concludes that rather than religious doctrine, the structure of church-state-society relations and the source and scope of religious tolerance played the central role in determining these religious groups' political attitudes and alliances.

According to Sigrun Kahl (2005), on the other hand, differences in the social doctrines of Catholicism, Lutheranism, and Calvinism were decisive in the evolution of European poor relief systems along differential trajectories. Doctrinal differences concerning salvation, work, charity, and the poor were "institutionalized into" different understandings and systems of poor relief in early modern Europe—hospitals in Catholic countries, centralized outdoor relief in Lutheran settings, and workhouses in Calvinist contexts—and continued to exert their influence in secularized institutions of poverty policy through path dependence.

Michael Young (2002) argues that both doctrinal and organizational elements of evangelical Protestantism were of major consequence for the rise of the first national social movements in the United States. The temperance and antislavery movements of the nineteenth century owed their organizational infrastructure to the centralized national network of benevolent societies established by the Protestant orthodoxy. The cultural efficacy of these movements, on the other hand, depended on a combination of the concept of "special sins of the nation" derived from orthodox covenant theology with the cultural schema of public confession popularized by revivalist upstart sects.

Other studies emphasize the interactions between the organizational and doctrinal aspects of religion. David Zaret (1985) explains the increasing salience of covenant theology in English Puritanism as the joint result of organizational pressure and ideological precedent. When Puritan clerics' organizational privileges were challenged by popular dissent in pre-Revolutionary England, they creatively adopted covenant theology based on antecedents in the Christian tradition. This doctrinal change helped absorb the challenges posed by the popular Reformation and at the same time served to settle the fears of social and political elites by emphasizing obedience to temporal authority.

In her study of the Second Vatican Council, Melissa Wilde (2004) emphasizes the successive influences of doctrinal and organizational elements on each other. Wilde argues that progressive and conservative bishops' divergent doctrinal stances on authority led to different organizational strategies on the two sides: while progressives' adherence to the doctrine of collegiality enabled them to build a consensus-based and effective organization early on, conservatives' opposition to this doctrine resulted in the formation of a hierarchical organization with a narrow scope at a relatively late point. The progressives' relatively effective organization in turn resulted in the successful implementation of their agenda, leading to significant transformations in church doctrine. Wilde's study shows that while religious doctrine may give rise to specific forms of religious organization, it may also change as a result of organizational elements; these two factors sometimes jointly produce outcomes in a chain of successive interactions.

Gorski's *The Disciplinary Revolution* (2003a), while paying close attention to doctrine and organizational form, focuses on a related but distinctive aspect of religion, namely, discipline. Discipline refers to the regulation of conduct through technologies of surveillance, including practices of self-regulation, mutual surveillance, and social control. Combining Weber's understanding of the ties between religion and discipline with Foucault's association of discipline and governance, Gorski systematically analyzes the impact of religious discipline on social order, state administrations, armies, educational institutions, and systems of poor relief in early modern Europe. Based on this analysis, he illustrates that disciplinary techniques and strategies spawned by Calvinism significantly increased the administrative efficiency and regulatory power of political authority both from below and from above, and thus played a central role in state formation.

How can religious discipline be situated with regard to doctrine and organizational form? Weber has famously demonstrated the links between the Calvinist doctrine of predestination and the ethic of work and self-discipline. Gorski stresses, on the other hand, that consistories, a committee of elders and church pastors for the moral supervision of congregations, were central to the development of Calvinist self-discipline. Thus, discipline is often rooted in religious doctrine, institutionalized in particular organizational forms, and in turn reinforced through these organizations. However, it is not reducible to either doctrine or organizational structure. In fact, Weber acknowledged that ascetic Protestant sects that engendered the same kind of discipline differed in their doctrines, which suggests that discipline is not a function of religious doctrine alone (Gorski 2003a, 26–27). We can thus identify religious discipline as a third channel through which religion has efficacy in history.

Whether they emphasize religious doctrine, religious organization, or religious discipline, most studies discussed previously follow in Weber's footsteps, not least in tracing the origins of modern Western social and political institutions to the religious history of early modern Europe. Their significant contribution to major areas in comparative-historical sociology—such as state formation, social movements, and welfare states—suggests that this line of research on the religious origins of Western modernity continues to have great potential, and the near future is likely to see more works in this strand.

However, in the rest of this chapter, I would like to discuss another line of comparative-historical research in terms of its potential contributions to the de-centering and re-centering of the sociology of religion. Most studies reviewed earlier focus on European and North American cases (although some explore the context of empire) and on denominations within Christianity. On the other hand, social scientists have produced many comparative-historical studies that focus on non-Western regions and non-Christian religions, such as analyses of Islamic parties (Schwedler 2007), Muslim social movements (Bayat 2007), and Latin American Christian Democracy (Mainwaring and Scully 2003). However, the comparative-historical literature on religion contains very few studies that compare cases across different world religions and regions. This vacuum is only recently being addressed by a handful of studies on fundamentalism (Riesebrodt 1993), religious parties (Kalyvas 2000, 2003; Tepe 2005, 2008; Altınordu 2010), and secularism (Kuru 2009). These cross-religious and cross-regional historical comparisons provide an especially promising avenue of research for the new sociology of religion. The next section will discuss the challenges and advantages of this line of research based on a detailed review of three cross-religious studies on religious parties.

Cross-Religious and Cross-Regional Comparisons

Our discussion thus far has focused on the existing and potential contributions of comparative-historical research to the new sociology of religion. Among the advantages of this perspective, I argued, is the ability to pin down how religion influences social and political change. In this section, I will seek to demonstrate that cross-religious comparisons facilitate such precision even to a larger degree as they involve cases with greater variation in doctrine, organization, and discipline. I also suggested that Western- and Christo-centric assumptions lead not only to the naturalization of concepts derived from the history of Western Christianity but also to assumptions of radical incommensurability between Western Christianity and other religious traditions, especially

Islam. The remedy against this dual fallacy, I argued, lies in cross-religious and cross-regional comparative studies, which facilitate the exploration of structurally similar processes across religious traditions without ignoring their specific characteristics.

In the remaining part of this chapter, I will seek to illustrate these points through a detailed review of three cross-religious investigations on religious parties: Tepe's study on the political ideologies of Judaic and Islamic parties in Israel and Turkey, my study on the rise of Catholic and Islamic parties in Germany and Turkey, and Kalyvas's study on the commitment problems of Catholic and Islamic parties in the emerging democracies of Belgium and Algeria. Although each study seeks to explain a different set of outcomes, considered together as an innovative strand of cross-religious and cross-regional research, they make key contributions to the new sociology of religion by provincializing the Western religious experience, challenging Christo-centric assumptions, and taking the inclusionary and democratic, as well as the exclusionary and antidemocratic, aspects of religion into consideration. Finally, not surprisingly for studies of religious parties, they all investigate the role of religion outside of congregations and examine the transformation of religious identities, discourses, and actors in the course of interactions within the political sphere.

Sacralizers and Internal Secularizers in Political Judaism and Islam

Sultan Tepe's cross-religious study comparatively examines the political ideologies of a set of Judaic and Islamic parties: Mafdal and Shas in Israel, and the Nationalist Action Party (NAP) and Felicity/Justice and Development Party (JDP) in Turkey.[3] The comparative analysis of religious parties within, as well as across, different religious and national contexts allows Tepe to identify two sets of discursive strategies. The sacralizers assign religious meanings to secular ideas and institutions. Through this process, they seek to reinforce hegemonic forms of nationalism and reconcile existing tensions between secular nationalism and religion. The internal secularizers, on the other hand, redefine religious terms in order to incorporate secular ideas into their religious-political discourses. However, they refract the meaning of these ideas in decisive ways in the course of this selective appropriation. While these discursive strategies do not constitute the only strands in these religious parties' complex and somehow eclectic ideologies, they carry distinctive implications in terms of their policy positions, democratic commitments, and exclusionary practices.

The ideology of the National Religious Party (Mafdal) in Israel was broadly defined by religious Zionism, a strand of religious nationalism based on the ideas of Rabbi Abraham Isaac Kook. As opposed to the ultra-Orthodox critique of Zionism as an obstacle to Jewish redemption through divine intervention, Mafdal saw the unity of the Jewish people under the Israeli state as a crucial stage in the path to collective salvation. Thus, the Israeli state assumed religious significance as the agent of Jewish redemption and Zionism was revalued as a religious project. This narrative depicted secular nationalists as unknowing contributors to Jewish redemption and thus legitimized them in religious terms.

This sacralization of secular ideas, institutions, and actors performed various political functions for Mafdal. Against the injunction of some ultra-Orthodox leaders to withdraw from politics and establish religious communities isolated from the secular world, Mafdal justified active participation in politics as a religious duty based on the religious essence of the national project. Furthermore, Mafdal's religious Zionism sought to supersede the conflict in Israeli politics between secular Zionism and Orthodox Judaism. This ideology allowed the party to cooperate with secular political elites despite their secularist policies, as observed in Mafdal's continuous participation in coalition governments between 1956 and 1992.

The sacralization of the Israeli state, land, and national unity also had tangible consequences for Mafdal's approach to major political questions. After the War of 1967, Mafdal encouraged Jewish settlements in occupied territories as a religious obligation. Since then, it has strictly opposed Israel's withdrawal from the occupied territories and fervently objected to the evacuation of Jewish settlements. In line with this position, the party also opposed the creation of a Palestinian state on what it considered the biblical land of Israel.

Sephardi Guardians of Torah (Shas), a religious-ethnic party established in 1984, adopted a complicated position vis-à-vis Zionism. While not critical of the Israeli state in toto, Shas denounced the version of Zionism promoted by the Labor Party as an ethnically exclusive ideology. According to Shas ideologues, the Israeli state in its foundational period promoted Ashkenazi hegemony and marginalized Sephardic Jews. Since the Sephardim were the bearers of the original cultural and religious traditions of the land of Israel, this led to the decline of religion in the country. Claiming that it represents real Zionism, the party advocated the restoration of the standing of Sephardim within the Jewish community and advocated the creation of an expanding community of Torah students.

Shas ideology defined religious Jews, secular Jews, and the non-Jewish people in Israel as distinctive communities and held the state responsible for their minimum welfare and harmonious coexistence. Rather than sacralizing the Israeli state or land, Shas emphasized the maintenance of the Jewish community as its main concern. In line with this view, the party accepted the role of secular expertise in matters that contribute to the preservation of the Jewish community.

Rabbi Ovadia Yosef, the spiritual leader of Shas, argued that land could be relinquished in cases where military and government authorities agree that withdrawal would facilitate the protection of Jewish life. Yosef based his ruling on the principle of *pikuach nefesh*, the Halakhic tenet that the protection of life overrides other religious considerations. This controversial religious opinion, interpreted by many political observers as an effort to strengthen the party's appeal as a coalition partner for secular parties, represented a novel position in ultra-Orthodox political discourse. Yossef's statement entailed not only the acknowledgment of secular expertise in a religious ruling but also the appropriation of the secular idea of "land for peace" into the religious discourse of the party. The political leadership of Shas similarly opposed additional settlements in occupied territories on the grounds that the resulting security problems would negatively affect the maintenance and expansion of the Torah community.

In Turkey, the NAP has increasingly emphasized religious identity as a central component of its ethnic nationalism. Seeking to reconcile the party's ethnic nationalism with Islam, NAP ideologues argued that the nation is a divinely ordained group, based on the Quranic verse on the creation of mankind as "distinct nations and tribes." Through the promotion of "the Turkish-Islamist ideal" as the official party ideology since the early 1990s, party leaders sought to attain a difficult reconciliation of Kemalist secular nationalism with Islam.

According to NAP ideology, Islamic beliefs and values had always been intrinsic to Turkish ethnic identity. Turkish culture contained proto-Islamic values (such as a monotheistic orientation and moral principles similar to Islamic ones) even before the rise of Islam; the conversion of Turks to Islam thus completed their spiritual growth. Through the ironic twist accomplished by this narrative, the pre-Islamic Central Asian ethnic roots—emphasized in secular nationalist historiography to play down the role of Islam in Turkish identity—were relinked with Ottoman-Islamic culture.

Ideologues of the NAP argued that throughout history the Turkish-Islamic tradition never gave rise to a theocratic state, including in the Ottoman era. In other words, secularism had always been a central component of Turkish Islam. Therefore, the perceived opposition between Islam and the secular Turkish state was a fallacy. As the sole institution capable of preserving the Turkish-Muslim community, the Turkish state took on a religious significance. In accordance with this notion, the NAP considered the maintenance of a strong state to be its highest priority.

The sacralization of the state and the national community had distinctive implications for the NAP's policy positions. Like Mafdal in Israel, the NAP regarded national and territorial unity sacred and thus took a rigid stance in all debates concerning group claims and territorial disputes. In line with its ideological orientation, the party advocated an uncompromising approach in the debates over the status of Northern Cyprus and strictly opposed Kurdish claims for a distinctive ethnic and political identity. According to the NAP's ideological framework, Kurds and heterodox religious groups such as the Alevis were to be included in the national community only to the extent that they accepted assimilation into the dominant Turkish-Muslim identity.

The National Vision (NV) movement was represented by five successive religious parties (National Order, National Salvation, Welfare, Virtue, and Felicity) in Turkish politics since 1970. The JDP, founded in 2002 by the reformist wing of the former Virtue Party, claimed to represent a break from the NV tradition; however, it still drew an important part of its cadres and ideology from this movement.

Like Shas in Israel, Felicity and the JDP had a community-centered rather than state-centered ideology. These parties argued that the official secularism of the Turkish state is not secularism in its true sense, and in fact violates the principles of Western secularism it claims to have adopted. Rather than remaining neutral toward religion and ensuring the freedom of religion, NV ideologues contended, the Turkish state sought to limit and control religious practice. They also observed that Kemalist secularism strengthened the state at the cost of society rather than supporting a civil society unrestrained by the state.

The NV politicians asserted that the Islamic tradition contains an authentic model of secularism that protects civil society. The Medina Charter, negotiated by the prophet Muhammad in the seventh century, guaranteed the freedom and peaceful coexistence of religious communities in Medina. The Ottoman state largely replicated this model with its millet system. Thus, an authentic form of secularism—incidentally also one closer to the gist of Western secularism than the existing Kemalist conception—is provided by the Islamic tradition. National Vision parties and the JDP thus appropriated the secular ideas of secularism, pluralism, and civil society into their religious-political discourses through a reinterpretation of Islamic history. In a process of internal secularization, they advocated these ideas as authentic aspects of the religious tradition.

This selective appropriation of secular ideas, however, also entailed their refraction in specific ways. Tepe observes that while they defended the rights of the religious community vis-à-vis the state, NV parties and the JDP were conspicuously silent on the rights of individuals within the community. Furthermore, these parties' assumption of unity within the religious community reinforced the power of hegemonic actors within the group. In other words, their conception of pluralism was limited to those who did not challenge the hegemony of orthodox Sunni practices within the Muslim community. As a result, these parties failed to develop an accommodating stance toward heterodox Islamic groups such as the Alevis and exhibited a skeptical attitude against their demands for equal recognition.

In Israel, conflicts over occupied territories and Jewish settlements, the status of the Palestinians, ethnic dynamics between the Sephardim and Ashkenazim, and the status of new immigrants were central issues facing both sacralizers and internal secularizers. In Turkey, the major problems at stake included state secularism, the Kurdish conflict, the accommodation of Alevis, and relations with the West, especially the European Union. Furthermore, there are major differences between the doctrines and traditions of Judaism and Islam. The idea of Jewish redemption (and disputes over how to achieve it) played a central role in the Israeli religious-political landscape, while Turkish religious politicians drew on references specific to Islamic and Ottoman history. Finally, each political regime entailed specific characteristics: the constitutional prohibition on religious parties in Turkey, for example, created distinctive complications for the articulation of party ideology.

Despite these differences, Tepe demonstrates that there were important parallels in the way religious parties in Israel and Turkey interwove religious and secular ideas. The political ideologies of Mafdal and the NAP attached religious meanings to dominant nationalist ideas and sacralized secular institutions, while Shas and NV/JDP ideologues selectively incorporated secular ideas by redefining religious terms and thus internally secularized their discourses. These discursive strategies gave rise to distinctive emphases and blind spots, categories of inclusion and exclusion, and attitudes of flexibility and rigidity.

Tepe's study demonstrates that cross-religious comparative analyses can be exceptionally productive for identifying general mechanisms in religious politics, without sacrificing attention to the specific characteristics of religious tradition and historical context. As she points out, "It is precisely the commonalities of religious parties based in different religions that help us to better understand their uniqueness" (2008, 344).

Revival, Reaction, and Politicization in German Catholicism and Turkish Islam

In a recent cross-religious comparative study, I sought to explain the rise of electorally successful religious parties (Altınordu 2010). To that end, I comparatively examined the trajectories of the German Catholic Center Party in the second half of the nineteenth century and the succession of Turkish Islamic parties in the post-1970 period. In the course of the late nineteenth century, the Center Party consolidated itself as the political party of German Catholics, receiving four out of every five Catholic votes in the Reichstag elections of 1874.

Similarly, the Islamic Welfare Party won striking electoral victories in Turkey in the mid-1990s, and its reformist spin-off, the JDP, formed a single-party government in 2002. Through a systematic comparison of these two cases, I seek to explain when and how electorally successful religious parties rise.

The study proposes a theory of "revival-reaction-politicization" to explain the outcome of successful politicization in these two cases separated by history, geography, and religious tradition. According to this theory, major religious revivals in both settings increased the public visibility, social influence, and autonomy of religion (revival). Informed by culturally entrenched discourses against the given religious movement, powerful social constituencies and state actors perceived the revival as a threat to their identities and interests. They thus engaged in countermobilization in civil society and enacted policies of repression at the state level against the revivalist movement (reaction). Given that existing political parties did not effectively represent concerns of religious defense, religious activists in response built a successful religious party based on the dense organizational web, influential religious authority, and strong religious identity constructed in the course of the revival (politicization).

In the German case, the mid-nineteenth-century Catholic Revival in Prussia was largely planned by the Roman Catholic Church and carried out by religious orders. Between 1848, when the revival activities were planned in a meeting of the German high clergy in Würzburg, and 1873, when Jesuits and other Catholic orders were banned on German territory, Jesuits, Franciscans, and Redemptorists organized hundreds of "missions for the people," local events that featured widely attended masses, sermons, and confessions, and rein- forced religious sentiments among the Catholic population. The missions were held in conjunction with an intense organization-building activity that led to the formation of religious associations of all sorts (Marianic sodalities, con- gregations, vocational associations) and restored clerical authority and confes- sional identity in secularized associations. The Catholic revival of the 1850s and 1860s thus successfully reversed the secularizing trends of the pre-1848 period in the German Catholic milieu.

In the second half of the 1860s, anti-Catholicism became strikingly salient in the German public sphere, with German Liberals and Protestant nation- alists taking the lead. Popular anti-Catholic mobilization culminated in the attack of a mob on a Dominican chapel and Franciscan orphanage in Berlin in 1869. This was followed by official state policies that sought to curtail the power of the Catholic Church. The *Kulturkampf*, a series of laws and policies implemented by the Prussian and Imperial German states throughout the 1870s and the first half of the 1880s, banned Jesuits and other religious orders from German territory, severely limited the autonomy of the Catholic Church in its internal affairs, subjected the clergy to a long list of strict requirements and regulations, and led to the arrest of clergymen who did not comply. In this era, public authorities frequently intimidated Catholics participating in pilgrimages, broke the public meetings of Catholic activists, censored Catholic newspapers, and convicted Catholic journalists.

In the wake of popular anti-Catholic mobilization, the new Prussian Center Caucus and the German Center Party were established in December 1870 and March 1871, respectively. While the Catholic clergy and population suffered from the Kulturkampf legislation, these policies proved largely ineffective and were gradually dropped in the late 1880s. Their significant result was rather the consolidation of the Center as a major political party. The party had achieved striking results in the Reichstag elections of 1871, but its success reached a peak in 1874—at the height of the Kulturkampf—when it received 83 percent of the Catholic vote. I argue that an important factor in the rise of a distinctively Catholic party in Germany was existing parties' unwillingness or failure to represent concerns of religious defense: while Liberals' anticlerical turn and their sponsorship of major Kulturkampf laws disqualified them as potential allies, Conservatives, divided into multiple groups and inconsistent in their response to anticlerical legislation, could not be trusted for the political representation of religious defense.

The Islamic revival in Turkey was initiated by religious orders in the 1970s and advanced under the favorable political environment of the 1980s. The military regime of 1980–1983 and the post-1983 government introduced mandatory religious education to public school curricula, significantly increased the number of religious functionaries employed by the Directorate of Religious Affairs, and established a large number of preacher schools. Religious orders also boosted their organizational activities in this period, setting up Quran courses; reading groups; charity foundations; women's, youth, and mutual aid associations; and student dormitories. The public visibility of Islam increased dramatically in the course of the revival, especially through the rising number of women wearing headscarves and nearly 30,000 new mosques built between 1973 and 1999.

The Islamic revival was perceived as a major threat by secularist state institutions and social actors. In the 1980s, a number of official regulations and decrees banned the wearing of the headscarf—the foremost symbol of the Islamic revival—in public universities, giving rise to an extensive pro-headscarf movement across the country. In the second half of the decade, public prosecutors indicted hundreds of religious activists in State Security Courts for "attempting to change the secular nature of the state." Between 1987 and 1994, secularist activists began to build a web of voluntary associations, which, in collaboration with state actors, led the mobilization in civil society against the Islamic revival. Following the victory of the Islamic Welfare Party in the national elections of 1995, the army imposed on the government a list of policy directives that aimed to bring the sources of the Islamic revival under state control and eventually forced Erbakan, the party's leader, to resign from his post as prime minister. The Turkish Constitutional Court banned the Welfare Party and its successor the Virtue Party in 1998 and 2001, respectively.

The first Islamic parties established by Necmettin Erbakan in the 1970s had a mixed electoral record, never surpassing 12.3 percent of the national vote in a society with an overwhelming Muslim majority. However, the confrontations of the late 1980s and early 1990s between the revivalists and the secularists, especially the heated headscarf conflict, created unique opportunities for the religious-political movement. Welfare emerged as the first party from the local elections of 1994 and won a plurality in the parliamentary elections of 1995. Following the Constitutional Court's dissolution of the Welfare Party and its successor the Virtue Party, the reformist wing of the party split from Erbakan's movement and established the JDP in 2001. In the November 2002 elections, the JDP won a landslide victory with 34.28 percent of the national vote and formed the first single-party government in Turkey since 1991. I argue that an important factor in the electoral success of distinctively religious parties in Turkey was right-of-center parties' adoption of policies conflicting with their traditional role of religious defense. In the early 1990s, these parties replaced important segments of their religious-nationalist cadres with liberals and adopted the alarmist secularism of republican parties in election campaigns. These developments added credibility to the Welfare Party's claim that it was the only party of and for Muslims in the Turkish political landscape.

I thus argue that in both the German and Turkish cases, successful religious parties emerged when major religious revivals confronted social countermobilization and state repression, provided that existing parties did not effectively represent concerns of religious defense. This cross-religious comparative analysis suggests that religious parties do not rise as a direct outcome of religious revivals. The cycle of conflicts between the revivalists on the one hand and secularist social groups and state institutions on the other is a crucial condition of successful religious-political mobilization. There are various reasons for this: (1) repressive policies create grievances that make the religious community more susceptible to political mobilization; (2) religious-political actors' claims to represent the religious community gain in credibility when these activists confront oppositional groups and the state in the name of the religious group; (3) the ethos of resistance in the face of perceived persecution allows the emergent religious-political groups to suspend their internal disagreements; (4) the resistance of religious authorities to politicization tends to wane in the face of anticlerical mobilization, as the cost of not acting politically in defense of religion now seems higher than the risks involved in politicization; and (5) public demonstrations, petitions, and other collective acts of protest in response to social discrimination and anticlerical state policies help build the religious-political constituency, which can be readily mobilized in elections.

The theory of revival-reaction-politicization further postulates that attacks on religious authority and practice are not likely to lead to the rise of a successful religious party in the absence of a preceding religious revival. Anticlerical social mobilization and state policies are often provoked by the increasing public presence of religion in the course of the religious revivals. Thus, in the absence of a major revival, the chain of conflictual interactions that fosters the rise of religious parties might not occur in the first place. More important, religious revivals create a strong religious identity, increase the social influence of religious authority, and build a dense web of religious organizations. Without a preceding religious revival, religious activists are likely to lack the cultural and organizational capacity required for the construction of a successful religious party.

By explaining the politicization of religion through a constellation of religious revival, social countermobilization, and political repression, the theory of revival-reaction-politicization avoids the pitfalls of reducing religious politics either to the religious or to the political alone. While establishing a contingent link between religious institutions on the one hand and political outcomes on the other, this cross-religious analysis suggests that politicization does not follow directly from religion-specific doctrines or regional political traditions; it results from the interaction of religious activism with established social elites and state power.

Religious Parties and Emerging Democracies in Belgium and Algeria

Stathis Kalyvas's study (2000) offers another comparative perspective on political Catholicism and political Islam. His comparative analysis of the Catholic party in late-nineteenth-century Belgium and the Islamic Salvation Front (FIS) in late-twentieth-century Algeria seeks to identify the conditions under which religious parties expected to win a mandate are integrated into emerging democratic systems.

The Belgian Catholic movement mobilized its constituents in protest of the anticlerical laws introduced by the Liberals in the late 1870s and early 1880s. While all Catholic political actors opposed anticlerical state policies, the movement brought together a moderate Conservative group that accepted the constitutional regime and denounced theocratic ambitions with a radical group of Catholic activists who rejected the Belgian constitution and refused to recognize the autonomy of the political sphere from religious authority and doctrine. While the moderates controlled the party in parliament, the radical minority had the upper hand in the Catholic associational network, exercised substantial influence in the Catholic press, and had the support of the lower clergy.

The Catholics won a landslide victory in the elections of 1884 and obtained a substantial majority in parliament. Although the incumbents had the capacity to subvert the electoral process using the state's repressive apparatus, they accepted the election results. This victory marked the transformation of the Conservative party into a confessional party. While the Catholic government reversed most of the anticlerical legislation of the previous decade, it did not seek a transformation of Belgium's secular and liberal political institutions. The Catholic party sustained its successful electoral record and remained in power without interruption until World War I.

The story had an entirely different course in the case of the Algerian FIS. Founded in 1989, this religious party criticized the existing regime, proposed Islam as the solution to the country's problems, and supported the introduction of *shariah*, but was generally vague in its policy positions. The moderate leadership, headed by Abassi Madani, publicly supported pluralism, accepted the differentiation between religious and political functions, and advocated the reform rather than the radical transformation of the political system. The radical strand within the party, epitomized in the figure of the younger preacher Ali Benhadj, fervently attacked the secular regime and called for the transformation of the Algerian polity in line with theocratic ideals.

The party achieved strong results in the municipal and regional elections of 1990, the first multiparty elections in Algeria since independence. Despite a series of conflicts between the party and the government over an electoral law, the first-round parliamentary elections eventually took place in December 1991 and resulted in the victory of the FIS, which received 47.2 percent of the national vote. The party was expected to achieve a large parliamentary majority in the second-round elections scheduled for January 1992. However, the military cancelled the elections and declared a state of emergency; the government subsequently arrested thousands of FIS activists and banned the party. The ensuing conflicts led Algeria into a major civil war.

Kalyvas's comparative analysis seeks to explain the divergent outcomes in these two similar cases. In both cases, the setting was an "emerging democracy" where the democratic rules of the game had not been consolidated and incumbents had the capacity to subvert the electoral process through military intervention. In both cases, the religious challengers expected to win the elections articulated an antisystem discourse, which in turn raised suspicions about whether they would seek a theocratic transformation of their respective polities once in power. To be more precise, the radicals within each group fueled these suspicions with their inflammatory discourses, while the moderates sought to signal their party's commitment to the fundamental structure of the political regime. What was the reason, then, that in one case there was a peaceful transfer of power to the religious party, leading to the consolidation of the democratic regime, while in the other case a military intervention sub-verted the electoral process, leading the country into a bloody civil war?

Kalyvas's explanation centers on the different degrees to which party lead-ers' signals of moderation possessed credibility in the two cases. The moderates in the Belgian Catholic movement succeeded in convincing the incumbents that they had secured control over the party and would not allow the radi-cals to set the agenda once the party came to power. Despite their substantial efforts to convey a moderate image, however, the leadership of the FIS failed to effectively silence the radicals within the movement. Thus, they were unable to assure the incumbents that a future FIS government would not subvert the political regime. Kalyvas argues that this decisive difference in the credibility of the signals in turn depended on differences in the institutional structure of Catholicism and Islam.

Before the elections of 1884 in Belgium, the Catholic Church decisively inter-vened in the intramovement struggles between the moderates and the radicals. Following Pope Leo XIII's statement in 1879 that the Belgian Catholics should refrain from attacking the constitution, the Belgian church openly began to back the moderates. The church eliminated prominent radicals, including the foremost radical ideologue Henri Périn, from the Catholic movement and pressured the Catholic press not to attack the constitution. Thus, by the time Catholics entered the elections of 1884, the moderates had decisively estab-lished their control over the movement, and the radical voices within political Catholicism had been silenced.

The moderate leadership of the FIS similarly sought to marginalize the rad-icals in the summer of 1991, suspending them from the party's nomination list, executive committee, and in some cases the party altogether. Unlike in the Belgian case, however, the Algerian moderates did not have recourse to a cen-tralized and hierarchical religious authority that would be able to effectively silence the radicals within the movement. In the period prior to the elections, participants chanted slogans calling for an Islamic revolution in events orga-nized by the party. Moreover, even some leading names in the party contin-ued to give mixed messages. As a result, the moderates' signals concerning the party's commitment to the regime did not have sufficient credibility in the eyes of the incumbents. The moderates did not seem to have complete control over the party, and the military was not willing to take the chance.

Kalyvas thus argues that the institutional structure of religion played the key role in determining the divergent outcomes in these two cases. Ironically, the centralized and hierarchical structure of religious authority in Catholicism enabled the integration of the Catholic party into the political system and fur-thered the consolidation of democracy in Belgium, while the more decentral-ized and plural authority structure of Islam was conducive to the breakdown of democratic politics in Algeria. This emphasis on the institutional structure of religious authority offers a fresh perspective on religious politics and democracy, considering that public and scholarly debates on the topic usually focus on the role of religious doctrine. The identification of this important factor was in turn made possible by the cross-religious comparative nature of the analysis. As Kalyvas (2000, 393) points out, "The crucial role of religious institutions is easily overlooked in case studies or nonanalytical comparisons (for example, between Islamist parties)."

Conclusion

What do these three studies reveal about the challenges and advantages of cross-religious comparisons? Compared to comparative analyses that limit themselves to the same religious tradition and region, cross-religious and cross-regional comparisons allow the selection of cases from a wider range of contexts. Thus, they provide an especially advantageous vantage point for identifying general mechanisms and constructing theories with a wide scope of validity. Conversely, where findings derived from a singular religious, geographical, or historical context have been asserted as general truths about religion, cross-religious and cross-regional comparisons can help determine the limits of their validity. From classical secularization theories that posit claims derived from the history of European Christianity in universal terms to religious economies models that advance general hypotheses largely based on the history of American Protestantism, sociologists of religion are rather familiar with such unwarranted generalizations.

Cross-religious comparisons also introduce significant degrees of variation along the axes of doctrine, organizational structure, and discipline. They thus allow the analyst to identify in a precise way how religion exercises influence in the political processes under consideration. The cross-religious comparative studies by Tepe, Kalyvas, and myself reviewed earlier all argue that we should not prejudge the role of religious doctrine in processes and outcomes involving religious parties. While assuming religiously motivated actors that seek to increase the social influence of religion and struggle to defend religious authority and practice, I argue that the rise of successful religious parties is the outcome of religious activists' interaction with social and political elites, rather than a function of religious doctrine. Kalyvas similarly argues that despite being embedded in different religious traditions, the leaders of the Belgian Catholic party and the Algerian Islamic Salvation Front faced very similar dilemmas. In the end, it was the institutional structure of religion rather than doctrinal factors that proved decisive for the outcome.[4]

While Tepe's analysis pays closer attention to doctrine due to her focus on religious parties' ideologies, she concludes that despite the specific nature of doctrinal elements, religious parties in Turkey and Israel interwove religious and secular ideas in similar ways. In fact, one could argue that in terms of discursive strategy, the internal secularizers in Israeli political Judaism and Turkish political Islam have more in common with each other than with the sacralizers in their respective national settings and religious traditions. Based on these findings, Tepe (2008, 344) notes that "[a]n unchallenged assumption that the impact of distinctive religious doctrines on politics is unique to those doctrines deprives us of knowledge that can only be gained by inquiring into how different religious doctrines can mold comparable political positions and how seemingly sui generis positions are actually shared."

Beyond these general observations about cross-religious analyses, the comparison of nineteenth-century European political Catholicism with contemporary political Islam in the Middle East raises a number of normative, political, and scholarly issues, especially with regard to the relationship between public discourses on Islam and academic research on religious politics.

When comparing European political Catholicism and political Islam in the Middle East, two axes of difference loaded with cultural preconceptions come into play. The distinction between Catholicism and Islam evokes deep-seated assumptions of fundamental differences between the political theologies, historical traditions, and authority patterns of Christianity and Islam. The distinction between Europe and the Middle East similarly calls forth culturally entrenched assumptions of categorical difference in terms of political tradition and historical progress. In most cases, it is these unquestioned cultural assumptions of incommensurability rather than purely analytical considerations that lead to the construction of separate explanatory frameworks for European/Christian and Middle Eastern/Islamic politics.

As discussed in the previous section, my study proposes a single theory to explain the rise of political Catholicism in Germany and political Islam in Turkey. Similarly, Kalyvas's analysis underlines that religious party leaders faced similar challenges and adopted analogous strategies in Catholic Belgium and Muslim Algeria, despite the divergent outcomes in the two cases. This strand of comparative research thus breaks the unspoken wall that separates the study of Islamic and Christian parties and contributes to the advancement of general theories on religious politics.

The resulting comparative perspective suggests that the dynamics that characterize contemporary Islamic politics in the Middle East are not incommensurable with European and Christian experiences. Kalyvas (2000, 392) observes that his comparative study "points to a European past which tends to be forgotten in the West and suggests that the resurgence of religion in politics is not as fundamentally removed from the western experience as is commonly thought." I similarly emphasize that "[w]hile Islamic politics at the turn of the present century is by no means an identical repetition of the European Catholic experience at the turn of the previous century, common assumptions on the *sui generis* nature of Islamic movements and Middle Eastern politics are equally misleading" (2010, 544).

In fact, there are striking similarities in the global public discourses on Catholicism in the nineteenth century and Islam today, which portray these religions as antimodern belief systems incompatible with democracy and individual freedom (Casanova 2005). The once salient assumption that Catholicism is inherently incompatible with democracy proved wrong, as church doctrine took a decisively democratic turn with the Second Vatican Council and political Catholicism evolved into Christian Democracy in the postwar era. As José Casanova (2005) points out, this Catholic history demonstrates the problematic nature of contemporary arguments concerning Islam's inherent incompatibility with modernity and democracy.

Finally, one may ask how this strand of cross-religious and cross-regional analysis relates to the Weberian tradition, which to this day constitutes the major social science paradigm for the comparative-historical study of religion. Max Weber's larger ambition within the framework of his sociology of religion was to develop a comparative analysis of the great world religions under the title *The Economic Ethics of the World Religions*. Influenced by the historical works of contemporary German Orientalists, Weber planned to develop a collection of studies— only partly realized by the time of his death—that would explore the divergent approaches to the conduct of life induced by different world religions, with a particular emphasis on their economic ethics (Kippenberg 2005). While Weber's "systematics of religion" offers a rich conceptual toolkit and a productive template for comparative-historical research on religion, the cross-religious and cross-regional studies reviewed in this chapter differ from this tradition in multiple respects.

The basic unit of analysis in the Weberian tradition is the religious (or denominational) tradition. Weberian studies proceed on the assumption that religious traditions give rise to particular patterns of economic and political conduct and (at least partly) explain major institutional outcomes in politics (e.g., the invention of revolutionary politics, the rise of modern state bureaucracies, the divergent structures of welfare systems in the West) with reference to the long-term and general impact of distinctive religious ethics. The cross-religious studies of religious politics I discussed previously, on the other hand, seek to explain more specific outcomes (e.g., the rise of electorally successful religious parties, the ability of religious parties to avoid military intervention, etc.) with reference to a shorter time frame. In their search for explanations, these analysts primarily focus on the interactions of religious actors with other political actors and on the parameters of the political context, rather than on the consistent effects of a distinctive religious ethics on the political conduct of religious actors.

This basic difference between the two paradigms of comparative-historical research also manifests itself in terms of divergent emphases on the similarities and differences across religious contexts. While the Weberian template of explanation, with its attention to distinctive religious ethics, tends to underline decisive differences across religions (or denominations), Tepe, Kalyvas, and I put more emphasis on the similar challenges faced and analogous strategies utilized by religious actors embedded in different religious traditions.

A second, and related, difference between these paradigms concerns the famous Weberian question: "why in the West?" While Weber's sociology of religion exhibits a genuine interest in and deep knowledge of non-Western religions, the preoccupation with the distinctiveness of Western modernity remains an underlying theme throughout his and his intellectual followers' studies on religion. The cross-religious and cross-regional comparative studies discussed in this chapter not only are unconstrained by this concern but also directly challenge deep-seated assumptions about the distinctiveness of occidental Christianity.

Despite these differences in research template and substantive concern, the Weberian project of the comparative ethics of world religions continues to have an immense potential for sociological research. Whether they investigate how differences in religious traditions shape divergent historical trajectories in the long term or focus on structurally similar processes across different religious contexts to explain outcomes of a more specific nature, detailed and systematic cross-religious comparisons offer a much needed alternative to the oversimplistic, essentialist, and ahistorical versions of civilizational analysis (e.g., Huntington 1996) that continue to exert a strong influence on public discourse and on some strands of scholarly work in today's world.

Notes

1. There are important predecessors to these comparative-historical works, foremost among them David Martin's *A General Theory of Secularization* (1978) and Michael Walzer's *Revolution of the Saints* (1982).
2. Gorski (2003a, 15) writes that "it is curious that previous work on early modern state formation has paid so little attention to religion." Similarly, Kahl (2005, 93) points out that "[t]he traditional welfare state literature is 'religion blind,' save for the occasional reference to Catholicism (in particular Christian Democracy)."
3. Tepe's analysis ends in 2005.
4. One would be right to point out, of course, that the centralized and hierarchical institutional structure of Catholicism is closely related to church doctrine.

References

Altınordu, Ateş. 2010. "The Politicization of Religion: Political Catholicism and Political Islam in Comparative Perspective." *Politics and Society* 38(4): 517–551.

Asad, Talal. 1993. *Genealogies of Religion: Discipline and Reasons of Power in Christianity and Islam*. Baltimore: Johns Hopkins University Press.

Bayat, Asef. 2007. *Making Islam Democratic: Social Movements and the Post-Islamist Turn.* Stanford, CA: Stanford University Press.

Berger, Peter L., Grace Davie, and Effie Fokas. 2008. *Religious America, Secular Europe? A Theme and Variations.* Aldershot: Ashgate.

Casanova, José. 1993. "Church, State, Nation and Civil Society in Spain and Poland." Pp. 101–153 in *The Political Dimensions of Religion*, edited by Said Arjomand. Albany: State University of New York Press.

Casanova, José. 1994. *Public Religions in the Modern World.* Chicago: University of Chicago Press.

Casanova, José. 2005. "Catholic and Muslim Politics in Comparative Perspective." *Taiwan Journal of Democracy* 1(2): 89–108.

Casanova, José. 2006. "Rethinking Secularization: A Global Comparative Perspective." *Hedgehog Review* 8(1–2): 7–22.

Chaves, Mark, and Philip S. Gorski. 2001. "Religious Pluralism and Religious Participation." *Annual Review of Sociology* 27: 261–281.

Conway, Martin. 1997. *Catholic Politics in Europe: 1918–1945.* London: Routledge.

Davie, Grace. 2002. *Europe: The Exceptional Case. Parameters of Faith in the Modern World.* London: Darton, Longman and Todd.

Finke, Roger, and Rodney Stark. 1988. "Religious Economies and Sacred Canopies: Religious Mobilization in American Cities, 1906." *American Sociological Review* 53(1): 41–49.

Fulbrook, Mary. 1984. *Piety and Politics: Religion and the Rise of Absolutism in England, Württemberg, and Prussia.* Cambridge: University of Cambridge Press.

Gorski, Philip S. 2000a. "Historicizing the Secularization Debate: Church, State and Society in Late Medieval and Early Modern Europe, ca. 1300–1700." *American Sociological Review* 65(1): 138–167.

Gorski, Philip S. 2000b. "The Mosaic Moment: An Early Modernist Critique of Modernist Theories of Nationalism." *American Journal of Sociology* 105(5): 1428–1468.

Gorski, Philip S. 2003a. *The Disciplinary Revolution: Calvinism and the Rise of the State in Early Modern Europe.* Chicago: University of Chicago Press.

Gorski, Philip S. 2003b. "Historicizing the Secularization Debate: A Program for Research." Pp. 110–122 in *Handbook for the Sociology of Religion*, edited by Michelle Dillon. Cambridge: Cambridge University Press.

Gorski, Philip S. 2005. "The Return of the Repressed: Religion and the Political Unconscious of Historical Sociology." Pp. 161–189 in *Remaking Modernity: Politics, History, and Sociology*, edited by Julia Adams, Elizabeth S. Clemens, and Ann Shola Orloff. Durham, NC: Duke University Press.

Gorski, Philip S., and Ateş Altınordu. 2008. "After Secularization?" *Annual Review of Sociology* 34: 55–85.

Huntington, Samuel P. 1996. *The Clash of Civilizations and the Remaking of World Order.* New York: Simon and Schuster.

Kahl, Sigrun. 2005. "The Religious Roots of Modern Poverty Policy: Catholic, Lutheran, and Reformed Protestant Traditions Compared." *European Journal of Sociology* 46(1): 91–126.

Kahl, Sigrun. 2009. "Religious Doctrines and Poor Relief: A Different Causal Pathway." Pp. 267–296 in *Religion, Class Coalitions, and Welfare States*, edited by Kees van Kersbergen and Philip Manow. Cambridge: Cambridge University Press.

Kalyvas, Stathis N. 1996. *The Rise of Christian Democracy in Europe.* Ithaca, NY: Cornell University Press.

Kalyvas, Stathis N. 2000. "Commitment Problems in Emerging Democracies: The Case of Religious Parties." *Comparative Politics* 32(4): 379–398.

Kalyvas, Stathis N. 2003. "Unsecular Politics and Religious Mobilization." Pp. 293–320 in *European Christian Democracy: Historical Legacies and Comparative Perspectives*, edited by Thomas A. Kselman and Joseph A. Buttigieg. Notre Dame, IN: Notre Dame University Press.

Keane, Webb. 2007. *Christian Moderns: Freedom and Fetish in the Mission Encounter.* Berkeley and Los Angeles: University of California Press.

Kippenberg, Hans G. 2005. "Religious Communities and the Path to Disenchantment: The Origins, Sources, and the Theoretical Core of the Religion Section." Pp. 164–182 in *Max*

Weber's Economy and Society: A Critical Companion, edited by Charles Camic, Philip S. Gorski, and David M. Trubek. Stanford, CA: Stanford University Press.

Kuru, Ahmet T. 2009. *Secularism and State Policies Toward Religion: The United States, France, and Turkey*. Cambridge and New York: Cambridge University Press.

Lepsius, M. Rainer. 1966. "Parteiensystem und Sozialstruktur. Zum Problem der Demokratisierung der deutschen Gesellschaft." Pp. 371–393 in *Wirtschaft, Geschichte und Wirtschaftsgeschichte. Festschrift zum 65. Geburtstag von Friedrich Lütge*, edited by Wilhelm Abel. Stuttgart: G. Fischer.

Mahmood, Saba. 2005. *Politics of Piety: The Islamic Revival and the Feminist Subject*. Princeton, NJ: Princeton University Press.

Mahoney, James, and Dietrich Rueschemeyer. 2003. "Comparative Historical Analysis: Achievements and Agendas." Pp. 3–38 in *Comparative Historical Analysis in the Social Sciences*, edited by James Mahoney and Dietrich Rueschemeyer. Cambridge: Cambridge University Press.

Mainwaring, Scott, and Timothy R. Scully, eds. 2003. *Christian Democracy in Latin America: Electoral Competition and Regime Conflicts*. Stanford, CA: Stanford University Press.

Martin, David. 1978. *A General Theory of Secularization*. New York: Harper and Row.

Masuzawa, Tomoko. 2005. *The Invention of World Religions: Or, How European Universalism Was Preserved in the Language of Pluralism*. Chicago: University of Chicago Press.

Riesebrodt, Martin. 1993. *Pious Passion: The Emergence of Modern Fundamentalism in the United States and Iran*. Berkeley: University of California Press.

Schwedler, Jillian. 2007. *Faith in Moderation: Islamist Parties in Jordan and Yemen*. Cambridge: Cambridge University Press.

Smith, Christian, ed. 1996. *Disruptive Religion: The Force of Faith in Social Movement Activism*. New York: Routledge.

Somers, Margaret R. 1996. "Where Is Sociology After the Historic Turn? Knowledge Cultures, Narrativity, and Historical Epistemologies." Pp. 53–89 in *The Historic Turn in the Human Sciences*, edited by Terrence J. McDonald. Ann Arbor: University of Michigan Press.

Somers, Margaret R. 1998. "'We're No Angels': Realism, Rational Choice, and Relationality in Social Science." *American Journal of Sociology* 104(3): 722–784.

Stamatov, Peter. 2010. "Activist Religion, Empire, and the Emergence of Modern Long-Distance Advocacy Networks." *American Sociological Review* 75(4): 607–628.

Stepan, Alfred. 2001. "The World's Religious Systems and Democracy: Crafting the 'Twin Tolerations.'" Pp. 213–253 in *Arguing Comparative Politics*. Oxford: Oxford University Press.

Tepe, Sultan. 2005. "Religious Parties and Democracy: A Comparative Assessment of Israel and Turkey." *Democratization* 12(3): 283–307.

Tepe, Sultan. 2008. *Beyond Sacred and Secular: Politics of Religion in Israel and Turkey*. Stanford, CA: Stanford University Press.

Walzer, Michael. 1982. *The Revolution of the Saints: A Study in the Origins of Radical Politics*. Cambridge, MA: Harvard University Press.

Wilde, Melissa. 2004. "How Culture Mattered at Vatican II: Collegiality Trumps Authority in the Council's Social Movement Organizations." *American Sociological Review* 69(4): 576–602.

Young, Michael P. 2002. "Confessional Protest: The Religious Birth of U.S. National Social Movements." *American Sociological Review* 67(5): 660–688.

Young, Michael P. 2007. *Bearing Witness Against Sin: The Evangelical Birth of the American Social Movement*. Chicago: University of Chicago Press.

Zaret, David. 1985. *The Heavenly Contract: Ideology and Organization in Pre-Revolutionary Puritanism*. Chicago: University of Chicago Press.

Zubrzycki, Geneviève. 2006. *The Crosses of Auschwitz: Nationalism and Religion in Post-Communist Poland*. Chicago: University of Chicago Press.

4

Religious Self-Constitution:
A Relational Perspective

MICHAL PAGIS

In this chapter, I will promote an understanding of religious self-constitution as a relational and embodied process. Though in recent years there has been a call for studying the emotional and experiential bases of religious practice, I argue that these calls are confined to a paradigm currently dominant in the sociology of religion, which anchors the self in the internalization of belief systems. In this common paradigm, the self is depicted as autonomous and dis-embodied with intact borders, a depiction that is based on the Christian notion of the soul as central to the modern understanding of the person. The notion of "internalization" assumes a strict separation between self and other, and the emphasis on belief, moral orders, and symbolic discourses neglects the relational and interactive aspects of self-constitution. Such an understanding of self and subjectivity is limited, especially when studying religious traditions that unlike Christianity may not involve a notion of a disembodied, personal soul.

The aim of the chapter is to de-center the emphasis on belief in the commonly used category of the religious self and re-center it on an approach that studies the self as an embodied process contextualized in ongoing social relations. To do so, I move away from the traditional empirical base of sociology of religion and work along three of the edges that were introduced in the opening of this volume. First, since the study of Christianity and especially Protestantism usually leads back to the common notion of the self as a disembodied soul, I move beyond studying Christianity and base my claims on examples taken from the practice of Buddhism. Second, the chapter is not based solely on the US context, but offers examples from other places around the world, including Israel and Mexico. Third, I move beyond studying congregations as the main social arena of religion, searching for other social spaces that are not necessarily community based: collective religious practice that does not produce a congregation, social relations with oneself and with one's body, and, last, social relations with objects that are a central part of solitary religious practice.

The chapter explores three dimensions of the embodied space in which religious selves develop: the importance of collective practice, the relation to the body, and the engagement with the material environment. Throughout the chapter, I offer examples from my ethnographic research on the practice of Vipassana meditation, a Theravada Buddhist meditation of mindfulness. These examples are further supported by references to ethnographic studies that explore other religious practices such as Muslim fasting or Christian prayer.[1]

Self, Belief, and Morality

Contemporary theories on the religious self commonly rest on a definition of self or personhood as an internalized structure of values and beliefs. This understanding rests on Charles Taylor's work on self and religion in the modern era. Taylor argues that the self equals an orientation in a moral space: "to know who you are is to be oriented in moral space, a space in which questions arise about what is good or bad, what is worth doing and what is not, what has meaning and importance to you, and what is trivial and secondary" (1989, 28). Morality, for Taylor, is a universal human need, prior to cultural diversity. People require a spiritual framework of orientation in order to act. Without this framework, human agency is impossible. We derive our sense of self from where we stand in relation to the higher good. In fact, according to Taylor, one of the basic human aspirations is "the need to be connected to, or in contact with, what they see as good, or of crucial importance, or of fundamental value" (1989, 42). He names this need to be in contact with the higher good an "aspiration for fullness." This aspiration can be met by building into one's life a pattern of higher action or a higher meaning or connecting one's life to a greater reality or story. Religion, according to Taylor, supplies a framework of orientation, an answer to the quest for spiritual higher goods.

When Taylor defines the self as an orientation in moral space, he specifically emphasizes the modern self, which he frequently opposes to the premodern self. As he claims, questions such as "Is my life worthwhile and meaningful?" and "Do our lives have unity?" are anchored in modern forms and images. And yet, even when emphasizing the historical specific context of his definition of the self, he constantly moves to universal claims. The modern aspiration for meaning, for example, is seen as having similarity with premodern forms, especially religious forms. The need for orientation in moral space is introduced as a universal human need. Due to this emphasis on morality and meaning making, Taylor (2007) equates religion with belief and faith. In the religious, premodern era, Taylor tells us, our sense of "fullness" was derived from God. In a modern, secular age, this sense of fullness can be related to a host of different sources and frequently to "sources which deny God" (2007, 26). Since the sense of fullness is, for Taylor, the main source for a sense of self, the religious self, its moral orientation, and religious belief are tied together.

Likewise, a morality-centered understanding of selfhood is strongly advocated by Christian Smith (2003) in his book *Moral, Believing Animals*. In this book, Smith offers a framework for human nature. Smith's main attempt is to counter the prevailing tendency in the "new program" of sociology of religion, which, according to Smith, rests on a rational-choice model of human action. He posits his model of humans as moral, believing animals in opposition to the idea that humans are "rational, acquisitive, exchanging animals" (p. 118). As Smith writes, "To be a human person, to posses an identity, to act with agency requires locating one's life within a larger moral order by which to know who one is and how one ought to live" (p. 118). Hidden in this framework of human nature is a model of human selfhood. For Smith, humans are unique in their ability to reflect on themselves, and this reflection takes the form of self-evaluations "based on external standards of good and bad, right and wrong" (p. 10). From this perspective, the self is anchored in the ability of human beings to judge and evaluate their actions in relation to internalized moral orders. The religious self is defined by the narratives, cosmologies, and beliefs that produce the external moral order in which the individual acts.

The understanding of selfhood as anchored in moral space and belief systems enables us to move away from an understanding of the person as a rational, autonomous being. As Smith rightly recognizes, people do not just follow their own egoistic interests—they have higher moral goals that are anchored in the culture that surrounds them. However, the portrait of the religious self as a structure of deep moral beliefs has three important limitations. The first is a separation of the self from its immediate interactional environment. The self, according to Smith, is not rational and autonomous, but it is certainly bounded. It is bounded since every individual is seen as a separate "mind" that operates according to an internalized moral system. The microsociological insight that there is no separation between self and other and that the subjective is always intersubjective disappears.

For example, when Smith discusses religious practice, the collective dimensions of the practice are not analyzed and practice becomes a mere vehicle of the religious system, since religious practice is understood as expressing "in dramatic and corporeal form a sacred belief system" (Smith 2003, 16). The emphasis on practice as expressing a sacred belief system leads to the second limitation of this view: a strong cognitive bias in the understanding of selfhood. Such an understanding, as Vásquez rightly recognizes in the first chapter of this volume, neglects "embodiment and the phenomenological-hermeneutic dimensions of religious practices" (Vásquez, this volume). The embodied dimension of the religious self is not ignored but is given a minor role. An analysis of

the religious self ends up being an analysis of belief systems or moral orientations instead of an analysis of bodily practice.

The aforementioned two limitations, relatively dis-embodied and decontextualized understandings of selfhood, lead to the third limitation of the
morality-based perspective. Religious self-constitution is understood as a process of adopting a moral order or a narrative. Conversion, from this perspective, equals a change in faith. Religious self-transformation is understood as
the point of adopting a new discourse, and this discourse is mainly located in
adopting a new set of beliefs (Snow and Machalek 1984). An example is the
classical Christian model of conversion as described in Augustine's confessions.
When Augustine read the Bible, he was flooded with light and reached a realization of the good. The words in the Bible led to a religious self-transformation.
What enabled this transformation was a narrative, a new orientation in moral
space, and this narrative was produced through turning inward and finding
God. His conversion is described as a solitary experience, decontextualized
from interactive space. This might indeed be one possible version of a process
of conversion. And yet, this model of conversion had become central to studies
of religion, commonly mistaken to be a universal model.

Interestingly, the understanding of self as highly reflexive, cognitive, and
anchored in morality has strong affinities with a Protestant understanding of
the soul. This may not be surprising. After all, the Reformation is considered
one of the most important steps in the making of modern culture. In some
cases, the constitution of religious selves may indeed be a dis-embodied, decontextualized experience. But in many cases it is not. And these are not cases
limited to premodern times when the self was porous, as Taylor (2007) might
argue, or to periods of coercive mass conversions. Even in the so-called late
modern age, religion is not always centered on orientation in a moral space.
The religious self is anchored in surrounding communities, social relations,
bodily experiences of pleasure or of self-mastery, and attachments to objects
and spaces. These are not all disconnected from faith or belief systems, but they
cannot be reduced to studying internalized moral structures. As we shall see,
even religious practices that are based on reflexivity, such as Buddhist meditation practice, and were adopted by modern practitioners are not necessarily
based on a shift in moral orientation, on an adoption of a new narrative, or on
a separate, solitary inner experience.

To summarize, religious practice, subjectivity, and experiences are often seen
as a reflection of religious discourse. From this perspective, moral order comes
first, and microinteraction second. Belief is central, and forms of interactions
are a derivative of belief systems. This emphasis on religion as an abstract symbolic system is firmly connected to the tendency to view culture and religion
as autonomous from the social worlds in which they are embedded (Smilde,
this volume). As Smilde shows, religion turns into an independent variable that

affects other dependent variables such as sociality. Here I would like to reverse the direction of causality. Instead of asking what does religion do, I ask what is the social and embodied space through which religion, and in particular the religious self, is constituted? It is important to note that the understanding of religion as semiautonomous is not limited to those who only emphasize morality. Even sociologists who do study religious practice usually use it as an index of religiosity or boundary marking or a signal of identity (e.g., Ammerman 2003; Warner 1997; McGuire 1990), but rarely as a constitutive element that is constantly at work. Since, as Bender (2012) writes, "the study of practice in the field centers on things (practices) rather than on processes (practicing)," the embodied microsociological dimension, which includes the embodied interaction with others, with oneself, or with the world, is rarely investigated.

In other words, religious selves are understood as *objects that can be measured* (i.e., measuring level of belief or frequency of practice) instead of being *processes that should be followed*. My argument in this chapter is that studying beliefs, values, or worldviews does not suffice for capturing the religious self and certainly cannot capture the actual embodied processes of religious self-constitution. To balance the tendency to focus on belief, I advocate a relational analysis of religious practice, one that can lead to insights regarding the embodied process through which selves are constituted. Religious practice happens in places and contexts where the body connects between one person and another, or between a person and the material world around him or her. This interaction is the place where religion takes place, and not in separate bounded minds. Siding with Lichterman's (this volume) claim that religion is public and not private, I explore the microsocial aspects of religion. To do so, I suggest putting aside, temporarily, the symbolic systems or religious doctrines and instead concentrate on behavior and experience. The justification for such a move is anchored in Collins's (2010) argument that theological doctrines are not necessarily the driving force behind different practical ethics. Taken to the extreme, I would like to side with Collins's claim that in fact "the religious practice determines the doctrine." This somewhat provocative claim opens a whole new field of study, in which behavior and experience are not a side effect of symbolic systems, but instead symbolic systems are the side effect of certain religious practices. The driving force behind religious ethics is the embodied social interactive process that is part of many religious practices.

Self, Reflexivity, and the Social World

From a microsociological perspective, the self is not an object. It is a process. Therefore, we cannot capture the self by specifying a static worldview or a set of beliefs. In microsociological theory, the notion of self refers to the ability of human beings to turn toward themselves, simultaneously being the observing subject and the observed object (Mead 1934; Rosenberg 1979; Gecas and Burke 1995; Weigert and Gecas 2003). The self, thus, is not a substance or an entity but instead a reflexive process based on an inner relationship.

Since the self here is defined as a process of inner relationships, it takes the form of social interaction. This social interaction can involve two or more parts that together conjure the self. Therefore, the central foundation of the theory of the self, and of this chapter, is the famous split of the person into a few components that interact with one another. For James (1981 [1890]), the self is split into two—the "I," the self as subject, meaning the present emergent and acting part of the self, and the "Me," the self as object, meaning the image of the self that is the outcome of self-reflection. As James claimed, the "Me" is based on the attitude of a social group toward the individual, on the image it produces of him or her, and thus we can have as many "Me's" as the social groups in which we are involved. Mead (1934) adopted James's structure by adding a third element—the generalized other. The generalized other is an attitude toward the self that combines together different groups, producing a general moral and normative view with which one judges one's actions. Wiley (1994) added a temporal dimension to Mead's model when splitting the self into the "I," the "Me," and the "You"—the "I" representing the present self, the "Me" the past self, and the "You" the future self. Others, such as Freud, Vigotski, and Bakhtin, have also offered different models of the self, always portraying the self as divided into a few parts that interact with one another.

Whatever the specific configuration of the self each of these authors portrays, they all agree that the split in the self that enables self-reflexivity is anchored in the social world since we always reflect upon ourselves through the eyes of others (Cooley 1902). In other words, it is only through taking the role of the other that we can become conscious of ourselves as both subjects and objects in the world. The individual "enters his own experience as a self or individual, not directly or immediately, not by becoming a subject to himself, but only in so far as he first becomes an object to himself just as other individuals are objects to him" (Mead 1934, 138). The self, therefore, is based on social interaction with others, in which we take the role of the other and view ourselves from different points of view. This ability to view ourselves from an external point of view enables both self-monitoring and self-knowledge as we become aware of our behavior as interpreted by others. It enables the production of the distance that is required for any process of reflexivity, a distance that enables us to open a relationship with ourselves.

The microsociological perspective on the self is not disconnected from morality and ethics. Morality, as a set of norms and values shared by a group of people, has a role in the process of self-reflexivity. As Mead argues, the ability to turn the gaze toward oneself is a crucial part in the formation of moral systems. Through taking the role of the other and gazing back toward the self, one can begin to monitor oneself in accordance to moral norms. As Mead (1934, 283) writes, "A person learns a new language and, as we say, gets a new soul. He puts himself into the attitude of those that make use of that language." This Meadian claim can lead us back to a symbolic-centered understanding of selfhood, one that is anchored in language-like structures such as belief systems and ignores the body. Indeed, as will be elaborated later, we need to adapt Mead's model into an embodied model of the self (Pagis 2009). Still, even for Mead, learning a new language is an interactive process. From a microsociological perspective, the process of self-judgment or self-monitoring is always connected to everyday processes of social interaction. We cannot, therefore, treat questions of religious conversion, for example, as decontextualized events. To get a new soul requires an interaction with others, and this interaction takes place in specific places and times.

Once we move to an understanding of the self as an interactive process, we not only introduce an important social dimension to the process of religious self-constitution but also introduce the embodied dimension. As long as the self is understood as an internalized structure of beliefs, this dimension is pushed to the side. The tendency to pay little attention to the body when relating to the self is anchored to the overall tendency to identify thought, cognition, rationality, knowledge, and interpretation as linguistic processes (Ignatow 2007). More specifically, classical and current understandings of hermeneutics "focus on discursive products and grasp meaning as the play of different linguistic signs" (Shalin 2007, 1). Since the self is a hermeneutic process, which includes knowledge and interpretation (i.e., self-knowledge and self-monitoring), it frequently falls under the category of discursive and symbolic mental processes, and self-reflexivity is frequently equated with inner conversations (i.e., Archer 2003). However, if the self is a process of inner interaction that can be translated to interaction with other people and with the world, then the body must take a more central role in inner self-relations. The body, after all, is the medium through which we interact with the world, the place where experiences are engrained. If we return to religious practice, then the body is both the subject and the object of many religious practices, be it fasting, praying, meditating, wearing religious outfits, or carrying religious icons.[2]

In recent years, the claim that thought, knowledge, and hermeneutics are based on linguistic and abstract signs has been challenged (e.g., Csordas 1990; Lakoff and Johnson 1999; Salins 2007; Pagis 2009, 2010b; Summers-Effler 2010). This challenge is based on a return to classical writings in phenomenology and pragmatism, specifically to Schutz, Merleau-Ponty, and Pierce. These scholars offer a theoretical base for studying the silent, nonverbal embodied forms of sociality that take place both in self-other relations and self-to-self relations. For example, Schutz's (1967) notion of "we-relations" is based on the constitution of a community of time and space in which subjective embodied experiences unfold together in a collective environment. Merleau-Ponty (2002 [c1945]) emphasizes embodied experience when claiming that the "body is a natural self," and Pierce (1960) extends our understanding of signs and interpretation to include nonlinguistic signs such as icons and indexes.

In what follows, I utilize their insights to develop an approach for the study of the relational and embodied space in which religious selves develop. Since the study of the self through religious practices is still a growing field, this chapter does not propose a comprehensive research program but instead offers an invitation for future research. The dimensions of the self I choose to explore are nonexhaustive and are part of a larger potential field of investigation. I explore three dimensions of the embodied sphere in which religious selves are constituted: the awareness of one's own embodied feelings, the bodily interaction with others, and the physical engagement with material objects.[3]

The Interactive Dimensions of Religious Self-Constitution

Although microsociological theory highlights the connections between the constitution of the self and social interaction, only a few studies follow the cultivation of selfhood as related to collective practice. Sociological studies assume that physical proximity to others involves mutual behavioral and emotional influence yet hide this process of mutual influence under vague notions such as socialization and internalization.[4] Religious practice offers a rich arena for investigating how self-other relations are coupled with self-to-self relations. Though many religious self-reflective practices are conducted in solitude, it is common that these practices include a social dimension. Meditation, prayer, and fasting, for example, can all be practiced alone, and yet collective meditation group sittings or collective prayers are an important part of the self-transformative process that takes place through religious practice (Targoff 2001; Cadge 2005). This collective practice forms an arena in which the bodily co-presence of different individuals plays a crucial role in producing and constructing selves.

I first encountered the importance of physical proximity to others in my ethnographic research on Vipassana meditation practice (Pagis 2010a). During this research, I realized that though meditation is frequently referred to as an individual and personal experience, practitioners still find that meditating in a group is beneficial to their practice. The movement between solitary and collective practice offered a puzzle, especially since the collective spheres in which meditation is conducted are silent spheres and therefore include very little overt social interaction. When looking at a collective group sitting, I observed

fifteen bodies sitting silently together, each concentrating on his or her internal sensations. This sphere produces the oxymoron of joint self-introspection.
One is asked to concentrate on inner feelings and ignore others and yet is positioned in close physical proximity to other meditating bodies.

When I asked people why they meditate together, I frequently received the
answer that together the meditations are deeper and stronger. In fact, when
going to a Vipassana meditation retreat lasting a few days, novice meditators
always share a meditation hall, while the more experienced meditators are allocated private meditation cells. The teaching method of Vipassana, therefore,
relies on physical proximity. Collective meditation has an important influence
on more advanced meditators as well. For example, when Ben, a Vipassana
meditator, first meditated in a private meditation cell, he found that in the
meditation cell he became tired and restless:

> I felt laziness and drowsiness. So for the majority of the time I decided
> to sit in the hall and not alone in the cell. It was very surprising—I
> would go to the cell, sit down, and suddenly I open my eyes, I do not
> feel like meditating. I tried fighting it, and it was really hard—I was
> not able to concentrate, I did not feel like meditating. So in the first
> days I tried to give the cell a chance and meditate there, but as the
> course continued I found myself more and more in the hall, where it
> was much easier to meditate.

The production of the peaceful and nonreactive self, the one encouraged by
Vipassana meditation practice, is thus strongly anchored in the physical proximity to others. This finding led me to analyze the mutual influence of practitioners in the meditation hall, searching for the mechanisms that connect self and
other in the practice of self-introspection. I realized that though all practitioners
sit silently in the meditation hall, there is a constant awareness of each other that
is key for the learning process of the kind of self-reflexivity taught in meditation.
The following descriptions, adapted from field notes, serve as examples:

> In one incident a loud cough was heard from the male side. As the
> man continued coughing, a woman in the third row moved her leg
> and changed her posture. Her movement was loud and activated two
> other movements—another woman moved her hand, and another
> straightened her back. In another incident, fifteen minutes before
> the end of a one-hour sitting a woman moved her leg. Almost concur-
> rently another woman sitting a few spots away straightened up, and
> her neighbor then took a deep, audible breath. In fact, once I became
> aware of this mutual influence of movement I suddenly found myself,

while in meditation, taking a heavy breath a second after the woman
next to me let out a heavy breath. (Pagis 2010a, 319)

Although it may seem that the physical proximity of others only disturbs meditation as people hear one another and react to one another, this is not the case. The
fact that movements tend to be clustered together teaches us that silence tends
to be clustered together as well. This mutual influence produces orchestras of
movement and nonmovement as the movement of one person triggers another,
and the silence of one person triggers another. Collective practice, therefore,
enables the silent production of an intersubjective space, producing what Schutz
(1960) refers to as a "community of time and space." This community is crucial
for the first steps of meditation training. Many novice meditators found that
when they had others around them meditating, they could easily meditate as
well. If in their rooms, they would get up in the middle of the meditation, which
they would not even consider doing during the meditation session in the hall.
When they did move, they tended to wait for a noise of another and only then
allowed themselves to stretch. If the meditation hall was completely quiet, they
were sometimes able to keep still for a whole hour. Since the silence of the body
is considered key for achieving a silent mind, the physical proximity to others
leads to higher levels of peacefulness and equanimity.

While the physical proximity of other bodies helps one to constitute a meditative self, this state is dependent on keeping the right balance between being
aware of others and being aware of self. Being too aware of the movements
of others or being too self-conscious becomes an obstacle. Meditators may
encounter such obstacles when sitting in certain places within the meditation
hall. For example, the first row is usually reserved for more advanced students
so that they may serve as role models of equanimity and silence. Tom, who
had taken a few meditation courses, was used to sitting in the front row. He
then took a more advanced meditation course in which he was one of the less
experienced meditators and therefore was moved to the third row. He found
that sitting in the first row had been an important facilitator of his ability to
reach high levels of concentration. In the third row, he tended to move more
and had difficulty concentrating. Thinking back, Tom felt that he had not been
conscious of the fact that others were observing him from behind, but somehow their presence behind him was extremely influential. Rachel, on the other
hand, had an opposite experience. When she was seated in the first row for the
first time (during her sixth meditation course), she was so conscious of the fact
that she was serving as a role model that she could not sit quietly. Her thoughts
so constantly revolved around the question "What do they think of me?" that
she ended up asking the teacher to change her seat.

These examples illustrate the kind of awareness required to produce
internal introspection. People in the meditation hall attend to their bodies

and minds through the bodies and minds of others. But to do so successfully, they need to find the right balance between being aware of others and
being aware of self. Being too aware of the movements of others becomes an
obstacle to self-introspection. This is because the others are not the object of
attention but are an instrument through which the religious self is produced.
This can be done only as long as others are kept in the periphery of attention, as a background, as the place from which one attends to something else
(Polanyi 1966).

The constitution of the self through the physical proximity of others is not
limited to meditation practice. Many religious practices include a movement
from solitary to collective practice. In her illuminating ethnographic study
of a Mexican Catholic convent, Lester (2005) follows the process of self-
transformation that accompanies the young women that join the convent.
When she examines the practice of prayer, she finds that though the women
are asked to repeat the same prayers daily in solitude and in silence (repeat-
ing the words in their heads), the vocalization of the prayer in a collective
environment carries a special meaning for the women. The following excerpt
from a conversation she conducted with Evelyn, one of the postulants, serves
as an example:

> I mean, you say the same prayers every day. It's pretty easy to memo-
> rize them because we say them over and over again. But once you get
> the words down, something else starts to come over it. Each time you
> say the Novena of Trust, for example, you can start to really think
> about what it is you are saying and what you are offering to God. And
> there is something really powerful about saying such things in front
> of your sisters: "I offer you all my being—my thoughts, my desires,
> my aspirations." Imagine it! Here you are opening yourself completely
> to God, and you're right there with everyone else. But that's just it.
> Everyone is doing the same thing. We are the daughters of God putting
> ourselves in His service, all of our voices joining together in one voice.
> It is a really beautiful thing. (p. 177)

This example again illustrates the importance of physical proximity to others
even in the intimate practice of submitting yourself to God through prayer.
Though Lester did not follow the embodied microsociological influence of
one woman over the other during collective prayer, I believe such an analysis
would reveal important social dynamics that are crucial in the constitution
of the submission of the self to God. Such moments reveal that religious
self-constitution is a complex process that involves much more than an
internalization of a stance in a moral space. What happens at that moment
of "joining together in one voice" that is essential for the maintenance of the

religious self? These moments, I claim, should be treated as equal in importance to the learning of religious doctrines or the performance of moral behavior.

Re-Embodying the Religious Self

When reviewing sociological studies that concentrate on self-reflexive practices, the emphasis on language as the main medium for self-reflexivity is highly visible. These studies concentrate on practices such as talking to others or to oneself, psychological therapy, writing in a diary, talk shows, support groups, or self-help literature (Davies and Harre 1990; Archer 2003; Rose 1990; Illouz 2007; Irvine 1999). This emphasis on linguistic and discursive practices of self-reflexivity is frequently linked to modern-Western culture, with its alleged emphasis on expressing the interior world through linguistic practices such as the confession (Foucault 1978). Whether or not the Western culture of the self is indeed predominantly based on discursive practices remains an open debate. Still, the end result of this linguistic monopoly is that the study of self-constitution neglects the centrality of the body in religious practices of self-reflexivity.

The study of religious practices reveals the different ways people can use the body as a reflexive medium. Religious practices frequently increase awareness to the body and to sensations, turning the practitioner's attention to his or her embodied state in the world. They are therefore based on producing a new kind of relationship with bodily sensations. The awareness of bodily sensations enables the practitioner to feel himself or herself feeling the world, to turn the self into an object through an embodied medium (Pagis 2009). Fasting, praying in certain positions, eating certain foods, bodily meditations, and yoga exercises are all examples of practices that turn awareness to certain bodily sensations. Through this awareness, the individual is instructed to monitor desires, emotions, and behavior. These practices, therefore, offer a rich arena for studying embodied forms of self-reflexivity.

When I began my research among practitioners of Vipassana meditation, I realized that the verbal and abstract understanding of the self does not capture the practice of meditation. Though Vipassana meditation is an introspection technique, and the word for meditation (in either Pali or Sanskrit) is best translated as "mental culture," there seems to be less of the mental and much more of the physical in the experience of meditation. Vipassana meditation is a reflexive practice, but this reflexivity is not abstract or discursive—it is anchored in the body. In meditation, to know oneself, one does not speak either with another or with oneself. Instead, self-knowledge is anchored in bodily sensations.

A dialogue I recorded between a teacher and a student illustrates this centrality of physical sensations:

STUDENT: "When I feel sadness I ask myself where this sadness is coming from?"

TEACHER: "Don't ask it, don't think about it."

STUDENT: "Not to think about it?"

TEACHER: "Observe sensations, sensations are the mind."

This dialogue exposes the Vipassana model of self-reflexivity, a model very different from the Freudian model of the "talking cure" so popular among sociologists of the modern culture of the self (e.g., Rose 1990; Illouz 2007). Instead of talking about yourself or writing your actions and feelings in a diary, you are asked to simply observe bodily sensations. As seen in this dialogue, students are specifically asked not to attach stories to their feelings. Utilizing Shweder's (1994) distinction between feelings and emotions, we can say that students are asked not to emotionalize their feelings, not to enter the cultural scheme common in Western cultures in which one attaches the title "sadness" to one's tears and searches for their cause.

Of course, the process of de-emotionalizing feelings is a cultural process and not a natural process. The new attitude toward bodily feelings that the teacher demanded from the student in the previous dialogue is anchored in a cultural world. If we decide to take a morality-based perspective, we can certainly analyze the connections between the attitude toward sensations that is practiced in meditation and central Buddhist tenets such as impermanence and not-self. But meditation is not just a vehicle for transmitting these tenets. For the people who practice meditation, the practice is a source of new inner self-relations, new ways of interacting with one's body, ways that involve emotions, attachments, pleasure, and pain.

Let me offer one example for the kind of embodied inner self-relationships that Vipassana meditation constructs. An excerpt from my field notes taken while participating in a Vipassana meditation course illustrates the details of the embodied loop of self-monitoring that constitutes this process:

> By now the sensations in the body are clear. I can feel them constantly. I saw a cockroach in the bathroom yesterday....I jumped back and let out a heavy breath. I didn't know what to do. For one moment I wanted to cry for help....I spent most of the night awake. The sensations on the body were so intense. Sensations creeping around, such unpleasant sensations, top to bottom. I cannot really describe them. Like being nauseous and a little sick and an unpleasant shivering. I attempted to direct my attention to these sensations, scan them slowly. It did help. Once in a while the picture of the cockroach entered my mind and

again I felt a strong desire to leave the room, and again I attempted to redirect my attention to the body. When I was truly observing the sensations I felt a relaxation—though the sensations were still unpleasant, they were suddenly bearable. (Pagis 2009, 274).

This example illustrates the phenomenological state meditators are in as they become sensitive to their bodily sensations. This embodied awareness enables a monitoring loop in which the observation of sensations—feeling them fully, but without taking action to correct the uneasiness or discomfort—relaxes the interpretation these sensations carry. This nonreactive observation produces a distance between the sensations and the self, a distance required for the process of self-reflexivity. The distance, in this case, is not created through the medium of language (as happens when you speak about what you feel) but instead is created through the medium of the body. By observing their sensations, meditators start feeling themselves feeling the world. The objectification of the self that is central to self-reflexivity, therefore, takes place through the medium of the body.

I do not mean to imply that meditation, as a self-reflexive process, is disconnected from discursive and symbolic spheres. The learning process of meditation requires language as meditation instructions are given verbally. At the same time, the practice itself is embedded in symbolic interpretations. But again, even when studying the symbolic interpretations that surround meditation, we find that we cannot assume an identity between practice and belief. The contemporary practice of meditation derives its meaning from a variety of discursive systems. During meditation retreats, meditation is introduced as a path to salvation, enabling one to detach from the self and realize the self's impermanent nature, thus basing the practice on Buddhist philosophy. But for the practitioners themselves, modern meditation practice is equally embedded in a general cultural discourse common in post-industrial Western cultures regarding the importance of peacefulness, freedom from attachments, and autonomous self-monitoring. Both discourses, the Buddhist and the late modern, play a role in producing the motivation for practice and building expectations for certain outcomes.

Meditation is one example of a religious practice that advocates awareness to the body. Turning to other ethnographies of religious practices, we can see similar processes of embodied self-reflexivity. Fasting, for example, is a common religious practice. Usually this practice is analyzed as a practice of moral asceticism and self-deprivation, and the self-constitutive dimension it holds is disregarded. In his ethnography of Muslim conversion, Winchester (2008, 1768) offers a glimpse of the self-reflexive aspect of fasting as was revealed to him while participating in a fast:

Before the fast, my fieldnotes largely represent me as a researcher acting and looking "outward." I, like most social scientists, am preoccupied

with the visual and sometimes aural field. I "see" acts of ritual prayer: I
"observe" myself and others taking off their shoes before entering the
mosque, I "hear" the reciting of Qur'anic verse. During my fast, however, my fieldnotes become more introspective. I "feel" my stomach
gurgling and rumbling: I "sense" the tiredness of my limbs: I "taste"
the dryness in my mouth.

As Winchester illustrates, fasting produces a shift in the medium through
which self-reflexivity takes place. From noting field notes that are oriented
toward capturing the happenings in the world around him, he shifts to a
sensory-based noting that is dominantly introspective. As he writes, fasting
enables an embodied form of awareness as "the visceral body ceases to recede
from consciousness and becomes a focal point of one's everyday experience"
(p. 1768).

Again, fasting is not disconnected from symbolic interpretations. An important part of fasting is to accept one's hunger and attempt not to fight it. In this
sense, the practice involves an attitude of detachment or distanciation from
desire not dissimilar to meditation practice. This is what makes fasting distinct from just being hungry. And yet, the previous description resonates with
descriptions of fasting in other religious traditions and with descriptions given
by women with eating disorders . Hunger, in this sense, is an embodied experience that has the potential to become a medium for self-reflexivity, and this
potential is utilized under many different symbolic traditions and discourses.

Lester (2005) offers similar observations on embodied practices when following young postulants in a Catholic Mexican convent. She shows how the different tasks and practices in the convent raise the postulants' awareness to their
bodies. For example, prayer in the convent is frequently accompanied with a posture of kneeling, a posture that produces pain. During prayer, the postulants are
required to observe and accept this pain without changing the posture or moving. As Lester writes, "The postulants learn to discipline their bodies to meet the
various requirements (such as rising at 4:45, eating food one dislikes, scrubbing
pots and pans, kneeling for hours in prayer and to become extraordinarily sensitive to the sensations this discipline produces exhaustion, nausea, resentment,
physical pain)" (p.178). Daniel (1984, 267) offers a similar description in his ethnography of a Hindu pilgrimage. Here, the awareness to the growing pain of the
journey, "caused by blisters under one's toenails and those on one's heels...the
pain arising from strained calf muscles and tendons...[t]he headache caused
by the heat of the noon sun," leads to a new phenomenology of the world and of
oneself and is a crucial part in the process of self-knowledge that is a part of the
pilgrimage (see also Haberman 1994). All these are examples of practices that
induce processes of embodied self-reflexivity, where religious transformation is
closely linked to one's relation to one's body.

Constituting Self Through Materiality

If we assume that religious selves are internalized moral structures, then religious dispositions, motivations, and attitudes are confined to the human mind. This, according to Smith, is what makes humans unique. However, if we adopt a relational view on the self in general, and on the religious self in particular, then religious dispositions, moods, and motivations extend beyond individual minds into the environment in which their bodies move and act. The idea that material objects can carry attitudes and dispositions may seem extraordinary, but this is only from a "modern" point of view in which minds are bounded and separated from the environment.

In his study of the scientific world, Latour (2005) tracks the relations between humans and objects, demonstrating how objects such as computers, physical particles, and chromosomes act as influencing agents in interaction. However, there is no need to go to the scientific sphere to find hybrid selves that extend into their environment. Likewise, the constitution of the religious self is an ongoing process of interaction with materiality. Religious practice is surrounded by material objects. Some are sacred objects that carry with them substances of the divine. Some are spaces that produce certain attitudes and motivations. If science is carried on the tracks of laboratories, so is religion carried in networks that connect humans and objects.

Take, for example, the meditation center. Meditation can be practiced everywhere. But the main place where people learn meditation, and the place where they reach deep meditative experiences, is the meditation center. This is also the place where people first learn to meditate, the place where they take meditation courses. The attempt to constitute a new self, or to cultivate certain dispositions, is thus done in a separate environment distinct from the atmosphere of everyday life. This separation serves two purposes. First, it detaches the person from the environment of everyday life, an environment that invites him or her to act in ways he or she might want to change. Second, the meditation center itself turns into a space that radiates, invites, and seduces one to meditate, cultivate calmness, move slowly, and gain insights on oneself. As such, it shares the logic of separate spaces that become attached to a successful performance of a certain act—be it reading in the library, working out in the gym, praying in the church, or researching in the laboratory.

The special environment of the meditation center leads many people to visit it for a few days "in order to absorb the rhythm and atmosphere." I frequently heard practitioners claim that upon entering the meditation center, they felt such a feeling of calmness that they immediately sat and meditated. The meditation hall, the most important building in the meditation center, frequently invites people to meditate even when empty. The meditation hall is painted completely white with blue mattresses and cushions on the floors. The dormitories are also painted white and are very simple. Simplicity, quietism, and peacefulness are integrated in the space. Since people who join meditation courses are isolated from daily activities and from their families and friends, the meditation center radiates solitude even though many people share it.

Some practicing meditators say that the meditation center is filled with energies and vibrations that influence practitioners. This conceptualization of energies depicts a self that is porous, open to the influence of the surrounding environment, a self that surrenders, extends itself, and allows the environment to enter it while at the same time allowing itself to take over the environment. But the conceptualization of energies is not necessary for one to feel the influence of the space. Many contemporary practitioners of meditation do not speak about energies and vibrations. These concepts are not a part of the way they interpret the world. And yet, they all agree that meditating in the meditation center is accompanied by a special effect. They frequently say that in the meditation center their sensations and perceptions suddenly become sharp and clear. The meditation center is built in a way that reduces stimulation of the senses. The colors are soft, the movements are slow, and the food is mildly spiced. The space is very quiet—people do not speak, and when they speak they tend to whisper. No cell phones are allowed; there is no television or Internet or newspapers. It is an environment that radiates seclusion.

The importance of materiality on the constitution of the meditative self is not limited to the meditation center. The most common object in the meditative world is the meditation cushion. In the Vipassana meditation center, all practitioners sit on similar meditation cushions. When visiting the homes of practitioners, I found that many practitioners sit on similar cushions as in the meditation center. In addition, many have fixed meditation places in the corner of one of the rooms. In this corner, they have the meditation mattress and cushion and a blanket to use as a cover in case it is cold. The mattress, cushion, and blanket are kept in the corner and are not put away in storage during the day. They therefore serve as reminders of meditation. When I myself attempted to meditate daily as part of my research, I frequently realized that this reminder is an important cue. Whenever I was lazy or too busy to meditate, the sight of the meditation corner would produce a feeling of guilt, and I would promise myself to meditate in the evening or the next morning.

Furthermore, the fixed meditation corners with the cushion and the blanket turn the actual material place of meditation practice into an anchor in the self-reflexive process of meditation. As one sits on the cushion, gets into the posture, and covers oneself with the blanket, the disposition of equanimity and introspection is generated. The familiar smell of the blanket, the well-known position in the room, the habitual posture—all these produce an association between material objects and an internal disposition that is supportive of meditation practice. These objects play a crucial role in generating the adequate meditative atmosphere.

The religious self, thus, is produced in interaction with the material world. Take, for example, the debate regarding the Muslim headscarf (*hijab*). This custom is frequently condemned by feminist scholars as representing women's oppression. The well-known ban in France that prohibits girls from wearing a headscarf to public schools was just one example of the negative perspective on this practice. The headscarf certainly carries many political and religious meanings: it represents levels of religiosity, women's shyness and docility, and Muslim patriarchy. However, a closer ethnographic analysis of the practice of wearing the headscarf, especially among those who do it voluntarily and without coercion, reveals that the headscarf plays an important role in the formation of self-to-self relations as women attempt to perfect their behavior in the virtue of shyness. As Mahmood writes, it serves as "a means to tutor oneself in the attribute of shyness" (2005, 158).

This headscarf, therefore, can serve a double function. First, it can serve a performative function: it signals others that you belong to a certain group and that you attempt to keep the ethical code of modesty (Rinaldo, unpublished). Yet at the same time, from a microsociological perspective, this performance to others is also a performance to self, one that serves as a constant reminder of the ideal self you want to reach. The scarf is thus an agent as it makes its wearer act in certain ways. The fact that the headscarf is worn around the head is more then just mere modesty—it is placed in a position where one can be aware of it continuously. The indexicality of the headscarf plays an important role when indexing women to perfect their behavior.

Another example is religious icons, such as the icons of saints. These objects, I suggest, take a central role in the relationships that surround the practitioner: the practitioner develops a relationship with the religious icon, a relationship that echoes the relationship with the saint represented in the icon. Thus, a practitioner can speak with the figure, regard it as sacred, or believe it holds special powers. Since, as discussed earlier, social interaction is firmly connected to internal self-relations, these objects also serve as tools in self-reflexive processes as they become mirroring agents that reflect the self. They are not mere objects. Religious icons are subjects. They are agents with whom one interacts; they carry with them qualities that invoke certain internal qualities.

Mead (1934) once wrote that physical objects can be analogous to social others. In this sense, we can take the attitude of a chair as an "invitation to sit down" (p. 279). The chair, Mead suggested, is a physical "Me." Mead claimed that our relation to the physical world is a social relation as we tend to treat objects as if they were social others. Mead, however, never elaborated on these ideas regarding the "Me" hidden in objects, or how exactly objects serve as tools in self-reflexive processes. Extending his notion of the invitation hidden in objects, we can think of the cushion not only as an invitation to meditate but also as an object that carries the attitude of meditation, including other qualities of meditation such as peacefulness and introspection. Likewise, the scarf carries the attitude of modesty and shyness, and the icon of a saint carries an attitude of his or her teachings (be it compassion or happiness). As such, religious objects are frequently used to create certain dispositions and moods, internally cultivating the attitude called for in the object.

I would like to stress that the fact that the material surrounding constitutes selves does not steal away the agency of the practicing person. On the contrary, in all the earlier examples people may choose to participate in an interaction event with the environment. They carry relics or icons. They wear the scarf. They create a meditation corner. When practitioners of meditation return to a meditation retreat once a year, they do so to submit themselves to the environment, in order to use the environment to maintain a certain selfhood. They actively use the material surroundings to produce dispositions, moods, and attitudes.

Conclusion: Going Beyond Religion

In this chapter, I suggested an approach for studying religious selves, an approach different from the common understanding of religious selves as internalization of moral orders. The relational and embodied perspective on the self takes into account the details and nuances of religious practice, following the interactive processes through which selves are constituted. This perspective is based on the claim that the self is not an object that can be measured but instead a process that should be followed. Throughout the chapter, I illustrated that though religious practices are not disconnected from symbolic systems, they are also not a mere reflection of moral orders and worldviews.

The fact that religious practice occurs in certain places and times with certain people and involves the body forces us to bring the social back in—to take the relational context of self-constitution seriously. I will now move one step forward in my call for a renewed understanding of selfhood. Throughout the chapter, I hinted that the limitations I described as belonging to the popular perspective on the religious self tend to appear in other sociological fields, ones that are not necessarily focused on religion. Thus, the modern understanding of the autonomous self, the one that is deeply anchored in the Christian understanding of the disembodied soul, is common throughout social sciences. Selves are understood as entities instead of processes. When relating to self-reflexivity, it is understood as an abstract linguistic process. People are assumed to hold an internalized structure of beliefs, values, and dispositions that is distinct from the surrounding social environment in which they act.[5] Minds are understood as separate from one another. The observations that we tend to spend time in the minds of others or to extend into the environment or that material objects can have agency are far from integrated into the mainstream sociological understanding of the self.

I would like to suggest that mechanisms similar to the ones described previously play a leading role in nonreligious spheres. In the case of the importance of collective practice, marathon runners, for example, frequently report that they tend to run faster when running in a group even if they are not competing with anyone. Sharing a breathtaking view from the top of a mountain or a joint walk through a museum are episodes with minimal social interaction in which the physical co-presence of the other is an important part of the embodied experience. Listening to music in a concert hall full of people—all these are examples of practices in which the co-presence of others is of crucial importance to the process of self-reflexivity that is enacted in the event. Similar analogies can be drawn in regard to the ongoing interaction with the body or with material objects. As I suggested earlier, the fasting of anorexic or bulimic people may be similar to religious fasting as both practices involve a strong embodied self-reflexive dimension. Likewise, we can find similarities between the culture of "working out" and religious pilgrimages as both involve putting the body in situations where attention is focused on sensations and a level of detachment and distanciation from pain is cultivated. Martial arts, dance, biofeedback, yoga, and even self-cutting are all practices that increase awareness to sensations and produce inner self-relations that are based on an embodied medium. Last, since our everyday life is based on relationships with objects, in some cases these objects can become self-reflexive tools and play a role in the constitution of the self. The deprived food of the anorectic can be a mirroring agent in regard to his or her own state. The biofeedback machine produces an icon of the self by offering an artificial map of the emotional state. The dance outfits may have a performative function, but they may also play a role in producing the appropriate mood.

The study of the constitution of religious selves can thus have an important impact on the general sociological understanding of the self. A close analysis of collective religious practice, from meditation to prayer, can teach us about the influence of physical proximity on the formation of inner states and how self-reflection is connected to self-other relations. Giving attention to embodied religious practices reveals that self-reflexivity is not necessarily discursive and can in fact be based on the reflexive capacity of the body. Analyzing the use of material objects in religious practice sheds light on the ways nonreligious dispositions and attitudes are associated with the material world. All these findings begin to form an empirical base on which important theorization on the self can take place.

Notes

1. Throughout the chapter, I follow Riesebrodt's (2010) definition of religious practices as practices that originated in religious traditions with the original aim of salvation. From this perspective, the study of contemporary meditation practice belongs to the sociology of religion, even though meditation practice is not always considered religious by practitioners but instead is considered a spiritual exercise or self-changing technique.

2. The emphasis on self-reflexivity and experience has become especially relevant in the study of late-modern religious practices. For example, when examining modern Buddhism, it becomes visible that meditation, as a self-reflexive practice, has only recently become central to Buddhist practice in both Asian and non-Asian locations (Gombrich 1983; Cook 2010). With the rise of meditation as a leading Buddhist practice, the experiential and embodied sides of Buddhist practice were turned central, while the symbolic and theoretical sides were pushed to the side (Jordt 2007; Sharf 1995).

3. A note on methodology: since the study of the self is a study of subjective experience, it cannot rely on positivistic forms of investigations and instead must use phenomenological and interpretive methods. The main methodology for studying processes of the self is therefore qualitative in nature. Since the study of self-constitution requires following individuals in different contexts of their lives, my opinion is that participant observation is the ideal methodology at hand. Furthermore, the participation aspect of participant observation enables the researcher to actually experience similar processes to those inhabited by his or her subjects of study. Such experience is crucial for understanding the phenomenological world in which the people we study reside and thus gain further insight into their self-to-self relations. All the examples I have chosen, therefore, are taken from in-depth ethnographies that follow religious practices and communities.

4. For examples of studies that do look into the collective process through which selves are constituted see Collins (2010) and Wacquant (2004).

5. The notion of the habitus, which became extremely popular in the sociology of culture, is one example of the common understanding of habits, dispositions, and values as internalized structures that have an autonomous standing regardless of social relations.

References

Ammerman, Nancy T. 2003. "Religious Identities and Religious Institutions." Pp. 207–224 in *Handbook of the Sociology of Religion,* edited by Michele Dillon. Cambridge: Cambridge University Press.

Archer, Margaret S. 2003. *Structure, Agency, and the Internal Conversation.* Cambridge: Cambridge University Press.

Bourdieu, Pierre. 1990. *The Logic of Practice.* Stanford, CA: Stanford University Press.

Bender, Courtney. 2012. "Practicing Religions." Pp. 273–295 in *The Cambridge Companion to Religious Studies,* edited by Robert Orsi. Cambridge: Cambridge University Press.

Cadge, Wendy. 2005. *Heartwood: The First Generation of Theravada Buddhism in America.* Chicago: University of Chicago Press.

Collins, Randall. 2010. *The Micro-Sociology of Religion.* Association of Religion Data Archives, Guiding Paper.

Cook, J. C. 2010. *Meditation in Modern Buddhism: Renunciation and Change in Thai Monastic Life.* Cambridge: Cambridge University Press.

Cooley, Charles H. 1902. *Human Nature and the Social Order.* New York: C. Scribner's Sons.

Csordas, T. J. 1990. "Embodiment as a Paradigm for Anthropology." *Ethos* 18: 5–47.

Daniel, E. Valentine. 1984. *Fluid Signs: Being a Person the Tamil Way.* Berkeley: University of California Press.

Davies, B., and R. Harre. 1990. "Positioning: The Discursive Production of Selves." *Journal for the Theory of Social Behavior* 20: 43–63.

Foucault, Michel. 1978. *The History of Sexuality*. New York: Vintage Books.

Foucault, Michel. 1997. *Ethics Subjectivity and Truth*, edited by Paul Rabinow. New York: New Press.

Gecas, Victor, and Peter J. Burke. 1995. "Self and Identity." Pp. 41–67 in *Sociological Perspectives on Social Psychology*, edited by Karen S. Cook, Gary A. Fine, and James S. House. Boston: Allyn and Bacon.

Gombrich, Richard. 1983. "From Monastery to Meditation Center: Lay Meditation in Contemporary Sri Lanka." Pp. 20–34 in *Buddhist Studies Ancient and Modern*, edited by Philip Denwood and Alexander Piatigorsky. London: Curzon Press.

Haberman, David L. 1994. *Journey Through the Twelve Forests: An Encounter with Krishna*. New York: Oxford University Press.

Hadot, Pierre. 1995. *Philosophy as a Way of Life: Spiritual Exercises from Socrates to Foucault*. New York: Blackwell.

Ignatow, Gabriel. 2007. "Theories of Embodied Knowledge: New Directions for Cultural and Cognitive Sociology?" *Journal for the Theory of Social Behavior* 37: 115–135.

Illouz, Eva. 2007. *Saving the Modern Soul Therapy, Emotions, and the Culture of Self-Help*. Berkeley: University of California Press.

Irvine, Leslie. 1999. *Codependent Forevermore: The Invention of Self in a Twelve Step Group*. Chicago: University of Chicago Press.

James, William. 1981 [1890]. *The Principles of Psychology*. New York: Dover.

Jordt, I. 2007. *Burma's Mass Lay Meditation Movement: Buddhism and the Cultural Construction of Power*. Athens: Ohio University Press.

Lakoff, George, and Mark Johnson. 1999. *Philosophy in the Flesh: The Embodied Mind and Its Challenge to Western Thought*. New York: Basic Books.

Lester, Rebecca J. 2005. *Jesus in Our Wombs: Embodying Modernity in a Mexican Convent*. Berkeley: University of California Press.

Latour, Bruno. 2005. *Reassembling the Social: An Introduction to Actor-Network-Theory*. New York: Oxford University Press.

Mahmood, Saba. 2005. *Politics of Piety: The Islamic Revival and the Feminist Subject*. Princeton, NJ: Princeton University Press.

McGuire, Meredith. 1990. "Religion and the Body: Rematerializing the Human Body in the Social Sciences of Religion." *Journal for the Scientific Study of Religion* 29(3): 283–296.

Mead, George H. 1934. *Mind Self and Society: From the Standpoint of a Social Behaviorist*. Chicago: University of Chicago Press.

Merleau-Ponty, Maurice. 2002 [c1945]. *Phenomenology of Perception*. London: Routledge.

Pagis, Michal. 2009. "Embodied Self-Reflexivity." *Social Psychology Quarterly* 72: 265–283.

Pagis, Michal. 2010a. "Producing Intersubjectivity in Silence." *Ethnography* 11: 309–328.

Pagis, Michal. 2010b. "From Abstract Concepts to Experiential Knowledge: Embodying Enlightenment in a Meditation Center." *Qualitative Sociology* 33: 469–489.

Pierce, Charles S. 1960. *Collected Papers*. Cambridge, MA: Harvard University Press.

Polanyi, Michael. 1966. *The Tacit Dimension*. London: Routledge.

Riesebrodt, Martin. 2010. *The Promise of Salvation: A Theory of Religion*. Chicago: University of Chicago Press.

Rinaldo, Rachel. Unpublished Manuscript. "High Heels and Headscarves: Women's Clothing and Islamic Piety in Indonesia."

Rose, Nikolas S. 1990. *Governing the Soul: The Shaping of the Private Self*. New York: Routledge.

Rosenberg, Morris. 1979. *Conceiving the Self*. New York: Basic Books.

Shalin, Dmitri. 2007. "Signing in the Flesh: Notes of Pragmatist Hermeneutics." *Sociological Theory* 25: 193–224.

Sharf Robert H. 1995. "Buddhist Modernism and the Rhetoric of Meditative Experience." *Numen* 42: 229–283

Shweder, Richard A. 1994. "You're Not Sick, You're Just in Love: Emotion as an Interpretive System." Pp. 32–44 in *The Nature of Emotion*, edited by Paul Elcma and R. J. Davidson. New York: Oxford University Press.

Summers-Effler, Erika. 2010. *Laughing Saints and Righteous Heroes: Emotional Rhythms in Social Movement Groups*. Chicago: University of Chicago Press.

Schutz, Alfred. 1967. *The Phenomenology of the Social World*. Evanston, IL: Northwestern.

Smith, Christian. 2003. *Moral, Believing Animals: Human Personhood and Culture*. Oxford: Oxford University Press.

Smith, Christian. 2007. "Why Christianity Works: An Emotions-Focused Phenomenological Account." *Sociology of Religion* 68: 175–178.

Snow, David A., and Richard Machalek. 1984. "The Sociology of Conversion." *Annual Review of Sociology* 10: 167–190.

Targoff, Ramie. 2001. *Common Prayer the Language of Public Devotion in Early Modern England*. Chicago: University of Chicago Press.

Taylor, Charles. 1989. *Sources of the Self: The Making of the Modern Identity*. Cambridge, MA: Harvard University Press.

Taylor, Charles. 2007. *A Secular Age*. Cambridge, MA: Harvard University Press.

Wacquant, Loic. 2004. *Body & Soul: Notebooks of an Apprentice Boxer*. Oxford: Oxford University Press.

Warner, R. Stephen. 1997. "Religion, Boundaries, and Bridges." *Sociology of Religion* 58(3): 217–238.

Weigert, Andrew J., and Viktor Gecas. 2003. "Self." Pp. 267–88 in *Handbook of Symbolic Interactionism*, edited by Larry T. Reynolds and Nancy J. Herman-Kinney. Walnut Creek, CA: AltaMira Press.

Wiley, Norbert. 1994. *The Semiotic Self*. Chicago: University of Chicago Press.

Winchester, Daniel. 2008. "Embodying the Faith: Religious Practice and the Making of a Muslim Moral Habitus." *Social Forces* 86: 1753–1780.

5

Studying Public Religion:
Beyond the Beliefs-Driven Actor

PAUL LICHTERMAN

Religion in Public, After All

Sociology has been shedding the old assumption that religion lives largely inside people's psyches in modern societies such as the United States. In classic statements of this older view, religious congregations constituted the one holdout of religion in an otherwise secular public realm, drawing congregants mainly out of rote (Luckmann 1967) or through effective salesmanship (Berger 1967), not by eliciting real religious conviction. Powerful criticisms of this view (Casanova 1994; Regnerus and Smith 1998) have ushered in the now-routine observation that religious identity and practice really do play roles in wider public life. As the introductory chapter observed, that means we should look for religious identity and practice beyond congregations. When we do, we find it in electoral politics, social movement activism, volunteering, and social service programs. With these unavoidable facts in mind, social theorist Jürgen Habermas has concluded recently (2005) that the United States is a "post-secular" society and religious reasoning of some kind is likely to inhabit its public life for the foreseeable future. Whether "post-secular" accurately describes the putatively changing character of society itself or only a change in our theoretical assumptions about society, it is fair to say that the privatization thesis is no longer a commonsense starting point for inquiry into religion.

The new starting point brings new, pressing questions: If religion is public after all, how do we look for it? How do we know who is a religious actor? A lot rides on our answers, including our understanding of when religion is "good" for society and what counts as religion to begin with—themes of concern throughout this volume.

Let's start with a brief illustration of the problem: In a large city, sixty community advocates, clergy people, and volunteers met over breakfast to trade ideas on what to do about homelessness in their urban neighborhood. The meeting opened with a welcome to "religious and nonreligious" people followed by a short prayer to an unnamed divinity. Participants identified with a variety of religious traditions or no religion at all. Some speakers embraced religious commitments; others criticized religious ideas or people. Some participants were clergypersons, but it would have been hard to tell only on the basis of what they said. Were they necessarily religious actors anyway? Should we categorize this as a religiously inspired gathering?

Researchers have often answered these questions by making assumptions about public religious actors in general. Using this "default model," we assume that we can locate public religious actors—whether individual or collective—relatively straightforwardly and that they manifest religious identities or sensibilities in a way that does not vary significantly by setting. After describing the default model, I introduce an alternative, "pragmatic" model[1] that focuses on action in settings. The case of the homelessness advocacy group pictured before will illustrate how settings shape religious expression.

Commonly we imagine religious actors as people driven by religious beliefs that motivate them in general, diffuse ways most of the time. Yet everyday life offers many examples of people who express religious sentiments in different ways in different social circles and who express it in some settings but not others. Sociological research has tended to neglect this variation; the approach I introduce here gives a more precise picture of where and how people voice religious culture in public.

The default model is an ideal type only. Some studies borrow from it implicitly if not explicitly, sometimes revealing changes in religious expression by situation despite relying on default conceptual language. Of course, some research on public religion—studies of congregations, for instance—are agnostic on the question of how exactly public actors express religion in everyday life (e.g., Chaves 2004) and have no necessary relation to either default or alternative models. Undeniably, studies relying on the default model have contributed greatly to our understanding of religion's social roles. Rather than counterpose a "bad" default position to a "good" alternative, the point here is to enlarge our sociological sensitivity to religion in everyday action and open new empirical questions difficult to entertain with the default model.

The puzzle of mixed, religious/secular settings that opened this paper is likely to become only more pressing. The number of Americans with no religious preference is growing (Hout and Fischer 2009; Kosmin and Keysar 2008), and interfaith or pluralistic religious projects and programs continue to spread (Wuthnow 2005). As Courtney Bender points out in her chapter, the prospects for religious pluralism in the United States are shaped historically by legal norms and political interests that promote some forms of religion over others, the forms that appear to comport well with congregationalism and liberal individualism. This chapter shows that cultural norms of group life, too, shape possibilities for public religious expression, whether interfaith or denominationally specific. When we relocate public religious expression from the edges to the center of our inquiry, we can learn a lot about how Americans negotiate religious pluralism in everyday life, as well as learning specifically where and how Americans do things with religion in public.

This focus on settings for public religious expression, rather than public religious actors, spotlights two of the other "edges" that shape this volume. First, it invites criticism and revision of some of the more optimistic portraits of religion's social roles. It finds that religion's effects on social ties are setting specific and variable; religious identity does not necessarily promote social networking even with coreligionists. Second, the pragmatic perspective apprehends "religion" itself in a way that may be counterintuitive given an emphasis on deep personal beliefs that is common in Christian, especially Protestant Christian, understandings that frequently have informed previous, American social research on religion.

The Default Model

The Religious Actor

The default model identifies and distinguishes religious and nonreligious actors. It does not suppose that religious people never change their religious commitments over the life course. Rather, its guiding assumption is that when religious identity or sensibility is manifest at all, it is not substantially affected by the setting. The default model's appeal has multiple supports. It is easy to take for granted partly because of a Protestant-derived, American cultural tendency to understand religion as identity-pervading belief (Neitz 2004), a faith deeply lodged in the self. Talk of "faith" or "sharing faith" may capture very clumsily the religious understandings of non-Christians, for example, Jews (Ammerman 2005). Yet these also are currently the terms of choice for polite, American talk about religion, and they too may well perpetuate an assumption even in some social research that real religion is constant and pervades the self. Epistemological assumptions about religion in sociology may have primed the default's appeal, too. As Manuel Vásquez argues in his chapter, sociology's self-understanding as a modern discipline has come at the cost of "othering" religion as a premodern, less-than-rational way of knowing and being. The actor who doesn't change by setting, who somehow escapes a modern society's differentiation of roles, sounds indeed like sociology's other. A full intellectual history of the default model goes beyond the bounds of this chapter, but we can find the model continually reappearing in American sociology of religion.

The privatization thesis that became modern common sense about religion (Lichterman and Potts 2009) at least implicitly if not explicitly depended on the stable religious self as a lynchpin of moral order. In Talcott Parsons's view, modern families socialized individuals to a kind of religion that consisted centrally if not wholly of prosocial values and an emphasis on individual responsibility (Parsons 1967, especially 418–421). Peter Berger's more well-known, more declensionist view of religion's socially integrative functions had it that religion unified society under a "sacred canopy" that was fraying in the glare of modern scientific thinking, voluntarism, and role segmentation (Berger 1967). Whether optimistic or pessimistic on the continuing role of religion's power in the modern world, both views saw religion as stable and unifying so neither would sensitize observers to variety in an individual's or organization's religious identity in different situations.

As the larger heritage of the privatization thesis—secularization theory—came under attack, some scholars packed previous assumptions of a unified and unifying religious self into their new research. Religion became a facilitator of wholeness and group empowerment in a pluralistic, fragmented world: religion, or spirituality, satisfied the "wholeness hunger" that a world of highly differentiated institutions and roles inevitably would bestow on individuals (Roof 1998; see Luckmann 1967). Religious identity might change over the life course, but any change from setting to setting still flew under an intellectual radar more attuned to whole-making religious selves. Religion could now be seen as having public, social functions, too: a strong, synthetic statement of this "new paradigm" (Warner 1993) observed that religion promotes group solidarity among immigrant and socially subordinate groups, perhaps most famously in the case of the American civil rights movement (Morris 1984). Substantiated by a large accumulation of research, this position turns our attention to group commonalities in religious selfhood. That can be a valuable move for some research questions; it simply does not highlight diversity in one individual's or group's modes of religious expression.

Both the new paradigm and a prominent alternative, neosecularization theory (Chaves 1994), explicitly represented themselves as social and institutional approaches to religion. Very recent moves to highlight everyday practices of religion have taken more inspiration from contemporary social theories of culture and communication (Ammerman 2003, 2007; Wood 2002; Besecke 2005), and like Wendy Cadge's investigation of hospital chapels in this volume, they find that public settings and not only the actors in them produce and influence meanings. With this more communication-centered, setting-sensitive approach, we can see, for example, how volunteers, some of whom express religious identities in other settings, feel their way hesitantly toward religious conversational topics while chopping vegetables and packing meals in the kitchen of an AIDS service organization (Bender 2003). The volunteers settle tentatively on a small number of "speech genres" that open, or funnel, some conversational space for religious expression in an organization that does not have an avowedly religious mission. Mutable religious identities have become harder to neglect, especially as researchers follow religious culture to workplaces, citizen groups, and other sites beyond the boundaries of officially religious institutions (Ammerman 2007).

Critiques of the Default Model

The default model has helped scholars investigate public religious actors to begin with instead of assuming public religion is vestigial and socially impotent. It complements common intuition and helps us ask some kinds of questions about religion's political and civic roles. Why should we complicate our notions of religious action? At least some of the reason is empirical: the default model misses some of religion's public roles by oversimplifying our notions of what people do with religion.

First, as Nancy Ammerman has put it, when studies consider religious identity "a singular guiding 'core' that shapes how others respond to us and how we guide our own behavior," they oversimplify variation in an individual's religious self-understanding and its consequences for action (Ammerman 2003, 209). Survey research on correlations between religion and public action necessarily rests on the assumption that religious people carry a core religious self—or else brackets the question of variability—in studies of religion and voting or volunteering, for instance. Close-up, qualitative studies often rely on a similar assumption of a core religious self. Studies of conservative social movement women, for instance, show women driven by a singular, alternative worldview or subculture and sense of religious self that is present across different settings, from national conferences, to local activist group conversations, to church settings and private interviews (Klatch 1987, 20–31; Press and Cole 1999). Leaving aside the notion of a singular religious self or subculture, more recent research on pro-life activists shows that the setting of an abortion protest can carry religious and/or nonreligious meanings for participants who identify religiously in other settings; the action is "polysemic" and does not rest on a single sense of religious self (Munson 2007).

Second, default assumptions encourage at least a soft or subtle form of "groupism," a tendency to attribute to members of a religiously identified organization the same shared religious sensibilities and identities. As Brubaker conceives it, groupism is the tendency to take "internally homogenous, externally bounded groups as basic constituents of social life" and the main actors in social conflicts (2002, 164). Harder or softer versions of groupism accompany studies of religiously inspired community organizing. Inferring that Christianity was a "shared yardstick," for instance, one study took a community organization to be homogenously religious because some members spoke dubiously about local elected leaders' religious virtues, and the organization sought out local churches willing to host announcements of the group (Lichterman 1996). A subtler kind of groupism accompanies another study that generalized that "religious commitments to community caring, family well-being, and social justice inspire and sustain political participation in IAF organizations" (Warren 2001, 4). Those religious commitments in turn are traced to different religious traditions said to be shared by clergy and lay members of congregations of different affiliations (pp. 191–210). One could infer a "group-ist" message from this combination of claims: groups pervaded by shared theology and uniform religiosity pursue community organizing. Yet, Warren's study also shows along the way how religiously-based community organizing must juggle overlapping social identities, especially racial identities, that can inhibit solidarity based on religious commonalities. It is harder to ask how religious identities intersect with or bracket racial ones if we already suppose that shared religious commitments pervade an organizing campaign—that the activists are "always" religious. Reasonably enough, a study that portrays a variety of influences on community organizing campaigns has limited space to devote to how exactly religious culture suffuses or is absent from different components or settings of a campaign. Asking that question would require research with a different lens on religion and settings.

Other research on religiously based community organizing moves further from groupism. We see community meetings with municipal leaders becoming powerful forums for "identity work" where, instead of "compartmentalizing themselves into a 'secular self' enacted in other settings," participants can integrate secular and religious identities (Wood 2002, 167). This remarkable observation on the power of settings comes with the quiet assumption that the prayer at these meetings "roots political work in the shared faith commitments of participants."[2] This kind of assumption may be difficult to leave aside entirely in research that aims to portray patterns in collectivities, but again, we can ask more about how religious identities, cues, or sensibilities work in collective action if we stop assuming that they are shared by everyone under study and always at work.

In the eyes of many academic and general audiences alike, the causal role often is the lead role in the sociological drama, and as a recent, comprehensive review points out (Smilde and May 2010), much recent sociological research on religion now treats religion as an independent variable. If religious expression is more setting specific than pervasive in individuals or groups, then we need to improve on default assumptions about causal relations between religion, self, and public action. Studies reviewed earlier are doing that using different conceptual metaphors of speech genre, polysemy, and identity work mentioned before. This emerging line of work already suggests the value of a pragmatic model of religion and public action, for which I introduce a method next.

A Pragmatic Model: A Focus on Style in Settings

The alternative approach is a "pragmatic" approach in a restricted sense of the term: it focuses on situated action and situated identities in settings (Mead 1934, 1964). Rather than follow the performance of religious or other texts (for instance, Burke 1969 [1945]), this approach starts with everyday action, similar to Goffman's studies of interaction (1961, 1959). The pragmatic approach, similar to many studies on the default model, treats religion as culture, not fundamentally different from other kinds of culture. In this perspective, religious culture is not silent beliefs, as popular common sense still has it, but patterned communication (Riesebrodt 2008; Ammerman 2003; Lichterman 2008). The pragmatic approach goes on to say that those patterns of communication—whether we call them vocabularies, discourses, or narratives, for instance—always are inflected by specific social settings (Eliasoph and Lichterman 2003; Lichterman 2005, 2007). This short chapter introduces some elements of a method we can use to study how settings enable and constrain what people can say and do religiously.

Group Style in Settings

Settings are structured by *group styles*. Group style is a concept from recent cultural sociology that improves the Goffmanian approach to settings. Group style is a pattern of interaction that arises from a group's shared assumptions about what constitutes good or adequate participation in the group setting. While Goffman treated culture mostly as a static backdrop, more recent work finds there are loose patterns of setting creating, which have their own histories and make up part of a society's cultural repertoire. Understandings about the floor of a setting sometimes are shared in many settings of the same type across a society. Group styles give settings their power to shape interaction and identity, in ways potentially different from how they would unfold outside the setting (Eliasoph and Lichterman 2003). Rather than say a group exists and has a style, from this viewpoint it makes more sense to say that people coordinate themselves and define the meaning of membership in different styles, creating different kinds of group. Different group styles elicit different abilities, perspectives, and even religious beliefs that individuals may not exercise or express outside the group.

For the scholar of religion, it is important to recognize that a group's style has a reality of its own. It is not simply a derivative or logical consequence of members' religious beliefs, or sacred texts. A new body of research is showing how group styles shape not only how people work together but also how people interpret their beliefs differently in different settings, how the same people welcome or eschew religious or political claims in different settings.[3] That is why we should investigate different settings for public religion, paying attention to how group style, the meaning of membership in a setting, itself shapes opportunities for religious expression. To discover group style, a researcher can focus on several aspects of action in common; for present purposes, two are the most important: First, organizations draw *boundaries* around themselves on a wider social map; those boundaries bring "the organization" itself into being, defining what is "inside" or "outside" it, who it is like, and who it avoids. Second, organizations sustain *bonds* that define a set of good members' obligations to each other.

To assess boundaries and bonds in relation to religious or potentially religious culture, the observer may pursue two related questions: What implicit understandings guide the actors' ways of relating to the potentially religious identities of others in the setting? And how do individual actors relate to their own potentially religious identities in the setting? The task, then, is not to figure out "what religion the participants have" or "how strongly they hold their religion," but how they construct religious identities and how they relate their religious commitments to those of others in a setting.

Demonstrating the Pragmatic Approach: The Case and the Method

Scenarios pictured in the following paragraphs come from a local community service group. Caring Embrace of the Homeless and Poor (CE) was a loose-knit group of congregational leaders and housing and homelessness advocates. A shifting core of members met monthly at an urban, mainline Protestant church with a decades-long history of engagement in progressive causes, located near a university in a neighborhood of working-class, Spanish-speaking residents and students. Monthly meetings gathered between five and twelve people who expressed different religious identities or no religious identity during meetings. The group's facilitator, Theresa, was the lead staff person for the hosting church's network of social advocacy projects and identified as a liberal Presbyterian. Other core participants included the hosting church's pastor, a long-time Lutheran pastor of a nearby congregation, a graduate student intern who avowed no particular religious identity, a Korean evangelical real estate agent, two members of a theater troupe made up of homeless and formerly homeless people who did not identify themselves in religious terms, the congregational liaison for a regional chapter of Habitat for Humanity who identified simply as Christian, and, early in the study, the community organizer from a citywide housing advocacy organization who expressed no religious identification at meetings. Neither the theater troupe members nor the community organizer identified themselves in religious terms during this study.

The group's main activity was a campaign to educate religious congregations about myths regarding homelessness and advocate that the real solution to homelessness is affordable housing. The Nails Project, as it was named, asked local religious congregations to collect nails, which CE would then donate to Habitat for Humanity, the large nonprofit organization that builds houses for low-income families. The group set a goal of collecting 74,000 nails, symbolizing the number of people homeless on an average night in the city. Many times the coalition's director described the Nails Project as a metaphor of action, as well as a symbol of the homeless problem's massive scope: the act of collecting 74,000 nails should send a powerful message that we can "turn homelessness into housing." During this study, the group had collected roughly 55,000 nails and had entertained several conversations about how to use the mountain of nails to dramatize the message: a media event could be staged to announce the donation of nails to Habitat for Humanity; CE members could bring wagons full of nails to city hall; members could build a portable display of nails alongside pictures and stories of homeless people in the city. None of these ideas materialized during the study. Nail collecting continued at a pace that the group's facilitator considered slow, while the group also kept members informed of homelessness- and housing-related meetings and protest events and became a stop-off point for a variety of homeless and community advocates looking to involve religious groups in their own projects.

Data for the case come from participant observation, the method of choice for studying how people enact religious identities in everyday settings in real time (Bender 2003; Lichterman 2008). I studied CE for 24 months; in addition to observing, I volunteered for outreach and other tasks and tried to get two congregations interested in hosting a speaker on homelessness from CE. To substantiate my argument about the power of settings, I contrast actors' expressions of religious identity or religious beliefs in the main organizational setting with the same actors' expressions of religious identity or belief outside that setting. As interactionists point out (Goffman 1961; McCall and Simmons 1978), conversational breaches or awkwardness, or a quick switch in conversational topic, is a good sign that shared understandings have been threatened or violated, and these interactional glitches too can help reveal the power of group style in a setting.

Inclusive Inspiration in a Community Education Project

Orchestrated Ambiguity and Inclusiveness

The default model bids us to see individuals or groups as carrying religious culture in monovalent ways. The following ethnographic scenarios would frustrate that effort. The first scene comes from a breakfast meeting sponsored by Caring Embrace of the Homeless and Poor, held in the basement meeting hall of the church that hosts the group and its director's office. The director planned this meeting to share ideas on how to deal with the growing presence of homeless people in the neighborhood surrounding the church. It included pastors or representatives from a variety of Protestant churches, both mainline and African American; a Catholic homeless shelter employee; several homeless or formerly homeless people from the city center; a rabbi from a Jewish college student organization; an affordable-housing developer and two affordable-housing advocates from a city-wide housing coalition; an imam from a local mosque; and several African American Muslims. Though many of the participants were clergy or religious leaders, their varied ways of avowing, alluding to, or ignoring religious identity make it very difficult to apply the default model. I quote from field notes at length to illustrate the great variety of ways people related to religion at this meeting.

> Theresa, the meeting director, asked the pastor of this church to make some opening comments. Pastor Frank W. said that "more and more [homeless] people are coming to our doorstep. . . . How can we make a compassionate response to homelessness? How can we make a compassionate response to poverty in this area? . . . How can we make a response with dignity? . . . How can we work together as religious people, as non-religious?" He added that "we all have resources to bring" to the issue—and he listed several qualities including "compassion" and "courage." Then he asked us to pray: "Thanks for the children," he said, "first of all . . . and thanks for the food we have today." There followed a mild petition to bless our work together, "and we ask in your name, amen." The prayer contained no specific names for the divine.

Theresa then asked us to do a go-around of introductory statements so that everyone could say a little bit about "what group we are from and why we are here." This go-around session took the great majority of the meeting time. Following are a sample of responses.

> Rabbi Kenneth from Campus Hillel: ". . . Instead of thinking of the campus as a fabulously wealthy university—let's think of homelessness [in this area] as an opportunity to learn about social consciousness."
>
> Thomas: He said that homelessness has grown so that now it included "people who used to be middle-class who are getting pushed down—on the verge of being on the street." He also described homeless people as "people trying to deal with issues alone, rather than getting together and working collectively."

Wes, pastor of a nearby mainline Protestant church: "I came here to learn, and to pray."

The pastor of St John's Episcopal: He told us there are people sleeping in his church yard. Homeless people tried to break in, to find a place to sleep for the night. He and his church people find themselves wondering, "Where are they from? How can we respond in an appropriate way?"

Two pastoral interns from St. Mark's introduced themselves. The second one described her church as "open all the time for people in need."

Two actresses from a theatrical troupe made up of homeless people said they were from "the other LAPD"—the Los Angeles Poverty Department. [This is a local, bitter joke in reference to the Los Angeles Police Department.] Each said she was homeless, lived downtown, and that "I'm a child of God, a social activist, a prayer warrior."

Francis, staff person with a housing advocacy organization: "Our response, traditionally, in many religious communities has been immediate service. But we need to broaden our imagination to think about what we can do to *end* homelessness."

A man from the "homeless artists local foundation" talked about himself, saying that he "had been homeless, but ten years ago spiritual principles were applied" and now he no longer was homeless. Later he said, "We need to do more networking with other churches. A lot of us don't realize that when we detach ourselves, our families still want us—they may be looking for us.... [I]t's an emotional issue.... I didn't realize how much people wanted me back."

The leader of a nearby mosque said there "was more need" than there used to be, and that homeless people were not all on drugs, but that rather it was "people down on their luck." He told us also that his mosque started a charter school.

Henrietta: She told us how when she was homeless, she and her family lived in their car. They parked it outside a church in Hollywood. She recounted to us how she told her children, "If these are good Christian people, they'll say something to us." Then she told us bitterly, "No one said anything. Children laughed and pointed at us!"

One of the prayer warriors agreed with the sentiment, saying she was "involved in church and then [became] homeless.... [I]t seems like there are instances where there is red tape...if you are not a member, and not a tithing member [then you don't get any help]."

It is extremely difficult to generalize about the religious or nonreligious character of the setting as a whole and hard to infer confidently the presence or absence of religious identities or motives in individuals as they are speaking. Speakers ranged from two "prayer warriors" and a man who "came to pray" to those who made no clearly religious comment at all. Some of the people were clergypersons, but one would not be able to guess that solely on the basis of what they said. For instance, Thomas, the man who said some homeless people were once middle class but had been pushed down the social ladder, was associate pastor of a large, mainline Presbyterian congregation. His comments and his appeal to collective action made him sound more like (nonreligious) housing advocate Francis than fellow mainline Protestant pastor Wes. We cannot know if Thomas was more motivated by social justice activism than religious piety or if Brown was more motivated by the power of prayer than the image of collective political action; staking these claims would require inferring basic, continuous motives, religious or irreligious, then using those to explain speech—making the kind of epistemological move that Ammerman warned against earlier. We know what we see and hear: it is safe to suppose that Thomas interpreted the breakfast meeting as an appropriate place to present a political activist's account of what is to be done, while Wes interpreted the stage for this meeting as one that welcomed prayerful reflection.

Dispensing with the question of whether or not the group "is" or "is not" a religious group, the pragmatic perspective would ask how participants collaborated in creating a kind of setting for both religious and nonreligious expression. The style that coordinated this setting featured fluid boundaries and an affirmation of individual voice. Pastor Frank set the stage to begin. "How can we work together as religious people, as nonreligious?" he asked. *The stage allowed us at the meeting to decide whether or not we wanted to sound religious or not and to decide whether or not someone else meant to be religious or not.*

In terms of group style, the pastor's comment bid us to make the *boundaries* between religious and secular fluid. This was not a "religious group" bringing religious compassion to a secular world; it was a group of caring people who may or may not claim religious identities. At the end of the session, Theresa validated all of the comments, from appeals to treating homeless people with dignity to calls for collective political action, saying that each had a place in an overall response to homelessness. The group's "map" welcomed a wide variety of caring responses into the circle of "we" who address homelessness.

Some individuals, like the homeless women from the theatrical troupe, interpreted the meeting as an opportunity to testify to their religious conviction; others, including pastors, did not. Others spoke in language easy for many Americans familiar with congregational life to associate with religion, such as "people in need." They may have spoken this way because they were motivated by Christian compassion. They may have spoken that way because they wanted to sound appropriately "churchy" at a meeting that included self-identified clergy in a church basement. We cannot know for sure, and that is the point: a pragmatic approach will not help us identify religious or secular motives that brought people to this meeting. Rather, it helps us study how people co-created a setting that could brook religious, nonreligious, and even antireligious identification. It tells us to listen to what people say about themselves in relation to religion—how they sustain boundaries between different kinds of religious or irreligious expression—rather than seek primary reasons or a deep sense of religious self behind what they say.

This stage invited participants to relate to their religiosity in a very individualized way. In terms of group style, the *bonds* holding together the participants in this setting were very personalized. They obligated each to hear the other respectfully *as individuals with personal inspiration,* necessarily as representatives of a creed or community, whether religious, irreligious, or antireligious. Pastor Frank set the tone when he said we all have resources to bring to the problem of homelessness and then named some which nonreligious or religious people might just as easily contribute, such as "courage." Whether or not people expressed strong opinions—as Henrietta did—no one tried to convince anyone else to adopt hers or his. Everyone got a hearing.

Ritual go-arounds of individual sharing will not sound remarkable to anyone familiar with the personalized style of bond common in contemporary American group life (for instance, Wuthnow 1994; Lichterman 1996), but this way of coordinating a group does not have any natural affinity with religious people. Some individuals on this stage perform as religious people in different ways in other settings, and those performances are not nearly as individualized. Pastor Thomas, for instance, participates in faith-based community organizing efforts, groups whose members all promote a shared, obligatory collective identity as "people of faith" who identify with Judeo-Christian traditions, not individuals who may or may not be "of faith" as in the case of CE's homelessness effort.

One might ask if the pragmatic approach works mainly when the people we study are "performing" in the conventional sense—trying to be polite in interfaith settings. Examining the group's monthly meetings suggests that a focus on the setting is useful even when the stage is much smaller and has a less diverse cast.

Inclusive Inspiration at Monthly Meetings

At monthly meetings, participants sustained the style of inclusive inspiration. Lines between religious and secular inspiration continued to be ambiguous. An awkward moment for the facilitator at the start of one meeting helps illustrate:

> At the start, Theresa was talking about a friend of hers with a terminal illness, muscle degeneration, who was at the point that she

could no longer move anything but her eyes and her mouth enough to talk. Theresa said this woman's daughter, also a family friend, carried pent-up anger at her mother and said her mother's illness seemed not to upset the daughter, but Theresa knew better. Theresa took off her glasses and wiped her eyes.

Theresa: "So whatever you do—pray, mediate, send energy—do it for them."

Raquel, the representative from Habitat for Humanity, asked, "What's her name?"

Theresa: "Marta, and Rita."

Raquel wrote down the names. I thought of the evangelical Protestant practice of taking names and praying for people.

Theresa took her glasses off and wiped her eyes again.

Chuck, the student from School of Social Work: "Will their names be able to get into the program [at Theresa's church, which hosted our meeting in the Peace Center Library] for Sunday worship?"

Theresa said they already had.

We still were waiting for the printed agendas for our meeting, which were not ready yet.

Theresa: "In some circles, it would be bad to come in unprepared—but I don't think that. I think it's part of our shared humanity."

Raquel gave her an understanding look.

Theresa signaled here that the stage was one for people with religious commitments, or spiritual commitments, or maybe humanistic and nontheistic ones. She recognized that it is irregular to lead meetings without being prepared and invited us to see beyond the unconventionality to "our shared humanity." The appeal would have sounded out of place at a corporate business meeting or school board meeting, and probably at many meetings where friends might gather (Bakhtin 1988). Theresa's appeal *might* suggest that this was a stage for subtle religious expression. Avowed Christian woman Raquel *might* have written down the names of Theresa's unfortunate family friends because she intended to pray for them. Once again, we could get stuck trying to infer a definite, first-moving sense of self behind statements and acts. It is safer to observe that the participants on the stage here—mainline and evangelical and African American Protestants, along with the observer known to a few members as Jewish—were maintaining a forum with fluid boundaries. It was a forum in which people *could* misguess each other's motives yet keep going, as long as all sincere, individual expressions of inspiration were safe. Identifying with religious faith was welcome though not mandatory, as long as any kind of inspiration, including faith in "our shared humanity," was welcome, too, and no individual needed to weigh in on another's inspiration.

On this inclusive stage, participants could affirm a religious teaching directly as long as they did not use them to promote some faiths to the exclusion of others. One of the very few direct endorsements of religious conviction during two years of field research was an inclusive-sounding interfaith affirmation as well:

> Raquel, a Christian, told us about a comment she heard a rabbi make about homelessness: "Their rabbi had one of the most profound statements I've ever heard on the morality of homelessness—or lack of morality of homelessness." The statement was that "If we are all made in the image of God, then the image of God sleeping on the street should be unconscionable." And, Raquel was amazed, her own pastor had said something almost exactly the same, in nearly the same words.
>
> Raquel: "When people from two completely different directions say almost the same thing—Wow, that is a truth!"

Throughout my time with CE, facilitator Theresa worked to make the group's identification with religion inclusive. Often she used the phrase "churches and synagogues and mosques" to describe both CE's audience and its own potential constituency. Since no one engaged with a mosque ever came to any of the monthly meetings I attended during twenty-four months and only two, short-term participants identified with Judaism, I inferred that the phrase symbolized the intent to project a diversely inspired, inclusive effort. At my first monthly meeting, she told the group, "Everyone out there is doing something—churches, synagogues, mosques, non-profits—but until there is a groundswell, we can't [change the policies]." Five months later, at a large breakfast meeting about homelessness like the one pictured earlier, she asked, "How many of you represent a church, synagogue, or mosque?" Two months later at a monthly meeting, affirming something that had come up at the breakfast, she said, "If every church, mosque, and synagogue takes a homeless family...there's more than 74,000 of these [congregations]." She was trying to say that there were more religious congregations than homeless people in our city. And at one of the last meetings I observed, Theresa was explaining CE's work to two participants, the interim pastor at a local Lutheran congregation and a long-time member of a nearby Episcopal church: "We all are doing things at our churches and mosques and synagogues, but we wanted to do something more collective."

Nonclergy, as well as clergy, members participated in more tightly bound religious groups and promoted more specific religious identities in settings *outside* CE meetings. Theresa told me several times *after* meetings that her type of Presbyterian church was different from the more theologically

conservative kind that some east Asian immigrant congregants were looking for; she identified with liberal Presbyterianism, not only inclusive spirituality in general. Yet she never suggested or implied CE members should
care about Presbyterianism. While touring me through her Korean evangelical church's museum of the Korean American experience, another member
referred proudly to "we Korean Christians" and explained to me the properly
Christian response to unappreciative homeless people she served. She said
she was willing to raise money for the poor because "the Bible is two-thirds
about money." Yet she never used Christian rationales to justify volunteering,
fundraising, or responses to unappreciative homeless people at CE meetings.
At a volunteer session for CE members at a Habitat for Humanity builders'
warehouse, Raquel said she would start our session according to the usual
Habitat custom, with a "scriptural reading." After reading the passage, her
voice breaking with emotion, Raquel talked about how the passage applied
to Habitat's work, and then another Habitat worker elaborated on the organization's Christian ministry. At CE meetings, in contrast, Raquel presented
herself as a churchgoer but never used biblical language to articulate her own
or the group's stance on housing and homelessness and never suggested we
start meetings, as some religious volunteer groups certainly do, with a biblical reading.

Since "inclusive inspiration" meant that specifically religious identity
was not mandatory but welcome within the limits of individualized expression, it took interactional work for participants who expressed *no* religious
identity, as well as those who did in other settings. Participants who distanced themselves from religious faith in other contexts did not do so in CE
settings. I never heard housing advocate Francis identify himself openly in
religious terms during this study—neither in CE settings nor at the housing organization I studied during the same period. Yet he spoke in the first
person plural when he urged religious people at the breakfast meeting pictured earlier to address homelessness in more political ways than by shel-
tering homeless individuals: "[O]ur response traditionally in many religious
communities has been immediate service—but *we* [my emphasis] need to
broaden our imagination to think about what we can do to end homelessness." A Methodist pastor already had said nearly the same thing to fellow
people of faith. Nonreligious community advocates quietly stood by when
CE participants identified themselves in religious terms. While participant-
observing the office of the housing advocacy organization that employed
Francis, I heard his co-worker Zina express disappointment that a core CE
member was religious. But neither Zina nor Francis or any other participant
questioned the value of basing homeless advocacy on religious identity during my observations at CE meetings.

Discussion

A certain Protestant Christo-centric view of "religion" and a focus on congregations would leave many public expressions of religion beyond our grasp. The pragmatic model helps us apprehend public religion and its ambiguities by turning our attention to group style in public settings rather than the actors we assume either are or are not religious. The pragmatic approach bids us to ask how people create social space for expressing religious views and identities and linking them to action. Many large, public disagreements over religion are disagreements over which styles of presenting religious identity are acceptable in which settings. Recent controversies over Muslim women's headscarves in France offer a quick, compelling example. French republicanism does not dictate whether or not French citizens should hold deep Muslim beliefs; the debate has been about which performances of religious identity are acceptable in public (Amiraux and Jonker 2006). If we want to know *how* religion acts as a resource or a facilitator of action in public, then the pragmatic model offers a more precise view than the default model of variation in religious identity and action.

What We Learn About Religious Pluralism

Classics in the sociology of religion (e.g., Berger 1967) treated pluralism as modernity's sandpaper, wearing down theological certainty, slowly erasing any sense of the sacred. Newer perspectives taught us to see religious pluralism as the opposite: an invitation to subcultural attachments in a world where there is no single, shared, sacred canopy but a multitude of warm, inviting tents each promising the power and joys of group belonging alongside the inspiration of believing (Warner 1993; Smith 1998). Berger's secularization thesis and the new paradigm have been concerned with why people do or don't continue believing when they know others believe differently. We need a different lens to focus on how believers relate to other believers and nonbelievers—with grudging tolerance, parity defined by the dominant group's terms, risky dialogue, or something else.

The pragmatic model of public religion helps us see religious pluralism as an ongoing accomplishment, a series of everyday moves that fall under the radar of theological questions and legal disputes. In a religiously diverse society in which religious commitment is highly voluntary, acts of pluralism become more ordinary and more unremarkably a part of what it is to act religiously in public (Joas 2008). That implies that performing pluralism is not only for liberal mainliners or mixed groups of religious, nonreligious, and antireligious people such as Caring Embrace but also for people who avow distinctive religious commitments. Studies of Catholic, Protestant, and Jewish volunteers at a Catholic-sponsored soup kitchen (Allahyari 2000) or evangelical church members of an "adopt a family" assistance program for ex-welfare-receiving families (Lichterman 2005) show that religious people work at creating settings that, while open to religious expression, are more ambiguous than the religious settings they would normally participate in as worshippers. From the actor's point of view, pluralism is not a corrosive external force so much as an ongoing, implicit agreement to make an image of religious others part of the religious self-understanding one enacts publicly.

How religious people coordinate action amidst different religious and non-religious people deserves much more research. We know, for instance, that theologically conservative Christians report less tolerant attitudes toward non-Christian religions than others, and we might infer that evangelical Protestants as a group are less likely to participate in interfaith action than others (Wuthnow 2005). Yet volunteers in the evangelical, adopt-a-family project pondered how to act together with the families for which they cared. They devised strategies that appeared to be part of a patterned group style, not ad hoc, but not easily predicted from theological teachings or denominational positions either (Lichterman 2005). A focus on group styles and settings can teach us much about what patterns interreligious public action takes and how those patterns include or exclude different identities and topics of discussion.

What We Learn About Social Ties

Some scholars have used the decline of the privatization thesis as an opportunity to highlight the prosocial roles of religion in public. They say that American religion promotes a vibrant civic life because religious Americans learn the arts of association in congregations and learn metaphors such as "children of God" that help them work together across social differences (Warren 2001; see Lichterman and Potts 2009). They laud congregations as rich stores of "social capital"—the networks and mutual trust that make citizenly collaboration possible (Putnam 2000; Smidt 2003). Social capital is a much used, much debated concept that has strongly influenced the way social scientists think about voluntary associations, governance, and economic development, to name just three areas.[4] When we focus on group styles and settings rather than religious actors and look beyond congregations, we learn more about conditions that may disable, as well as enable, religious people's networking for civic ends.

The example of the Nails Project in CE shows that it is not religion, but one's preferred style of relating to religion in specific settings that determines whether or not religion helps people recruit social networks for collective action. The director of Caring Embrace, for instance, knew many local leaders in her city's social activist and religious circles. She attended a large variety of different organizations' meetings and events related to homelessness, afford-able housing, gentrification, and urban redevelopment. Through her, CE should have had access to a lot of religious social capital since she was known widely as an activist who led her church's social justice center and had access to its phone lists, administrative staff, and money. The reputation of Theresa's church grew out of many years of public support for progressive, sometimes contentious viewpoints. The church gave not only moral encouragement but also physical protection to students protesting university expansion plans, and decades ear-lier it took care of property forcibly abandoned by Japanese residents ordered to internment camps. The social justice center's schedule of activities read like a chronicle of progressive causes. Two mainline Protestant pastors who attended CE meetings said at different times in the same words that getting congrega-tions to collect nails for an awareness-building project on homelessness "should be a no-brainer."

Yet the fluid and inclusive style of the religious setting that the director preferred kept her from attracting a wide range of religious people, even in liberal Protestant churches, to work together on the project. The Nails Project realized relatively little benefit from the director's potential social capital: the simple if tedious quest to collect 74,000 nails was still in pro-cess after two years, many months behind its projected schedule. Theresa hesitated to make her inspiration the *guiding* inspiration of CE; she wanted hers to be one of a variety of voices. The director may have had a lot of social capital in an abstract sense, but the group style that she preferred in settings of religious people made it difficult to prevail upon other people even for a good cause.

In this way, religion research contributes wider sociological insights. Social capital doesn't empower people by itself. Rather, social ties empower collec-tive action depending on how people create settings for mobilizing those ties. Studying religious people teaches us about how different forms of group cohe-sion can lead to powerful campaigns that sway governmental leaders or to good-willed group efforts that frustrate members' own goals.

Notes

1. This is a partial exposition, designed for this volume. For a fully developed argument about the two models and more extensive case comparisons, see Lichterman (2012).
2. Wood notes later (Wood 2002, 179) that community organizers themselves span some range of opinion on how important religious culture is for faith-based organizing.
3. For the main expositions of this viewpoint and methodological guidelines for using it, see Eliasoph and Lichterman (2003), Lichterman (2005), and Eliasoph (2011). For other applications of the group style concept to cases in the United States, South America, and

Europe, see Lichterman (2007, 2008, 2012), Mische (2008), Faucher-King (2005), Yon (2009), Luhtakallio (2012), and Citroni (2010).

4.   The discussion here refers to Robert Putnam's distinctive version of the social capital concept, the most widespread one. For extensive reviews and critiques, see Somers (2005) and (Lichterman (2006).

References

Allahyari, Rebecca. 2000. *Visions of Charity*. Berkeley: University of California Press.

Amiraux, Valerie, and Gerdien Jonker. 2006. "Introduction: Talking About Visibility—Actors, Politics, Forms of Engagement." Pp. 21–52 in *Politics of Visibility: Young Muslims in European Public Spaces*, edited by G. Jonker and V. Amiraux. New Brunswick, NJ: Transaction Publishers.

Ammerman, Nancy. 2003. "Religious Identities and Religious Institutions." Pp. 207–224 in *Handbook for the Sociology of Religion*, edited by M. Dillon. Cambridge: Cambridge University Press.

———. 2005. *Pillars of Faith: American Congregations and Their Partners*. Berkeley: University of California Press.

———, ed. 2007. *Everyday Religion: Observing Modern Religious Lives*. New York: Oxford University Press.

Bakhtin, Mikhail. 1988. *Speech Genres and Other Late Essays*. Translated by Caryl Emerson and Michael Holquist. Austin: University of Texas Press.

Bender, Courtney. 2003. *Heaven's Kitchen: Living Religion at God's Love We Deliver*. Chicago: University of Chicago Press.

Berger, Peter. 1967. *The Sacred Canopy: Elements of a Sociological Theory of Religion*. Garden City, NY: Doubleday.

Besecke, Kelly. 2005. "Seeing Invisible Religion: Religion as a Societal Conversation About Transcendent Meaning." *Sociological Theory* 23(2): 179–196.

Brubaker, Rogers. 2002. "Ethnicity Without Groups." *Archives Européennes de Sociologie* XLIII(2): 163–189.

Burke, Kenneth. 1969 [1945]. *A Grammar of Motives*. Berkeley: University of California Press.

Casanova, Jose. 1994. *Public Religions in the Modern World*. Chicago: University of Chicago Press.

Chaves, Mark. 1994. "Secularization as Declining Religious Authority." *Social Forces* 72: 749–775.

———. 2004. *Congregations in America*. Cambridge, MA: Harvard University Press.

Citroni, Sebastiano. 2010. "Inclusive Togetherness: A Comparative Ethnography of Cultural Associations Making Milan Sociable." Ph.D. Dissertation, Department of Sociology, Università degli Studi di Milano-Bicocca.

Eliasoph, Nina. 2011. *Making Volunteers: Civic Life After Welfare's End*. Princeton: Princeton University Press.

Eliasoph, Nina, and Paul Lichterman. 2003. "Culture in Interaction." *American Journal of Sociology* 108: 735–794.

Emerson, Robert, Rachel Fretz, and Linda Shaw. 1995. *Writing Ethnographic Fieldnotes*. Chicago: University of Chicago Press.

Faucher-King, Florence. 2005. *Changing Parties: An Anthropology of British Political Party Conferences*. New York: Palgrave Macmillan.

Goffman, Erving. 1959. *The Presentation of Self in Everyday Life*. Garden City, NY: Doubleday.

———. 1961. *Encounters: Two Studies in the Sociology of Interaction*. Indianapolis: Bobbs-Merrill.

Habermas, Jürgen. 2005. "Religion in the Public Sphere." Paper presented at the Fourth Annual Kyoto Laureate Symposium, University of San Diego, March 4.

Hout, Michael, and Claude S. Fischer. 2009. Unchurched Believers. *The Immanent Frame*. http://blogs.ssrc.org/tif/2009/10/01/unchurched-believers/ (accessed June 11, 2010).

Joas, Hans. 2008. "Religion in the Age of Contingency." Pp. 21–35 in *Do We Need Religion?* Translated by Alex Skinner. Boulder, CO: Paradigm Publishers.

Klatch, Rebecca. 1987. *Women of the New Right*. Philadelphia: Temple University Press.

Kosmin, Barry, and Ariela Keysar. 2008. *American Religious Identification Survey*. Hartford, CT: Trinity College.

Lichterman, Paul. 1996. *The Search for Political Community*. Cambridge and New York: Cambridge University Press.

———. 2005. *Elusive Togetherness: Church Groups Trying to Bridge America's Divisions*. Princeton, NJ: Princeton University Press.

———. 2006. "Social Capital or Group Style? Rescuing Tocqueville's Insights on Civic Engagement." *Theory and Society* 35(5/6): 529–563.

———. 2007. "Invitation to a Practical Cultural Sociology." Pp. 19–54 in *Culture, Society and Democracy: The Interpretive Approach*, edited by Isaac Reed and Jeffrey Alexander. Boulder, CO: Paradigm Publishers.

———. 2008. "Religion and the Construction of Civic Identity." *American Sociological Review* 73: 83–104.

———. 2012. "Religion in Public Action: From Actors to Settings." *Sociological Theory* 30(1): 15–36.

Lichterman, Paul, and C. Brady Potts, eds. 2009. *The Civic Life of American Religion*. Stanford, CA: Stanford University Press.

Luckmann, Thomas. 1967. *The Invisible Religion: The Problem of Religion in Modern Society*. New York: Macmillan.

Luhtakallio, Eeva. 2012. *Practicing Democracy. Local Activism and Politics in France and Finland*. Basingstoke: Palgrave Macmillan.

McCall, George, and Jerry Simmons. 1978. *Identities and Interactions*. New York: Free Press.

Mead, George Herbert. 1934. *Mind, Self, and Society*. Chicago: University of Chicago Press.

———. 1964. *On Social Psychology*, edited by Anselm Strauss. Chicago: University of Chicago Press.

Mische, Ann. 2008. *Partisan Publics*. Princeton, NJ: Princeton University Press.

Morris, Aldon. 1984. *The Origins of the Civil Rights Movement*. New York: The Free Press.

Munson, Ziad. 2007. "When a Funeral Isn't Just a Funeral: The Layered Meaning of Everyday Action." Pp. 121–135 in *Everyday Religion: Observing Modern Religious Lives*, edited by Nancy T. Ammerman. New York: Oxford University Press.

Neitz, Mary Jo. 2004. "Gender and Culture: Challenges to the Sociology of Religion." *Sociology of Religion* 65(4): 391–403.

Parsons, Talcott. 1967. "Christianity and Modern Industrial Society." Pp. 385–421 in *Sociological Theory and Modern Society*. New York: Free Press.

Press, Andrea, and Elizabeth Cole. 1999. *Speaking of Abortion*. Chicago: University of Chicago Press.

Putnam, Robert. *Bowling Alone: The Collapse and Revival of American Community*. New York: Simon and Schuster.

Regnerus, Mark, and Christian Smith. 1998. "Selective Deprivatization among American Religious Traditions: The Reversal of the Great Reversal." *Social Forces* 76: 1347–1372.

Riesebrodt, Martin. 2008. "Theses on a Theory of Religion." *International Political Anthropology* 1(1): 25–41.

Roof, Wade C. 1998. *Spiritual Marketplace*. Princeton, NJ: Princeton University Press.

Smidt, Corwin, ed. 2003. *Religion as Social Capital*. Waco, TX: Baylor University Press.

Smilde, David, and Matthew May. 2010. *The Emerging Strong Program in the Sociology of Religion*. New York: SSRC Working Papers.

Smith, Christian. 1998. *American Evangelicalism: Embattled and Thriving*. Chicago: University of Chicago Press.

Somers, Margaret. 2005. "Beware Trojan Horses Bearing Social Capital: How Privatization Turned Solidarity into a Bowling Team." Pp. 233–274 in *The Politics of Method in the Human Sciences*, edited by G. Steinmetz. Durham, NC:Duke University Press.

Warner, R. Stephen. 1993. "Work in Progress toward a New Paradigm for the Sociological Study of Religion in the United States." *American Journal of Sociology* 98:1044–1093.

Warren, Mark R. 2001. *Dry Bones Rattling: Community Building to Revitalize American Democracy.* Princeton, NJ: Princeton University Press.

Wood, Richard. 2002. *Faith in Action.* Chicago: University of Chicago Press.

Wuthnow, Robert. 1994. *Sharing the Journey.* New York: Free Press.

———. 2005. *America and the Challenges of Religious Diversity.* Princeton, NJ: Princeton University Press.

Yon, Karel. 2009. "Quand le syndicalisme s'éprouve hors du lieu de travail: La production du sens confédéral à Force ouvrière." *Politix* 22: 57–79.

6

Pluralism and Secularism

COURTNEY BENDER

Religious pluralism is a fact of American society. But what kind of fact is pluralism and the heterogeneity that it frames? Since the founding of the country Americans have praised their nation's religious diversity and held it up as a measure of America's commitments to freedom. Yet the "religious diversity" that Americans identify and take pride in is far from stable. Nor, for that matter, is its political value. We can, for example, note how the mid-twentieth-century's "Judeo-Christian" and "Protestant-Catholic-Jewish" America transformed into a "new multireligious public square" in the wake of changes in immigration law—and, at the same time, how celebrations and concepts of American religious diversity changed in the public sphere as well (Cadge and Ecklund 2007; Eck 1999; Prothero 2006). The concomitant restructuring of Protestant denominations (Wuthnow 1988; Chaves 2011) and growing numbers of nominally religious or "spiritual not religious" Americans (Hout and Fischer 2002; Bender 2010) have shaped quite different arguments and analyses of religious pluralism and likewise different arguments about its positive or negative effects. The lack of sociological consensus on what types of religious diversity matter in framing discussions about the conditions creating religious pluralism or its effects (Chaves and Gorski 2001), is thus itself a matter for further inquiry. It calls attention to the ongoing ways that the sociological observation of religious pluralism and the political valence of the term in public discourse continue to be deeply intertwined (Wuthnow 2005; Hutchison 2003).

While the diversity of American religions pose significant challenges to any who embark on empirical research, the political and social uses of "religious pluralism" and sociology's ongoing role in shaping those discussions presents an additional layer of complexity. This is all the more so when we observe that a diverse range of sociological studies of American religious pluralism share a deeply sedimented and taken-for-granted conception of the social conditions that generate religious pluralism. Currently, three competing sociological models of religious pluralism (free market, multicultural recognition, and neo-institutional) begin with the position that religious pluralism takes shape within a free and unregulated civil sphere, or civil society. While they quibble on the details, this vision of an unregulated civil sphere shaped by secularizing forces is taken on faith: it is posited rather than examined or contextualized. While they agree on little else, they nonetheless all begin with a position that religions operate freely in American civil society.

The strong, shared conviction that American religions operate freely has shaped a robust disciplinary scaffolding that presents little opportunity for a sustained analysis of these central claims. Contemporary sociological scholarship on religious pluralism rarely asks the sociological questions of how "religion" is socially constructed (and shaped and regulated) within an American secular society that is committed to certain kinds of governance and citizens, or how "pluralism" that takes shape within it relates to these forms. These questions become more pressing as religious diversity in the United States becomes more politically charged, and as scholarship in a range of disciplines actively questions the historical and contemporary limits of religious pluralism. For example, legal and religious historians and anthropologists have demonstrated how American claims of religious freedom and plurality have also worked to exclude some religious actors from public life (Fessenden 2007; Hamburger 2002; Goldschmidt 2006). Others have noted how American law and public policies limit claims to free religious expression and transform the ways that groups understand the character, quality, and authority of their own religious "traditions" (McNally 2010; Leavelle 2010). These shifts compel a closer inspection of the underlying concepts of religious freedom in American secular society that shape sociological discourse.

My principal goal in this chapter is to highlight the shared ground on which contemporary sociological visions of religious pluralism take shape. I argue that current approaches to pluralism developed in response to classical secularization theory's failure to account for the persistence of religiousness in the religiously plural United States. Observing that religious pluralism did not diminish religious fervor as secularization theory predicted, sociologists turned this theory on its head. They adopted a view wherein the diminishing state-church monopoly and the expansion of a civil society differentiated (and thus freed) religion from other institutions. Religious groups were and are thus free to begin and end, thrive and fail, without regulation by the state. This framework shares stronger affinities with liberal political theory's conceptions of religion and civil society than it does with classical sociological approaches, I argue. I work briefly through John Locke's and Jean-Jacques Rousseau's arguments about religion and polity to identify their resonance with contemporary sociological models, and to similarly highlight the limits of these frameworks which are not often noted. This chapter ends by considering how approaches shaped by theories of secularism may offer an opportunity to revive a broadly sociological approach to investigate these compelling issues.

Three Sociological Approaches

Until very recently, sociologists and secularization theorists viewed religious plurality as either a sign of or a harbinger of secularization. Durkheim (1995) and Weber (1958) both linked modern societies' increasing institutional differentiation, bureaucratically organized divisions of labor, and rationalization of law and politics as components of secularization. Religion became more private, more a matter of choice. That is, it became simultaneously more plural and less public (see also Casanova 1994). Through the 1960's, numerous sociological investigations supported these theoretical claims: empirical studies that noted the declining value of specific religious identities as meaningful social markers (Herberg 1955); intermarriage rates were rising (Yinger 1967); the salience of religious differences in civic life seemed to be on the wane (Gans 1967, 1979). The modern industrial or white-collar workplace, public schools, the bowling league, the veteran's association, and the block association were no longer defined, according to these sociologists, along religious lines. Most sociologists observing American religion noted that while nominal religious identity mattered in the public world of the Protestant-Catholic-Jewish America, strong sectarian commitments and identity were on the wane.

Peter Berger's *Sacred Canopy* (1967) reinvigorated the classical theoretical bases of these empirical claims, pointing throughout to the links that connected the plurality of religions to secularization. Berger argued that modern individuals participated in a variety of social settings and institutions that required them to switch through multiple worldviews or meaning structures. Religion became one among others, losing its power as an overarching system of meaning. Modern people confronted and came to terms with a new and profound awareness of the limitations of their religious worldviews, which weakened the plausibility and authority of their beliefs even as it also opened up new possibilities for secular belonging and ethics (Cox 1965; Taylor 2007).

Much as we can read Berger's 1967 thesis as a theoretical response to empirical research heralding the declining robustness of religion in the Protestant-Catholic-Jewish milieu, we can read the voluminous recent work on American religious pluralism as a response to the failure of Berger's arguments. The "new" flourishing of religious activity in the United States since the 1960s has often been taken as a prima facie refutation of Berger's analysis and the classical secularization theory on which he draws. That said, the three models of pluralism discussed below share Berger's view that religion is differentiated and private. That is, they agree that "religion" in modern society is self-evidently identifiable and, through processes of differentiation, increasingly disentangled from state control and state regulation. Free market models of religious pluralism make these claims most clearly, and so we turn to them first.

Pluralism 1: Competition in Religious Markets

In the late 1970s, sociologists of religion began to argue (contra Berger, Weber, and Durkheim) that the absence of a state-sanctioned religious monopoly and the resulting "freedom" of religious actors did not lead people to fall away from religion but, on the contrary, created a setting of competition and religious vitality. A "free market" allowed for religious innovation and expansion and the flourishing of multiple sacred umbrellas, which activated more religious fervor than the tepid plausibility structures of a state-church monopoly. In this "supply side" frame, individuals with diverse religious interests had more likelihood of finding a religious group that suited their tastes (or more possibilities for starting their own) within an entrepreneurial system (Finke and Stark 1988, 1992). Religious competition for participants who sought to have their (already identifiable) religious needs met increased the distinctions among various groups.

These models and the data that undergirded them were hotly debated through the 1980s and 1990s. Data on membership in churches were analyzed and reanalyzed. Supply-side proponents continued to make strong theoretical claims about the explanatory purchase of an individual and rational religious actor who could seek out the best compensatory religions within a changing religious marketplace. Critics, on the other hand, convincingly demonstrated that the theory could not be supported by the quantitative data once they were properly analyzed (for a review, see Chaves and Gorski 2001). Notwithstanding these nails in the proverbial coffin, the "story" of American religious pluralism as a development of the monopoly-less "free market" of American religious organizations has been a robust chestnut in the arsenal of pundits' views of American religiosity (see, for example, Dennett 2004). It remains a particularly powerful argument, I believe, because of its clear alignment with a variety of American understandings of religious freedom that operate at the level of discursive belief.

Before moving on, we should note an obvious point about this particular set of analyses. The free-market analysis of religious pluralism and freedom addresses a plurality of American Christianities and, more specifically, American Protestantisms. These arguments about religious pluralism rely almost exclusively on data compiled from varieties of Christian groups. The models take a conception of religious belonging (voluntary membership in a congregation that the believer himself or herself chooses) as the norm into which other forms of membership are adapted or translated in order for analysis to proceed. The historical numeric majority of Protestants aside, theory operates with a clear definition of normal American religion that aligns quite well with Protestant organizational forms and membership norms and that has difficulty historically comparing (or even including) the religions of indigenous people, slaves, and non-Protestants (Jews, Catholics, and so on) in its "story" of religion in America. The broader claim that religious pluralism as competition is best captured by focusing on "American Christianities" shows that, no matter who the nominal losers are, the true "winners" in the United States are the various free-standing, voluntary American Christian groups who enjoy a constitutional and legal, as well as political, framework where the Protestant norm is legalized within a secular conception of "religion." This model of religious pluralism is not interested in addressing the political and public struggles of religious groups that are organized around other kinds of filiation (land, practice, piety, kinship) to position themselves within a system that may, indeed, favor some kinds of religions over others.

Taking the broader picture, we might say that if the story of "competition" is somewhat evocative of the history of American Protestantism, this story nonetheless begs questions about who can participate in the "free market" of religion, how its borders and limits are distinguished, and the legal, political, and civic work required to *become* "competitors" (the history of American Catholicism provides one pertinent example; Hamburger 2002). The free market model does not, for this reason, address the conditions or the social norms that normalize some kinds of religion as actors in this free market, and others (including those that organize membership around kinship, land, practice or piety) as improperly adapted to the market. It thus begs the question: what are the structures external to "religions" themselves that make some not only "winners or losers" but also, beyond that, participants or nonparticipants in this rigged game?

Pluralism 2: Multireligious Public Spheres

One would expect scholars whose work investigates the extensive American multireligious landscape, including Asian religious groups and others, to present a robust critique of the free-market model of pluralism, and some of them do. However, the focus of critique, insofar as one exists, is on the free market model's individualistic views religion, which stand in contrast to the types of religious identities and experiences that are highlighted in work focusing on growing religious diversity in the United States. That is, this body of research frequently emphasizes how the religious experiences, identities and activities of non-Christian and non-European immigrant religious groups do not align with the norms of American Protestant focus on individual belief, and emphasize how religious organizations and community interactions provide connections and resources for immigrants (Cadge and Ecklund 2007).

Numerous sociological works studying new immigrants observe that immigrants often take on a stronger or more invested religious identity upon immigrating to the United States. These studies frequently emphasize how religious identities, religious associations and networks, and religious resources establish immigrants in transnational networks, where religious identity is salient and powerful. These transnational actors seem to be quite distinct from the American religious actors that emerge in free market analyses of religious pluralism. Indeed, sociological studies of immigrant religions rarely address how, or even whether, immigrant religious groups might intersect in the religious free market.

In contrast, sociological studies of the "new" multireligious United States emphasize different kinds of religious identity altogether. Largely eschewing questions of religious choice (with some exceptions, see Chen 2008) this scholarship emphasizes how religion can be mobilized (or can be a burden)—much as racial or ethnic identity is. Religion for immigrants is a resource and a right, rather than a choice. It can be protected, it can gain legal recognition, and it operates in a broader field of American rights and identities. Although as Prema Kurien (2007) notes this scholarship often problematically frames immigrants' religious "identity" as self-evident and given, much like "race" and "ethnicity," it nonetheless calls attention to a wider range of ways that religion operates in American public life than free market positions. Religion, as a constitutive part of identity politics, seems poised to challenge and deepen the claims of free market pluralism.

A "multireligious pluralist" narrative may be opposed to the politics of the free-market model but, all the same, does little to challenge it. It rarely depicts the "new" religious groups as being in any kind of competitive position in relation to other religious groups in America. Focus on self-determination, internal community interactions, and the like have yielded very little scholarly research that addresses, much less challenges, the free-market model's tacit understanding that voluntary religions are more competitive and robust than those that are not. Without addressing this claim directly, the sociological analysis of American religious minorities often frames immigrant religious groups as transnational actors that are not fully anchored to the American political context, uninterested or incapable of competing for adherents or resources. This story of new immigrants thus provides a complementary and fractured story of American religious pluralism. In this milieu, it is possible for some American religions to compete with each other for adherents who are not religiously, racially, or ethnically marked, and at the same time for immigrants encumbered by various commitments that keep them from becoming free to find resources in religious commitments.

Stating that the public sphere is multireligious begs the question of which religions, and which actors, find it easier or more difficult to articulate their place within it. As much of the focus on new immigrant religious communities begins within those communities and seeks to consider how individuals engage others in either civil society or other "public" settings, this literature

does not always address the ways that immigrants come to find themselves acting *as* religious (as opposed to ethnic, national, or racial) actors while engaging
those actors. This focus suggests that such actors are "religious" without need
of translation or transformation when they reach American shores, and their
religious aspirations, maladapted or otherwise, appear to be an issue related to
the specific religious traditions rather than to the social structures that distinguish and designate religions (and religions of certain types) as relevant social
identities.

Pluralism 3: De Facto Congregationalism

A third approach to the study of American religious pluralism emerges out of
cultural and institutional responses to supply-side religion models as well. In
the grounding text of this perspective, R. Stephen Warner (1994) described
the processes of "de facto congregationalism," wherein religious groups entering US society since the nineteenth century transform their religious organizational structure into a congregational model. This argument identifies the
religious field as primarily congregational (voluntary, not-for-profit, semiautonomous organizations). According to Warner and others, new entrants to this
field took on voluntaristic and communal forms due to a variety of pressures,
including legal ones. As Warner argues, becoming a legitimate religious actor in
the United States means conforming to already existing structural norms.

De facto congregationalism has much to recommend it. Unlike free-market
and multireligious pluralist models, it calls attention to a range of social institutions and isomorphic pressures that contribute to shaping all religious
traditions in the United States into similar forms. Warner calls attention (as
neo-institutional theory does) to the ways that earlier entrants into a field—in
this case, Protestants—provide the norms to which later entrants to the field
are pressured to conform. This theory helps explain why Catholics and then
Jews, and later on other religious groups, form congregational-style communities in the United States—and likewise points quite clearly to an approach to
religious pluralism that pays attention to the regulating power of both civic/
historical and legal norms.

Despite this promise, many of the scholars who have drawn upon the de
facto congregationalism model remain wedded to a view of American secularity as lacking cultural or "theological" norms. Sociologists do not argue that
religions in the American public sphere conform to the historical norms that
govern all religions within it, but rather claim that the American secular sphere
enables all religions to pursue their goals freely. New entrants into this public
sphere are certainly changed by participating within it, but the transformation that they encounter is one of becoming more free and authentic religions.
Once religious communities are unencumbered by the cultural and political

weight that is experienced elsewhere, they can voluntarily work out the norms, principles and ethics that shape their communities. The result, according to Fenggang Yang and Helen Rose Ebaugh (2001), is that religious groups become more theologically open, more tolerant, more voluntary, and thus better versions of themselves.

To be clear, recent uses of de facto congregationalism emphasize how religions change when they come to the United States. New immigrant religions frequently experience pressure to conform to the dominant congregational models found in the United States. But rather than arguing that this social milieu transforms religions into more American versions of themselves, or perhaps even "Protestantized" versions, sociological research has emphasized the freedom of voluntary participation. This makes groups not more American or Protestant but, rather, more culturally and religiously authentic and free renditions of their traditions. As Yang and Ebaugh argue, adopting a congregational form encourages religious communities to work out for themselves what it means to be Muslim, Hindu, or Christian without the intervention or gaze of state-sanctioned religious authorities or other external pressures. They argue that where religion is free and voluntary, religious groups find themselves becoming more conscientious and self-aware religious practitioners and are provided new opportunities to distinguish the "cultural" from "religious" elements of their practices. Religious practitioners thus confront their traditions in a more authentically religious way.[1]

Nancy Ammerman's *Pillars of Faith* makes a similar argument. Noting that American congregational life flourishes "[w]ithout state regulation—but also without state support" (2005, 254), "each group could embody its religious impulses in the pragmatic organizations that the American experiment made possible. It was a system born of the Protestant impulse, but nurtured in the pragmatic and pluralist democracy of the United States" (2005, 256). The relationship between religious pluralism, secularity, and religious freedom articulated in this model is more complex than that offered in free-market and multicultural pluralism, but it ultimately turns the question of religious "flourishing" or failure on religious communities themselves. Or, as Ammermen puts it, "without state authorities to enforce orthodoxy, each group's attempt to create a more nearly perfect spiritual community was free to find its own fertile soil or perish" (2005, 254).

Pluralism through the Lens of Secularism

The three models present nominally different views of the relation between religious pluralism and the secular American society that fosters it. This is perhaps not surprising, given that each responds to real changes in American religion ongoing since the 1960's's, and likewise to the real failures of classical secularization theories to account for them. The transformation of the socio-logical narrative over the last two generations shifted from viewing pluralism as a harbinger of religious decline to observing it as a key element of religious flourishing. American sociologists of religion now consistently agree that the flourishing of religion in the United States, its pluralities, and its possibilities are shaped by and likewise contribute to a free civil society.

The limitations of these models and in particular, their claim to religion's lack of regulation become clear once we begin to look a bit more closely. The *multireligious* model emphasizes relations among religious groups in a civil society but gives little attention to the question of why (or how) some groups and not others come to be identified as a religious actors with legitimate claims or practices (see McNally 2010; Moore 2011). *Free-market* models describe religion as being most vital in a free market that lacks state regulation, and more actively assert that the US model works best for religion as it most closely embodies this ideal. But the claim that all religions are, or can be, participants in the "free market" ignores the range of regulations barring entry to the market, and the norms that call into question the very religiousness of those who are so regulated. Sociological studies of *de facto congregationalism* share a vision that American democratic processes leave open the possibility that all religions can (and, through isomorphism, may) join in the organizational field of American religious pluralism. We cannot take it on faith, however, that religions in the American public sphere transform into more free and authentic "religions" without inquiring more deeply into the claims that American secular society is itself norm free.

From Secularization to Secularism: Rethinking the Place of Pluralism

The assertion that religions become better versions of themselves in the American context only makes sense if the American secular civil society is conceptualized as an arena lacking cultural norms, laws, or social processes that impinge on religious groups. This claim suggests that the structures of American civil society, secularized and organized by constitutional rights to free expression and a separation of church and state, allow all religious groups to be self-determining and free, and only regulate those who stand to limit others' freedom (Harcourt 2011). In recent years, research in the history, anthropology, and comparative sociology of secularism have challenged these claims.

Where secularization models viewed secular society as an inevitable process wherein religion and its authority receded, leaving public life and secular space in its wake, recent analyses of the historical creation of secular societies identify the dynamic changes that took shape in these transformations. Studies of secularism analyze the specific historical developments, actors, and discourses that alter the relationships between religion and secularity, transforming both in the process. They argue, contra secularization theory, that secularizing processes do not displace religion or privatize it necessarily, but rather refashion it (in specific, historically identifiable ways), even as religious interests and groups variably engage with, embrace, or fight against new assignations.

"What is distinctive about secularism [as a method or mode] is that it presupposes new concepts of religion, ethics, and politics, and new imperatives associated with them," writes Talal Asad (2003, 2). Asad and others call for stronger analysis of the political doctrines, discourses, and institutional structures that reconfigure the relations between religion/religions and secular states (Jakobsen and Pellegrini 2008; Mahmood 2005; Sullivan 2009). As a complex and dynamic set of historical processes, they note how the secular is "neither continuous with the religious that supposedly preceded it (that is, it is not the latest phase of a sacred origin) nor a simple break from it (that is, it is not the opposite, an essence that excludes the sacred)" (Asad 2003, 25). This allows us to ask what kinds of religions—singular or plural—are able to develop and flourish within varying "secular" societies, and likewise how various secular visions (of human rights, of political action, of "reason" or "rationality") develop through a translation of specifically theological-religious concepts into universal or humanistic concepts (Smith 2003; Gorski and Altınordu 2008).

Both scholarship on secularism and sociological scholarship on pluralism respond to the same social conditions that find classical secularization theory lacking. Yet by focusing on the interlocking dynamics that take shape to form secular and religious interests, identities, and capacities in modern societies, studies of secularism enable scholars to ask questions that recent studies of pluralism do not. Indeed, insofar as sociological studies of pluralism remain in the orbit of classical secularization theory's claim that "secular" societies are what emerge as religions recede or become privatized, it becomes difficult to investigate the social processes that shape secular norms and their relations to religion. Studies that begin with a focus on investigating the shape of American secularism in contrast allow us to ask not only "what kinds of religious interaction and pluralities shape what kinds of democratic civil society?" but also, importantly: "What kinds of secular political and social forms produce what kinds of religious pluralism?"

These questions prompt us to reflect upon the articulation of freedom that shapes contemporary sociological analyses of religion. In broadly rejecting classical secularization theory's narrative of the negative connection between pluralism and religious vitality, contemporary sociological writing on pluralism comes closer to aligning itself with classical political theory's liberal models of natural religious freedom, the liberal subject, and particular notions of toleration. While a close analysis of the alignments between sociology and liberal political theory is beyond the scope of this chapter, the pages that follow highlight some shared understandings of religion that, refracted through each other, raise questions about the secular imaginations of democracy that are buoyed in recent sociological analyses.

Natural Religious Freedom and the Free State: Locke, Rousseau, and Marx

John Locke's *A Letter Concerning Toleration* (1983) is widely heralded as a seminal political document identifying the religious rights of subjects or citizens within a liberal state. Locke's treatise argues that it is the state's duty to provide for citizens' freedom of religious conscience, while also articulating the importance of that religious conscience in forming citizens who will adequately perform their duties toward the state. Locke argues for the goods that come with toleration of multiple religious views and, likewise, the state's role in providing the rights of voluntary assembly to worship together.

Locke's argument for religious tolerance makes the rather strong argument that religious toleration toward the other is both a condition of and a sign of a good polity. Both multiple religious beliefs and operating toleration are necessary for the functioning of liberal states. Yet at the same time, Locke views areligion and maladapted religion to both be grave threats to political freedom. Toleration cannot therefore be extended to atheists, as "Promises, Covenants, and Oaths, which are the Bonds of Humane Society, can have no hold upon an Atheist" (1983, 50–51). Catholics and "Mahumetans" are likewise excluded, as their religious beliefs "deliver themselves up to the Protection and Service of another Prince." In Locke's view, Atheists can have no bond to the state, as they do not exercise a moral code; Catholics and Muslims also can have no true bond to the state, as they serve another master. All such parties are politically excluded as they are enemies of a state that values religious toleration.

Locke sets the definition of religion and of religious toleration in clear and recognizable relief. From our vantage point, it is evident that Locke views non-Protestant religions as challenging the very terms of religious toleration. Toleration extends to the multiplicity of Protestant groups that share (in Locke's estimation) the theological understanding that religion is a matter of personal conviction that bonds men together in society. This realm of tolerance allows real religion to thrive, by pressing to the margins all religions that stand in the way of toleration. Hence, religion that is overly infected by the state and tradition (Catholicism, Islam, Judaism) does not allow men to cultivate free conscience; on the other hand, areligion (atheism) dissolves men's attachments to and natural duties toward society. It is only when those maladapted possibilities are excluded that both men and religion can be free. In this kind of society, voluntary religious groups can focus on the salvation of men's souls and the cultivation of social sentiments that promotes political (and also religious) freedom.

The limited and quite exclusionary practices of "toleration" that are built into Locke's argument turn the problem of religious pluralism and toleration on its head. In brief, Locke might be said to argue that the state, with its interest in making sure that it protects individuals' religious consciences and freedom of belief, has every right to exclude religions that appear to refuse to their own adherents the capacities to choose freely. The "freedom" of religion offered by liberalism sorts religions into those that are naturally free and those that maladapted to freedom. Locke's views are clearly exclusionary and do not map onto contemporary practice. Nonetheless, Locke's arguments are quite familiar to twenty-first century Americans. The claims that some religions are maladapted to real freedom, and others are adapted to it, remains part of the secular claims about religious pluralism. We might thus pause with political theorist Anthony Marx, to note that while Locke's "selective form of toleration would be hailed as a purely liberal principle is its incredible enough" the fact "that this sleight of hand would be celebrated on face . . . suggests that Locke's successors were less conscious of the limits of liberalism than was he" (2003, 179).

Arguments for free religion reverberate somewhat differently in Jean-Jacques Rousseau's classic liberal treatise *On the Social Contract* (1764) and expose another articulation of the naturalization of true, free religion under the free liberal state. Rousseau's liberalism begins with an indictment of European political societies, which he sees as the outgrowth of the development of private property. The "true founder" of civil society, he argues, was "the first person who, having enclosed a plot of land, took it into his head to say this is mine and found people simple enough to believe him." Thus, the very first moments of society were ones of slavery and abuse. Society brought with it "crimes, wars, murders . . . miseries and horrors." But on the other hand, social intercourse also allowed humanity to develop language, reason, and other higher faculties. To overcome the evils and inequalities of social life and allow the goods of social life to emerge, Rousseau argues, means agreeing to a social contract. Citizens form a social contract by submitting to a joint concept of shared sovereignty (what Rousseau calls the "general will"), where each person "gives himself whole and entire." Orienting one's actions and reason according to the general will rather than to self-interest leads to a society where the best interests of the "general" population bring about true social freedom (1987, 60). And, as Rousseau further argues, citizens can be properly educated to use reason and to listen to what he believes is a naturally given, prerational, and deeply human sentiment or moral compass: if citizens can be so educated, they will not need to be "forced to be free" (1987, 148, 150).

Rousseau's chapter on religion (it is his argument "on civil religion") appears at the end of this political-social fantasia. Rousseau's interest in religion thus develops both from his assessment of the limits of reason to compel moral action and his desire that all citizens orient themselves to something more than their own self-interest. As he writes, it is "of great importance... that each citizen have a religion that causes him to love his duties," and it is religion's role to make sure that this happens (1987, 226). Similarly to Locke, Rousseau takes a very nominal view on what all men must believe (though he believes they must believe something). Likewise, he argues that these opinions are for the most part "outside the province of the sovereign" and "none of their business, so long as they are good citizens in this life" (1987, 226). The state needs religion, we see: its primary utility is to engender love of fellow man and love of duty to the state.[2]

While this sounds (to some) to be a not so veiled argument for a nominal theocracy where religion is fully subservient to the state, Rousseau argues otherwise. It is worth paying close attention to the way that Rousseau distinguishes between civil religion and theocracy, as much depends on his view of natural religion, which emerges in this chapter and undergirds his understandings. "On Civil Religion" begins with a genealogy of the world religions, in which Rousseau narrates a story of religion's role in politics in the premodern world. In this world, nations and gods were the same, so that despite the efflorescence of various deities, religion was united in a system (paganism) or what he calls the "single, identical religion in the known world" wherein "each religion was uniquely tied to the laws of the state which prescribed it" (1987, 221).

According to Rousseau, this world system was disrupted by Jesus' introduction of a religion that espoused "a spiritual kingdom," one that was not tied to or wedded to a particular nation, people, or land. The development separated the theological system from the political system. Insofar as Christians remained only wedded to a spiritual kingdom, Christianity was tolerable, but as soon as Christianity began to make temporal claims and challenge "this world's" kingdoms, it led to a breakdown in social unity and to more war and strife than humans had heretofore experienced.

Rousseau uses this genealogy of world religions to articulate a typology of models of existing relations between religions and the state (1987, 223–224), each of which fails to offer what he believes is necessary for the flourishing of a liberal, equal society. He immediately dismisses Catholicism and other religions that make a claim over temporal authority as "bizarre" and "worthless." Any religion that attempts to stand side by side in a state of tension with political order—which offers men two laws, two homelands, and two authorities—and any religion that prevents them from being "simultaneously devout men and citizens" will "break up unity," Rousseau states. He argues, "All institutions that place man in contradiction with himself are of no value" (1987, 223). This critique brings Rousseau close to a position of posing theocracy as the preferred form, insofar as he is most favorably disposed

to religions that unite law, love, duty, and the state. But Rousseau finds theocracies deeply lacking. They are "based on error and lies, makes [citizens]
credulous and superstitious" (1987, 224). Given that they are not based on
universal human moral sentiment but rather on the conjured religious imaginations of these states' leaders, theocracies are "bloodthirsty and intolerant,
so that men breathe only murder and massacre" (1987, 224). It is impossible
to support the social compact, which depends on reason and on the ability of
all citizens to use that reason in concert, with a religion based on lies.

It might also be tempting to imagine that Rousseau is arguing for voluntary, privatized Christianity as the best form of religion. But once again
Rousseau finds much to criticize: "The pure and simple religion of the Gospel"
is a spiritual religion, one that induces men to give up their duties and love for
the state and to not care at all about things of the world. Christianity cannot
make good citizens or a good society. "A society of true Christians would no
longer be a society of men," he argues (p. 224). As a "completely spiritual religion," it cannot be concerned with things in the world, and in this sense, "true
Christianity" is also antithetical to the development of the social compact and
its freedoms.

This theological argument about true Christianity is quite interesting given
Rousseau's own biography and relations with religion. However, it also allows
him to assert a political claim about what Christianity has historically made
possible—namely, the rediscovery of the individual moral compass or human
sentiment within each person—while also claiming that such human sentiment is human, and not specifically Christian. While Jesus' claims to the spiritual kingdom initially divided the kingdoms and led to disunity and strife,
these claims also paved the way for the development within the free state for
this underlying religious sentiment to be reactivated. Much as private property
led initially to slavery, wars, and horrors but also enabled humans to reach the
more enlightened and reasonable free state of the social contract, so, too, did
Christianity initially lead to slavery and war, even though it eventually enabled
humans to recover their true, free spiritual nature (Willhoite 1965).

It appears, then, that civil religion *is* true and free religion. It is the "real"
religion that emerges once men are unencumbered from theocratic and misleading Christian modes of religiosity. This unencumbering is a gift that the
good society grants to its citizens. Civil religion can be displayed in various
rituals and rites, mores, and "sentiments of sociability" (1987, 226). But it
is grounded, fundamentally, on a deist's romantic creed: "the existence of a
powerful, intelligent, beneficent divinity that foresees and provides; the life
to come; the happiness of the just; the punishment of the wicked; the sanctity
of the social contract and of the laws" (1987, 226). These are the elements of
religion that are written in the "good and great volume" of nature. As Rousseau
argues in *Emile*, "there is no excuse for not reading this book, for it speaks to

all in a language they can understand" (1911, 259). Rousseau, like Locke, ends with a strong call for religious toleration in the free society. Like Locke, he advocates for a form of toleration within the liberal social compact where religious freedom is allowed yet subordinated to the state. It extends, of course, to freedom and liberty of opinion that both believe are "natural" to humans, and that emerge once despotism is thrown off. Rousseau, like Locke, is quick to remind readers that some religions do not shape free citizens: these religions are inimical to the liberal state.

Religious freedom and political freedom support each other. Unlike thinkers and writers who preceded them, Rousseau and Locke are not arguing for theocratic or mono-religious polities—on the contrary, freedom of religious opinion and religious sentiment is both central to and a representation of the human freedoms that *secular* liberal democracies (or social contracts) provide. It is in this philosophical context (shaped through specific considerations of toleration in the development of European state building) that we observe religious toleration and pluralism developing as a central feature of secular liberal societies. The existence of religious heterogeneity and tolerance is presented as evidence that a state is secular and that people have gained the kinds of religious and personal freedoms that secular states provide.

Yet we also see that these arguments about religious freedom (and free religion) are closely tailored to historically developed understandings of religious subjects and religious subjectivities, political identities, and actual violence against and among religious and political groups (A. Marx 2003; Nexon 2011). The liberal state explicitly and deliberately gives to religion, religious groups, and religious individuals their own autonomy in deciding what to believe and how: in so doing, they also argue that they are not fiddling with religion but rather letting free religion (and free persons) operate within the space of civil society. After all, as both Locke and Rousseau (and many other liberal writers after them) make evidently clear, the freedom of all to associate with others who believe similarly is the apotheosis of both religious freedom and political freedom. They argue that liberal secular democracies uniquely allow true, real, and good religion to flourish.

Karl Marx's critique of liberal civil society and its freedoms or rights to property and religion (among others) places the political consequences of the naturalized religion of liberal political theory into relief. Marx's "On the Jewish Question," written in response to nineteenth-century German debates about Jews' citizenship, argues that, contrary to many Germans' view, the status of the Jew as a political actor (or citizen) is not dependent on an internal quality of "Jewishness" or the distinctiveness (or deficiencies) of Jewish identity or theology, as there exists no such natural condition. He argues, instead, that these identities are directly related not to qualities of religiousness but rather to the "state in which the Jew lives" (1972, 30). As long as a citizen's religious identity remains an issue, the state itself is not secular. Marx argues, however, that the secularity of the state does not mean that religious identity ceases to matter. Pointing to the United States, he notes that where constitutions do not define citizens in relation to religious identity, the Jewish question "loses its theological significance." The political issue is no longer about the so-called internal qualities, ideas, or properties of religious traditions or the political character of their adherents. Religion instead becomes a matter more akin to "secular" question, where religion is one more marker of distinction and division.

This should not be taken as a positive shift, in Marx's view, because while Jewishness ceases to be a theological issue for the secular state, religion nonetheless remains of interest to the liberal state. Religion and religious identity become part of a package of political rights and voluntary actions that compose civil society. Just as the act of privatizing property does not transform property into something that the state has no interest in, so Marx argues that the privatization of religion does not make it free to be left to its own devices. Making religion "private" shifts it to "civil society" where religion, much like property, becomes a site of new capacities for social and political distinction (see also Johnson 2011). Even as religious difference becomes a mark of freedom and distinction, it is simultaneously the case that in this setting "the adherent of a particular religion... finds himself in conflict with his citizenship and with other men as members of the community." For, if "man emancipates himself politically from religion by banishing it from the sphere of public law to that of private law," then "religion is no longer the spirit of the state.... Religion has become the spirit of civil society, of the sphere of egoism, of *bellum omnium contra omnes*. It is no longer the essence of community, but the essence of difference" (Marx 1972, 35). While the liberal political state thus depends on religious difference and toleration as a sign of its own capacity to allow freedoms, these differences (and the limits of that toleration, defined politically) are also a product of this relationship. They are not the fulcrum of a natural freedom that emerges with the separation and privatization of religion, but rather a refashioning of both freedom and religion in the framework of a new set of social and political demands.

As Marx (along with Durkheim and Weber) observed, secular societies and politics identify (and alter) religions that are most amenable to their given ends. The traditions of liberal political philosophy have determinedly argued that free states make religions free, and that these freedoms are only enjoyed without state interference (or religious interference). And this argument has been galvanized by a set of conditions and a set of distinctions that continue to operate with great effect today—namely, that real "religion" supports and is supported by liberal democratic civil society with minimal difficulty.

American Secularism, American Pluralism

American secularism shapes and is shaped by the coordination and regulation of religious difference and, likewise, coordination of narratives of religious pluralism and religious freedom. Despite narratives that frame religions in the United States as free, rules regulating religion remain potent, and perhaps more so insofar as the logics that shape them are naturalized and normalized through numerous social institutions, including the social sciences. What takes shape is a form of "religion" that is valuable for our polity, one that we can, within our visions of freedom, claim not only to be free but also to advance freedoms, whether in the individual or in the world. This is a particular kind of religion as we can see by looking at the struggles within American religious history to shape and enforce these forms and to furthermore convince various actors that such enforcement is actually "free" and "liberating" and even (as in the case of isomorphic pluralism) "authentic." It also conforms and aligns with the "spiritual not religious" post-traditional authority of religious individualists.

William Hutchison (2003) observed that while differences tolerated in the early republic were real, they were also reinforced by a strong cultural and linguistic consensus. Between 1620 and 1820, Hutchison notes, 95 percent of European settlers in the Americas were Protestant. Of these, 90 percent represented the Calvinist wing of the Reformation, and 85 percent were English speaking. While they were "religiously diverse," early Americans clearly and evidently shared a broad cultural framework: "a dissenter could hold wildly heretical opinions and yet be tolerated so long as he or she was 'our sort of person,'" Hutchison writes (2003, 32). This shared cultural framework and the religious tolerance that it supported was not extended to either Africans or to Native Americans, whose religious liberties were curtailed not just as a matter of course, but often because their religious practices were feared as demonic, seditious, or both (Fessenden 2007; Norton 2005). The language and expression of religious tolerance and its performance by a Protestant plurality made it possible for nineteenth-century Americans to interpret the growing religious violence that accompanied the mass migration of Catholics to the United States in the 1830s and beyond as "problems" that were instigated by nondemocratic Catholic religious others. In the colonial period, "pluralism" reinforced and established certain kinds of Protestant religiosity as uniquely able to participate in American secularism and, increasingly, to pose as a more authentic kind of general religiosity that other religions could emulate. The "problem" of Catholic violence could be solved by transforming Catholics into more tolerant American Catholics—or by returning them to their homelands (see Haefeli 2010).

Questions of pluralism, citizenship, and religious freedom preoccupied Americans in the late nineteenth and early twentieth century as senators, judges, and missionaries publicly debated the question of whether Asians should be able to immigrate or be granted citizenship. Questions revolved around whether Chinese or Indian religious ideas were inimical to freedom, and whether as a result their devotees could attune themselves to the "freedoms" and civilization that American democracy allowed (Snow 2007; Goldschmidt and McAlister 2004). Mirroring and extending the critiques and questions that continued even through the twentieth century to dog the "democratic possibilities" of Catholicism (Fessenden 2007; Hamburger 2002), the notion that non-Christian others could not participate in American pluralism showed clearly how notions of politics, religion, and freedom intertwined. That these arguments about pluralism are now conjoined to public commentary about the ability or inability of Muslims (and moreover "Muslim nations") to secularize should come as no surprise.

The practices of American secularism have shaped a particular, historically embedded understanding of religious pluralism. It is expansive, but that expansiveness has embedded within it a set of norms and distinctions, as well as limits and regulations. All of these practices and understandings are undertaken with the freedom of religion in view. Its practices shape citizens and the religious forms that are amenable to their political development. Some, having noted the narrow and limited origins of pluralism's political framework, argue that these problems are issues of the past. The secularist model of plurality that was built on Protestant difference and excluded all others eventually "opens up" to include Catholics and "Asians" and "Muslims" as well. Yet this is not the case. The arguments about religious freedom are connected tightly to, and indeed built upon, the negative comparisons and active restrictions and exclusions of multiple religious groups from its trajectory, even in the present. As Saba Mahmood puts it, "The political solution that secularism proffers . . . lies not so much in tolerating difference and diversity, but in remaking certain kinds of religious subjectivities (even if this requires the use of violence) so as to render them compliant with liberal political rule" (2006, 328).

We need not belabor the point that religion is regulated in American society. But with this in mind, the absence of even a cursory articulation of the numerous social structures, legal conditions and cultural norms that create the American plural landscape is even more striking. If we take the relationship between "religion" and "politics" to be a good one, we cannot, nonetheless, stake the claim any longer that this relationship is one that emerges when secularization frees religion from politics and political cultures. If, as legal scholar Winnifred Fallers Sullivan (2010) argues "the religion that is desired by government today, all governments—is a religion that will produce pious— but not too pious—healthy-minded, and productive citizens," then sociologists might inquire further into the secular political processes and legal cultures that might promote such plural pieties.

Conclusion

Understanding religious pluralism in the American context requires explicit and sustained empirical attention to the structures and contexts of American secular norms, which make certain kinds of pluralism both possible and natural to those who participate within them—as well as for those who don't. Insofar as sociologists of religion uncritically adopt these views rather than call attention in their studies to the impact that they have on the objects and subjects they pursue, they leave numerous questions about the shape of American religious life, and its political implications both in the United States and abroad, wholly untouched. At best, our current practices and norms have led to an atrophying of our understanding of how religion matters in the United States and why; at worst, our practices reproduce the unnamed, naturalized civil religion of plural freedoms that is exported as the fulcrum of democratic practice.

To make the shift in thinking from secularization to secularity, from a focus on given religious heterogeneity to an approach that couples these observations with studies of the structures that give heterogeneity its shape, from a celebration of given pluralism to a questioning of its "imaginative failures," will require that we assess the current theories of religion that sociologists have drawn upon in the wake of classical secularization theories' apparent inability to provide adequate understandings of pluralism. More sociologically robust concepts and models are available to us through the reframing of religion around the questions and issues of secularism in the United States and its powers and effects. Concepts of religion, plurality, toleration, and democracy are ones that we may hold sacred as citizens of a particular country. But this is all the more reason to redouble our attention to the secular and religious projects that continue to sacralize them.

Notes

1. Ammerman states, "[S]ome non-Protestant traditions have complained that they have been 'Protestantized' as they have accommodated to American culture. Whatever else that has meant, they are right that they have been pushed to adopt a basic commitment to live peacefully alongside religious others" (2005, 256). Others have suggested quite different analyses of the relationship between Protestantism and pluralism (Anidjar 2006; A. Marx 2003; Kaplan 2008).

2. With this context in place, we can likewise better understand the "Durkheimian" emphasis that Robert Bellah gave the term "civil religion" in his epochal essay. Where Bellah emphasizes the prophetic role that civil religion can perform, to return a nation to its proper course, it is clear throughout Rousseau's writings that religion should always be subordinate to the polity, although this is qualified by his also clear linking of religion to a natural sentiment that precedes reason and society (Willhoite 1965).

References

Ammerman, Nancy. 2005. *Pillars of Faith: American Congregations and Their Partners.* Berkeley: University of California Press.

Anidjar, Gil. 2006. "Secularism." *Critical Inquiry* 33: 52–77.

Asad, Talal. 2003. *Formations of the Secular: Christianity, Islam, Modernity.* Stanford, CA: Stanford University Press.

Bellah, Robert N. 1967. "Civil Religion in America." *Daedalus* 96: 1–21.

Bender, Courtney. 2010. *The New Metaphysicals: Spirituality and the American Religious Imagination.* Chicago: University of Chicago Press.

Bender, Courtney, and Pamela Klassen, eds. 2010. *After Pluralism.* New York: Columbia University Press.

Berger, Benjamin. 2010. "The Cultural Limits of Legal Tolerance." Pp. 98–125 in *After Pluralism: Reimagining Religious Engagement,* edited by Courtney Bender and Pamela Klassen. New York: Columbia University Press.

Berger, Peter. 1967. *The Sacred Canopy.* Garden City, NY: Doubleday.

Cadge, Wendy, and Elaine Howard Ecklund. 2007. "Immigration and Religion." *Annual Review of Sociology* 33: 359–379.

Casanova, Jose. 1994. *Public Religions in the Modern World.* Chicago: University of Chicago Press.

Chakrabarty, Dipesh. 2001. *Provincializing Europe.* Princeton, NJ: Princeton University Press.

Chaves, Mark. 2011. *American Religion: Contemporary Trends.* Princeton, NJ: Princeton University Press.

Chaves, Mark, and Philip Gorski. 2001. "Religious Pluralism and Religious Participation." *Annual Review of Sociology* 27: 261–281.

Chen, Carolyn. 2008. *Getting Saved in America: Taiwanese Immigration and Religious Experience.* Princeton, NJ: Princeton University Press.

Connolly, William. 2005. *Pluralism.* Durham, NC: Duke University Press.

Cox, Harvey. 1965. *The Secular City.* New York: MacMillan.

Curtis, Edward. 2009. *Muslims in America: A Short History.* New York: Oxford University Press.

Dennett, Daniel. 2006. *Breaking the Spell: Religion as a Natural Phenomenon.* New York: Viking Press.

Durkheim, Emile. 1995. *The Elementary Forms of Religious Life.* New York: Free Press.

Eck, Diana. 1999. "The Multireligious Public Square," Pp. 3–20 in *One Nation Under God? Religion and American Culture,* edited by Marjorie Garber and Rebecca Walkowitz. New York: Routledge.

Eck, Diana. 2007. *What Is Pluralism?* The Pluralism Project. http://www.pluralism.org/pluralism/what_is_pluralism.php (accessed March 21, 2007).

Fessenden, Tracy. 2007. *Culture and Redemption.* Princeton, NJ: Princeton University Press.

Finke, Roger, and Rodney Stark. 1988. "Religious Economies and Sacred Canopies: Religious Mobilization in American Cities, 1906." *American Sociological Review* 53: 41–49.

Finke, Roger, and Rodney Stark. 1992. *The Churching of America, 1776–1990: Winners and Losers in Our Religious Economy.* New Brunswick, NJ: Rutgers University Press.

Gans, Herbert. 1967. *The Levittowners: Ways of Life and Politics in a New Suburban Community.* New York: Vintage.

Gans, Herbert. 1979. "Symbolic Ethnicity." *Ethnic and Racial Studies* 2: 1–20.

Goldschmidt, Henry. 2006. *Race and Religion Among the Chosen Peoples of New York.* New Brunswick, NJ: Rutgers University Press.

Goldschmidt, Henry, and Elizabeth McAlister. 2004. *Race, Nation, and Religion in the America.* New York: Oxford University Press.

Gorski, Philip, and Ateş Altınordu. 2008. "After Secularization?" *Annual Review of Sociology* 34: 55–85.

Gunn, T. Jeremy. 2009. *Spiritual Weapons: The Cold War and the Creation of an American National Religion.* Westport, CT: Praeger.

Haefeli, Evan. 2010. "Toleration." *Religion Compass* 4: 253–262.

Hamburger, Philip. 2002. *The Separation of Church and State*. Cambridge, MA: Harvard University Press.

Harcourt, Bernard. 2011. *The Illusion of Free Markets: Punishment and the Myth of Natural Order*. Cambridge: Harvard University Press.

Herberg, Will. 1955. *Protestant Catholic Jew*. Chicago: University of Chicago Press.

Hicks, Rosemary. 2010. "Creating an 'Abrahamic America': Cold War Political Economy, Pluralism, and Cosmopolitan Sufi Muslims in New York After 2001." PhD dissertation, Columbia University, New York, NY.

Hout, Michael, and Claude S. Fischer. 2002. "Why More Americans Have No Religious Preference: Politics and Generations." *American Sociological Review* 67: 165–190.

Hurd, Elizabeth Shakman. 2007. *The Politics of Secularism in International Relations*. Princeton, NJ: Princeton University Press.

Hutchison, William. 2003. *Religious Pluralism in America: The Contentious History of a Founding Ideal*. New Haven, CT: Yale University Press.

Jakobsen, Janet R. 2010. "Ethics After Pluralism." Pp. 31–58 in *After Pluralism: Reimagining Religious Engagement*, edited by Courtney Bender and Pamela Klassen. New York: Columbia University Press.

Jakobsen, Janet R., and Ann Pellegrini, eds. 2008. *Secularisms*. Durham, NC: Duke University Press.

Johnson, Paul C. 2011. "An Atlantic Genealogy of 'Spirit Possession.'" *Comparative Studies in Society and History* 53: 393–425.

Kaplan, Benjamin. 2008. *Divided by Faith: Religious Conflict and the Practice of Toleration in Early Modern Europe*. Cambridge, MA: Harvard University Press.

Klassen, Pamela, and Courtney Bender. 2010. "Habits of Pluralism." Pp. 1–28 in *After Pluralism: Reimagining Religious Engagement*, edited by Courtney Bender and Pamela Klassen. New York: Columbia University Press.

Kurien, Prema. 2007. *A Place at the Multicultural Table: The Development of an American Hinduism*. New Brunswick, NJ: Rutgers University Press.

Leavelle, Tracy. 2010. "The Perils of Pluralism: Colonization and Decolonization in American Indian Religious History." Pp. 156–177 in *After Pluralism: Reimagining Religious Engagement*, edited by Courtney Bender and Pamela Klassen. New York: Columbia University Press.

Locke, John. 1983. *A Letter Concerning Toleration*. Indianapolis: Hackett Publishing.

Mahmood, Saba. 2005. *The Politics of Piety: The Islamic Revival and the Feminist Subject*. Princeton, NJ: Princeton University Press.

Mahmood, Saba. 2006. "Secularism, Hermeneutics and Empire: The Politics of Islamic Reformation." *Public Culture* 18: 323–348.

Marx, Anthony. 2003. *Faith in Nation: Exclusionary Origins of Nationalism*. New York: Oxford University Press.

Marx, Karl. 1972. "On the Jewish Question." Pp. 26–52 in *The Marx-Engels Reader*. New York: Norton.

McNally, Michael. 2010. "Native American Religious Freedom Beyond the First Amendment." Pp. 225–251 in *After Pluralism: Reimagining Religious Engagement*, edited by Courtney Bender and Pamela Klassen. New York: Columbia University Press.

Moore, Rick. 2011. "The Genres of Religious Freedom: Creating Discourses on Religion at the State Department." Pp. 223–53 in *History, Time, Meaning and Memory: Ideas for the Sociology of Religion*, edited by Barbara Denison and John Simpson. Leiden and Boston: Brill.

Nexon, Daniel. 2011. "Religion and International Relations: No Leap of Faith Required." Pp. 141–167 in *Religion and International Relations Theory*, edited by Jack Snyder. New York: Columbia University Press.

Norton, Mary Beth. 2005. *In the Devil's Snare*. New York: Knopf Press.

Philpott, Daniel. 2002. "The Challenge of September 11 to Secularism in International Relations." *World Politics* 55: 66–95.

Prothero, Stephen, ed. 2006. *A Nation of Religions: The Politics of Pluralism in Multireligious America*. Chapel Hill, NC: University of North Carolina Press.

Rousseau, Jean-Jacques. 1911. *Émile*. New York: E.P. Dutton.

———. 1987. *The Basic Political Writings*. Indianapolis: Hackett Publishing.

Smith, Christian, ed. 2003. *The Secular Revolution: Power, Interests and Conflict in the Secularization of American Public Life*. Chicago: University of Chicago Press.

Snow, Jennifer. 2007. *Protestant Missionaries, Asian Immigration, and Ideologies of Race 1850–1924*. New York: Routledge.

Sullivan, Winnifred Fallers. 2009. *Prison Religion*. Princeton, NJ: Princeton University Press.

Sullivan, Winnifred Fallers. 2010. "We Are All Religious Now." Pp. 82–97 in *After Pluralism: Reimagining Religious Engagement,* edited by Courtney Bender and Pamela Klassen. New York: Columbia University Press.

Taylor, Charles. 2007. *A Secular Age*. Cambridge, MA: Harvard University Press.

Warner, R. Stephen. 1994. "The Place of the Congregation in the American Religious Configuration." Pp. 54–99 in *American Congregations, Vol. 2: New Perspectives in the Study of Congregations*, edited by James P. Wind and James W. Lewis. Chicago: University of Chicago Press.

Warner, R. Stephen. 2006. "The De-Europeanization of American Christianity." Pp. 233–255 in *A Nation of Religions: The Politics of Pluralism in Multireligious America*, edited by Stephen Prothero. Chapel Hill: University of North Carolina Press.

Weber, Max. 1958. "The Protestant Sects and the Spirit of Capitalism." In *From Max Weber: Essays in Sociology* New York: Oxford Galaxy.

Willhoite, Fred H., Jr. 1965. "Rousseau's Political Religion." *Review of Politics* 27: 501–515.

Wuthnow, Robert. 2005. *America and the Challenges of Religious Diversity*. Princeton, NJ: Princeton University Press.

Yang, Fenggang, and Helen Rose Ebaugh. 2001. "Transformations in New Immigrant Religions and Their Global Implications." *American Sociological Review* 66: 269–288.

Yinger, J. Milton. 1967. "Pluralism, Religion and Secularism." *Journal for the Scientific Study of Religion* 6: 17–28.

7

Religion on the Move: Mapping Global Cultural Production and Consumption

PEGGY LEVITT

Just as computers and cell phones have transformed the way we do business, so they are transforming the way the "word" travels. The Christmas season of 2004 was the first time that Italian Catholics could receive free video transmissions of Pope John Paul's Midnight Mass and his Christmas day message on their cell phones. In fact, the Holy See stays close to its faithful by texting "The Papal Thought of the Day" to subscribers. The service, available in Italy, Ireland, Malta, Britain, and the United States, costs 30 cents a message. Christians are not the only ones engaged in high-tech proselytizing. The British-based Islamic Prayer Alert Service, which sends out 70,000 messages a month, reminds its subscribers of prayer times and regularly sends them inspirational quotes from the Qur'an. The service costs more—25 pence a message or about $1,700 a year—but 65 percent of the revenue is donated to charity (Curnow 2005).

Technology is just one engine propelling religions on the move. Migrants, pilgrims, social movement members, and scholars all carry religion. Religious objects, narratives, and spirits circulate actively and frequently within and between the layers of religious social fields. Yet we still talk of national religions—of American Protestantism or French Islam—or of self-contained, discrete congregations, organizations, or social movements. We assume that religious practices and organizations obediently respect national boundaries. We take stasis and boundedness as the default categories for organizing religious life while, in fact, many religious ideas and practices are often and unabashedly in motion.

In keeping with the overarching objectives of this volume—to de-Christianize, de-Americanize, and de-congregationalize the study of religion—this chapter argues for the need to study religious movement and connection and proposes a way to analyze what happens when circulating religious elements encounter what is already in place. It is a conceptual roadmap, not an empirical analysis.

Rather than assuming that religious life stays primarily within contained spaces (be they religious traditions, congregations, or nations), I start from the assumption of circulation and linkages. I see religion not as a packageable, stable set of beliefs and practices rooted in a particular bounded time and space, but as a contingent clustering of diverse elements that come together within to-be-determined spaces riddled by power and interests. The resulting assemblages, made up of actors, objects, technology, and ideas, travel at different rates and rhythms, across the different levels and scopes of the social fields in which they are embedded. How can we explain what happens at these "sites of encounter" where what is circulating and what is in place come together? What social and political work gets done, and whose interests are served when religion is conceptualized as a cohesive, bounded system as opposed to an unruly, clumsy collection that is constantly on the move?

I am not proposing that religious objects and practices travel unencumbered. God may need no passport, but religious beliefs and believers regularly encounter obstacles and roadblocks along their way. Rather, I argue that continuing to study religion within discrete containers and taking for granted the boundaries and levels of the appropriate spatial units of analysis blinds us to important ways in which contemporary religious life is actually lived and the power hierarchies that shape it. Our research would be more productive if we began by looking empirically at the borders and layers of the spaces that concern us. How they are connected (or not) to other actors and objects in the social field is an open question. It might be that there are few ties or little movement. But assuming stasis and boundedness a priori risks overlooking important dynamics and producing an analysis that is incomplete.

I am, by no means, the first to take up these questions. Many studies assert that aspects of religious life are "on the move" and that some kind of encounter—be it hybridization, syncretization, convergence, or transculturization—takes place (Ortiz 1940; Starkloff 2002). Others suggest ways of thinking about the spaces, networks, or flows that drive religious movement (Ebaugh and Chafetz 2002; Yang and Ebaugh 2001; Mooney 2009; Hagan 2008, Hüwelmeier and Krause 2009). In general, this work stops short of explaining what happens at these sites of encounter where what is moving bumps up against what is already there. We need a way to unpack and explain that contingent clustering, which holds the local, the national, the global, and all the layers of social experience in between in conversation with each other. We need a way of identifying systematic patterns of convergence, if they exist, and of explaining how power and history create them. We need to understand why some things move easily while others fail to launch or get blocked along the way.

This chapter begins by laying out a transnational optic that helps elucidate aspects of these social relations and processes. I then outline how I understand "religion" and the carriers, geographies, and pathways that influence religious assemblage construction. I use examples from my own work and the work of other colleagues to make my case. I conclude with a discussion of how religious and ethnic movement compare and reflect on how these different diversity markers are conceived and managed supports existing power hierarchies.

Conceptualizing Religion

Rule makers created the category "religion" at a particular epistemological moment to dominate and control the powerless, formally institutionalizing what had, in many cases, been disparate, messy, contested sets of practices and thereby allowing the colonizer or Christian majority to better control the "Other" (Chidester 1996; Asad 1993 Masuzawa 2005). The British, for instance, created the label "Hinduism" out of a varied, informal set of beliefs and practices so that "Hindus" were easier to manage and dominate. Doing so cemented false dichotomies such as tradition and modernity, the public and private, and religion versus politics that privileged certain ways of being and belonging while marginalizing others (Vásquez 2005). The analytical categories scholars used missed many of the informal, folk, and material aspects of religion: embodied practices, emplaced institutions, and sacralized artifacts. They imposed an order and cohesiveness on a wide range of beliefs and practices that, in fact, only came together in unique ways at specific moments (Euben 2006).

A much needed corrective comes from recent scholarship that calls attention to how particular religious configurations converge at particular times and places, explores why certain discourses, practices, and institutions are called "religious," and asks how they interact with the "nonreligious" (Bender and Klassen 2010). This research asks what interests are served by understanding religion in this way and what kinds of institutional and legal responses to public religion and religious pluralism have developed in response.

Assemblage theory provides a way of thinking about these heterogeneous and emergent constellations by stressing relationships over structures, change over stability, and variable scope over delimited space (Deleuze and Guattari 1987; Legg 2010; Marcus and Saka 2006). Unlike the metaphorical "tree" and the elements that move through its branches and roots extending upward and downward from a grounded center, the central organizing metaphor is the rhizome. The rhizome has no fixed bounds or conceptual limits and is based on the idea of multi-directionality and diversity. Any point of a rhizome can be connected to any other, and must be (Deleuze and Guattari 1987). Furthermore, when parts of rhizomes break off, they can survive on their own, meandering and re-forming or uniting with others, but always along lines that trace back.

While the "de-territorialization" of assemblages is a central focus, assemblages also settle, have periods of stability, and re-territorialize (Legg 2010).

I find it generative to think of the contingent encounter between religious actors, practices, and objects as assemblages that come together in loose or tightly coupled ways. The image of the meteor that casts off and accrues elements as it travels through space captures its circulatory quality. We can think of anything from individual religiosity to the constitution of global religious organizations as produced by this conditional clustering. The basic core of the assemblage may be well defined and agreed upon or barely held together. How tightly organized it is and what attaches and detaches from it as it travels is context specific and ever changing.

A Transnational Optic

Religion is just one aspect of contemporary social life that operates across borders. Social movements mobilize constituencies around the globe. Economies are organized around transcontinental investment, manufacturing, and consumption chains. And tandoori chicken has become one of London's foods of choice.

This is not new. One need only think of colonialism and imperialism, missionary campaigns, anti-slavery and workers' movements, or jazz to realize that human social formations and processes have always been trans-border and trans-boundary to varying degrees. But because the social sciences came of age at roughly the same time as the current nation-state system, many of the analytical categories we use assume that the nation is the automatic and logical organizing container of contemporary experience.

Methodological nationalism is the tendency to accept the nation-state and its boundaries as a given (Wimmer and Glick Schiller 2003). However, while nation-states are still extremely important, social life does not obey national boundaries. To capture these dynamics, we have to trade in a national optic for a transnational one or use both simultaneously. Social life takes place within the context of social fields that are multi-sited and multi-layered, encompassing structured interactions of differing forms, depth, and breadth (Levitt and Glick Schiller 2004). National social fields remain within national boundaries, while transnational social fields connect actors, through direct and indirect relations, across borders. Neither domain automatically takes precedence; rather, determining the relative importance of national versus transnational social fields is an empirical question. Religious assemblages potentially come together within and are made up of elements circulating within these transnational spaces.

Seeing how these constellations take shape and identifying the sites and sources from which they are created requires a transnational optic. Such studies would identify the parameters of the appropriate social fields and the connections between the actors and institutions within and beyond them. They would treat individuals and groups not as closed containers rooted in local sites but would see them instead as potential sites of clustering and convergence which, once constituted, circulate and recirculate, uploading and downloading as they travel. The resulting configurations are not purely local, national, or global but nested within multiple scales of governance, each with its own logic and repertoires of institutional and discursive resources.

A transnational optic helps identify the actors, ideas, and technologies that are the *carriers* of religion. It calls our attention to the real and imagined, past and present *geographies* through which religion travels and the pathways and networks that guide the elements circulating within them. Finally, it produces a clearer picture of how and why religious assemblages are created at these *sites of encounter.*

Toward Religion in Motion

Carriers of Religion

Most aspects of religious life are potentially mobile. Bodies, spirits, deities, and souls move. Modes of religious organization and social movements travel. Ideas, practices, and symbols also circulate. These goods have multiple carriers: objects and ideas piggyback onto or permeate seemingly nonreligious objects and ideas. This is the stuff from which assemblages are made. Religion also strongly influences individuals' migratory journeys, including how they travel, what it means to be pious and respectable once they arrive, and how values and practices are transmitted and change along the way (Hagan 2008). Finally, religion speaks clearly to the unrooted, often unstable quality of contemporary life. Its narratives of individual redemption and universal transcendence provide tools for understanding transitions between youth and age, poverty and wealth, or tradition and change. It's not a surprise, then, that religion and movement are so deeply implicated.

People are one important source of religion in motion. But individuals move for different amounts of time across varying distances, producing different levels of contact with the people with whom they interact and the places where they travel. Not everyone moves with the intention of permanent settlement, nor are they allowed to. Migrants, as well as pilgrims, tourists, professionals, students, religious leaders, and scholars, also carry faith.

Religions themselves propel movement. In some communities, movement is required of members in good standing: for Mormons, some evangelical

Christians, or the members of Tablighi Jamaat, part of being religious is spreading the word. Movement is part of the group's collective history and how it understands its calling today. Modes of organizing religious life also travel. Highly structured religious communities, such as the Catholic Church, follow their members by simply transplanting their transnational corporate structure from one context to another (Levitt 2007).

Traveling objects and rituals also carry faith and their symbolic value and meaning often change dramatically along the way (Durand and Massey 1995; Oleszkiewicz-Peralba 2007). Migrating deities and spirits can themselves be socially mobile. Sinha (2005), for example, found that lower class devotees worshipped the Hindu God Muneeswaran in India, while aspiring middle class migrants worshipped him in Singapore (see also Lambek 1993; Meyer and Moors 2006; Hüwelmeier and Krause 2009).

Religious status, piety, and authority are also negotiated across time and space. Richman (2005) found that Haitian migrants used faith to extricate themselves from one sacred space and reinsert themselves into another. Although many of her respondents were Catholic, they also believed in *lwas* or "saints" who could afflict and protect members of their descent groups. But as people grew unwilling to spend large sums of money on the *lwas'* care, they converted to Protestantism to liberate themselves from these ritual obligations.

Geographies of Circulation

To understand how and why these different religious carriers move and cluster as they do, we need to take into account the geographies within which they circulate—the intersecting planes and networks that constitute transnational social fields and their boundaries. Things travel through what Lefebvre (1991) called "textures" of space, contours of representational regimes, and signifying practices by which spaces are made places and filled with meaning. Different regimes of governance operate within these scales. Appadurai (1996) might call these religio- or sacroscapes. In Castells's (2004) "network society," sets of interconnected nodes with no clear center or periphery constitute the social boundaries within which circulation takes place.

Some terrains are clearly more stable than others. The social fields connecting Mexico and the United States, Britain and South Asia, or Germany and Turkey have relatively long and consistent histories. In contrast, less developed, uncertain social fields, such as those plagued by civil unrest or climactic disaster, are more difficult to navigate. Not only can communication be hampered, but also what travels may be more likely to stray or encounter obstacles along the way. In some parts of the world, religious elements circulate in the context of failed states and markets, while in others they encounter strong states and booming economies where governments actively regulate public religious expression and land use.

The geographies that religious actors and objects traverse are not virgin territories. Spaces become places because of their history, politics, and culture. They are deeply rutted. Just as each new eruption of lava slowly settles into the cracks and crevices of the volcano, so new cultural infusions have to accommodate themselves to the existing terrains. New overlays land on pockmarked geographies, enabling some things to travel easily while inhibiting others.

For instance, contemporary Hinduism travels primarily within a British postcolonial space. Its carriers, who move between Europe, the United States, the Caribbean, South Asia, and Africa, enact their religious lives against a common meta-cultural frame that is still influenced in subtle and not-so-subtle ways by British colonial assumptions about law, governance, and social cohesion. A common ethos and set of social dynamics characterize life in South Asia, Trinidad, and East Africa although they bump up against very different local backdrops. Circulating religious elements and actors land in terrains that are similar but different, familiar yet strange.

So how and why does Hinduism take shape in London, Kenya, and Fiji given that it lands in places that are distinct yet connected at the same time? How is the religious assemblage constituted in each place given that its core basic elements encounter very different national and global repertoires? How does Islam take shape when it moves from South Asia to the Middle East as opposed to England or the United States?

Arriving at a satisfactory answer requires taking all of the ideological and governance structures at work within transnational social fields into account. The broadest, most overarching are global norms (or what neo-institutionalists or world polity theorists call "global culture"), which include models for the organization and regulation of religious life, a notion of rights based on personhood rather than citizenship, and ideologies about religious freedom and pluralism (Lechner and Boli 2005). Global culture is a resource, because it is a repository actors draw upon, but it is also a constraint because it limits the range of options they can choose from and pressures people to conform to them.

National context and history also matter (Bramadat and Koenig 2009). Countries have unique philosophies of integration and narratives about who they are and who can belong (Favell 2001). Their different *religious, ethnic, and racial diversity management regimes* reflect deeply ingrained assumptions about how much "they" can become part of "us." The United States tells itself it is a country of immigrants founded on principles of religious pluralism that has always been successful at making newcomers into Americans. Sweden tells itself it is a secular society where everyone is equal. America expects its newcomers to believe in some version of Judeo-Christianity. In Sweden, talking about, let alone publicly expressing, religious identity is far less common because labeling difference is seen as marginalizing rather than empowering the newcomer.

National incentive structures reward the embrace of certain kinds of identities and the constitution of certain groups (Bloomraed 2006). In the United States, minorities are expected to embrace the terms of abiding, unchanging cultural and racial essences. Accepting ethnic or religious labels or formally establishing a legal nonprofit religious community can enhance access to resources and state protection and support. That is why the Garifuna become adept at the language of "ethnic" culture (Johnson 2007) and Indian Americans embrace Hinduism as a way of taking "their place at the multicultural table" (Kurien 2007).

Physical geographies exist alongside, and sometimes supersede, imagined and remembered sacred landscapes that have topological properties of their own. Some believers think of themselves as living, first and foremost, in the kingdom of God or the Muslim *Ummah*. They are *religious global citizens* who abide by a different set of rights and responsibilities in territories populated by co-religionists (Levitt 2007). The salient landmarks are shrines and pilgrimage destinations rather than national museums and monuments.

Others feel part of a historical landscape, a religious chain of memory connecting them to the past, present, and future (Hervieu-Léger 2000). When Cuban Americans bring their newborns to be baptized into the Cuban nation at the national patron saint shrine they erected in Miami, they are locating them in this imagined landscape formed by the past, present, and future. They induct these infants into a Cuba that existed in Havana, exists in Miami in the present, and they hope to reclaim in Cuba in the future (Tweed 2006).

Sites of Encounter

Religious assemblages circulate through diverse geographies encountering people, ideas, and practices along the way. What explains how and why what lands and what is already in place come together as they do? How do we explain the constant accretion and shedding that happens as religious assemblages travel—the things that spin off and attach to the tail of the meteor.

One broad set of factors influencing these sites of encounter is the *social status of the carriers and the receivers*, be they individuals or organizations. Some research suggests that "marginal men," who take risks because they are less constrained by social norms, are more likely to adopt radical innovations (Rogers 2003; Strang and Stroule 1998; Wejnert, 2002). Others find that powerful, respected individuals are better able to pressure their peers to change their behavior. When individuals are financially or emotionally dependent on someone, they are more likely to do what that person says. Similarly, organizations that perceive themselves as similar should look and act similarly

(DiMaggio and Powell 1983; Dobbin, Simmons, and Garrett 2007). When a congregation or denomination sees itself as sufficiently like another, it is more likely to mimic the behavior of its peer.

Adoption and convergence at one site or level of a social field can spill over into other levels. McAdam and his colleagues (2001, 331) talk of *scale shift* or episodes of contention that migrate from the local to the translocal and to the national. The messages and activities of religious leaders and teachers also *scale up and out*. The same rules and rituals that protect believers from evil in a homeland will also protect them across the world. So the woman who won't eat certain foods or who does not interact with men wards off impurity in India and the West, protecting herself from the heathen neighbor in Ahmedabad and the materialistic, alcohol-drinking colleague in America. The devotee who used to do *bhakti pheri* or proselytizing in poor villages in Gujarat but who now spreads the word in Boston and Atlanta is also scaling out. Allowing women to be leaders at the local mosque scales up when they also become leaders in regional and national governance.

A second broad set of influences affecting what happens at religious sites of encounter is the *difference between the objects or rituals in motion and those that are already in place*. By this I mean not only how easy it is to package, communicate, and transmit what is circulating but also how distinct it is from existing practice.

Some rituals and objects are clearly more portable than others and some messages more transposable. Fasting, praying, singing, making offerings, playing music, and dancing can happen anywhere with certain adjustments. Some packages are also more appealing than others, like the Islamic educational materials children quickly embraced because they resemble Disney characters (Mandeville 2001). Werbner (2005) sees charisma as portable. While the plots of the stories about the Sufi saint she studies were tailored to local circumstances, the narratives were paradigmatic. They were "marked by a recurrent 'global' plot and a localized here and now narrative" (Werbner 2005, 286). Because their underlying structure is the same, they were portable and powerful in Morocco, Iraq, Pakistan, or Indonesia; their comparable semiotic logic makes them easy to carry and transmit. Likewise, Johnson (2007) described the Garifuna who carried beach sand from Honduran villages to use in ritual events in New York City. While migrants' ties to Honduras weakened, their connections to other places, ancestors, and powers grew. By using objects in the same ways as they had in the past, migrants signaled a direct link to memory, but by also using them more symbolically in new contexts, they distinguished between memory and the present, allowing a generic "ancestor" to travel, rather than someone specific.

Portability and adoption also depend, in part, on boundaries or the difference between what is already in place and what is new or different. Boundaries can be high because adoption requires a major change and there are therefore significant barriers to entry. Or they can be low when what comes to ground has a lot in common with what is already there. Boundaries can be thick, creating tight, dense data packets that travel easily and efficiently, or they can be thin, creating leaky packages that have more difficulty moving because they are given to spillage. Written traditions travel in packages that are literally bounded, while stories transmitted orally are more likely to change when they are translated and told over and over again. Some boundaries are only permeable for a short time or to a small amount of input (think about the sperm that must fertilize the egg quickly or lose its strength; once the sperm crosses the cell wall, the membrane becomes impermeable again). Similarly, ideas and behaviors loose steam and fall out of fashion. What Herbert Simon (1984) called bounded rationality, or the ability to take in only so much information at once, is also at play. Individual and organizational adopters can only process and respond to so much input. Finally, boundaries tend to be selectively permeable, only permitting things with particular shapes and textures to cross them. Ideas and practices that are too "round" to fit within metaphorically square-shaped gates simply cannot pass.

The *frequency and strength of contact* between circulating elements and elements in place also influence the nature of the encounter. One aspect of this is how ideas and objects get introduced into the field. Think of the allergy sufferer who rubs cortisone cream onto her skin as opposed to the person who uses an inhaler. The drug's impact is enhanced when it is introduced directly into the bloodstream. The student who belongs to a religious community during her four years abroad has a different kind of encounter than her second-generation peer, from a similar background, who was actively raised in a religious household. The tourist brushes up against the surface of religious life, while the pilgrim, although also a short-term visitor, engages with it more reflectively. Hearing something once from a visiting pastor or teacher does not have the same impact as listening to the same preacher week after week. Likewise, convincing one or two congregation members that churches should be governed democratically will have a different effect than if the entire congregation votes to change its governance structure. If a change catalyst emanates from several sources, such as the local, regional, and national denominational offices, it may also be more likely to take hold.

The *characteristics of the pathways or channels* that religious elements traverse, whether they are real or mediated, also affect sites of encounter. Faith moves through religious organizational structures of different strengths and scope. Most Sunni Muslim mosques are stand-alone; they do not form part of large organizational hierarchies. Other religious organizations involve some kind of center(s)/periphery(ies), whereby the "mother institution" or headquarters exerts some control over its members. How tightly structured these networks are and how much the "center" directs its outposts strongly influence the circulation of religious goods.

Ideas and practices traveling through hierarchical institutionalized structures like the Catholic Church traverse clear, protected channels. Powerful individuals sanction their journey and strictly regulate what moves in an effort to protect brand integrity. When objects move through weaker, more informal institutions, they are more vulnerable to interference and challenge. Alternative, unsanctioned practices are more likely to permeate their boundaries and pose obstacles. At the same time, it is sometimes easier to traverse less formally structured paths.

Finally, the nature of the circulatory encounter depends on *the presence of exogenous elements* that stimulate, enhance, or cancel out its effect. Certain ideas and practices travel together in a kind of partnership, producing an interaction effect. Sometimes their relationship is parasitic; what is introduced piggybacks onto a host that it decimates as it travels. The idea that a pious woman can work outside of her home is unlikely to be adopted if it circulates hand in hand with the idea that working women cannot be good mothers. Other flows cancel each other out, like the pastor who encourages his immigrant members to become politically active but also tells them they should participate, above all, in the kingdom of Christ (Levitt 2007). Finally, other ideas and practices depend on each other symbiotically for survival. Achieving a more equal gender balance at home is a precursor for women to become more active leaders in their temples and churches.

An Empirical Example

So far, I've described various carriers of religion in motion, the geographies and pathways through which they travel, and some of the factors affecting what happens when religion on the move encounters ideas and practices already in place. Now, I turn to an empirical example.

Consider the issue of female piety. Several competing sets of loosely coupled assemblages concerning gender and women's rights circulate widely. Each time they come to ground, they encounter regional and local social justice ideologies, gender norms, and organizational ecologies that strongly influence if and how they are appropriated and vernacularized. In some cases, their connection to the global is quite tenuous, while in others, international references and substance remain strong.

A neoliberal assemblage promoting privatization, structural adjustment, democracy, capitalism, human rights, the rule of law, transparency and accountability, and gender equity through institutions like the World Bank and the Ford Foundation is perhaps most familiar. A fundamentalist religious assemblage based on gender complementarity, tradition, conservatism, and authority that gets spread through religious networks like the Tablighi Jamaat and evangelical Christian groups is a second example. A third "anti-globalization" assemblage coalesces around anti-consumerism and anti-materialism, environmentalism, fair trade, and living locally and simply. Each of these assemblages has its own narrative and set of technologies associated with women's roles and gender relations. Religious actors and movements appropriate and trade on these discourses. They are sources of the new and different or foils against which actors take the measure of their own piety and power.

Farhat Hashmi, the leader of the Al-Huda International Welfare Foundation (commonly known as Al-Huda), a nongovernmental organization founded in Pakistan in 1994 to help women become more observant Muslims through better education, constructs female piety transnationally. Global culture, and the women's rights package that forms part of it, clearly informs her work, as do local conditions and national gender regimes.

While Al-Huda now works with men, prisoners, the sick, and the poor, the majority of its members are still wealthy, urban, educated Pakistani housewives and young women. They attend one of the nearly 200 schools Dr. Hashmi created to increase religious literacy among women. Many students knew little about Islam prior to enrolling and lived what they now consider to be un-Islamic lives. They attend school for one or two years, receive a diploma, and then create similar courses, using similar materials, for other women in their neighborhoods, workplaces, and communities. This multiplier effect, the thinking goes, will slowly remake the Pakistani religious landscape.

Dr. Hashmi plays to all sides of the gender struggle by combining elements of the neoliberal and fundamentalist global values assemblages. She builds on local norms, respecting the limits they impose while also pushing beyond them. Her lectures appeal to women's desire for empowerment, but it is an empowerment that leaves certain basic rules intact. While in the past only poor, uneducated men attended Islamic schools, she believes that women can get an Islamic education too, encouraging them to read the Qur'an and make it relevant to their lives. And while she does not expect Pakistani women to become en masse mosque goers any time soon, she provides them with ways to engage collectively and publicly through study and prayer.

Depending on one's point of view, Farhat Hashmi is savior or enemy. Her supporters claim that she brings women back to Islam by getting them to veil themselves and adapt more conservative practices, but that she also encourages them to personalize their relationship with their faith. She acknowledges her primarily middle-class constituents' socioeconomic gains while at the same time addressing the disappointments of middle-class secular life. She enables women to return to tradition without giving up all of their freedoms. According to Sarah Karim, a 45-year-old devoted Farhat Hashmi follower, "My life changed when I learned about Dr. Hashmi. She helps women be part of Islam together, but in a way that respects our national culture and obeys the rules of our faith."

Critics claim Dr. Hashmi preaches an intolerant, conservative brand of Islam that verges dangerously close to groups like the Taliban. According to Tariq Ramadan, a 50-year-old opponent, "Farhat Hashmi has filled the streets of Karachi with *Ninja Turtles* (referring to the many women now wearing the *Niqab* which completely covers their faces). She is importing Islamic practices from the very conservative heart of the Middle East and it is sending our country back to the Dark Ages." As the ranks of her supporters grow, the country's secular and moderate religious spaces are shrinking, increasing the damage already wrought by larger geopolitical forces. To her detractors, Dr. Hashmi is moving Pakistan in the wrong direction.

The Al Huda example reveals how ideas and practices circulating throughout a particular transnational religious field come together and are vernacularized. Dr. Hashmi combines and adopts rhetorics from various women's rights assemblages in ways that defy straightforward characterization because they include reformist and progressive messages. Encouraging women to engage collectively with Islam is a radical move, but one she makes in ways that are culturally appropriate and responsive to the Pakistani context. She speaks of empowerment and rights at the same time that she speaks of tradition and gender complementarity—generally discourses placed in opposition to each other. Her message respects the hard-worn freedoms of Pakistani middle-class women, as well as their desire to return, on their own terms, to the religious fold.

Vernacularization or Not

Farhat Hashmi creates a unique religious assemblage through vernacularization. Circulating elements and those in place come into contact, but they have to be actively vernacularized or appropriated and transformed to be used in a particular place. Translation and vernacularization are different processes. While translators communicate to be understood, vernacularizers communicate to make something understandable and applicable to a specific context. There are at least three types of vernacularization: the act of building on the imaginative space, momentum, and power of particular global frames without using them directly; the act of translating global ideas so they are locally appropriate and applicable to new issues; and the act of taking core concepts, articulating them in locally appropriate ways, and modeling new ways to put them into practice (Levitt and Merry 2009). Dr. Hashmi does all three.

Some circulating elements within transnational social fields never get appropriated. They enter the social field, encounter what is already there, but maintain their integrity within it. This is transmission without vernacularization; what circulates does not challenge the status quo. Such are the Charismatic Catholic groups that migrants establish in the parishes where they settle that are within the local church but not of it, therefore changing or being changed little by their surroundings. There are also cases in which what is already in place is more compelling than what is introduced. While members of the Bhaghat Samaj (a Hindu subcaste in Gujarat State in India) knew about discourses of global human rights and social justice, when they discussed the kinds of charitable projects they wanted to undertake, they described their choices in Gandhian terms (Levitt and Merry 2009) They argued that individuals had the right to food, shelter, and self-sufficiency. They did not reference the global language of development, modernity, and equality because the local social justice models already in place were too compelling.

A second scenario is that circulating elements are integrated into the social field with little lasting impact. Because they are too small or too different, not enough people appropriate them to have a significant effect. These are the members of radical sects or new religious movements who introduce their beliefs to the broader public but find few takers.

A third, more common scenario is that circulating culture is gradually vernacularized such that eventually the parent cannot be distinguished from the offspring. Vernacularization occurs continuously through an unending uploading and downloading, accretion and shedding. Assemblages of all sizes take shape and are appropriated by individuals and groups. If, at first, there was an identifiable core and periphery, the periphery soon becomes a source of beliefs and practices that strongly influence the rapidly disappearing center.

For example, the first Gujaratis to bring Hinduism and Islam to Johannesburg brought a version of their faith that has since been transformed by its constant recirculation between homeland, host land, and other places where the Indian diaspora settled. Brazilian evangelical pastors who migrated to the Boston area belong to religious communities first introduced to Brazil by missionaries in the late nineteenth century that they are now reimporting back to the United States (Levitt 2007). In each of these cases, history, structure, and ideology all influence how vernacularization takes shape.

Conclusion

In this chapter, I have argued that scholarship on religion needs better tools with which to capture how people, ideas, and objects circulate through transnational social fields. Because of the impoverished nature of our conceptual vocabulary, many studies of religion assume a stasis and one-way movement that is inaccurate. The assemblages produced by religion on the move do not arise from a single "world culture," nor do they circulate unidirection-ally through a single, stable geography. Human and material elements come together in specific historical and political contexts. What results is a new mix, which shifts and recombines form and content before it travels once again. This chapter is an attempt to rewrite the dictionary and to chart ways to identify systematic configurations across time and space.

One way to further this agenda is to compare the ways in which religion is conceptualized and travels to the circulation of other kinds of identities and allegiances. What is it about this particular geopolitical moment that explains why religion and ethnicity are understood and deployed as they are? What work gets done and whose interests are served by these genealogies and uses?

On the one hand, we might see religion as more easily bound, carried and tamed than ethnicity. A common set of beliefs is spelled out and codified in the Qur'an, the Bible, or the Gita, which are all collective reference books. Even if most people know little about what is actually in them, they can always look it up. Many received some kind of basic literacy training as children. These cen-tral religious texts make it easy for faith to travel: they are not only inher-ently packageable but also portable (e.g., the Jews carrying the Ark through the desert). Religions also have clear rituals and prohibitions on behavior. In fact, for many followers, part of being religious means engaging in frequent collec-tive rituals and performances led by official experts in formal organizational spaces that reinforce the group.

In contrast, there are no clearinghouses specifying the official meaning or membership requirements of Italianness or Irishness. While there are national stories and founding myths and rich traditions of passing them on to children, they are not codified or authorized in quite the same way as their religious equivalents. Italy, as the incarnation of Italianness, does not fit neatly within two covers. Its rituals of belonging are often private and individualized. There is no central authority or collective structure within which they are enacted. There is no official way to convert outsiders.

The semiotic logic of religiosity also differs from ethnicity in ways that make it more conducive to movement. It is more open to multiplicity because most faiths include narratives about syncretism and movement. While there may be one authorized version of faith, the lived, everyday reality of religious life reflects constant combining and boundary crossing. In contrast, contemporary nation-states and their political and legal systems have been, until recently, based on the assumption of singular membership. Even today, critics of dual citizenship complain that belonging to two countries is like bigamy: it's not possible to be married to two countries at the same time. While in the United States hyphenated identities are common, many European countries actively reject the possibility of being Moroccan-French or a Pakistani-Dane. Even in the American context, the underlying assumption is that the Italian and the

American side of the hyphenated equation are relatively self-contained, discrete partners.

But in reality, in this particular nation-state moment in which global governance structures, capital, and migration are on the rise and challenge national borders, not just aspects of religious life, but also ethnicity and by default nationality assume forms that are actually more similar than we think. We see a proliferation of global religious organizations and movements and, it could be argued, a rise in *religious global citizenship*. People live in one place but sometimes also claim rights and exercise responsibilities in a worldwide imagined community of faith. These religious communities challenge nation-state sovereignty when followers obey calls that seemingly contradict national interests.

More and more, though, ethnicity and nationality are also constituted across borders. Increasing numbers of nation-states not only grant long-term membership without residence but also actively encourage it because they depend on the economic and political power of their citizens living abroad. Mexicanness is produced not only in Mexico but also by the millions of Mexican Americans living in the United States, just as Indianness is a negotiated contest between nonresident Indians of varying power living all over the world. Ethnic and national organizational architectures organize and regulate the diaspora, which is alternatively viewed as a resource and a threat.

Therefore, in many ways religion and ethnicity are equally misunderstood. They are both analytic categories created and deployed to organize and contain difference, albeit in different ways in colonial, post-colonial, and global contexts. They are generally thought to be rooted in nations and containable when, in fact, in the everyday lives of ordinary individuals, they are in flux within and beyond nation-states. They are treated as analytically distinct when they are often constituted and deployed together. There is, then, in both cases, a major disjuncture between how aspects of ethnic and religious life are actually lived and how they are conceptualized, regulated, and rewarded legally and politically.

The words we use to talk about society and the methods we use to study it perpetuate the existing power hierarchy. They enable leaders and policymakers to continue to insist that religion and ethnicity are nationally constituted and manageable when, in fact, they often cross national boundaries. They are part and parcel of the illusion that at least some ethnic and religious bodies are still and controllable when, in fact, they move frequently and far way. These discourses reinforce national unity and the geopolitical status quo. They make it more difficult to see and talk about the fact that people embrace all kinds of competing loyalties and responsibilities, and that this does not automatically mean they are not loyal and responsible to the places where they live. The methods and conceptual tools outlined here fundamentally call into question the enduring strength of the container society and bring to the fore how the categories and analytical strategies we use perpetuate our inability or unwillingness to let it go.

References

Appadurai, A. 1996. *Modernity at Large: Dimensions of Globalization*. Minneapolis: University of Minnesota Press.

Asad, T. 1993. *Genealogies of Religion*. Baltimore: Johns Hopkins University Press.

Bender, C., and P. Klassen. 2010. *After Pluralism*. New York: Columbia University Press.

Bloomraed, I. 2006. *Becoming a Citizen*. Berkeley and Los Angeles: University of California Press.

Bramadat, P., and M. Koenig, eds. 2009. *International Migration and the Governance of Religious Diversity*. Montreal, Canada: McGill-Queens University Press.

Castells, M., ed. 2004. *The Network Society: A Cross-Cultural Perspective*. Northampton: Edward Elgar.

Chidester, D. 1996. *Religion and American Popular Culture*. Berkeley and Los Angeles: University of California Press.

Curnow, R. 2005. "Wireless: Dial-A-Prayer, Upgraded." *International Herald Tribune* (online version), January 17. http://www.iht.com/articles/2005/01/16/business/wireless17.php

Deleuze, G., and F. Guattari. 1987. *A Thousand Plateaus: Capitalism and Schizophrenia*. Minneapolis: University of Minnesota Press.

DiMaggio, P. J., and W. W. Powell. 1983. "The Iron Cage Revisited: Institutional Isomorphism and Collective Rationality in Organizational Fields." *American Sociological Review* 48(2): 147–160.

Dobbin, F., B. Simmons, and G. Garrett. 2007. "The Global Diffusion of Public Policies: Social Construction, Coercion, Competition, or Learning?" *Annual Review of Sociology* 33: 449–472.

Durand, J., and D. Massey. 1995. *Miracles on the Border*. Tucson: University of Arizona Press.

Ebaugh, H.R., and J. Saltzman Chafetz, eds. 2002. *Religion Across Borders: Transnational Immigrant Networks*. Walnut Creek, CA: AltaMira Press.

Euben, R. 2006. *Journeys to the Other Shore*. Princeton, NJ: Princeton University Press.

Favell, A. 2001. *Philosophies of Integration: Immigration and the Idea of Citizenship in France and Britain*. New York: Palgrave, in association with Centre for Research in Ethnic Relations, University of Warwick.

Hagan, J. 2008. *Migration Miracles*. Cambridge, MA: Harvard University Press.

Hervieu-Léger, D. 2000. *Religion as a Chain of Memory*. Cambridge, UK: Polity Press.

Hüwelmeier, G., and K. Krause, eds. 2009. *Traveling Spirits: Migrants, Markets and Mobilities*. New York: Routledge Press.

Johnson, P. 2007. *Diaspora Conversions*. Berkeley and Los Angeles: University of California Press.

Khagram, S., and P. Levitt. 2007. *The Transnational Studies Reader*. New York: Routledge Press.

Kurien, P. 2007. *A Place at the Multicultural Table: The Development of American Hinduism*. New Brunswick, NJ: Rutgers University Press.

Lambek, M. 1993. *Knowledge and Practice in Mayotte: Local Discourses of Islam, Sorcery and Spirit Possession*. Toronto, Canada: University of Toronto Press.

Lechner, F., and J. Boli. 2005. *World Culture: Origins and Consequences*. New York: Wiley and Blackwell.

LeFebvre, H. 1991 [1974]. *The Production of Space*. Oxford: Basil Blackwell.

Legg, J. 2010. "Transnationalism and the Scalar Politics of Omperialism." Paper presented at the New Directions in Transnational Studies Conference, Tufts University, March 23, 2010.

Levitt, P., and N. Glick Schiller. 2004. "Transnational Perspectives on Migration: Conceptualizing Simultanity." *International Migration Review* 38: 1002–1040.

Levitt, P. 2007. *God Needs No Passport: Immigrants and the Changing American Landscape.* New York: The New Press.

Levitt, P., and S. Merry. 2009. "Culture in Motion: The Vernacularization of Women's Rights in India." *Global Networks* 9 (4): 441–461.

Mandeville, P. 2001. *Transnational Muslim Politics: Reimagining the Umma.* London: Routledge.

Marcus, G., and E. Saka. 2006. "Assemblage." *Theory, Culture, and Society* 23(2–3): 101–106.

Masuzawa, T. 2005. *The Invention of World Religions.* Chicago: University of Chicago Press.

McAdam, Doug, S. Tarrow, and C. Tilley. 2001. *Dynamics of Contention.* Cambridge: Cambridge University Press.

Meyer, B., and A. Moors, eds. 2006. *Religion, Media and the Public Sphere.* Bloomington and Indianapolis: Indiana University Press.

Mooney, M. 2009. *Faith Makes Us Live.* Berkeley and Los Angeles: University of California Press.

Oleszkiewicz-Peralba, M. 2007. *The Black Madonna in Latin America and Europe: Tradition and Transformation.* Albuquerque: University of New Mexico Press.

Ortiz, F. 1940. *Cuban Counterpoint: Tobacco and Sugar.* New York: A. A. Knopf.

Richman, K. 2005. *Migration and Voodoo.* Gainesville: University of Florida Press.

Rogers, E. M. 2003 [1962]. *Diffusion of Innovations.* 5th ed. New York: Free Press.

Roy, O. 2006. *Globalized Islam: The Search for a New Muslim Ummah.* Paris: CERI.

Simon, H. 1984. *Models of Bounded Rationality.* Cambridge, MA: MIT Press.

Sinha, V. 2005. *A New God in the Diaspora?* Copenhagen, Denmark: NIAS Press.

Starkloff, C. 2002. *A Theology of the In-Between.* Milwaukee, WI: Marquette University Press.

Strang, D., and S. A. Stroule. 1998. "Diffusion in Organizations and Social Movements: From Hybrid Corn to Poison Pills." *Annual Review of Sociology* 24: 265–290.

Tweed, T. 2006. *Crossing and Dwelling.* Cambridge, MA: Harvard University Press.

Vásquez, M. 2005. "Historicizing and Materializing the Study of Religion: The Contribution of Migration Studies." Pp. 219–242 in *Immigrant Faiths: Transforming Religious Life in America,* edited by K. I. Leonard et al. Lanham, MD: Altamira Press.

Wejnert, B. 2002. "Integrating Models of Diffusion of Innovations: A Conceptual Framework." *Annual Review of Sociology* 28: 297–326.

Werbner, P. 2005. *Pilgrims of Love.* Indiananopolis Indiana University Press.

Wimmer, A., and N. Glick-Schiller. 2003. "Methodological Nationalism, the Social Sciences, and the Study of Migration: An Essay in Historical Epistemology. *International Migration Review* (37):576–610.

Yang, F. and H. R. Ebaugh. 2001. "Transformations in New Immigrant Religions and Their Global Implications." *American Sociological Review* 66: 269–288.

PART TWO

EXEMPLARY CASES:
EMPIRICAL EXAMINATIONS

8

Difficult Dialogues:
The Technologies and
Limits of Reconciliation

DAWNE MOON

Projects known as *dialogue* or *reconciliation* build on the common ground between members of historically adversarial groups to help overcome vicious cycles of retaliation. They do so by helping people to *relate,* in Martin Buber's (1970 [1923]) sense of the term, to those they perceive as "Other," and thus to transform through interaction how they define themselves. While some posit that the deep interpersonal understanding that reconciliation fosters is actually central to most or all religious traditions, reconciliation projects can also facilitate a mode of non-institutional spirituality, thus inviting us to explore one of the sociology of religion's "edges" this volume seeks to re-center. In this mode, participants may see institutional religion as fallible and human but see reconciliation as bringing contact with something transcendent and universal—a truth long known in their particular religious heritage, and others as well, but forgotten in many institutions. Such reconciliation projects may be experienced as "spiritual" rather than "religious," transforming selves precisely by bringing together people who might normally be institutionally segregated. At the same time, instances such as those I discuss here can only arise when they are explicitly distanced from politics, and thus paradoxically they may reproduce the very hierarchies some participants wish to overcome.

While this research ventures outside of congregations and looks at movements that cross religious boundaries, its real force lies at a different edge of the sociology of religion by helping us to locate the ambiguous effects of the "spiritual"-feeling efforts at dialogue or reconciliation and the ways these efforts can both inspire and frustrate desires for political transformation and equality. It has been argued that lasting political transformation depends on changes in how people identify themselves as members of a group in relation to other groups (Todd 2005). Not all participants are drawn to reconciliation/dialogue because they want to effect political change, however; many simply are tired of political conflict and the violence it involves. For these dialogue efforts to be fully effective, they need parties from either side of a historical conflict, and this is why it resides at a point of tension. To elucidate this tension, I begin by exploring how these groups can be effective; I then explore the limitations of dialogue, focusing on the paradox that emerges when the groups in question are characterized by an imbalance of power or privilege.

I compare observations from two studies of religious and religio-ethnic communities. The more recent is a qualitative study of American Jews' understandings and experiences of anti-Semitism and how it relates to politics, particularly around the Israeli-Palestinian conflict.[1] I compare some of the findings from this study with findings that emerged in my earlier ethnographic research on debates about homosexuality within the United Methodist Church (Moon 2004, 2005a, 2005b). In the broader study of American Jews and their understandings and experiences of anti-Semitism, I used voice-recorded intensive interviews with a snowball sample of thirty-two respondents, ranging from one hour to three-and-one-half hours.[2] Here I focus on two closely related organizations that were a subset of this research, an international dialogue and peace organization called Listening with Love, and a loose network of local groups called Palestinian-Jewish Reconciliation Circles that meet monthly, usually in different members' homes, to share their stories and practice listening attentively to each other in order to overcome suspicion, defensiveness, and hatred.[3] Interviews were grounded in and supplemented with participant observation in workshops and public forums, including a two-weekend training session with Listening with Love and a four-day retreat organized by the core members of a Reconciliation Circle. I also draw here from interviews with members of an organization called Jews for a Just and Lasting Peace, which engages the conflict in the Middle East at the political level, but whose members echo some principles of dialogue. Because these concepts grew out of a study of Jews, I have so far interviewed a relatively small number of Palestinians. While Palestinian perspectives will be the focus of future research, critiques that have emerged in the current research have been sufficient to point to some of the tensions inherent in dialogue and reconciliation.

Discussions of the Israeli-Palestinian conflict are invariably controversial, especially when one discusses power. To be sure, there is a huge range of opinion among Israelis, Palestinians, and others who identify with either or both groups, and this chapter explores some of the middle ground. However, the basic conflict might be roughly summarized as follows. To many Palestinians, Israel is a militarily strong occupying government founded unjustly and illegitimately on Palestinian lands, and now funded largely by the United States, whose forces have and continue to dispossess and dehumanize people in the West Bank and

Gaza by taking away their livelihoods; cordoning them off into isolated areas
where water, food, and medical treatment are scarce and difficult to access; tear-
ing down people's homes at will; appropriating their land; imprisoning people
indefinitely without charge; and consigning people to refugee camps. While
Palestinian citizens of Israel are treated better and have some rights, they experience discrimination, for instance, in unrecognized Arab towns that receive
inferior government services. To many who identify with the state of Israel,
Palestinians are a group of Arabs, politically backed (but perhaps abandoned
when it comes to humanitarian support) by the entire Arab world, determined
to eradicate the Jewish presence in the Middle East and killing Israelis in random terrorist attacks to make their point.[4] During the Nazi Holocaust, which
was one among many large-scale attacks on Jews historically, many Jewish
refugees literally had nowhere to go; shiploads of people were turned away from
the United States and other countries and sent back to Europe to face whatever dangers they might. The state of Israel, born in the wake of World War II,
became both a symbol of redemption and a desperately needed refuge. That refuge is a tiny country, the size of New Jersey, subject to attacks, both violent
and discursive. Some have argued that the state of Israel is subject to a "new
anti-Semitism" that uses the same tropes as traditional anti-Semitism but on a
global scale: they see the Jewish state being verbally attacked and delegitimated,
held accountable for offenses that draw little international notice when committed by other countries, and scapegoated for offenses committed by many governments (Chesler 2003; Dershowitz 2003; Foxman 2003). Many of my Jewish
interview subjects identified to some extent with the state of Israel, and at the
same time, many were critical of its treatment of the Palestinians.

My interview pool was not representative of the American Jewish public.[5]
Most of the Jews I spoke to in this research came from families that ardently
supported the state of Israel, but many respondents experienced a feeling of
awakening when they learned of the Palestinian perspective. Some went to Israel
and saw the way Palestinian citizens of Israel, as well as residents of the West
Bank or Gaza, were treated. For others that feeling came when they saw a play
or read a book that prompted them to question the definition of the situation
with which they had grown up, and for others yet it was simple exhaustion with
all the violence that led them to look for a way to bring about peace or prompted
them to find out "the other side of the story." Some have come to the conclusion
after looking into the situation that Israel has the upper hand in relations with
the Palestinians in terms of wealth and military power. Rather than seeing ter-
rorism against Israel as one among many examples throughout world history of
anti-Semitism—the term David Norman Smith (1996) reserves for the mythol-
ogization of Jews as chimeric monsters (controllers of the world economy and
media, eaters of Christian children, and the like)—some see attacks on the
state of Israel as part of an ordinary conflict like other international conflicts

over ordinary issues including borders and resources.[6] Given that the Israeli-Palestinian conflict is one of the two main factors Cohen and Eisen (2000) see as contributing to a decline in the centrality of the state of Israel to American Jews, it is likely that these findings may become more relevant in the future.

Theorizing the Self in Interaction

This chapter explores the intersection of politics with the self, which sociological theories of the self have generally ignored. Mead (1967 [1934]) argued that to be a person means internalizing the generalized other's view of the "me," seeing myself as others see me. He argued that we only become persons in interaction, that each human organism (his term) is at once an individual "I" and an embodiment of his or her society, an object to himself or herself as much as to those around him or her. But for all his importance and influence in sociology, Mead's concept of the generalized other is a bit too simple.[7] The concepts of Martin Buber (1965, 1970 [1923]) help us to understand the transformation of the self that can occur in dialogue to produce intersubjectivity between parties who once viewed each other as Other, as outside their moral world. Like Pagis's study of Vipassana meditation (this volume), attention to Buber's analysis helps us to rethink Mead's conception of the self and its relationship to the generalized other.

For Buber, the inherent duality of humanity is not "the I and the me," as it is for Mead, but two kinds of "I." He distinguishes the "I" in an *I-it* experience—when the other is regarded as an object of contemplation, of discovery, even of affection—from the "I" in an intimate, *I-you* (*Ich-Du*, often translated as *I-thou*) *relationship*.[8] For Buber, a relationship with the intimate you occurs when for each person the other is "infinitely there," touching the core of the self. It may sound a bit mystical, but as a sociologist, Buber insisted that the communion between souls that can happen when they relate in what he calls *dialogue* is a real occurrence, much as the communion people experience in collective effervescence is a concrete, empirical reality in Durkheim's (1995 [1912]) theorization. As Buber explains in his 1929 essay "Dialogue,"[9] to engage in dialogue is to open oneself to being touched at the core, stepping out of the "armor" we wear in everyday life. For Buber, when someone "says" something to me, in a song, a sermon, a lecture, or a conversation, for instance, he or she touches me at the core. *To be attentive* is Buber's term for being open to such a connection.

Buber is careful to point out that *I-it* interactions are essential, and not necessarily negative; asking a professor to explain a concept, for instance, or asking for directions or medical advice is essential to functioning in the world, but a problem emerges when this kind of interaction is mistaken for relating. For Buber, the *I* of the *I-it* experience is the ego, who "occupies himself with his My: my manner, my race, my works, my genius," while the *I* of the *I-you* relationship is the person, who is open to "infinite conversation" (1970 [1923], 114). He remarks:

> Egos appear by setting themselves apart from other egos.
>
> Persons appear by entering into relation to other persons.
>
> One is the spiritual form of natural differentiation, the other that of natural association.
>
> The purpose of setting oneself apart is to experience and use . . . .
>
> The purpose of relation is the relation itself—touching the You. (1970 [1923], 112–113)

For Buber, *relating* to another person transforms the self; its lack of instrumentality and its mutual understanding resonate with Habermas's concept of communicative rationality. We have all probably had such moments, though like affect, they are difficult to know in another or to describe in any way resembling "objectivity."

Buber distinguishes true relating from imitations. He distinguishes "genuine dialogue" from "technical dialogue," which is solely concerned with gaining objective understanding, and "monologue disguised as dialogue," in which "two or more men, meeting in space, speak each with himself in strangely tortuous and circuitous ways and yet imagine they have escaped the torment of being thrown back on their own resources" (a description that evokes graduate seminars a bit more than any of us might like; 1965, 19). Under this heading, he includes *debate,* in which "in the speaking are so pointed that they may strike home in the sharpest way, and moreover without the men that are spoken to being regarded in anyway present as persons"; *conversation,* marked "solely by the desire to have one's own self-reliance confirmed by marking the impression that is made"; and other facsimiles of dialogue that separate people rather than connect them (1965, 19–20). These distinctions acknowledge that genuine dialogue can be difficult to achieve, especially when egos intervene. I suggest that egos are not the only thing that can intervene; hierarchies of authority can prevent relating, even as relating can disrupt hierarchy.

The dialogue groups I observed work by getting people into a room together with those they view as opponents and keeping them all coming back. Such processes thus depend on participants not becoming too alienated or threatened, even if the legitimacy of their tacit authority is challenged. Since discussions of politics can easily degenerate from *debate* into shouting matches that could drain participants of energy for no reward, dialogue groups walk a fine line. As Amanda Udis-Kessler (2008) demonstrates in her study of the United Methodist General Conference of 2000, when opponents convene to make policy decisions without the transformation of consciousness that comes from relating to each other in Buber's sense, the interaction can feel like a war between groups from utterly different moral worlds (see also Hunter 1992). Thus, dialogue groups endeavor to avoid politics, focusing on giving each participant the time and space to "tell their story," speaking "from their hearts." In doing so, they give participants the opportunity to humanize each other, to see each other as members of the same moral community (Baumann 1989; Fein 1979; Tavuchis 1991). Broadening the moral community changes the "generalized other" one internalizes, and thus changes the self by internalizing the gaze of, rather than repudiating, those once deemed anathema.

Relating Versus Knowing One

Buber's distinction between relating and experiencing helps us to understand a puzzle that emerged in my earlier research on debates about homosexuality in the United Methodist Church, or UMC. I would ask my interview respondents how they had come to their current views. Those who believed that homosexuality was sinful cited a range of things: the Bible, their comfort about their convictions (which, as one woman remarked, God would surely disturb were she on the wrong track), their knowledge that God loved order and that homosexuality flouted it. In contrast, I was struck by pro-gay church members' recurring accounts of gay people close to them: a brother who had come out recently; a gay friend, relative, or child; a speaker who expressed pain at being shut out of the church. In spite of the mainstream lesbian, gay, bisexual, and transgender (LGBT) movement's strategy of "coming out," encouraging every LGBT person to make her or his sexual orientation or gender identity known to friends, coworkers, neighbors, and everyone else, it seemed a facile truism that "knowing one" made all the difference. After all, plenty of members of the congregations I studied also knew gay men or lesbians and still believed homosexuality to be sinful—in their view, wanting to be nice to gay men and lesbians at the expense of upholding the word of God was understandable, but sinful, and would condemn to hell those one should be helping to find salvation. Similarly, in Udis-Kessler's study, pro-gay "inclusionists" chanted slogans such as "See our people" and "Know your people" (2008, 64) and tried to encourage delegates to get to know LGBT participants, but neither strategy moved those who believed that knowing gay people was beside the fact that homosexuality was sinful. Again, the assumption that "knowing one" was sufficient to change minds led pro-gay members to make an argument that seemed irrelevant to their opponents.

When my research moved into the arena of American Jewish understandings of anti-Semitism and its relationship to Middle East politics, I finally understood what I had been seeing. Again, the theme of "knowing one" came back. For instance, Julia, a 57-year-old Jewish environmental activist and art-ist, told me about how reading Israeli geographer Meron Benvenisti's (2002) *Sacred Landscape* opened her eyes to the Palestinians' experience of Israel, a country she had loved since her childhood. She remarked:

> And you know it's a great sadness to me, one of the first things I'll often say to a Jewish person if they have a lot of, you know, what I would say are misperceptions, I would say, "Have you, do you have any Palestinian friends? Do you even know any Palestinians?" And almost across the board, no. They might have met a Palestinian shopkeeper. They never exchanged stories. After I read that book I went around and I would meet Palestinians in many places, there are lots of them here and as soon as they might say where they were from, Ramallah or Hebron or somewhere, I would say, "My name is Julia, I'm Jewish, I'm really sorry." And instantly, every one of them, from old, grizzled men to young girls, all, just filled with the anger of the Palestinian cause, would embrace me. Every one of them would open their heart immediately, just by my saying that, just saying, "I understand what happened to your people, and I'm sorry." And one couple of brothers in Taos, New Mexico, they brought out the Qur'an and showed me where Muhammad says, "See, he says we're supposed to all be like broth-ers, Christian, Jew, and Muslims across the board." Just saying I'm a Jewish person and I'm sorry for what happened to them. I couldn't help it. I just felt so terrible.[10]

Nicholas Tavuchis (1991) argues that apology is an effort to reestablish mem-bership in one's moral community when one has violated its norms, saying:

> [A]pology expresses itself as the exigency of a painful re-membering, lit-erally of being mindful again of what we were and had as members and, at the same time, what we have jeopardized or lost by virtue of our offen-sive speech or action. And it is only by *personally* acknowledging ultimate responsibility, expressing genuine sorrow and regret…that the offender simultaneously recalls and is re-called to that which binds. (1991, 8)

In Julia's case, the apology is to people who are often seen as belonging to a dif-ferent moral community; Julia's apology is in effect a claim that she and those to whom she is apologizing *do* belong to the same moral community, a claim affirmed in the New Mexico men's invocation of the Qur'an. It is not simply "knowing one" that makes the difference; *relating,* in Buber's sense, implies see-ing another as part of one's moral community, or as Habermas might say, as part of one's lifeworld.

Julia described a trip she had taken to Israel with Listening with Love (LWL), an international organization that seeks to foster relating between members of historically opposed groups. The organization offers training and practice sessions to teach antagonists to hear and understand each other so they may move beyond the cycle of mutual suspicion, hatred, and defensiveness. Listening with Love posits that human beings are all linked by a core, fundamental "essence" of "values that we all share," including love, safety, compassion, beauty, courage, creativity, freedom, friendship, generosity, joy, truth, trust, and the like, and its organizers facilitate dialogue between Jews and Arabs, Jews and Germans, and other historically antagonistic groups. The organization also offers training sessions so that people may learn their techniques and apply them in their daily lives. At the training session I attended, facilitators presented their model: each human being has a *core*, which has been wounded by life's disappointments, injuries, injustices, and attacks. *Defenses*, or what Buber (1965, 10–11) calls "armor," have grown to protect those wounds and the vulnerable core, but they can be counterproductive as they often prevent people from relating to each other, or in LWL's terms, from seeing each other's "true self." The organization teaches that the extreme of defenses arguing back and forth at each other is war, but when people can open themselves to each other, telling their stories and being heard, then peace is possible.

The process thus resembles the evangelical Protestant process of racial reconciliation that Emerson and Smith (2000) discuss. In their account, which summarizes Yancey's (1998) analysis, reconciliation as it was defined by the early founders of the movement takes place in four steps: (1) developing primary relationships across racial lines, (2) recognizing social structures of inequality, (3) whites' repenting "of their personal, historical, and social sins," and (4) African Americans' willingness to forgive, individually and corporately, when asked, repenting of anger and whatever hatred they hold toward whites and the system (see Emerson and Smith 2000, 54–55). As Emerson and Smith found, however, the recognition of social structural imbalance implicit in the model brought a political element into reconciliation that cohered in no way with white evangelicals' worldview and thus found resistance. Efforts at reconciliation without acknowledgement of social structural hierarchies could result in blacks feeling that their white counterparts were making a shallow effort at best. Emerson and Smith describe the beginnings of reconciliation theology in the late 1960s and early 1970s, saying:

> Some of the white elite evangelicals attempted reconciliation, but incompletely. The problem with whites' conception of reconciliation, many claimed, was that they did not seek true justice—that is, justice both individually and collectively. Without this component,

reconciliation was cheap, artificial, and mere words. It was rather like a big brother shoving his little brother to the ground, apologizing, and then shoving him to the ground again. (2000, 58)

Later, I will explore similar political tensions in the dialogue/reconciliation movements I discuss here, but first it is important to acknowledge that even when the process is incomplete, it can have some of its desired effects. First, dialogue and reconciliation processes can indeed help to humanize adversaries, which may be no small feat. At a retreat organized by the Palestinian-Jewish Reconciliation Circle, a Palestinian-American woman I estimated to be in her thirties who was active in the movement spoke of having been raised on stories of what "the Jews" did to her family in 1948—taking their homes, making them into refugees. She felt she was raised to hate, but she didn't want to raise her own children that way, so the Reconciliation Circle offered her the opportunity to overcome that legacy without having to forget the past. Others, who had never had the opportunity to talk to someone from the other side of the Israeli-Palestinian conflict, became friends with them and felt hope that peace was actually possible. At a press conference after the event, an Israeli woman whose son was serving in the Israeli army spoke of having met a 16-year-old exchange student to the United States from Iraq:

> He said, "Don't hate me, but growing up, my parents taught me that we have to hate you, that you are awful people." After a half hour of wonderful dialogue, he said, "I'm sorry I feel this way; you are actually sweet." We greeted each other every morning with a smile and a kiss; now I'm going home to tell my son that peace is possible. [Reconstructed in notes]

While simply learning that adversaries are human might seem so simple as to be banal, it can actually be profoundly terrifying, troubling one's worldview and pre-existing relationships. Ken, a 69-year-old retired pediatrician and the organizer of a Reconciliation Circle, remarked on the "great courage" it can take to participate, mostly because of the fear of what one's "own people" would say. He commented:

> We're talking about fear. Fear, part of it is fear not only of the Other, but also of your own people.... You're seen as a traitor, you're seen as naïve, you're seen as not intelligent, which is a terrible thing in the Jewish community. You're seen as on the Left. Oh my goodness. It takes great courage to move out to the Other. You take flak from your own people, usually.

To illustrate this difficulty, Ken told me about an incident with a local newspaper:

> The most powerful criticism dynamic that I have had is, a couple of years ago, in the local Jewish newspaper, there was exaggerated demonization of the Palestinian people, the Palestinian schools, and the Palestinian textbooks. And I am familiar with the university-based research about those things. And this article was hateful. And there was a photograph of like a 3-year-old Palestinian with a Kalashnikov, semiautomatic rifle that somebody took somewhere... [a]nd the point was, "They're teaching all their children to kill all the Jews." And I just couldn't [let that go], so I wrote an OpEd, an opinion-editorial, and I simply quoted the Israeli academicians and their findings of the Palestinian textbooks, and schools.... I just quoted academics, but [people in the area] projected the worst things onto [my wife] and me, and onto the Reconciliation Circle. They took out ads, actually, in the newspaper.... And, they just called us all the names, you know: naïve, traitors, um, Arab-sympathizers....

In his comments, he demonstrated the effectiveness of the dialogue techniques he had honed in the Reconciliation Circle, saying:

> And you know what I did? I phoned every one of them. And you know what? The ads disappeared, in two weeks the letters were over, and I would say I'm still in relationship with the people who wrote them. I phoned them and I really listened to them. I asked them what their stories were, I got into their frame of reference. They felt heard. I felt understood. I told them what my motive was. It wasn't done from a distance of blaming or fist-[shaking] across a campus green.

In addition to humanizing the Other, Ken reveals how such processes can impart skills for de-escalating conflicts, as well as building relationships with past adversaries.

Habermas's distinction between the formal world and the lifeworld is instructive. The lifeworld is what constitutes mutual understanding, while formal world concepts constitute a reference system about which mutual understanding is possible (1981, 126). The lifeworld is the realm of the taken-for-granted and, in Buber's terms, of the real relationships that shape us at the core, while the formal system is a realm of solely *I-it* interactions. To problematize the lifeworld is to destabilize a person's whole worldview and problematize the core of the person, as happens when people observe a reality that does not conform to their symbolic imaginary: when people from either side realize that the Israeli-Palestinian conflict is not the battle between good and evil they may have assumed it to be, or when they realize homosexuality is not actually the derangement or evil it symbolizes in heterosexist common sense.

Dialogue humanizes the Other, transforming the self in the process. When dialogue works best, participants come to see each other not as representatives of evil forces that have been out to destroy them, but "as human beings"; in other words, like apology in Tavuchis's formulation, dialogue allows people to see each other as members of the same moral community. Even people who have hurt and killed others, such as Combatants for Peace (the real name of an organization of former Israeli soldiers and Palestinian fighters), can come together, admit to the harm they have caused others, and explain why it seemed justified at the time, as well as how they have since come to see otherwise. People who seemed to occupy the formal world, the world of objects—violent, oppressive, frightening, selfish, impure, chaotic—enter into the lifeworld, the realm where mutual understanding is possible, the realm of *relating*. Regarding the Israeli-Palestinian conflict, dialogue participants come to see people who "love peace" as part of the "us," while they see those who seem to prefer war— governments, war profiteers, the hateful—as the redefined outsiders. They do so at some risk, however—they risk the security of their old view for the unknown. In Ken's words, they risk alienating their "own people"; they stand to forego a relatively popular position of "we're good, they're evil" for a rarer one, and most frighteningly for detractors, they risk making themselves open and vulnerable to people who could exploit their weaknesses.

When Jewish people such as Ken and Julia *related* to Arabs and Arab Americans, and when Arabs related to Jews, they regarded the Other as part of their moral community, and it was simply implausible that an entire people could be inherently violent, less loving, or less deserving of a happy life. Similarly, *relating* to someone who was gay or lesbian, in my earlier research, made the stigmatization of gays and lesbians seem preposterous, dangerous, and profoundly unfair. When respondents, including some members of the conservative congregation I studied, *related* to gay men or lesbians, it became implausible to them that God could find gay intimacy more sinful than heterosexual intimacy or find gay people to be less capable than heterosexuals of doing God's work. The distinction between knowing and relating helps to explain why pro-gay strategies fail to transform those who believe homosexuality is sinful—*relating* emerges organically; like collective effervescence, it cannot be simply willed into existence among the unwilling.

The Politics of Dialogue

To introduce the concept of dialogue, Buber tells a story about a meeting he attended in 1914, where someone raised an objection to too many Jews being nominated to help form an international organization. Sensing anti-Semitism on the part of the objector, Buber raised his own objection. He writes:

> I no longer know how from that I came to speak of Jesus and to say that we Jews knew him from within, in the impulses and stirrings of his Jewish being, in a way that remains inaccessible to the peoples submissive to him. "In a way that remains inaccessible to you"—so I directly addressed the former clergyman. He stood up, I too stood, we looked into the heart of one another's eyes. "It is gone," he said, and before everyone we gave each other the kiss of brotherhood.... In this transformation dialogue was fulfilled. Opinions were gone, in a bodily way the factual took place. (1965, 5–6)

In Buber's account, speaking from his heart to someone open to him transformed the man, his objection, and their relationship. But what if the Christian man had *not* been open to Buber's words? What if he felt a personal stake in maintaining his authority as a Christian to decide how many Jews should be permitted into their group?

What those who called Ken a traitor may have sensed was that in addition to humanizing the other and teaching skills for de-escalating conflict, dialogue can inspire people to learn about power dynamics they hadn't known about, a step Yancey sees as crucial to early reconciliation theologians' process. For instance, Julia, who had gone on the trip to Israel with LWL, remarked:

> One reason I went on this trip is that I felt that so many Jews didn't have the full story. That we had been given a lot of information that didn't allow us to see and understand the humanity of the other side and their suffering.... I wanted to go and with my own eyes and ears come back with the stories that I could then bring back to Jews. And part of me felt like, "Well, Israel doesn't really need the American Jews," but it turns out so much money is coming from American Jews that's going into terrible projects, that are making things worse, that Israel desperately needs an enlightened American Jewish public. In fact, the American Jewish [public] is more pro-Zionist than the Israelis by and large. Because we're blinder, because we're not living there and not seeing and understanding the complexity, the great complexity, the chaos and confusion and the suffering on all sides.

Similarly, 42-year-old Lisa belonged to Jews for a Just and Lasting Peace (JJLP), an organization that seeks to work in solidarity with the Palestinians.

Having grown up with a grandfather she admired and saw as a model of Jewish ethics, she had always understood that being Jewish meant both fighting racism and supporting the state of Israel. She experienced a moral crisis upon her first visit to Israel and Gaza when she was in her twenties, having seen Israelis treat Palestinians in ways she could only describe as profoundly racist. She told me of the difficulties she had with her father over the Israeli-Palestinian conflict, given their family's intense commitment to Zionism. Lisa remarked:

> [My partner] is very close to my dad, and she said, "The thing about your dad that's so funny, is that if he were traveling and met a Palestinian family over dinner he would fall in love with them, and he'd be the first person sitting there crying, listening to their story. He would so, on a heart level, connect to them." And so for people like that, which is most of us really, that's an important thing that he has to experience, to get to break through this ignor—you know, naïveté.

For Lisa and others, as for the reconciliation theologians Yancey discusses, humanizing the other was a tremendous first step, but insufficient. When I told Lisa that some of her comments resembled those of members of the Reconciliation Circle, she remarked:

> I haven't done [Reconciliation Circle work], but the critique is there's no political analysis. And what I'm talking about, just trying to talk to people in your family, just trying to get through that, the barrier is emotional. But of course what you need to get it to is the actual political analysis of how we can make it better....I mean my hope would be, with the dialogue groups, [that] people realized we need some more, *real*, fair peace negotiations. That it's actionable, instead of, you know, a warm and fuzzy feeling. But yeah, I think all that has to happen.

This politicization speaks to a tension involved in dialogue or reconciliation. Talking about one's own feelings and experiences and telling one's personal story are the means; participants are urged to avoid talking about politics, precisely because "politics" involves polarization, needing to win, and armoring instead of opening oneself to the other. Yet deep beneath the surface, the ends seem to have a political aspect—once people learn to humanize each other, they may well come at some level to advocate political transformation. They may even come to understand their own people as benefiting from an imbalance of power and privilege. If they state that outright, then those who oppose such analyses will object to dialogue. But if they do not, they do a difficult dance, as 69-year-old JJLP member Diane remarked about her own experience at a previous Reconciliation Circle retreat:

> They put us in little talking groups, at different times, and I was with an Israeli Jew and an Israeli Palestinian, who lived neighboring towns, and who had just put a niche in their fenced off area and some of the parents and some of the children were doing projects together, and being nice to each other. And you could see, they were both extremely nice men, and you could see how very fond they were of each other. The question [we were given to discuss] was something like, "What's causing this rift, or this conflict?" and they were very careful, you know, the Israeli Palestinian didn't say that what's causing this conflict is that we're being oppressed and persecuted, and I said, "It seems to me you can't have balance. You're talking about a mighty military power and a basically unarmed people trying to hold on." And so that, I find that troublesome. That *that* truth has to somehow be managed, within a dialogue. But on the other hand, there were some profound connections made. And it's, you know, I have read that Palestinians in the territories [of the West Bank and Gaza] only see Jews with guns, pushing them around, and Israelis only see Palestinians in suicidal bomb gear. So they don't know each other. They never see each other. So, I have mixed feelings about it, but it was an amazing experience.

A story from my field notes taken at a later Reconciliation Circle retreat helps to illustrate the complications of this kind of organized "relating." The event was the fourth annual retreat of this sort, hosted at a Jewish summer camp, but it was a much larger affair than it had been in years past, which presented some logistical problems for the organizers. With roughly 200 people in attendance, only a quarter were Arab or Arab American. The group was broken into groups of four for the first workshop of the day to allow each group member to speak uninterrupted for a minute about his or her feelings about each of a number of emotionally—and politically—loaded terms, including "right of return," "suicide bomber," and "Jerusalem," but many groups had no Arabs, mine included. Dora, a Canadian Jewish woman who was approximately 45 years old, and Orit, a 17-year-old Israeli woman, both expressed disappointment that our group had no Arabs. "I wanted to talk to some Arabs," Dora commented, "I wanted to hear their perspective." While Buber might see such claims as verging on *I-it*, objectifying experiences, the women's reactions were understandable. People invested a good deal of time and money, and traveled great distances, to come to this event, and they hoped to learn something new from it—to relate to Arabs. As it became clear to the organizers that some groups were without Arabs, the events were quickly reorganized. For the next session, our group was merged with a group that included Ali, a 30-ish Palestinian high school teacher from Jerusalem, and May, a Palestinian American woman who was about 45 years old whose father had helped organize the event. Ali started the discussion off, asking how our group's morning discussion had gone.

> "It wasn't that interesting," said Dora, "We all pretty much agreed on things."
>
> "Oh," challenged Ali, "so you all agreed that the Palestinian right of return would be a bad thing!"
>
> "Well, I just don't know what would happen to us, to Israelis, to Jews," said Orit. "What would happen?"
>
> "No one ever thought to ask what would happen to the Palestinians when the state of Israel was created on our land. Why should anybody ask what will happen to Israeli Jews now?"
>
> "But it's my home," Orit replied. "Where would we go?"
>
> "It was the Palestinians' home before. No one asked where we would go."[11]

The conversation continued in that vein with Ali at the center and members of the group taking turns asking him a question or presenting an alternative viewpoint, to which he would then respond. Facilitators circulated among the groups and would say things like, "Try not to talk about politics. Just focus on your feelings," as they walked by ours. At the time, I felt annoyed by the whole exercise. I was annoyed with Ali for assuming he knew what I thought, without giving me or anyone else a chance to actually speak his or her mind. I was annoyed that he had set the terms of the discussion. I was annoyed at the way he seemed to steamroll over a 17-year-old. As I reflected on the experience that afternoon, I thought about it another way: here was a Palestinian man visiting from West Jerusalem, coming to a Jewish camp, in the numerical minority, with Jewish prayers painted in brightly colored signs on the walls, in the United States, a major source of monetary and military support for the state of Israel. Everyone ostensibly came to work for peace, but what leads to peace? Talking about your feelings? Or asking questions about equality and what one sees as preventing it? Would it even be possible for him to talk about how he felt about the Palestinian right of return without talking about "politics"? Would such a discussion feel like anything more than "cheap, artificial, and mere words" (Emerson and Smith 2000, 58)?

Our discussion that afternoon felt like a failure, by the organizers' standards, because no one gave voice to any breakthroughs. No one embraced and said, "Now I know peace is possible." It felt pointless; it enacted Buber's description of *debate* with remarks "so pointed that they may strike home in the sharpest way, and moreover without the [people] that are spoken to being regarded in any way present as persons" (1965, 19). No one from our group was asked to speak at the concluding press conference. We were not a testament to the healing and transformative power of dialogue. Whenever I tried to find Ali later to see if he might sit down with me for an interview, he seemed to always miss my gaze and walk on. This is the paradox: as Habermas describes, formal world systems—politics—are entirely outside the lifeworld, although for Ali it might have been impossible to discuss his feelings without discussing the inescapable political realities into which he was born. Like Lisa, he might have found it more pressing to discuss actionable, concrete realities rather than the feelings of those who seemed to him to control his world with laws and military power. To open himself to dialogue in the way Buber describes could have been unthinkable in this context.

An anecdote from my previous fieldwork might help to shed light on Ali's situation. Because so many pro-gay members of religious communities come to their views through relating—to children, friends, siblings, and the like— pro-gay movements often rely on the strategy of asking gay men or lesbians to speak informally to a group of interested members, a class, or a discussion group. But given that putative heterosexuals bear no stigma for their orientation and are often in the numerical majority that makes policy, such events can feel like an audition—either for oneself or on behalf of the entire stigmatized group—for full entry into the moral community, particularly if saying the wrong thing can affect the decisions of those with the authority to make policy. While this strategy may introduce the issues to people and inspire further thought and inquiry, I have neither seen nor heard of it changing many minds, particularly in cases where people are already firm in their convictions. Such forums seem more often to produce what Buber would call *technical dialogues* or *monologues disguised as dialogue*.

Midway through my research in United Methodist congregations, Jenny, a friend and key informant, invited me to join her at her parents' church where she had been invited to speak as a lesbian about what inclusion in the church meant to her. We had discussed my analysis that gay men and lesbians in my study were repeatedly cast as being pained and how "gay pain" became the reason for many members to welcome them into the church, and she was determined not to fall into that pattern; she was not in pain, and she believed there were compelling theological reasons for the church to welcome LGBT people. But the structure of the event itself *caused* a sort of pain, or at least a demonstration of pain. As the event began about twenty people sat in a circle and Jenny was introduced. She had prepared remarks around the theme that human beings cannot always know God's will, but that God can surprise people, calling us to do things that go against societal expectations. She began by reading scriptural stories of prophets and disciples being called to drop everything they knew in life and heed God's surprising call. But before she had completed her first sentence, she was in tears. She struggled to get her message out while crying, and soon several others, myself included, were crying as well and someone had to be dispatched to find a box of tissues. The very question at stake, the purpose for the gathering, was the question she had hoped to take as already answered: whether she had equal access to God's revelation, whether she was a full person in the eyes of God and the church, whether the stigma she bore resulted from social conventions or timeless truth. It is difficult for a community discussion of who belongs in the community—of who can speak for the community and who can only, at its discretion, speak *to* it—to produce conditions of full equality within that community since the question itself prefigures some members' exclusion.

In Udis-Kessler's (2008) research, inclusionists thought that if conservatives just "knew our people," they would change their minds; in the inclusionists' lifeworld, God makes some people gay, and same-sex love and intimacy teach people more about God's love. This knowledge comes from the *relating* that happens in the lifeworld, so their knowledge cannot be explained to their opponents in any satisfactorily objective-seeming terms. Those who believe homosexuality is sinful, on the other hand, see homosexuality and all it symbolizes to them (selfishness, carnality, politics, chaos, and the like; see Moon 2004) as firmly entrenched in the formal world—what evangelicals consider the fallen, human world. They cannot enter intersubjectivity with inclusionists because their prior understanding of homosexuality and what it symbolizes does not permit entrance into the realm of relating into their moral community. The symbolic violence LGBT people and their supporters experience in Udis-Kessler's study is the violence of being forcibly shut out of their lifeworld, their church, by those with the authority to do so—in terms of votes and tradition. In my own research (2004, 2005a), this pain became the admission price for the lifeworld to which they thought they had belonged all along: for gay and lesbian members to be seen as truly belonging in the church, they must perform pain; they cannot present themselves as whole persons simply seeking what any church member seeks in church. But to be forced to represent only one aspect of one's personhood—and a wounded aspect at that—is not relating; one's "whole self" is not quite welcome, but only the broken parts that fit within a particular, strategic narrative. That scenario becomes another of what Buber calls "faceless specters of dialogue" (1965, 20), in which one cannot relate or be related to because parts of oneself are silenced and one must take care to appear a certain way.

Returning to Ali at the retreat, to what extent does dialogue feel like "auditioning" for membership in the moral community of people who have a greater say than oneself over policies and the distribution of resources? As Diane asks, to what extent do some people's personal stories seem too "political" for

dialogue, and what happens to dialogue when aspects of some personal stories are unspeakable? The goal of the weekend was to foster relating, and it
succeeded in many cases. To relate to people previously outside one's lifeworld
context involves some kind of feeling of sacrifice, for everyone involved. But
to what extent might such an event feel to Palestinians the way it can feel for
a gay person to be asked to speak to a group of people who may or may not
believe that he or she is a living symbol of sin, fallenness, and carnality? To
what extent might such a conversation feel like an audition to be recognized as
fully human or a much-needed opportunity to convince those who might have
more political leverage that there is something profoundly unfair happening
that needs to be changed?

On a hike after the incident at the retreat, I spent some time getting to
know a friendly man who was around 50 years old, a Jewish man named Saul.
He expressed an interest in political discussions, so I asked him whether
he thought there was anything odd about trying to talk about something
like the Palestinian right of return without talking about politics. He gave it
some thought and got back to me later, saying:

> I was thinking about what you said and I had a conversation with a
> woman named Bobbie. She had a communication problem with a man
> that left her feeling misunderstood. They talked about it later and
> cleared it up. I think it's good that we leave politics aside and focus on
> just trying to *understand* each other. [Reconstructed in notes.]

He had a point, but after the event when I interviewed Jamil, a Palestinian
involved in a Reconciliation Circle, he hesitated to answer many questions
and repeatedly referred me instead to a local Palestinian advocacy group. I
left our two-hour interview with the distinct impression that as a spokesper-
son for reconciliation, he did not feel he could say anything verging on the
political.

The Paradox of Dialogue

As Buber argues about relating, Habermas argues that in communicative
action, people are transformed. He writes:

> Communicative action is not only a process of reaching understanding;
> in coming to an understanding about something in the world, actors
> are at the same time taking part in interactions through which they
> develop, confirm and renew their memberships in social groups and

their own identities. Communicative actions are not only processes of interpretation in which cultural knowledge is "tested against the world"; they are at the same time processes of social integration and of socialization. (1981, 139)

When a new grouping is formed, in the case of the Reconciliation Circle, or when the group's stated membership criteria are in flux, in the case of Protestant homosexuality debates, the collectivity and participants' personal self-concepts are redefined. But in cases like these that can be prefigured by tacit speech-rules about what can and cannot be said, particularly about power relations, these redefinitions are not complete, real though they may feel to those at the unacknowledged top of the hierarchy. These hierarchies, when unspoken, can be tacitly reproduced as well, particularly if there are double standards about who can tell his or her own story in his or her own way, whose story is legitimate, and what kinds of personal truths are too "political" to be uttered. In those cases, stigmatization is reproduced, even as those closer to the top of the hierarchy genuinely feel that they have transformed, given of themselves, or made themselves vulnerable in the name of reconciliation. The gag rule impedes those at the bottom from being fully expressive, from feeling understood, and perhaps from being transformed in the process. As Buber (1988 [1965]) posits, genuine dialogue is free from needing to *appear* a certain way to another. However, if people are allowed to "discuss politics," then the whole concept of dialogue could easily revert to the polarized conflict dialoguers commit to sacrificing and transcending. This is the paradox.

There are solutions to this paradox. One is to avoid dialogue altogether, ridiculing it as naively idealistic or banal or seeking to discredit its participants as traitors. On the other hand, some maintain that politics and relationship come together; they commit to solidarity and can hear political critiques of their own power and privilege without feeling personally attacked. Politicization can light a path forward. When genuine dialogue occurs, people feel transformed, spoken to, understood. But the line between genuine dialogue and the imitations Buber discusses is not always clear. When genuine dialogue happens, social hierarchies that were previously naturalized can come to seem profoundly arbitrary and unfair. But since dialogue cannot be objectively assessed, a semblance of it can renaturalize the hierarchies it fails to demystify. Still, dialogue and the relating that takes place in it are real phenomena that we need to consider when we think about hierarchies in communities and when we think about the relationship between social power and the self. Indeed, when we ignore it, we cannot understand the social change that happens, and does not happen, in communities bound by relationship.

Taking reconciliation/dialogue seriously calls us to consider the boundaries people draw between social convention and timeless truth, lines straddled by both institutional knowledge (religious and otherwise) and extra-institutional forms of knowledge (religious and otherwise). If sociologists consider only institutional religion in our studies of how people make their lives meaningful, we close our eyes to the fact that to be defined as "truth" one must define it—whatever one believes it to be—as transcendent. In that sense, religious and nonreligious contexts overlap considerably (and where a person feels at home depends on where one has found truth). Acknowledging that considerable overlap, we can see more clearly the profound ways in which those with more privilege to define the terms of dialogue can—as they try sincerely to express what feels deeply true to them—delegitimize others' truths, and silence the very people with whom they wish to reconcile.

Acknowledgment

I wish to thank Jonathan VanAntwerpen, Steve Warner, and the editors of this volume for helpful comments and feedback, and the respondents who gave me the gifts of patience and insight as they made this project possible.

Notes

1. As Gamson (1992) discusses, the naming of this conflict is itself highly controversial. Given that many of the Arabs most directly implicated in this struggle identify as Palestinian and are identified by other respondents as such, I use this term. I thus refer to the conflict as the Israeli-Palestinian conflict.
2. In addition, I conducted two focus groups involving another twenty-seven respondents.
3. To protect confidentiality, names and some identifying details of people and organizations have been changed.
4. Helpful summaries of the ideological and political tensions appear in Lerner (2003) and Ruether and Ruether (2002).
5. For a more representative study of American Jewish attitudes, see Cohen and Eisen (2000).
6. British legal scholar Anthony Julius has argued that the state of Israel's founding father Theodor Herzl envisioned that with their own state, Jews would have "ordinary enemies," fighting over ordinary things like borders and resources (Julius 2007; see Herzl 1988 [1896], chapter IV).
7. Habermas (1981) makes a similar argument but does not discuss Buber.
8. While *Ich-Du* is conventionally translated as *I-thou*, Kaufmann argues that this translation, with the archaic quality of "thou," fails to capture the familiarity of *Du*, the intimate you that a child would use with his or her parents or that intimate friends use, which is what Kaufmann argues that Buber intends.
9. Printed in Buber (1965).
10. Respondent quotations are from recorded interviews unless otherwise noted and have been edited for readability (for instance, by removing extraneous utterances such as "um" and "like").
11. These discussions were reconstructed in field notes.

References

Baumann, Zygmunt. 1989. *Modernity and the Holocaust.* Ithaca, NY: Cornell University Press.

Benvenisti, Meron. 2002. *Sacred Landscape: The Buried History of the Holy Land Since 1948.* Berkeley: University of California Press.

Buber, Martin. 1965. *Between Man and Man.* New York: Macmillan Publishing Co.

———. 1970 [1923]. *I and Thou,* translated by Walter Kaufmann. New York: Simon and Schuster.

———. 1988 [1965]. *Knowledge of Man.* New York: Harper and Row.

Chesler, Phyllis. 2003. *The New Anti-Semitism: The Current Crisis and What We Must Do About It.* San Francisco: Jossey-Bass.

Cohen, Steven M., and Arnold M. Eisen. 2000. *The Jew Within: Self, Family and Community in America.* Bloomington: Indiana University Press.

Dershowitz, Alan. 2003. *The Case for Israel.* Hoboken, NJ: John Wiley and Sons.

Durkheim, Emile. 1995 [1912]. *Elementary Forms of the Religious Life.* New York: Free Press.

Emerson, Michael O., and Christian Smith. 2000. *Divided by Faith: Evangelical Religion and the Problem of Race in America.* New York: Oxford University Press.

Fein, Helen. 1979. *Accounting for Genocide.* New York: Free Press.

Foxman, Abraham H. 2003. *Never Again? The Threat of the New Anti-Semitism.* San Francisco: Harper.

Gamson, William A. 1992. *Talking Politics.* New York: Cambridge University Press.

Habermas, Jürgen. 1981. *The Theory of Communicative Action, Vol. 2: Lifeworld and System: A Critique of Functionalist Reason.* Boston: Beacon Press.

Herzl, Theodor. 1988 [1896]. *The Jewish State.* New York: Scopus.

Hunter, James Davison. 1992. *Culture Wars: The Struggle to Define America.* Basic Books.

Julius, Anthony. 2007. "When Legitimate Dissent Crosses the Line." Keynote address given at Finding Our Voice: The Conference for Progressives Constructively Addressing Anti-Semitism, San Francisco, January 28.

Lerner, Michael. 2003. *Healing Israel/Palestine: A Path to Peace and Reconciliation.* Berkeley, CA: Tikkun Books.

Mead, George Herbert. 1967 [1934]. *Mind, Self, and Society from the Standpoint of a Social Behaviorist.* Chicago: University of Chicago Press.

Moon, Dawne. 2004. *God, Sex, and Politics: Homosexuality and Everyday Theologies.* Chicago: University of Chicago Press.

———. 2005a. "Emotion Language and Social Power: Homosexuality and Narratives of Pain in Church." *Qualitative Sociology* 28(4): 325–347.

———. 2005b. "Discourse, Interaction, and the Making of Selves in the US Protestant Dispute over Homosexuality." *Theory and Society* 34: 551–577.

Ruether, Rosemary Radford, and Herman J. Ruether. 2002. *The Wrath of Jonah: The Crisis of Religious Nationalism in the Israeli-Palestinian Conflict.* 2nd ed. Minneapolis, MN: Fortress Press.

Smith, David Norman. 1996. "The Social Construction of Enemies: Jews and the Representation of Evil." *Sociological Theory* 14(3): 203–240.

Tavuchis, Nicholas. 1991. *Mea Culpa: A Sociology of Apology and Reconciliation.* Stanford, CA: Stanford University Press.

Todd, Jennifer. 2005. "Social Transformation, Collective Categories, and Identity Change." *Theory and Society* 34: 429–463.

Udis-Kessler, Amanda. 2008. *Queer Inclusion in the United Methodist Church.* New York: Routledge.

Yancey, George. 1998. "Reconciliation Theology: Results of a Multiracial Evangelical Community." Paper presented at the Color Lines of the Twenty-First Century Conference, Chicago; cited in Emerson, Michael O., and Christian Smith. 2000. *Divided by Faith: Evangelical Religion and the Problem of Race in America.* New York: Oxford University Press, 54–55.

9

Negotiating Religious Differences in Secular Organizations: The Case of Hospital Chapels

WENDY CADGE

"Little remnants of past worlds." That is how a vice president at Simon Medical Center described the hospital's two chapels.[1] Built years ago when what is now a large academic medical center included hospitals of two different religious traditions, what was the Protestant chapel retains its original appearance down to the cross, stained glass windows, pews, organ, and denominational hymnals. Rarely used, these spaces are physically distant from the hubs of hospital activity.

Not far away, hospital staff and visitors flow into and out of an interfaith chapel off the lobby at Overbrook Hospital. Moved and renovated several times as the hospital grew and merged with others, this chapel includes twenty movable chairs, artificial plants, a piano, and no fixed religious symbols. A sign on one wall points toward Mecca for Muslims wishing to pray, and prayer rugs and texts from a range of religious traditions are on a shelf at the back of the room. Electric light enters the room through artistically rendered stained glass windows steeped in nature imagery, and no sounds are audible save the air moving through the building's heating and cooling systems. While few people attend the daily interfaith prayer services chaplains hold in this chapel, many more enter throughout the day to pray, sit quietly, or write a prayer in the hospital's prayer book.[2]

Sociologists who study religion frequently focus on the dynamics of religious congregations rather than asking how religion is present and negotiated outside of congregational settings. Most people in the United States spend more of their daily lives outside than inside of congregations, as well as in other organizations such as schools, workplaces, community centers, hospitals, and sports leagues. Many of these other organizations are formally secular, raising questions about how, if at all, these organizations accommodate people's religious and spiritual beliefs and practices.[3] Conflicts like a California hospital's struggles to accommodate Hmong patients or a Tyson poultry plant in Tennessee considering replacing the paid holiday of Labor Day with Id-al-Fitr to accommodate Muslim workers make the news or end up in courts, but little is known, absent these conflicts, about the everyday practices of secular organizations around religion and spirituality (Fadiman 1998; Greenhouse 2008a, 2008b).[4]

I build on the noncongregational edge and loosely illustrate what Paul Lichterman (this volume) describes as a pragmatic approach to how religious identities are articulated and performed by focusing on how one set of organizations that are not congregations—hospitals—respond to religion and spirituality in daily organizational practice. I describe what Nancy Ammerman calls the "social worlds" in large, mostly secular hospitals "in which religious ideas, practices, groups and experiences make an appearance" (Ammerman 2007a, 6). I view hospitals as strategic sites for capturing how the religious ideas and practices "in motion" that Peggy Levitt describes in this volume rest in a single location, revealing notions of religion, inclusivity, and diversity at play in the minds of the people regulating the space. This approach pushes scholars to see that religion is a property not just of individuals, organizations, and/or nation-states, but of the public spaces in each where religious ideas and practices collide and must be negotiated—not as a secondary, but as a fundamental component of what religion is. If we overlook these and other places where religion inserts itself in the interstices of seemingly secular spaces, we run the risk of overlooking crucial aspects of what religion is and the ways it is present, and perhaps tellingly patterned, in different social locations.

While I could focus on hospital policies, hospital chaplains, the work of hospital staff, or the experiences of patients and family members in this chapter—all of which may include religious and spiritual dimensions—I concentrate specifically on the physical spaces hospitals demarcate for religious or spiritual purposes in their buildings.[5] I consider the history of these spaces—usually called chapels or meditation rooms—and analyze their locations, physical appearances, and daily use.[6] I start with the assumption that contemporary religious negotiations take place in historically and demographically pluralistic contexts (Klassen and Bender 2010).[7] This assumption leads me to pay particular attention to what religion is in these spaces—how it is "inflected by specific social settings" in Paul Lichterman's words (this volume)—and how religious differences and diversities are welcomed, negotiated, or ignored. As Courtney Bender argues in an earlier chapter, the forms of religious pluralism that take shape in American public life and in sociological imaginations are not 'natural,' but rather are shaped in the interaction of specific secular and religious forms and interests. I shift familiar questions about hybridization and syncreticism from their usual focus on individuals and religious traditions to organizations,

broadening the question of what counts as religion and how particular symbols, ideas, or practices from different religious traditions come to rest in these
seemingly secular spaces.

Despite often being called interfaith, the actual appearance and use of hospital chapel spaces vary significantly. While some like those at Simon Medical
Center were built within particular religious traditions and remain so, others have been renovated—in light of increasing religious pluralism—as part
of efforts to make spaces more welcoming, flexible, and inclusive to a broader
range of religious people and practices. Such renovations typically include
removing fixed religious objects—both explicit symbols like crosses and
implicit symbols like pews—and introducing plants, nature imagery, and/or
abstract art and designs. Chapels built in the last twenty years were generally
designed to be what chaplains call "interfaith" from the start, including either
a range of religious symbols or, more commonly, none as chaplains and hospital
administrators strive to create spaces they think will be utilized by a range of
people, including those with no spiritual or religious background.

Looking at these developments over time, what is notable is the extent to
which religious symbols and objects have been removed or made flexible in
chapels so that the spaces, at least theoretically, can accommodate a range of
people and their practices.[8] Rather than multifaith spaces shared by people and
symbols from a range of religious and spiritual traditions, hospitals have more
often created what they call interfaith spaces focused on new symbols—of
nature and art—though sometimes continuing to reflect underlying Christian
templates and assumptions.[9] These templates likely reflect the assumptions
about religion held by the disproportionate number of (liberal) Protestant
chaplains who lead chaplaincy departments and make decisions about chapel spaces, and what Robert Wuthnow and Wade Clark Roof have described as
Americans' broader mix-and-match approach to spirituality and religion writ
large.[10] To the extent that the chapels analyzed here reflect those in a broader
set of hospitals or other secular organizations, they show religion existing in
the interstices of secular organizations as patterned by the (changing) norms
of the cultures in which they exist. Broader comparison with such spaces in
prisons, the military, or schools or with hospitals around the world would provide the analytic leverage needed to more systematically analyze how, as freeze
frames of religious negotiation in motion, they act and are acted on by their
surroundings.

In this case, these spaces point to a particular response to religious pluralism in American life that is less about recognizing and naming diverse religious
beliefs and practices, including none, and more about efforts to remove religious
symbols and create generic spaces that will accommodate people and not offend.
Perhaps this reflects Americans' comfort with mixing and matching different
religious ideas outside the boxes of their religious organizations, or perhaps it

suggests an approach to religion that tries to emphasize similarities across differ-ent traditions rather than pointing out differences in how meanings are assem-bled. Regardless, it shows what is overlooked in approaches to religion that either do not look beyond congregations or look at religion in public life so amorphously as to miss the ways religious pluralism is in play in secular organizations.

Brief Background

Relatively little is known about chapels, prayer, or meditation spaces in con-temporary American hospitals or secular organizations more generally.[11] The term *chapel* was first used in the twelfth century and comes from the word *capella*, or "cloak." According to the etymology in the *Oxford English Dictionary*, the cloak of St. Martin "preserved by the Frankish kings as a sacred relic" was "borne before them in battle and used to give sanctity to oaths." The term was then "applied to the sanctuary in which this was preserved under the care of its *cappellani* or 'chaplains,' and thence generally to a sanctuary containing holy relics, attached to a palace, etc., and so to any private sanctuary or holy place, and finally to any apartment or building for orisons or worship, not being a church...." Initially consecrated and having an altar, the originally Christian term *chapel* has come to describe "a room or building for private worship in or attached to a palace, nobleman's house, castle, garrison, embassy, prison, monastery, college, school, or other institution" (Oxford English Dictionary 1989).[12]

A few historical studies describe specific university, military, and prison chapels in the United States, but none trace chapels historically or compare chapels within or across organizational sectors. In their research in the United Kingdom, sociologists James Beckford and Sophie Gilliat make some of these contemporary comparisons, describing the shrinkage of chapel spaces in UK prisons since the 1950s and movements toward multipurpose and religiously neutral spaces (Beckford and Gilliat 1998). In the United States, they explain, principles of nonestablishment do not allow tax dollars to be used to build separate religious facilities in federal or state prisons. Current policies stip-ulate that "the space assigned for group prayer and worship should be large enough for the congregation, functional and neutral in design" (Beckford and Gilliat 1998, 184). This neutrality implies that spaces should not contain per-manent symbols from one religious tradition that might be seen as an affront by others. While hospitals in the Veterans Health Administration in the United States have similar guidelines about religiously neutral chapel spaces, private hospitals generally do not.

Little is known about the history of chapels in American hospitals. Early hospitals including Pennsylvania Hospital, New York Hospital, and

Massachusetts General Hospital do not appear to have had chapels. New Haven Hospital utilized Gifford Chapel, which temporarily housed some of the 200 soldiers sick with typhoid sent to the hospital during the Spanish American War.[13] Hospitals started by religious groups in the nineteenth and twentieth centuries were probably more likely than secular hospitals to have chapels.[14] Reflecting the rise of religiously run hospitals, architect Edward Stevens wrote in his 1921 *The American Hospital of the Twentieth Century*, "as a large part of the smaller hospitals today are being maintained by one or another religious society, it very often follows that the provision for a chapel must be incorporated into the plans of the institution" (Stevens 1921, 89). Larger hospitals, Stevens noted, often had chapels set away from the main buildings clustered with laboratories, classrooms, rooms for autopsies, and the morgue. Some were built as mortuary chapels, structurally linking religion and death from the start. With time, Stephen Verderber and David Fine (2006) argue that chapel space was "downsized to a waiting room off a bleak corridor," though there is no systematic historical evidence of this transition or when it took place (p. 26).[15] Some of the hospitals described here may buck this trend, adding chapels, especially after hiring their first professional chaplains, between 1940 and the present.

In 1974, the American Hospital Association reported that of the 3,038 hospitals with chaplain services (43 percent of all hospitals), 98 percent provided some kind of worship space or office facility for chaplains. The survey reported that 55 percent had a chapel for use by all denominations, 19 percent had a chapel for use by one denomination, 22 percent had an additional prayer chapel or meditation room, and 13 percent had a prayer chapel or meditation room only (Kuby and Begole 1974). The American Hospital Association's *Manual on Hospital Chaplaincy* published in 1970 pointed to the importance of hospital chapels, describing "space for religious services for inpatients" as "one of the most important requirements in facilities for a chaplaincy program" (38). The space could be one or more chapels or a multipurpose room that would "demonstrate the hospital's appreciation for the various religious faiths" (39). While the religious affiliation of some hospitals would determine the chapel's design, the authors encouraged other hospitals to form interfaith committees with consultants from major religious groups in the area to, in their words, "help determine the symbols used in designing the furnishings" (39). They encouraged hospitals to put chapels in central locations accessible to inpatients and visitors alike and wrote of current "trends" in hospital chaplaincy that favored interfaith spaces, "with symbols and designs clearly representative of all faiths" (39). For example, "A reading center in the chapel may contain various kinds of devotional materials, various editions of the Bible, and some Jewish prayer books. . . ." (40). Little has been written about hospital chapels since the 1970s, with the exception of newspaper articles that describe hospitals' recent efforts to turn Christian chapels into interfaith spaces for prayer and meditation (Creager 2000).

One Set of Teaching Hospitals

To learn more about contemporary hospital chapels, I focus here on fifteen teaching hospitals in one state.[16] These hospitals range from large academic medical centers with more than 600 beds to small community hospitals with many fewer. While many—like hospitals nationally—have religious roots, only two currently have religious affiliations, both Catholic. The majority of patients treated in these hospitals are Catholic and Protestant, reflecting the demographics of the region. To learn about chapel spaces, I visited them and interviewed the director of chaplaincy at each hospital.[17]

All of these hospitals have one chapel and half have two. Hospitals with two chapels either merged like at Simon Medical Center and retained each chapel or built a second chapel or meditation space that is more interfaith than the first. One of the Catholic hospitals, for example, has a Catholic chapel just inside the main entrance. The chapel was named and dedicated by the local cardinal and includes all of the symbols common in a Catholic church. To accommodate non-Catholics, the hospital recently built an interfaith meditation chapel in another area, noting in information for visitors that "The purpose of the chapel is to offer patients, families, staff and visitors a quiet place for retreat and prayer." Similarly, another hospital with religious roots has a Protestant chapel with pews, lecterns, and other trappings of a Protestant church. They built an interfaith prayer room also in an effort to reach out to non-Protestants. Both the original and second chapels in these hospitals were built with financial support from donors—often hospital auxiliary groups—noted on plaques in the spaces.

While some of the chapels have formal names, usually connected to donors, the majority are simply called chapel or interfaith chapel. Four include the word prayer or meditation in their names. At Queens Hospital, the director of chaplaincy specifically decided not to name the chapel when it was first built twenty years ago despite financial support from several donors. Based on his time at the institution, he explained, "I realized how sensitive spiritual issues are . . . and how inclusive a chaplaincy department needs to be . . . not just from the chaplain's perspective but the entire institution's perspective." Believing that putting a name on any sacred space sends a "message that someone owns a piece of it," he decided against a name. He thought about not even calling it a chapel because the word might not be familiar for all. "We can't just say 'House of the Spirit,'" he concluded, though, and settled on chapel because the term "is pretty accepted in the culture."

This chapel and about half of those I learned about are located in hospital lobbies or other central areas. At the others, chaplaincy directors are trying to move chapels to such central locations. Describing the current chapel as "not very centrally located" and in an "awful space," one director spoke of trying to secure "a new space that's closer to the ED [emergency department] and close to the front [of the building] so it's more accessible." It is the directors of chaplaincy departments, who have historically been disproportionately Protestant, that negotiate the location for the chapel when needed and primarily tend to chapel spaces in consultation with hospital administrators.[18]

A Continuum

To better understand the appearance and use of chapel spaces, I describe several examples in more detail. I view these chapels as existing along a continuum—from those that were started and remain within particular religious traditions to those that were renovated to be interfaith, or that were founded as interfaith from the start. These spaces are not externally regulated. What is evident, therefore, is a very slow process of institutional isomorphism as ideas about the appropriateness of so-called interfaith spaces slowly circulate, probably more through the networks of hospital chaplains than hospital administrators who tend to work together on their designs.

Tradition Specific

Most of the hospitals that were started by religious groups continue to have tradition-specific chapels. These chapels look like Protestant churches, Catholic churches, or Jewish synagogues and do not house texts, symbols, or objects from other religious traditions. This was the case in the two Catholic hospitals. Both were dedicated by bishops or cardinals and are recognized as chapel spaces within their respective diocese. Materials about the chapel at St. Francis Hospital name the cardinal that consecrated the altar, the patronage of the space, and members of the hospital and local diocese who made its construction and consecration possible. Catholic symbols including a crucifix, statue of Mary, statues of other saints, and other items are in the space. Without knowing how they got there, visitors would not likely know they were in a hospital chapel rather than a local Catholic church. While one of these hospitals built a second interfaith chapel as described earlier, the other did not.

Renovated from Tradition Specific

Other chapels initially built in particular religious traditions—usually Christian—have been renovated to make space for a wider range of religious people, symbols, and/or practices. Many directors removed tradition-specific objects or made changes they believed would make the spaces more flexible. A chapel originally built as part of what was then a Protestant hospital was in the process of being renovated when I learned about it. Believing that the "pastoral" thing was to "share" the space, the current director explained, "they're going to leave the stained glass and the altar and everything else, but we're going to take out the hard pews and put in soft chair pews that lock together and change the carpeting and have it so it's moveable . . . so that it's a little more comfortable for a larger group." Rather than aiming to serve the Protestants who historically had services in this space, the director especially hoped that physicians might use the space to relax and prepare for surgeries." He hoped to "tie it into the OR [operating room] so that docs can go in there and look at a surgery when they need to." These renovations have not all been welcomed, especially by staff that, in the director's words, "sort of interpret this as [the chapel] somehow being closed." "I don't," he said. "I interpret it as opening up and making better use of the sanctuary space for things of medicine and healing." In an effort at compromise, the director agreed to keep the default chair arrangement in the new space as soft pews. The use of soft pews and continued presence of stained glass windows and the altar will maintain the chapel's Christian template even after the renovation.

At other hospitals, chapels have been renovated more dramatically, with altars and stained glass windows being removed or changed. Twenty years ago the chapel at Creek Hospital, built as a Christian space, was used primarily for Catholic services. When the current director arrived, she led a redesign to, in her words, create a "space that's accommodating [to] a variety of religious traditions." Unlike some of the more recently built chapels that are symbol free, this director created a multifaith space actively drawing in objects from a range of religious traditions. Most notably, a system of curtains and pulleys was built at the front of the chapel such that a large cross with images on it (for Catholics), a plain wooden cross (for Protestants), or a Star of David (for Jews) can be put in place at the front of the room absent the other two. A sign also points toward Mecca, and prayer rugs and prayer times are available. Because some Muslims are not comfortable with human images, a light behind the stained glass window in the chapel that contains such images can be turned off so the images cannot be seen. The director explained, "We have a light put onto this [window] so that for Muslims who don't want images, human images in their space, we can do that." The chaplains also try "to keep all the images away from the side [of the room] that faces Mecca," she explained. The chapel houses "scriptures of written traditions, including the Koran, and a variety of New Testaments." These objects join prayer shawls and Sabbath candles for Jews and cushions for Buddhists on a shelf at the back. The materials needed for Catholic and Episcopal communion are also available in the chapel.[19]

Constructed as Interfaith

Most of the chapels built in the last twenty years were constructed to be interfaith from the start, with some slowly shedding underlying Christian templates
along the way. Physical space for a chapel was part of the original plans for
the Overbrook Hospital building when it was designed more than twenty years
ago. Ten years before that, the hospital's first chaplain began calling for an
"interdenominational chapel," describing his vision as an "aesthetically attrac-
tive building" that would provide "the ground for private meditation, comfort,
and beauty in the midst of chaos." He hoped that the chapel would welcome
people from all religious traditions, though he described it in largely Protestant
terms—reflecting his own background—saying he hoped the space would have
seating for fifty and include a place for an organ, a choir, eight instrumental-
ists, an altar, a font, a robing room, and a sacristy.

His vision was scaled back significantly when the building was designed; the
first chapel was a small fifteen-by-fifteen foot room with an altar/communion
table and a few chairs decorated in reds and gold located near the main hospital entrance. The chaplain described the first chapel as "interdenominational,
and not exclusively Christian," even though it centered on an altar/commu-
nion table and members of other religious traditions were not involved in its
design or opening. The chapel was consecrated by a local Episcopal bishop and,
even before the consecration, the chaplain held the first service there bless-
ing bibles donated by the Gideon Society for all patient beds in the (secular)
hospital. The chapel has moved twice since its original opening and has shifted
from having some Christian religious symbols to having few. "In an attempt
to become interfaith and respectful," Pat, the current director, explained,
"we became neutral." The interfaith orientation of the chapel is signified by
a series of interlocking circles on paper signs displayed in a glass case outside
the door. The middle circle says interfaith, and the words "Islam," "Hinduism,"
"Buddhism," "Christianity," "Unitarianism," and "Judaism" are in circles with
pictures of tradition-specific symbols around each. The room's stained glass
windows have a nature theme, reflecting a part of the world important to their
original donor.

Like at Overbrook, interfaith chapel spaces at other hospitals include few
religious symbols and fair amounts of nature imagery, especially nature and
light motifs. At Central Hospital, a confessional booth, baptismal font, and
organ were pushed against back walls in ways suggesting their infrequent use
and stained glass sun catchers with images of flowers and bugs were on windows at the front, the focal point of the room. At Queen's Hospital, a stained
glass screen was the main image in the chapel. The director explained, "I like to
think of it as a metaphor for pastoral care at the hospital: a prism that serves
people of many different faiths—a symbol of peace and hope." At Main Hospital,

the chapel had to be called a "meditation room" and could not "have any visible signs of any particular faith or denomination," according to the director. Absent religious symbols, the room is oriented around a round blue and yellow stained glass art piece hanging prominently at the front of the room.

Use

Regardless of how they appear, there are several commonalities in how hospital chapel spaces are used. First, in pamphlets, on web pages, and in interviews, chaplaincy directors emphasize that chapels are open to all people. This broad message of welcome seems to be present regardless of who might actually feel comfortable in a particular chapel space given its appearance and their beliefs or practices. A chapel constructed when what is now a secular hospital was Jewish and not renovated since, for example, has a small signed posted inside that reads this "chapel is a public space. Everyone is invited to use this space without exception for personal prayer, meditation and reflection at all times including when other formal worship and meditation experiences are underway." The fact that the space looks like a Jewish chapel does not deter the broad welcome. Many chaplaincy departments similarly note that chapels are available twenty-four hours a day or, in one case, that the chapel has never been closed since it was first opened more than fifty years ago, including when it was moved from one physical location to another. Whether, especially in interfaith chapels, spaces have been created that feel inviting to a range of people versus unfamiliar to most is an open question, as is the extent to which chapel spaces are theoretical versus actual sites of religious encounter.

Second, with the exception of the Catholic hospital that built a second interfaith chapel to accommodate non-Catholics, hospitals implicitly assume that people from a range of religious and spiritual backgrounds, including those without such backgrounds, can and will share space when they use a chapel. While some Muslims, Orthodox Jews, and members of other groups do not tend to be comfortable sharing sacred space based on their own rules about how it must be sacralized, these differences are generally overlooked, much as the early chaplain at Overbrook Hospital did not see calling the first chapel space "interdenominational" and having it consecrated by an Episcopal bishop as incompatible. At only one of these fifteen hospitals was a group other than the group who founded the hospital granted their own space, and that was in the creation of a Muslim prayer room—separate from the chapel—for both staff and visitors. Also rarely mentioned by directors are traditional Catholics or members of other religious traditions for whom an interfaith chapel absent religious symbols might be a quiet place to rest but not sacred with the symbols, texts, or consecration by leaders of their traditions.

Third, in juxtaposition to their increasingly interfaith appearances, almost all of these hospitals offer sparsely attended religious services in particular traditions, more for families and staff than for patients.[20] Most directors of chaplaincy departments recognize that as patient stays have declined and the health conditions of those admitted to hospitals have become more acute, it is largely staff and families who use chapels. As one director explains, "If patients are able to get down to a service [in the chapel], they're in a cab going home or being transported home.... They'll never see any other place in the hospital but the OR and their bed.... [T]he nature of health care has changed."

Despite these changes, all of these hospitals hold religious services that are sparsely attended except on Catholic holy days, especially Ash Wednesday, when they are moved from chapel spaces to larger auditoriums. Most hospitals hold Catholic mass either daily or weekly. At one smaller hospital, an exception, the only Sunday afternoon mass in the area is offered at the hospital and people come from outside to attend. As the priest explains, "In the city there are no more Sunday afternoon or evening masses so people come to my 4 o'clock mass on Sunday. That's in the auditorium. Looks like an operating theater, but we do it there. I don't care, but that is where we do it." A few hospitals hold interfaith services daily or weekly and a few others offer Jewish, Muslim, or other services including "guided imagery for spiritual centering and relaxation" at one and centering prayer at another. On special occasions, including Thanksgiving, Martin Luther King Day, Christmas, and other specific holidays, some hospitals hold services. At several hospitals, services are broadcast to patient rooms from the chapel. All services are organized and led by the hospital chaplain.

Several hospitals have also started to hold memorial services to honor, in the chapel, the memories of patients and staff who die. One hospital had a memorial wall in the chapel with a sign across the top that read, "We will remember you always with love." Below were notes and letters, written on scraps of paper and even parts of cafeteria trays, saying things like, "For R. may she rest in peace," "I will always love and miss you," and "Please pray for DJ and AL. They both went to heaven to be with God. I love them both." Other hospitals had annual memorial services to honor patients who died, as well as services for staff, especially well-known or long-term staff, when they passed away.

More than for formal services, most chapels seemed to be used informally throughout the day. A few directors described particular staff members who use the chapel as part of their regular routines, stopping on their way into work, for example, to say a short prayer. I frequently saw staff members in scrubs and white coats sitting quietly in these spaces. Visitors and family members seemed to use the spaces more, some spending five minutes and others thirty minutes or more. Mostly I saw people sitting quietly crying, sleeping, or praying silently to themselves. Almost all of these chapels had prayer books inside that invited people to write and leave a prayer, worry, or concern. These books were also a focus of activity as people often entered and wrote a prayer and then sat for a few minutes before leaving (O'Reilly 2000; Cadge and Daglian 2008). Not surprisingly, chapels more centrally located in hospitals seemed to be used more often than others, and interfaith chapels almost always had more people in them than those that were tradition specific. Given the number of people who move through these hospitals on a daily basis, only a small minority likely utilize chapel spaces, however, with most using them privately and in their own ways rather than engaging with others in the space.

Conclusion

Hospital chapels are one of many ways religion and spirituality are negotiated in contemporary American hospitals. While the spaces have shifted from tradition specific to more interfaith over time, they continue to display ambivalence on several levels. First, despite renovations and attempts to create more interfaith and welcoming spaces, some—not all—retain traditional Christian or Jewish motifs in their stained glass windows, pews, and orienting objects like altars. Others have replaced these Christian motifs with abstract stained glass and nature images—implicitly, as well as explicitly, removing religious symbols from the spaces as underlying Protestant assumptions fade. Second, despite a movement toward interfaith spaces, the majority of hospitals continue to offer poorly attended services—most especially Catholic mass—sometimes in symbol-less physical spaces. While the few hospitals that also offer services in Protestant, Jewish, Buddhist, and other religious traditions could theoretically include objects and symbols from those traditions in their chapel space, this is uncommon.

More generally, the chapel spaces described here reinforce arguments about ambivalence around religion and spirituality in hospitals more generally. Anthropologist Francis Norwood points to these ambivalences in her study of hospital chaplains. To find places for themselves between medical and religious forms of power, she argues, chaplains have to distance themselves from religion—which is often not welcomed in hospitals more generally—and make strategic choices that foster their presence in an otherwise foreign environment (Norwood 2006). The directors of chaplaincy departments are perhaps struggling with similar challenges in trying to create chapel spaces in hospitals that will not be seen as too explicitly religious, that create space for as many people and their practices as possible, and that do not offend as religion and religious symbols sometimes do in public life.

To the extent that the patterns here are evident in a broader range of hospital chapels or in chapel spaces in airports, universities, the military, and prisons, it suggests a response to American religious diversity outside of congregations that is less about bringing together a range of religious traditions and symbols and more about removing them from public view. This generification of religion can be seen as a new form of civil religion within organizations connected to the interests of teaching hospitals, if not private or state interests more generally. With the exception of Creek Hospital, the responses of the hospitals described here are less multifaith than interfaith, consistent with what James Beckford and Sophie Gillat found in UK prisons even despite the differing relationships between religion and the state.

Both substantively and methodologically, the case of hospital chapels points to the importance of considering how religion and spirituality are negotiated in daily life outside of congregations. As a third "edge," these spaces and questions about religion outside of congregations bring academic and political conversations about the appropriate role of religion in public life into conversation with how it is actually present—in its complexity or, as these hospitals suggest, its supposed neutrality. They show that religion is a property not just of individuals, organizations, and/or nation-states, but of the public spaces in each where religious ideas and practices collide and must be negotiated—not as a secondary, but as a fundamental component of what religion is and does.

Notes

1. The hospitals described here are identified by pseudonyms and identifying details are either omitted or slightly changed.
2. For more information see Cadge (2012), chapter 3.
3. See related discussions in DiMaggio (1998) and Ammerman (2007b). For exceptions see Bender (2003); Grant, O'Neil, and Stephens (2004); Miller (2007); and Gorski and Altınordu (2008).
4. Research that has been conducted about religion outside of religious institutions focuses on schools, prisons, and the military. For example, see Sullivan (2009), Beckford and Gilliat (1998), and Beckford (2001). Court cases also focus in these areas.
5. See also Cadge (2012). A large and growing body of literature focuses on relationships between religion, spirituality, health, and medicine—for a review see Cadge and Fair (2010). Little of it pays attention to the organizational and institutional dimensions, however, and nothing has been written about hospital chapels. In focusing on chapels, I aim, like Thomas Gieryn, to create a "space for place in sociology" (Gieryn 2000).
6. Related nonpublic spaces in these hospitals include rooms previously used for ritual circumcisions or spaces that used to be mortuary chapels. Some hospitals also have private rooms where Muslim staff can pray. Most chaplains also have office space, which I do not discuss in this chapter.
7. See also Prothero (2006).
8. Chapel transitions are mirrored in the professional development of hospital chaplaincy from its Protestant origins to recent attempts to support all people through presence, active listening, and other forms of spiritual, instead of just religious, support (Norwood 2006; VandeCreek and Burton 2001).
9. This is also the case in some UK prisons (see Beckford 2005).
10. This is perhaps not unlike dominant frameworks in the sociology of religion at large, as outlined in the introductory chapter to this volume.

11. Despite a literature about sacred space in religious studies, nothing has been written about chapels as sacred spaces (Chidester and Linenthal 1995; Nelson 2006; Jones 2000).
12. See also discussion of the term in Beckford and Gilliat (1998, 25).
13. This is described in the 1998 Annual Report from Yale-New Haven Hospital.
14. See Risse (1999, chap. 10) and also (Fine 2003).
15. In a subsequent book, Verderber studied similar spaces in hospices, comparing their warm spaces to cold chapel spaces in hospitals (Verderber and Refuerzo 2006).
16. This is close to the complete population. Missing hospitals did not respond to repeated invitations to participate. I exclude from the sample hospitals affiliated with the Veterans Health Administration because they are subject to different regulations.
17. Jennifer Dillinger assisted me with these interviews and visited several hospitals I did not, sharing with me photos and descriptions of the spaces.
18. The chaplains interviewed work in departments called pastoral care, chaplaincy, or, less frequently, spiritual care services and are paid either directly by the hospital or by the local Catholic diocese or Jewish synagogue council.
19. Pointing to the need for tradition-specific spaces, the director of chaplaincy at this hospital also spoke of how she and her colleagues support the creation of such spaces. "For instance," she explained, "we have the only succa in the medical area, and we had a blast building it, and the doctors and families and patients come from all over the medical area to eat, and have text study."
20. I have been able to locate little information about such services historically (see Bassett 1976). In the archives of the Association for Professional Chaplains, there is occasional correspondence about the types of religious services held in different kinds of hospitals.

References

American Hospital Association. 1970. *Manual on Hospital Chaplaincy.* Chicago: American Hospital Association.

Ammerman, Nancy, ed. 2007a. *Everyday Religion: Observing Modern Religious Lives.* New York: Oxford University Press.

Ammerman, Nancy. 2007b. "Studying Everyday Religion: Challenges for the Future." Pp. 219–238 in *Everyday Religion: Observing Modern Religious Lives*, edited by Nancy Ammerman. New York: Oxford University Press.

Bassett, S. D. 1976. *Public Religious Services in the Hospital.* Springfield, IL: Charles C. Thomas.

Beckford, James, and Sophie Gilliat. 1998. *Religion in Prison: Equal Rites in a Multi-Faith Society.* New York: Cambridge University Press.

Beckford, James A. 2001. "Doing Time: Space, Time Religious Diversity and the Sacred in Prisons." *International Review of Sociology* 11(3): 371–382.

———. 2005. "Muslims in the Prisons of Britain and France." *Journal of Contemporary European Studies* 13(3): 287–297.

Bender, Courtney. 2003. *Heaven's Kitchen: Living Religion at God's Love We Deliver.* Chicago: University of Chicago Press.

Cadge, Wendy, and M. Daglian. 2008. "Blessings, Strength, and Guidance: Prayer Frames in a Hospital Prayer Book." *Poetics* 36: 358–373.

Cadge, Wendy, and Brian Fair. 2010. "Religion, Spirituality, Health and Medicine: Sociological Intersections." Pp. 341–362 in *Handbook of Medical Sociology*, edited by Chloe Byrd, Allan Fremont, Stefan Timmermans, and Peter Conrad. Nashville: Vanderbilt University Press.

Cadge, Wendy. 2012. *Paging God: Religion in the Halls of Medicine.* Chicago: University of Chicago Press.

Chidester, David, and Edward T. Linenthal. 1995. *American Sacred Space.* Bloomington: Indiana University Press.

Creager, Ellen. 2000. "Prayer Rooms in Hospitals Acknowledge Power of Faith." *Dayton Daily News*, City, May 27, p. 4C.

DiMaggio, Paul. 1998. "The Relevance of Organization Theory to the Study of Religion." Pp. 7–23 in *Sacred Companies: Organizational Aspects of Religion and Religious Aspects of Organizations*, edited by N. J. Demerath, Peter D. Hall, Terry Schmitt, and Rhys H. Williams. New York: Oxford University Press.

Fadiman, Anne. 1998. *The Spirit Catches You and You Fall Down*. New York: Noonday Press.

Fine, Steven. 2003. "Arnold Brunner's Henry S. Frank Memorial Synagogue and the Emergence of 'Jewish Art' in Early Twentieth-Century America." *American Jewish Archives Journal*. 2: 47–70.

Gieryn, Thomas F. 2000. "A Space for Place in Sociology." *Annual Review of Sociology* 26: 463–496.

Gilliat-Ray, Sophie. 2004. "The Trouble with 'Inclusion': A Case Study of the Faith Zone at the Millennium Dome." *Sociological Review* 459–477.

———. 2005. "'Sacralising' Sacred Space in Public Institutions: A Case Study of the Prayer Space at the Millennium Dome." *Journal of Contemporary Religion* 20(3): 357–372.

Gorski, Philip, and Ateş Altınordu. 2008. "After Secularization?" *Annual Review of Sociology* 34: 55–85.

Grant, Don, Kathleen O'Neil, and Laura Stephens. 2004. "Spirituality in the Workplace: New Empirical Directions in the Study of the Sacred." *Sociology of Religion* 65(3): 265–283.

Greenhouse, Steven. 2008a. "Muslim Holiday at Tyson Plant Creates Furor." *New York Times*, August 6, A(0), p. 20.

———. 2008b. "Tyson Plant Reinstates Labor Day as Holiday." *New York Times*, August 9, A(0), p. 16.

Jones, Louis. 2000. *The Hermeneutics of Sacred Architecture: Experience, Interpretation, Comparison, Two Volumes*. Cambridge, MA: Harvard University Center for the Study of World Religions.

Klassen, Pamela E., and Courtney Bender. 2010. "Introduction: Habits of Pluralism." Pp. 1–30 In *After Pluralism: Reimagining Models of Religious Engagement*, edited by Pamela E. Klassen and Courtney Bender. New York: Columbia University Press.

Kuby, Alma M., and Catherine M. Begole. 1974. "AHA Surveys Chaplaincy Programs." *Hospitals: The Journal of the American Hospital Association* 48: 98–102.

Miller, David W. 2007. *God at Work: The History and Promise of the Faith at Work Movement*. New York: Oxford University Press.

Nelson, Louis P. 2006. *American Sanctuary: Understanding Sacred Spaces*. Bloomington: Indiana University Press.

Norwood, Frances. 2006. "The Ambivalent Chaplain: Negotiating Structural and Ideological Difference on the Margins of Modern-Day Hospital Medicine." *Medical Anthropology* 25(1): 1–29.

O'Reilly, JoAnn. 2000. "The Hospital Prayer Book: A Partner for Healing." *Literature and Medicine* 19(1): 61–83.

Prothero, Stephen. 2006. *A Nation of Religions: The Politics of Pluralism in Multireligious America*. Chapel Hill: University of North Carolina Press.

Risse, Guenter B. 1999. *Mending Bodies, Saving Souls: A History of Hospitals*. New York: Oxford University Press.

Stevens, Edward F. 1921. *The American Hospital of the Twentieth Century*. New York: Architectural Record Company.

Sullivan, Winnifred F. 2009. *Prison Religion: Faith-Based Reform and the Constitution*. Princeton, NJ: Princeton University Press.

VandeCreek, Larry, and Laurel Burton. 2001. "Professional Chaplaincy: Its Role and Importance in Healthcare." *Journal of Pastoral Care* 55(1): 81–97.

Verderber, Stephen, and David J. Fine. 2000. *Healthcare Architecture in an Era of Radical Transformation*. New Haven, CT: Yale University Press.

Verderber, Stephen, and Ben J. Refuerzo. 2006. *Innovations in Hospice Architecture*. New York: Taylor and Francis.

10

Negotiating Pluralism in Québec: Identity, Religion, and Secularism in the Debate over "Reasonable Accommodation"

GENEVIÈVE ZUBRZYCKI

Once nicknamed "the priest-ridden province," Québec is now a strikingly secular place. During the 1960s' so-called Quiet Revolution, the Québécois dramatically rid themselves of Catholicism, amputating what a new generation of social activists and political figures came to see as a gangrenous limb preventing the healthy development of the nation.[1] The building of a modern provincial welfare state and the laicization of social services such as education, health care, and welfare were accompanied by the profound and extremely rapid secularization of society characterized by a stringent critique of the Catholic Church, a drastic decline in religious practice, and even a significant incidence of clergy renouncing their vows to re-enter secular society. Many today thus often perceive religion as either an atavistic residue of the past surviving at the margins of society or imported from "outside" by recent waves of immigrants.

Yet religion, it turns out, is present not only in the lives of "others" but also as a skeleton in Québec's closet that is often experienced as phantom limb pain. This became apparent in the debates over the religious practices of cultural minorities, which were at the center of public life from 2006 to 2008. Although framed in the media and certain political circles as a contest between the secular majority and religious minorities, my analysis of the debates reveals that what was at stake was as much about Québec's religious past as it was about its present religious landscape and the challenges it poses for a self-avowed secular society. The debate about the increasing visibility of religion in the public sphere became a debate about the very identity of Québec, which reinvented itself forty-some years ago with the wholesale rejection of Catholicism. By looking at what at first glance seems to be about religion and immigration, we actually uncover a much wider social problematique. Analyzing the challenges of Québec's religious "present" allows us to uncover how the Québécois are coming to grips with their religious past and dealing with the limits of social and historical change.

The Québécois case is also helpful to think about the meaning and stakes of religious pluralism and secularism in contexts very different from that of the United States or France, which offer the prevailing models. Courtney Bender's analysis (this volume) of the specific context in which pluralism emerged and is defined in the United States is an important intervention because in spite of being context specific, those normative templates are exported with the pretention of universality. Other societies must grapple with those models, adapt them to their specific conditions, and "sell" them to their own populations and the international community as not only more befitting to their situation but also as "equally legitimate" as the models first defined elsewhere. Pluralism, "variously specified as cultural, political, legal, or religious, has come to represent a powerful ideal meant to resolve the question of how to get along in a conflict-ridden world" (Bender and Klassen 2010: 1) and has become a core value of democratic societies and the liberal state. Québec, as I will show through my analysis of the debates over reasonable accommodation, is currently trying to find its own way between the French, American, and Canadian models of laïcité, pluralism, and multiculturalism.

In this chapter, I analyze the debates over reasonable accommodation to show the multi-layered articulations between national identity, religion, secularism, and pluralism. This chapter is thus framed by two or even three of the edges identified by the contributors to this volume: it focuses on a non-US and noncongregational case, as well as discusses the ways in which religion is critically engaged in a society reexamining its past, present, and potential futures.

Debating Religion in Québec

The debate over the place of religion in Québec was ignited in the fall of 2006 and winter of 2007 when several incidents involving religious minorities and Québec's secular majority made provincial headlines: In one, frosted-glass windows were installed at a Montréal YMCA at the request—and expense—of ultra-Orthodox Jews who wished to protect young boys walking to their neighborhood yeshiva from temptations posed by the sight of women exercising at the gym. In another high-profile episode, fathers attending their children's swimming exam were asked to leave the pool area because their presence caused discomfort to Muslim women enrolled in a swimming class at the same time. In a third case—it was reported in the press—the menu of a popular commercial "sugar shack" (where maple syrup is typically produced in the spring and traditional dishes—many with pork—are served family style) was changed to accommodate the dietary needs of Muslim patrons. In yet another case, two ambulance attendants were asked to leave the cafeteria at Montréal's Jewish General Hospital where they were about to eat their lunch because they had not purchased their food there and the area where they were seated was considered kosher.

The four cases briefly outlined concerned private individuals and their dealings with specific institutions—most of which were public, such as the Montréal YMCA, the recreation center, and the General Jewish Hospital, but which also included private ones, such as the sugar shack. Many other cases, however, involved issues related to the use of—and arguments over what constitutes—public space. They concerned, for example, ongoing disputes between some neighborhood residents and the city of Montréal regarding the loosened application of parking regulations on the Shabbat; broken city codes with the erection of Sukkahs during the Jewish festival of Sukkot; or the deployment of elaborate *eruvim* in Outremont, a neighborhood where the coexistence of ultra-Orthodox and Francophone Gentile communities has not always been easy (Stoker 2003).

These are only a few from a long list of "incidents" that punctuated the last few years, incidents that were widely reported in Québec media and that were often closer to rumors and half-truths than actual, "factual" events.[2] In most cases, the problem prompting vocal opposition in the public sphere was not so much religious minorities' discomfort with, or request to, curtail widely accepted practices of the host society (such as coed swimming pools)—or even the request for special permissions or for the loosening of certain rules at specific moments (such as parking regulations or the erection of temporary religious structures)—but rather the perception of public institutions' *over* accommodation of what were not considered by most to be "reasonable" expectations. Why should fathers be asked to leave the swimming pool area? Why should the ambulance personnel be prohibited from eating their ham and cheese sandwiches at the hospital cafeteria? Why should certain (religious) communities be allowed to violate city codes, and members of other communities given special "dispensations" allowing them not to wear protective helmets on construction sites or allowing them to carry weapons to schools (as in two other famous cases concerning Sikhs) (Stoker 2007)? Where do the private and public spheres begin, and how much should a host society, itself a minority within Canada, accommodate minorities living within it? What are, in other words, the limits of "reasonable" accommodation?

Before discussing the debates about reasonable accommodation, it is important to first define "reasonable accommodation." Strictly speaking, a reasonable accommodation is "an arrangement that falls under the legal sphere, more specifically case law, aimed at relaxing the application of a norm or statute in favour of an individual or a group of people threatened with discrimination for one of the reasons specified in [Québec's Charter of human rights and freedoms]" (Bouchard and Taylor 2008a, 289). The duty of accommodation demands that discrimination be present on at least one of the thirteen grounds recognized by the Québec Charter: some are circumstantial (such as pregnancy or marital status); others are permanent traits of an individual (such as sex, skin color, or disability); yet others are sociocultural (such as language or religion). Discrimination alone, however, is not sufficient for an accommodation to take place because "the duty of accommodation is limited by the realism of the request, that is, by the ability of the organization to accommodate." The reasonable accommodation of a given request is therefore mitigated by the notion of "undue hardship." In other words, the duty of accommodation is assessed in relation to the weight of inconvenience posed to the organization to which the request is addressed (Bouchard and Taylor 2008a, 63).

It is difficult to paint an accurate picture of the accommodation requests made by members of diverse religious groups because many of those requests and their accommodations are made on an ad hoc basis between student, parents, and teacher; employee and employer; and so forth. While that type of solution, legally speaking, is not considered an accommodation per se (but rather a "concerted adjustment"), any demand for the relaxing of a rule or request to accommodate specific needs of an individual or community on the basis of religion was referred to, in the public sphere, as a request for "accommodation."

The media widely commented on what it quickly named "La crise des accommodements," and the "crisis" entered the social and political spheres. The municipal council of Hérouxville, a small village in Mauricie (population 1,338), adopted a "lifestyle code" that potential immigrants would have to comply to were they to come reside there. The document outlined "normal" and acceptable practices in Québec (most of them espousing liberal values and emphasizing gender equality) and controversially stated that "stoning women or burning them alive [was] prohibited, as [was] female genital cutting," a xenophobic statement that was widely reported in international media outlets, as well as vehemently ridiculed and criticized at home. While Hérouxville became a source of embarrassment and synonymous with small-town bigotry that was in no way representative of Québec as a whole, Mario Dumont, then leader of a conservative political party, nevertheless decried in a clever neologism that the Québécois were afflicted by "aplaventrisme"—from à plat ventre, "flat on one's belly." In a widely disseminated open letter, he wrote that they suffered from "spinelessness" since they passively acquiesced to the requests of those who should be the ones to adapt, of those who "when in Rome, should do as the Romans do."[3] Around the same time, however, André Boisclair, then leader of the left-leaning and separatist Parti Québécois, noted that no one had ever requested the removal of the crucifix at the National Assembly even though, in his personal opinion, that religious symbol had no place at such an institution. Although both declarations may not appear to be related, or perhaps related only in the context of political games and contests, they are faces of the same coin—that of an ongoing debate about the identity of Québec at a moment of profound transformation.

In response to public confusion and discontent over the hazy boundaries of "reasonable accommodation," in February 2007 Québec Premier Jean Charest announced the establishment of the Commission on Practices of Accommodation Related to Cultural Differences. The Bouchard-Taylor Commission, as it is commonly called after the names of its commissioners, sociologist Gérard Bouchard and philosopher Charles Taylor, visited sixteen regions of the province in fall 2007 for a total of thirty-one days of public hearings where private citizens, as well as local and regional organizations, presented briefs to the commissioners. The commissioners heard 241 private testimonies and received more than 900 briefs representing over 6,000 pages of documents. Twenty-two "citizens' forums" (adopting a town-hall-meeting format) were organized throughout the province, which attracted 3,423 participants. All hearings were taped and discussed on evening news programs, and the citizens' forums were televised "live" on Radio-Canada (the French-language branch of the Canadian Broadcasting Company [CBC]). In addition to those testimonies and briefs, over sixty province-wide organizations such as political parties, trade unions, professional associations, women's groups, ethnic minorities' coalitions, and religious institutions presented briefs to the commissioners during a week-long hearing in Montréal at the very end of the process. Between August 2007 and January 2008, the commission also operated a website where briefs could be downloaded and provided a space where the public could engage in exchanges. The website was visited more than 400,000 times (Bouchard and Taylor 2008a, 17). The commissioners produced a 310-page report assessing the situation and made thirty-seven recommendations to the government. The much-awaited report was officially made public on May 22, 2008—but only after a few pages of the report had been leaked out to the press, creating a media frenzy and provoking a whirlwind of political commentaries, accusations, and counteraccusations.[4]

This public consultation and forum was charged with exploring and explicating the meaning and practice of Québec's official secularism in the face of increasing religious pluralism created by diverse immigrant populations. While the high-profile cases briefly mentioned earlier and the outpouring of protest they generated may suggest that the "crisis" was primarily about immigration and integration, the public hearings revealed that it was also about the Québécois' own relationship to their past Catholic identity and the challenges pertaining to their national(ist) project within Canada. Public debate was not solely about the challenges faced by a secular host society and its religious "guests," but one about the very identity and secularity of Québec. Indeed, the year-long investigation of "reasonable accommodation" turned out to be the most significant critical interrogation about Québécois' national identity in the last forty years as political figures, public intellectuals, artists, business-people, and ordinary citizens all lent their voices to the commission's work. Québec, so to speak, was on the couch.[5]

My analysis is based on briefs submitted to the commission,[6] observation of the commission's work, informal interviews with participants and key actors,[7] and a review of important interventions in the press and blogosphere during and after the debate. Unlike other places where similar debates are currently under way—France, Great Britain, Spain, Germany, the Netherlands, Denmark, and the United States, in Québec the issue of secularism is intrinsically related to that of the "national question" (i.e., national independence), which is especially complex and a much-debated issue in that society. The debate over reasonable accommodation and the meaning and challenges of religious pluralism in Québec more broadly can thus only make sense when triangulated with national identity and the history of Catholicism in Québec; with the transformation of that relationship in the 1960s' Quiet Revolution; and in the post–Quiet Revolution and post-separatism Canadian context. This historicization is necessary to provide a fuller picture of the issues at stake in the debate and provides the structure for the remainder of this chapter.

The Longue Durée ... From French Canada to Québec

Catholicism has been historically central in defining the French Canadians' national identity against the Anglo-Protestants surrounding them on the North American continent. Colonial domination by this Other, following the British Conquest of New France in 1759, further reinforced the role played by Catholicism in ethno-national identity, while the failure of the Patriots' Rebellion—a series of republican uprisings against the British colonial power in 1837—was crucial in solidifying the ideological and institutional dominance of the Catholic Church in French Canadian society. The crushing of the rebellion left a void of elites able to carry the liberal torch, creating an ideological vacuum that the clergy energetically filled. The Catholic Church emerged as the institution best able, in French Canadian society, to create, sustain, and disseminate a national project. That project was defined in ethno-religious terms centered on the idea of *survivance*, or cultural preservation. The goal was not to change the political structures and free the (French Canadian) nation from the British Empire, but to ensure the nation's very *survival* within the new system by keeping the identity of its members alive. Assimilation was to be resisted on two intertwined fronts: through the preservation of the French language and

Catholicism bolstered by a demographic "counterattack" fought through the active glorification of large families, a strategy commonly referred to as "the revenge of the cradle."

The Rebellion also ensured the institutional dominance of the Catholic Church in Lower Canada indirectly by making evident to the British colonial authorities that they could not rule effectively without the loyalty of its conquered subjects and the help of the clergy, now their only elites. A marriage of convenience between the British colonial authorities and the church hierarchy was thus established: the church worked diligently at fostering the Canadiens' loyalty to the crown, while in return the British colonial authorities allowed the confessionalization of education, health, and welfare in French Canada, turning the church into a de facto "crypto-state." From roughly 1840 until 1960, such was the structure of domination in French Canadian society.

The death, in 1959, of Québec's Premier Maurice Duplessis, who had ruled the province of Québec for almost a quarter of a century and whose political tenure was characterized by rabid corruption and quid pro quo relationships with the Catholic Church and big business, served as a catalyst for a wholesale rejection of that status quo. A new political elite was elected with the slogans "Things must change," "Now or never," and "Masters in our own house." Thus began a decade of profound transformations that not only pulled out Québec from Duplessis's era of so-called Great Darkness (*Grande noirceur*) but also effected a radical rupture with a traditional past and marked Québec's forceful entry into modernity.[8] That decade was marked by profound structural, social, political, economic, cultural, and religious transformations known as the Quiet Revolution, which exerted a long-lasting impact on Québécois national identity and its relationship to Catholicism and religion more broadly.

At one level, the Quiet Revolution marks the birth of the Québécois nation,[9] as the articulation of a new political project around independence led to the rejection of the pan-American ethno-religious "French Canadian" identity and the adoption instead of a civic and secular "Québécois" identity resting on language and delimited by the province's boundaries (Breton 1988; Bouchard 1999). Catholicism was abandoned as an important or even a desirable marker and secularism instead was enshrined as a key value (and virtue?) of the newly defined nation.

A new generation of intellectuals, politicians, artists, and social activists also explicitly rejected the notion of ethno-religious "survival"; the goal was not to survive but to *develop*. The Quiet Revolution's modus operandi was thus to *catch up* ("rattrapage") and modernize. The church, which controlled most social services, supported political authorities, promoted large families, and glorified an agrarian economy of subsistence, was no longer perceived as a bulwark, but rather as a barrier to the achievement of that goal. The new provincial state was to be the instrument of modernization and national development, adequately equipped to represent the interest of the "new" Québécois nation within Canadian federal structures.

The 1960s were therefore marked by important structural transformations, chief among them the building of a modern provincial welfare state and the laicization of social services such as education, healthcare, and welfare, taken over by the state. This institutional marginalization of the church was accompanied by a significant and rapid secularization of society, characterized by a stringent critique of the church, a drastic decline in religious practice, and even a significant incidence of clergy renouncing their vows to re-enter secular society.[10] Within ten years, churches that once thronged with people several days a week now sat empty. Some were later bulldozed; others were sold to developers who transformed them into condominiums or hotels; others remained only to be transformed from sites of ritual practice into sites of "cultural heritage"— a phenomenon to which I return later. These transformations were occurring just when the church itself, during the Second Vatican Council, was critically reassessing its role in modern society, which facilitated its retreat from the political and social spheres.

As religious practice tumbled, so did fertility: in 1959, Québec had the highest birth rate of all the provinces in Canada. By 1972, however, it had the lowest, with less than half of what it had been at the end of the 1950s (Christiano 2007, 34–35). While in 1957 the typical French Canadian woman in Québec had on average four children, by 1970 fertility had dropped to 2.09 children per woman, below the 2.1 standard required for population replacement (Christiano 2007, 34). While decreases in fertility are common in the Western world in that period, the extent and rapidity of the drop in Québec is unusual. And when many thought it could not get lower, in 1986, the rate hit a record low at 1.4 children per woman, what demographers call "low-low fertility," creating a wave of insecurity about the future of the nation, a nation increasingly described in the media and political discourse as "endangered" (*en voie de disparition*). In 1989, a documentary entitled "To Disappear" was widely advertised before it was shown on Radio-Canada, generating an intense discussion in the public sphere. Its official synopsis declared:

> Within 25 years at the most, some demographers predict, the French Canadian nation will be moribund. THEN IT WILL DISAPPEAR. Unless [the nation] starts to make more children and welcomes immigrants desiring to truly integrate. Two eminently political options. By comparing experiences in other regions of the world with the situations prevailing in Québec, this vast analysis of the state of the nation warns against mistakes to avoid and proposes solutions that could, it seems, save the French people of America from extinction.[11]

This insecurity about the future of the nation must also be put into the context of the results of a Referendum on the Sovereignty of Québec held on May 20, 1981, in which 40.44 percent of Québec voters voted for, and 59.56 percent voted against giving a mandate to the Québec government to negotiate the province's sovereignty from the rest of Canada. The 1980s were therefore marked not only by the realization of the demographic impact of the Quiet Revolution but also by the injuries left by an acrimonious battle between supporters of the "yes" and "no" camps, serious soul searching by the "sovereignists," and complex and contested negotiations between Québec and the rest of Canada to constitutionally recognize the distinctiveness of Québec within Canada.

It is in that specific political context and cultural climate that Québec governmental agencies actively encouraged the immigration of Francophone populations to Québec to keep the delicate linguistic balance in the province and the relative weight of Québec within the Canadian federal structures.[12] The recent influx of immigrants, however, has brought religion "back on the table" as many of them are significantly more religious than the Québécois, and many are also non-Christian, which has forced the Québécois to reflect on secularism and their rapport to Catholicism, which many thought they had left behind for good.[13] The debate over religion and secularism is, moreover, no longer only an "internal" one—that is, a debate among "Québécois of French Canadian descent"—but one that now involves a dialogue with the Other.

The Bouchard-Taylor Report and Reactions in the Public Sphere

Over 75 pages of the Bouchard-Taylor Commission's full report, 310 pages long, were devoted to the factual description of dozens of cases that had been reported in the press or brought up during the commission's audiences to set the record straight. It also contained a detailed portrayal of actual practices in the field of education and health, where most of the need for accommodation is felt, and potentially also where most of the tensions can occur. The goal was to demystify both the extent and nature of requests for accommodation and the alleged over-accommodation of those requests by public institutions.

Tellingly, only six of the thirty-seven recommendations made by the commissaries in their report to the government pertained to religion directly. The other recommendations concerned educating the population about immigrants, integration practices (including greater assistance for employment), linguistic policies, and the promotion of interculturalism, Québec's response to Canadian multiculturalism.

Multiculturalism is a system founded on the respect and promotion of ethnic diversity within a given society. That system is widely criticized in Québec for several reasons. First, it is perceived as poorly adapted to the province's particular situation and the specific challenges it faces. Contrary to the rest of Canada, where about a third of the population is of British descent, in Québec about 80 percent of the population self-identifies as Québécois of French Canadian descent. There is thus a strong attachment in that province to that ethnocultural group's history, traditions, and language, especially when the position of that language in North America is, for obvious reasons, rather precarious. Second, multiculturalism is commonly understood as an ideological program meant to drown Québec's distinctiveness, as the Québécois become, in the "Canadian mosaic," an ethnic community among many others. By emphasizing diversity over continuity, Québec somehow loses its historic status of "founder." Finally, since the Quiet Revolution, the Québécois have come to understand themselves as a majority in their own province, while remaining a minority within Canada.[14] That double status makes their relationship to multiculturalism and to immigrants especially complex.

For all these reasons, Québec political and cultural elites advocate a different model of interethnic relations in the province, "interculturalism," which attempts to marry ethnocultural diversity with the continuity of the francophone ethnocultural "kernel." As the report explained, in the interculturalist model, "the respect of diversity is subordinated to the necessity to preserve the francophone culture of Québec." A key stake for the future of the nation, the authors of the report argued throughout, was the successful integration of immigrants. According to them, that outcome was most likely through a continued "open secularism" rather than through the adoption of the French republican model, which they considered and referred to as "rigid" and "radical."

The report therefore recommended the continued goodwill of public agents and authorities to accommodate religiously motivated requests, as long as they did not threaten the neutrality of the state and gender equality, two core values of Québécois society. Concretely, the report proposed that the beneficiaries of state services could continue to wear outward signs of their religious faith and request accommodation to specific needs on a case-by-case basis. State agents such as teachers and doctors could also wear such symbols in the exercise of their functions insofar as it did not prevent them from accomplishing their duty. So, for example, the report proposed that it was appropriate for a Muslim teacher to wear the hijab in the classroom, but that wearing the niqab or the burka was not, and therefore should be prohibited because these specific religious garbs interfere with the teacher's communication with children and thus cause prejudice to the population served by the state.

The report, however, recommended that state agents who occupy positions representing state authority—such as judges, police, prison guards, and the president of the National Assembly—be prohibited from wearing religious symbols because their very positions "embody the necessary neutrality of the state." In the same vein, the report also recommended the removal of some problematic remnants of Catholicism in the public sphere, including a large crucifix over the seat of the speaker at the National Assembly in Québec City, to truly create a secular society where religious "others" could find their own place: "In keeping with the notion of the separation of Church and State, we believe that the crucifix must be removed from the wall of the National Assembly" (Bouchard and Taylor 2008c, 60). This crucifix was installed there by Maurice Duplessis in 1936 and suggests, according to Bouchard and Taylor, "a special proximity between the legislative power and the majority's religion." "It seems preferable," they thus noted, "that the very site where elected representatives deliberate and legislate not be identified with a specific religion. The National Assembly is the assembly of the entire population of Québec" (my translation of a passage in the full-length version of the French-language report, Bouchard and Taylor 2008b, pp. 152–153).

Just hours after the report was officially made public, Prime Minister Charest proposed a motion to retain the said crucifix *as symbolic of Québec's religious heritage and culture*, its collective memory—not, as Charest declared at the National Assembly, as symbolic of the religious beliefs of individual deputies. Though the nation is not primordially constituted and certainly changes, Premier Charest argued, it remains historically and culturally construed, and that history has enduring power.[15]

The prime minister's reaction was in line with other policies developed in the 1990s to preserve religious heritage as cultural patrimony. After churches had been bulldozed, sold, and transformed into condominiums, or simply had fallen into neglect for lack of support from "parishioners" who no longer went to church, the state decided in the 1990s to "invest in religious patrimony." The government of Québec allocates financial aid and provides expertise to preserve and maintain any elements of religious buildings and sites (structures, materials, furniture, artifacts and artwork, landscape, and monuments) recognized as having "patrimonial value." (See figure 10.1.)

Since 1995, thus, the government of Québec has spent $254 million in restoring "religious patrimony."[16] As stated on the website of the Conseil du patrimoine religieux du Québec:

> For the Conseil, Québec religious heritage appears to be a founding heritage, if we take in consideration that religious preoccupation and religious buildings have been present since the origin of Québec society. Among our entire cultural heritage, it is the most universal, the most diversified, and the richest. It is also the most visible and the most spread out over the territory. It represents a major expression of the

Figure 10.1 Back of what remained of St.-Vincent-de-Paul church, Québec City, in 2008. Abandoned, the church and the site were sold to developers who plan to build a large hotel complex. Graffiti artists painted the interior walls of the facade, visible from the lower town. Pressure groups and committees on patrimony managed to have the city mandate that the façade of the church be incorporated into the hotel structure, but the decision was finally overturned and the façade was demolished on February 20, 2010. Photograph by Geneviève Zubrzycki.

culture of Québec and an important element of our identity, expressing the social, ethical and philosophical values of our society.[17]

Religious heritage is therefore enshrined as a collective "good" and a value, sacralized through the notion of *cultural* patrimony. In an attempt to inform and educate a public that no longer practices, the state has also put forth aware-ness campaigns, posting large banners on religious sites whose preservation is funded by the state with the slogan "Our cultural patrimony, it's sacred!" (See figures 10.2 and 10.3). Another document, a report published in June 2006 by the Commission de la culture, was entitled *Croire au patrimoine religieux [To believe in religious patrimony]*. What matters here is not belief in religion, but belief in religious past qua culture. The state, in this reframing, funds not religion, but the *memory* of a religious *past* transformed into the broader and putatively neutral notion of cultural patrimony.[18] It is through "cultural patrimony" and "culture" more broadly, then, that many secular—and even atheist—Québécois remain "Catholic" and continue to perceive non-Catholic religious groups as "other." By stressing the past, such strategies reaffirm the predominance of the majority group while confirming that religion indeed "belongs to the past." Churches become museums to act as a counterweight to a threatening plural religious mosaic.

For the Charest government,[19] the report was thus going too far in proposing to remove religious symbols from the Parliament in order to stress the religious neutrality of the state. The government instead promoted Québec's religious heritage reconfigured as cultural patrimony. For the separatist opposition, both the government's "position" and the "open secularism" advocated in the Bouchard-Taylor report are unacceptable. That political formation and many of their adherents advocate instead for a French-type republican model of secularism in which not only the state and its representatives but also citizens in the public sphere are secular.

The report was thus hotly debated, but it was more or less ignored by policymakers. The issue of secularism has not disappeared, however. In March 2010, sociologist Guy Rocher, a key actor of the Quiet Revolution, initiated and cosigned the Declaration of Intellectuals for Secularism. The authors argued in that document for "the necessity of an explicit legislative recognition of the Québec state's secularism, and the inherent prohibition for State representatives to wear conspicuous religious signs." The authors also demanded that Québec's de facto secularism be instituted de jure and justified that demand with historical precedents and historical imperatives: "If the idea of a secular State predates the Patriots, one cannot claim that it is a defensive reaction against recently arrived minorities. . . . Secularism is part of Québec's historic landscape and its recent achievements define Modern Québec." They insisted that "[s]ecularism is not a rejection of pluralism" but is rather "an essential condition for it. It is the only way for the equal and fair treatment of all convictions because it favors nor accommodates none; atheism no more than religious faith. Thus understood, pluralism is neither that of minorities nor that of the majority. It is also the necessary condition for gender equality." Finally, the Declaration concluded with the forceful statement that "[i]f withdrawal into oneself is not the solution, self-denial is not better. It is important to define the framework of case-based practices

Figure 10.2 Notre-Dame-des-Victoires church, Place Royale, Québec City, 2008. It is one the oldest stone churches in North America; the construction of the church was started in 1687 and completed in 1723. Initially dedicated to L'Enfant Jesus, the church was renamed Notre-Dame-de-la-Victoire after the Battle of Québec, and Notre-Dame-*des*-Victoires in 1711, when the sinking of a British fleet was given miraculous signification. It is an important symbol of French resistance and victories over the British. Photograph by Geneviève Zubrzycki.

of accommodations through our collective values, otherwise the piecemeal requests for accommodation risk of shattering in pieces the collective accomplishment of our entire society."[20]

By May 6, 2010, more than 3,100 university professors, teachers, doctors, and artists had signed the Declaration, and a few months later in October it was submitted to the Parliamentary Commission examining the proposed Bill 94, "An Act to establish guidelines governing accommodation requests within

Figure 10.3 Under the government-sponsored poster informing passersby that the church had received a $78,000 subvention as part of the patrimony program, another plaque, permanently affixed to the wall, informs (French-speaking) visitors that "Place Royale [is] the cradle of New France. Here, on these grounds, Samuel de Champlain founded Québec City in 1608." Photograph by Geneviève Zubrzycki.

the Administration and certain institutions." That bill is currently being examined and debated at the Legislative Assembly.[21]

Conclusion

What does this analysis teach us about Québec? For one, Catholicism as a religion may have lost its centrality in Québec society, but when encountering religious "others," the Québécois remain Catholic in their secularism. By that I mean two things: First, the secularism of the Québécois is informed by their past Catholic identity; that is, despite relegating Catholicism largely to the past, Catholicism continues to inform "who they are" in a broad cultural way. Second, Québécois remain "Catholic in their secularism" precisely because they *rejected* Catholicism in favor of secularism during the Quiet Revolution. Their story is one of *overcoming* Catholicism. As a result of that specific historical trajectory and the cultural valence of its narrative, they often tend to view religion—the category as such—with suspicion.

Québec may well have undergone a thorough secularization, therefore, but religion survives either in defining a collective "us, former Catholics" against a certain "non-Catholic them" or as an "irreligious us" against a "religious them." The commissioners' recommendation to remove the crucifix at the national assembly along with earlier requests by left-leaning separatist politicians, however, suggests an awareness of the tension between a secular Québécois identity and its Catholic French Canadian origins. Just as the crucifix remains in place "as a symbol of Québec's religious heritage and cultural patrimony," a profound ambivalence defines the Québécois' relationship to their religious past. (See figure 10.4.)

It is within this context that the meaning of pluralism in Québec emerges and that the challenges of building a plural society in Québec become a little clearer. The debate over reasonable accommodation in Québec was not "just" about "religion" or about "the religious and the secular." It was a reexamination of the way in which the secular was born in that society, a reflection on the religious and political systems out of—and against which—the secular was born. Just like "Catholicism" carries a range of significations, occupies diverse social spaces, and achieves various levels of political valence in different national and historical contexts, secularism is defined in relation to specific religious systems and articulated in relation to specific political structures, themselves historically constituted.

What looked like a debate about a secularism threatened by the religious otherness of immigrants, then, was also—if not primarily—about the examination of Québec's religious past and its forceful break with it during the 1960s' Quiet Revolution. The religions "at the center" of the debates were the "usual suspects" in similar debates occurring in Western Europe—Islam, Orthodox Judaism, and Sikhism. But, as I showed, it is the religion "at the edge" of that debate, Catholicism, that truly informed the debates. While suspended outside the frame of the discussion, that silent religion was the "default" taken-for-granted norm against which the others were compared and evaluated. The crisis over reasonable accommodation was shaped by the past dominance of Catholicism and the church in Québec, and the negative

Figure 10.4 Cartoon that appeared in the neighborhood newspaper *Le Plateau* on October 10, 2007. "Accommodations are fine, but we've had our share of religion in the past.../So going back is out of the question/QUÉBEC IS A SECULAR LAND!/ Thank God..." © Pascal Elie.

valuation of that religious past, on the one hand, and the realization that this past is an important one, on the other. Caught in the middle were Québec's "religious others."

Beyond the case, however, this analysis shows how important it is to study "religion beyond religion," that is, to study religion as it is imbricated in various social, political, and cultural processes. Religion may have seemed to be at the center of the debates over reasonable accommodation, but it was actually at the edge; "the nation" was at the core, a core nevertheless defined through and in opposition to that religious edge. The point is if we were to look at these debates from a narrowly "religious" perspective, we would miss the intricate and subtle ways in which religion matters in Québec. It was by placing religion at the edge in my analysis and broadening the question—in which the religion/secularism issue is but one among many to study—that the full significance of the religion/secularism issue actually takes on all its signification.

Acknowledgment

Research for this chapter was generously funded by grants from the University of Michigan's Office of the Vice President for Research, the University of Michigan's Rackham Graduate School, and the American Sociological Association's Fund for the Advancement of the Discipline. I am grateful to Elizabeth Young for her research assistance, to Gérard Bouchard for illuminating conversations, and to the editors of this volume and Paul Johnson for their helpful comments and suggestions.

Notes

1. A note of nomenclature is necessary: as early as the eighteenth century, the descendants of French settlers in Canada called themselves "Canadiens," an ethnonym reflecting their budding national identity as distinct from their French ancestors. They started calling themselves "Canadiens français" in the early nineteenth century when the British who settled in Canada after the Conquest (1759–60) began to describe themselves as "Canadians" (Frenette 1998, 9). The term "Canadien français," however, fell out of usage in Canada in the 1960s when the French Canadians in Québec started thinking of themselves as Québécois, a spatial narrowing of their mental national map that also provoked the redefinition of other French-speaking Canadians' identities (Franco-Ontarians, Franco-Manitobans, Fransascois, and so forth). Despite the pervasive use of the term in (non-Canadian) English, there exists no operative "French Canadian" identity since the 1960s. Moreover, contrary to what is often assumed outside of Canada, the term "Québécois" does not suggest one's political commitment to Québec's independence. It is a descriptive rather than a normative political term. In this chapter, therefore, I speak of "French Canadians" to denote the descendants of French settlers in Canada until the 1960s.
2. Detailed accounts of those cases and dozens more—of the events themselves and how they were reported in the press—can be found in two chapters of the Bouchard-Taylor Commission's final report: "Chronology of a Crisis" and "Perceptions and the Reality of Accommodation (Bouchard and Taylor 2008a, 45–76).
3. Dumont had many times, prior to the "crisis," skillfully linked the issue of immigrant integration to that of history and national identity. In 2006, he declared in an interview to the *Journal de Montréal* that "[The Québécois] cannot defend [their] identity with one knee on the ground; [they] fought with too much zeal to carry their identity and language through the centuries on this continent for all that to stupidly disappear because of a demographic decline" (Nov. 19, 2006).
4. Pages were dropped anonymously to the English-language Montréal daily *The Gazette*, which added another layer to the "leak" and discussion about the intent of the person leaking the pages.
5. An entire literature devoted to the "crisis" and the commission's work has mushroomed during and after the commission's work. They included journalistic accounts, personal memoirs and opinion pieces, social scientific analyses, and even psychoanalytic ones.
6. My research assistant and I read and systematically coded a sample of the briefs, representing a third of the entire corpus of all briefs submitted and made available for download on the commission's website (now closed down). The French- and English-language versions of the report (full and abridged) could also be found there.

7. I observed the commission during a week-long series of hearings and meetings in Montréal on November 26–30, 2007, which also included two evening citizens' forums (one in French, the other in English). Radio-Canada's coverage of the hearings, the press conference upon the publication of the report, parliamentary discussions of the report, and various interviews with the commissioners and politicians can be watched at http://www.radio-canada.ca/nouvelles/National/2007/09/10/004-Bouchard-Taylor-Antenne.shtml. During my week-long observation of the commission's hearings in Montréal, I also conducted informal interviews with participants who presented briefs, as well as with "ordinary citizens" present at the hearings. I have also discussed the commission's work and the debate on several occasions with Gérard Bouchard, who co-chaired the commission.

8. While this historical interpretation is a key feature of the Québécois national narrative, several studies in the last twenty years have critically reexamined the putative chiaroscuro that contrasts the Duplessis years' "Great Darkness" with the Quiet Revolution's "light." They reject the notion of the Quiet Revolution as a rupture and radical beginning, emphasizing instead continuity with the liberal tradition in Québec (Bourque, Duchastel and Beauchemin1994; Gagnon and Sarra-Bournet 1997; Bélanger, Comeau, and Métivier 2000; Bouchard 2005). That literature stresses the legacy of the Patriots' liberal movement and identifies the roots of the Quiet Revolution in the 1940s' and 1950s' liberal activism of *Cité Libre,* an anticlerical, pro-union publication cofounded in 1950 by Pierre Elliott Trudeau (Behiels 1985); in religious movements within the Catholic Church itself (Meunier and Warren 2002); or in *Le Refus Global* ("Total Refusal"), an antiestablishment and antireligious manifesto published in 1948 by a group of artists and intellectuals who advocated the total rejection of all conventions and promoted free thinking. Calling for "an untamed need for liberation," the manifesto incited "resplendent anarchy" and criticized the "cassocks that have remained the sole repositories of faith, knowledge, truth, and national wealth" (http://www.geocities.com/Athens/Forum/5462/refusglo.html, accessed May 29, 2008). Although this type of opposition to the church existed before the 1960s, it became more meaningful during that decade because it coincided with, and found its home in, political developments.

9. I am following Anderson's definition here (1983).

10. In Montréal, for example, participation in Sunday Mass dropped by almost two-thirds in the 1960s, from 88% in 1957 to 30% in 1971 (Hamelin 1984, 277). For an instructive account and perceptive analysis of Catholicism's trajectory in twentieth-century Québec (in English), see Baum (1991) and Christiano (2007).

11. http://www.onf-nfb.gc.ca/fra/collection/film/?id=4665 (accessed December 14, 2009). The demographic impact of the Quiet Revolution remains to this day a common concern, as expressed in one verse of a hit song called "Dégénérations"—the title playing on the decline of generational transmission and its "degenerative" aspects. The song nostalgically recounts the achievements of previous generations and critically assesses the moral void left behind by the baby boomers' Quiet Revolution: "Your great-great grandmother had 14 children/Your great grandmother had almost as many/And your grandmother had three, which was plenty/Then your mother didn't want any—you were just an accident/Now you, girl, change partners all the time/When you screw up you save the day by aborting/But some mornings you wake up crying/After dreaming at night of a large table surrounded with children" (Mes Aïeux, "Dégénérations," 2007).

12. Québec has control over immigration to its territory and regards prior knowledge of French as an important factor in reviewing immigration applications. Approximately 40 percent of immigrants settling in Québec therefore know French (about 25 percent know only French, about 15 percent know both French and English, 20 percent know English only, and 40 percent know neither French nor English; http://www.micc.gouv.qc.ca/fr/recherches-statistiques/index.html, accessed December 14, 2009).

13. Haitians, who are francophone and Catholic, have been relatively successfully integrated into Québec society and have not been the object (or subject) of debates during the investigation on reasonable accommodation.

14. Approximately 80 percent of Québec's population is French speaking, self-identifying as descendants of French settlers in Canada. That group constitutes about 25 percent of Canada's population.

15. Akin to Nicolas Sarkozy's notion of "positive secularism"—*laïcité positive*.

16. http://www.patrimoine-religieux.qc.ca/en/aidefinanciere/soutien.php (accessed December 9, 2011).

17. http://www.patrimoine-religieux.qc.ca/en/aidefinanciere/principes.php (accessed December 9, 2011).

18. The state does not solely fund the restoration and preservation of Catholic sites, and the website of the Conseil is careful, in its visuals, to showcase religious patrimony of other religious communities. It funds projects of diverse religious communities insofar as they are recognized as religious patrimony. By reason of the sheer number of Catholic sites in Québec, however, the latter constitute the overwhelming majority of projects funded.

19. Charest is the chief of the Liberal Party. Despite its name, that party is on the right of the Parti Québécois, the separatist party in Québec. Contrary to what is often assumed, nationalists in Québec are on the left, and federalist parties, such as the Liberal Party, are more conservative socially, economically, and culturally.

20. http://www.quebeclaique.org/ (accessed April 2, 2011).

21. http://www.assnat.qc.ca/fr/travaux-parlementaires/projets-loi/projet-loi-94-39-1.html

References

Anderson, Benedict. 1991. *Imagined Communities: Reflections on the Origins and Spread of Nationalism*, New York: Verso.

Asad, Talal. 1999. "Religion, Nation-State, Secularism." Pp. 178–196 in *Nation and Religion: Perspectives on Europe and Asia*, edited by Peter van der Veer and Hartmut Lehmann. Princeton, NJ: Princeton University Press.

Asad, Talal. 2003. *Formations of the Secular: Christianity, Islam, Modernity*. Stanford, CA: Stanford University Press.

Balthazar, Louis. 1986. *Bilan du nationalisme au Québec*. Montréal: L'Hexagone.

Baril, Daniel. 2007. "Les accommodements religieux pavent la voie à l'intégrisme." *Ethique Publique* 9(1): 174–181.

Baubérot, Jean. 2007. *Les laicités dans le monde*. Paris: Presses Universitaires de France.

Baum, Gregory. 1991. *The Church in Quebec*. Outremont: Novalis.

Beauchemin, Jacques. 1995. "Nationalisme québécois et crise du lien social." *Les Cahiers de Recherche Sociologique* 25. 101–123

Beauchemin, Jacques, Gilles Bourque, and Jules Duchastel. 1991. "L'Église, la tradition et la modernité." *Recherches Sociographiques* 32: 175–197.

Bédard, Éric. 2005. "De la difficulté à penser le conservatisme canadien-français." *Recherches Sociographiques* 46: 453–471.

Bégin, Paul. 2007. "Laïcité et accommodements raisonnables." *Ethique Publique* 9(1): 158–165.

Behiels, Michael D. 1985. *Prelude to Quebec's Quiet Revolution: Liberalism Versus Neo-Nationalism, 1945–1960*. Kingston, Ontario: McGill-Queen's University Press.

Bélanger, Yves, Robert Comeau, and Céline Métivier, eds. 2000. *La Révolution Tranquille 40 ans plus tard: un bilan*. Montréal: VLB éditeur.

Bender, Courtney, and Pamela E. Klassen, eds. 2010. *After Pluralism: Reimagining Religious Engagement*. New York: Columbia University Press.

Berger, Peter L., ed. 1999. *The Desecularization of the World*. Grand Rapids/Cambridge: Wm. B. Eerdmans Publishing Co.

Bock-Côté, Mathieu. 2007. "Behind Secularism, the Nation: Looking Back at the Controversy of Reasonable Accommodations and the Crisis of Québécois Multiculturalism." *GLOBE: Revue Internationale d'Etudes Québécoises* 10(2): 95–113.

Bosset, Pierre. 2005. "Le droit et la régulation de la diversité religieuse en France et au Québec: une même problématique, deux approches." *Bulletin d'Histoire Politique* 13(3): 79–96.

Bouchard, Gérard. 1999. *La Nation québécoise au futur et au passé*. Montréal: VLB éditeur.

Bouchard, Gérard. 2005. "L'imaginaire de la Grande Noirceur et de la Révolution Tranquille: fictions identitaires et jeux de mémoire au Québec." *Recherches sociographiques* 46:411–436

Bouchard, Gérard, and Charles Taylor. 2008a. *Building the Future: A Time for Reconciliation. Report*. Québec: Gouvernement du Québec.

Bouchard, Gérard, and Charles Taylor. 2008b. *Fonder l'avenir. Le temps de la conciliation. Rapport*. Québec: Gouvernement du Québec.

Bouchard, Gérard, and Charles Taylor. 2008c. *Building the Future: A Time for Reconciliation. Abridged Report*. Québec: Gouvernement du Québec.

Bourque, Gilles, Jules Duchastel, and Jacques Beauchemin. 1994. *La société libérale duplessiste, 1944–1960*. Montréal: Presses de l'Université de Montréal.

Breton, Raymond. 1988. "From Ethnic to Civic nationalism: English Canada and Quebec." *Ethnic and Racial Studies* 11:1, 85–102.

Casanova, Jose. 1994. *Public Religions in the Modern World*. Chicago: University of Chicago Press.

Chaves, Mark. 1994. "Secularization as Declining Religious Authority." *Social Forces* 72: 749–774.

Christiano, Kevin J. 2007. "The Trajectory of Catholicism in Twentieth-Century Quebec." Pp. 21–61 in *The Church Confronts Modernity: Catholicism Since 1950 in the United States, Ireland, and Quebec*, edited by Leslie Woodcock Tentler. Washington, DC: Catholic University of American Press.

Clément, Eric, and Marc-Alain Wolfe. 2008. *Québec sur le divan: Raisonnements de psys à l'heure des accommodements*. Montréal: Voix Paralelles.

Côté-Boucher, Karine, and Ratiba Hadj-Moussa. 2008. "Malay Identity: Islam, Secularism and Preventive Logic in France and Quebec." *Cahiers de Recherche Sociologique* 46: 61–77.

Dillon, Michele. 2007. "Decline and Continuity: Catholicism Since 1950 in the United States, Ireland, and Quebec." Pp. 239–267 in *The Church Confronts Modernity: Catholicism since 1950 in the United States, Ireland, and Quebec*, edited by Leslie Woodcock Tentler. Washington, DC: The Catholic University of America Press.

Dufour, Valérie, and Jeff Heinrich. 2008. *Circus Quebecus: sous le chapiteau de la Commission Bouchard-Taylor*. Montréal: Les Éditions du Boréal (April 1, 2008).

Dumont, Fernand. 1971. *Idéologies au Canada français*. Québec: Presses de l'Université Laval.

Dumont, Fernand. 1986. "Histoire du catholicisme québécois, histoire d'une société." *Recherches Sociographiques* 27: 115–125.

Dumont, Fernand. 1993. *Genèse de la société québécoise*. Montréal: Boréal.

Eid, Nadia F. 1978. *Le clergé et le pouvoir politique au Québec: une analyse de l'idéologie ultramontaine au milieu du XIXe siècle*. Montréal: Hurtubise.

Ferretti, Lucia. 1999. *Brève histoire de l'Église Catholique au Québec*. Montréal: Boréal.

Fournier, Marcel. 2001. "Québec Sociology and Québec Society: The Construction of a Collective Identity." *Canadian Journal of Sociology* 26(3): 333–346.

Frenette, Yves. 1998. *Brève histoire des Canadiens français*. Montréal: Boréal.

Gagnon, Alain-G., and Michel Sarra-Bournet, eds. 1997. *Entre la Grande Noirceur et la société libérale*. Montréal: Editions Québec-Amérique.

Gagnon, Nicole. 2000. "Comment peut-on être Québécois?" *Recherches Sociographiques* 12(3): 515–566.

Gaudreault-Desbiens, Jean-Francois. 2009. "Religious Challenges to the Secularized Identity of an Insecure Polity: A Tentative Sociology of Quebec's Reasonable Accommodation Debate." Pp. 151–175 in *Legal Practice and Cultural Diversity*, edited by Ralph Grillo. Surrey, England and Burlington, Vermont: Ashgate.

Geadah, Yolande. 2007. *Accommodements raisonnables: droit à la différence et non différence des droits*. Montréal: VLB.

Guindon, Hubert. 1988. *Québec Society: Tradition, Modernity, and Nationhood*. Toronto: University of Toronto Press.

Hall, John A. 2001. "Liberalism and Statelessness: Québec in Contexts." *Scottish Affairs* 42–53. [Special Issue "Stateless Nations in the 21st Century: Scotland, Catalonia and Quebec," edited by J. MacInnes and D. McCrone.]

Hamelin, Jean. 1984. *Histoire du catholicisme québécois: Le XXe siècle*. Vol. 2 (De 1940 à nos jours). Montréal: Boréal Express.

Handler, Richard. 1988. *Nationalism and the Politics of Culture in Quebec*. Madison: University of Wisconsin Press.

Heap, Ruby, Pierre Savard, Fernand Dumont, Jean Hamelin, and Nicole Gagnon. 1986. "Débat: le Catholicisme au XXe siècle." *Recherches Sociographiques* 27: 101–131.

Hughes, Everett C. 1943. *French Canada in Transition*. Chicago: University of Chicago Press.

Koussens, David. 2009. "Neutrality of the State and Regulation of Religious Symbols in Schools in Québec and France." *Social Compass* 56(2): 202–213.

Kuru, Ahmet T. 2007. "Passive and Assertive Secularism: Historical Conditions, Ideological Struggles, and State Policies toward Religion." *World Politics* 59(4) 568–594.

Lamonde, Yvan. 2000. *Histoire sociale des idées au Québec*. Saint-Laurent, QC: Fides.

Lamonde, Yvan, and Claude Corbo. 1999. *Le rouge et le bleu: une anthologie de la pensée politique au Québec de la Conquête à la Révolution Tranquille*. Montréal: Presses de l'Université de Montréal.

Lemieux, Raymond. 1990. "Le catholicisme québécois: une question de culture." *Sociologie et sociétés* 22: 145–164.

Lemieux, Raymond. 2006. "Catholicisme et fonction identitaire: du 'Canada français' au Québec contemporain." In *Le Canada français: son temps, sa nature, son héritage*, edited by G. Gagné. Québec: Nota Bene, 29–41

Létourneau, Jocelyn. 1997. "La Révolution tranquille, catégorie identitaire du Québec contemporain." Pp. 95–108 in *Duplessis: entre la Grande Noirceur et la société libérale*, edited by Alain-G. Gagnon and Michel Sarra-Bournet. Montréal: Québec/Amérique.

Mann, Susan, 1988. *The Dream of Nation: A Social and Intellectual History of Quebec*. Montréal: McGill-Queen's University Press.

Martin, David. 1978. *A General Theory of Secularization*. New York: Blackwell and Oxford.

Martin, David. 2005. *On Secularization: Towards a Revised General Theory*. Surrey, England and Burlington, Vermont: Ashgate.

Meunier, E.-Martin and Jean-Philippe Warren. 2002. *Sortir de la " Grande noirceur ". L'horizon personnaliste de la Révolution Tranquille*, Sillery: Septentrion.

Milot, Micheline. 2002. *La laïcité dans le nouveau monde. Le cas du Québec*. Turnhout: Brepols.

Milot, Micheline. 2005. "Les principes de laïcité politique au Québec et au Canada." *Bulletin d'Histoire Politique* 13(3): 13–27.

Norris, Pippa. 2004. *Sacred and Secular: Religion and Politics Worldwide*. New York: Cambridge University Press.

Potvin, Maryse. 2008. *Crise des accommodements raisonnables: une fiction médiatique? Montréal:* Athena.

Routhier, Gilles. 1997. *L'Église canadienne et Vatican II*. Saint-Laurent, Québec: Fides.

Saint-Pierre, Jocelyn, and Michel Sarra-Bournet. 2001. *Les nationalismes au Québec du XIXe au XXIe siècle*. Sainte-Foy, QC: Presses de l'Université Laval.

Stoker, Valerie. 2003. "Drawing the Line: Hasidic Jews, Eruvim, and the Public Space of Outremont, Quebec." *History of Religions* 43(1), 18–49.

Stoker, Valerie. 2007. "Zero Tolerance? Sikh Swords, School Safety, and Secularism in Québec." *Journal of the American Academy of Religion* 75(4): 814–839.

Swidler, Ann. 1986. "Culture in Action: Symbols and Strategies." *American Sociological Review* 51: 273–286.

Sztompka, Piotr. 1993. *The Sociology of Social Change*. Cambridge, MA: Blackwell Publishing.

Taylor, Charles. 2007. *A Secular Age*. Cambridge, MA: The Belknap Press of Harvard University Press.

Tentler, Leslie Woodcock, ed. 2007. *The Church Confronts Modernity: Catholicism Since 1950 in the United States, Ireland, and Quebec*. Washington, DC: Catholic University of American Press.

Thériault, Joseph-Yvon. 1999. "La nation francophone d'Amérique: Canadiens, Canadiens français, Québécois." Pp. 111–137 in *Dislocation et permanence: l'invention du Canada au quotidien*, edited by C. Andrew. Ottawa: Ottawa University Press.

Thompson, Bernard. 2007. *Le Syndrome Hérouxville ou les accommodements raisonnables*. Montréal: Momentum.

Venne, Michel, ed. 2000. *Penser la nation québécoise*. Montréal: Québec-Amérique.

11

Revisiting Religious Power:
The Korean Evangelical Church as
a Disciplinary Institution

KELLY H. CHONG

Recent efforts by students of religion within and outside of sociology to rethink conventional approaches to studying religion have opened up a number of innovative avenues for reconceptualizing religion in the modern world. One such notable approach has been the call for the study of religion as "lived" (Hall 1997). Although to study religion as "lived" signifies a number of things, the heart of this approach lies in moving away from the traditional focus on the "official" aspects of religion toward observing and analyzing the myriad ways religion is experienced, understood, imagined, and practiced by ordinary people in their everyday contexts. Grounded on the assumption that religious beliefs can hardly be studied apart from human activity and the practices of everyday life, these approaches are concerned not only with uncovering what religions look like in their multiplicity but also with the dimension of lived practice, that is, with what people *do* with religion, how "particular people, in particular places and times, live in, with, through and against the religious idioms available to them in culture" (Orsi 1997, 7). This methodology, which takes people seriously as actors capable of creatively (re)interpreting and (re)fashioning religion according to their local circumstances, has necessitated efforts to fundamentally reconceptualize what religion is, generating challenges to some cherished analytical categories in the study of religion—for instance, Christo-centrism, a focus on institutional or positive aspects of religions—and what it means to be "religious" in the modern world.

Owing to its emphasis on lived practice, another important hallmark of this approach has been what one scholar has referred to as the "hermeneutics of hybridity," (Orsi in Hall 1997) an interpretive lens that is committed to avoiding easy, functionalist explanations about what religion does and to embracing instead the unpredictable nature of religious creation and activity, including the unstable, ambivalent, and contradictory aspects of the sacred as it becomes the site of reworking and improvisations by the actors. As in many studies employing this kind of approach, one notable implication of this methodology has been to uncover and shine light on the various liberatory and transgressive possibilities of religion, as when religious idioms, for example, are shown to be appropriated in unexpected and innovative ways by the actors than in ways and for ends sought by those in positions of authority.

At the heart of this methodological and interpretative reorientation, one can discern the recent shift in the thinking about religious power, which follows the wider reconceptualizations of power that have occurred in the academy over the last few decades. In particular, this reorientation takes cue from what can be broadly characterized as "poststructuralist" approaches to power, which, grounded in the ideas of such thinkers as Michel Foucault (1990 [1978]), foreground "de-centered" conceptions of power in which culture is seen as a field of both the inscription of and resistance to power (Rubin 1996). This line of theorizing also draws inspirations from what Sherry Ortner (1984) has labeled "practice theory," a school of theorizing that advocates an "action-based approach" to analyzing human behavior centered on the "doing subject" (seen as an active strategizing/calculating agent), or what Ortner calls the "strategic model" of human action.

As some scholars have pointed out, however, this strong imperative on the charting and politics of practice inherent in this approach have also resulted in interpretive orientations that sometimes tend to overemphasize agency, improvisation, and resistance at the expense of religion's "complicity in sustaining structures and patterns of alienation and domination" (Orsi 1997, 15). Although there is no question that this interpretive redirection has been critical in complicating our view of religion as more than simply an "opiate of the masses," it is important to be mindful that the articulation between religious idioms and potentialities for power and/or resistance is always a socially and historically specific matter. Taking seriously, then, the multiplicities and the complexities of lived experiences of religions as they emerge in different social contexts, I suggest that what is needed is a more balanced analysis of the meaning, operation, and effects of "power" as they play out within diverse religious contexts.[1]

Drawing upon my ethnographic study of South Korean evangelicalism and women's religious practices conducted between 1996 and 2006, I propose in this paper to revisit the important question of religious power. In the poststructural approach mentioned earlier, one way that religious power, and power in general, has been conceptualized is as that which is nonlocalized, multidirectional, and mobile; in this perspective, power is not seen as one-sided or monolithic, even when we can and do speak of dominance or oppression, because power is not seen as a property or possession of one group or another, but that which circulates within a social body or institutions. As Foucault reminds us (1990 [1978], 90–95), power, understood thus as a "multiplicity of force relations," is furthermore always exercised in relation to "mobile points" of resistance, which is necessarily inscribed in the very exercise of power. But in works on religion that make use of this nonbinary, nonhegemonic view of power, what is often overshadowed are direct investigations of the *disciplinary* effects and nature of power and the fact that religious institutions must be seen first and foremost as regulatory and normalizing institutions whose aim is to effect specific constitution of subjects. Like the family, school, or medical establishment, religion is one of the myriad institutions in modern society that can and often do serve as agents of repressive power, which, through the deployment of specific sets of disciplinary techniques that enable repressive, as well as productive, operations of power, work to govern and regulate human mind and behavior. Thus, as Orsi (1997, 15–16) observes, when speaking of religious institutions and power, it may not be enough to speak of religious subversion and resistance unless we also speak of how these movements of opposition may be at the same time idioms of discipline; that is, "just as we have learned to understand the way power operates in the modern discourse and practices of freedom, so we might consider the ways that religious idioms, even those that appear oppositional to participants and to ethnographers, are themselves deeply, subtly, and inevitably implicated in strategies of social and psychological discipline" (p. 15).

By showing the complex ways in which Korean evangelical women practice and appropriate their faiths, I highlight in this chapter the dimensions and operations of religious power that often remain underexplored in discussions of lived religion—its disciplinary dimensions. In doing so, this chapter addresses in particular two of the "edges" with which this volume is concerned: pursuing critical engagement with religion and exploring religious experiences outside of the US context. While the religious beliefs and practices of the female believers in my study, and the dynamics of religious power at work within their churches, do embody the dialogic tension between regulation and resistance, discipline and empowerment, the clear limits of evangelicalism's transformative possibilities for women—possibilities that lie especially in its capacity to heal and uplift—reveal the formidable potency of the normative and regulating dimensions of religious power, spotlighting the complicit relationship between religion and social discipline, between the sacred and the power of culture (Hall 1997; Ammerman 2007; McGuire 2008).

By focusing on both the discursive and spiritual processes by which the boundary-transgressing powers of the feminine are redomesticated and proper Confucian-evangelical feminine subjectivities reconstituted, I illustrate how the church's technologies of gender discipline articulate with and transpose upon what Foucault calls the "technologies of the self."[2] In particular, I explore a core set of discursive and spiritual disciplinary technologies—especially as deployed in small-group contexts such as cell meetings, Bible study, and specialized seminars on the family and marriage—that are employed by the church for the purposes of generating a specific feminine religious habitus.[3] While fully acknowledging the empowering, even subversive, possibilities of these believers' encounters with the sacred, both in the realms of the spiritual and the domestic as I explore extensively elsewhere (see Chong 2008), I empha- size in this article the regulatory/disciplinary dimensions of women's religious experiences, particularly as these relate to women's continued embeddedness in the family/gender regimes of South Korea. This underscores our need for critical engagements with religion that illuminate religion's complex and con- tradictory roles across different social and religious spaces in the contempo- rary world: its role as a source both of empowerment and of disempowerment and conflict.

The observations and analyses presented in this chapter are based largely on ethnographic data and interviews gathered from a study of two large, middle- class evangelical churches in Seoul—one Presbyterian and the other Methodist (the two largest denominations in South Korea)—but incorporates my obser- vations and studies of more than twenty evangelical churches in Seoul.[4] As I make clearer in the following pages, although South Korean evangelical churches are by no means monolithic in their beliefs, the ideologies of gender and family espoused by the vast majority of the churches and the patriarchally oriented institutional culture of these churches are, even across denomina- tional lines, remarkably similar, as are their predominantly middle-class char- acteristics. Thus, although this study does not make claims of generalizability to all Protestant churches in South Korea, the study's findings do reflect an important set of core dimensions of middle-class women's experiences and encounters with evangelicalism and patriarchy in South Korea.

Women and Korean Evangelicalism

Ever since evangelical Protestantism entered Korea in the late 1880s by way of Western missionaries, women and the church have developed a knotty rela- tionship. In light of the extreme position of subordination endured by Korean women under the traditional Confucian social structure, scholars, on the one hand, give evangelicalism due credit for its role as an emancipatory force for women. In addition to facilitating general literacy among ordinary people by translating the Bible into the native vernacular *hangeul* (native Korea alpha- bet), evangelicalism played a critical role in pioneering women's education in

Korea by founding modern girls' schools and universities; many early female
leaders and intellectuals of the country were Christians and products of these
missionary-established educational institutions. By employing lay women as
church workers, the church also offered women—many of them belonging to
poor, marginalized groups such as widows and unmarried women—unprec-
edented economic and professional opportunities outside of the domestic
sphere. On the other hand, the fundamentally conservative nature of the missionaries' views and activities in Korea are not denied; despite the progressive
effects of the missionaries' activities for women, it is no secret that the missionaries' goals were in no way aimed at elevating women above the conventional notions of womanhood, and despite their genuine impulses to improve
the lot of Korean women, the missionaries' ultimate purpose was to promote
evangelization through education (Choi 2009; Kang 1996; Yi 1985).

Expressive of the syncretic blending of orthodox, evangelical traditions of
the early revivalist missionaries with native cultural elements, as well as the
church's relative isolation from the liberal theological developments occurring
in the West through the twentieth century, the Protestant church that evolved
in Korea over the last century has been a distinctively patriarchal institution,
both culturally and theologically (Clark 1996; Martin 1990; Ro and Nelson 1995;
Suh 1985). Some scholars estimate that presently, as many as 90 percent of
Protestant churches in South Korea can be described as conservative-evangelical
(Lee 2006). Within this context, women, despite their numerical predominance
and pivotal importance to the church's survival and growth, have come to
occupy an unquestionably subordinate status and role within the church organization and hierarchy.

Their subordinate positions notwithstanding, Korean evangelical women's
relationship to the official beliefs and doctrines of the church is, and has been,
a highly complex one. As a generation of women caught in the maelstrom of
post–World War II social changes, changes that have induced far-reaching
destabilization of the structures and relations of gender and family, many
women in my study seek church involvement both as a way to cope with personal sufferings arising from a range of difficult domestic dilemmas *and* as a
strategy for resolving these intractable domestic challenges. These dilemmas—
ranging from problems of loveless marriages, intense conflicts with husbands
and mothers-in-law, and unmanageable domestic burdens to frustrations from
unfulfilled individual aspirations—stem from the fundamental contradictions
of the modern patriarchal family and the wider gender system, centered particularly upon the acute discrepancy between the profound transformations in
women's expectations/horizons about family/marital relations and the ongoing traditionalist demands on women.

In this situation, women's evangelical beliefs and practices serve a distinctly
empowering role in their lives. Evangelical faith, first of all, serves as a critical

spiritual resource for women, particularly in its capacity to foster psychic/emotional healing from the injuries inflicted by the patriarchal family system, as well as to promote a sense of empowerment that enhances the ability of women to deal better with difficult situations. By enabling the women to access divine power through various institutional activities, institutional involvement in the form of church service furthermore helps to reinforce such empowering and self-transformative processes by providing women with the opportunity to expand themselves beyond the domestic arena, gain a measure of personal self-fulfillment, and be rewarded and recognized for their accomplishments in this nondomestic arena. As an important and unique community institution, the evangelical church is particularly important in a society lacking in a wide array of other institutional mechanisms for helping women to deal with domestic challenges.

Despite their prominent role in Korean women's struggle for deliverance from patriarchal oppression and control, the evangelical churches in my study must, however, be recognized first and foremost as vehicles for propagating the traditionalist ideologies of gender/family, which are ultimately aimed at maintaining and restoring the cohesion of the existing family and gender arrangements. Whereas women successfully appropriate the evangelical beliefs and practices in various ways in their efforts to resist and cope with the injuries and restrictions of the patriarchal system, they are also, within the churches, confronted with a powerful set of religiously sanctioned views on gender and family that are aimed at effecting specific kinds of feminine subject formation and at redomesticating women to the family/gender system. I will examine first the contours of this ideology, then the key disciplinary technologies employed by the church to generate a lasting habitus of submission in women, actuated through what I refer to as the technologies of group confession and criticism, combined with key techniques of psychological/behavioral/spiritual discipline focused on helping women locate and renounce deep-seated, transgressive desires and embrace obedience.

Smarty Women: Diagnosing the Contemporary Family Dilemma

The views on gender and family encountered in the evangelical churches of this study have one main goal: the stabilization of contemporary family relations through the transformation of female behavior and consciousness. The churches do, to be sure, attempt to "reform" men as well, but there is no mistaking the fact that the bulk of the attention is focused on facilitating female accommodation to the church-sanctioned order of family and gender as a means of ensuring family stability. In other words, the churches provide women with an array of important channels or "outlets" through which to cope with the problems and conflicts of the patriarchal family while seeking ultimately to bring about the resolution of these conflicts by securing women's recommitment to the principles of patriarchal gender relations.

According to the official discourse espoused by the churches in my study, one of the most vexing issues in contemporary Korean society is the problem of the family. Along with an array of other social problems of perennial concern to South Koreans such as national division, political repression, economic insecurities, and governmental corruption, the problem of the modern family is, as manifested by increasing levels of marital conflicts and youth problems, a serious expression of the crisis facing Korean society today. These family problems, according to the churches, are a reflection and manifestation of the general degradation of the wider social and moral order, a decline in traditional values, and a turn away from the fundamental principles of human relationships as defined by the Confucian system—in particular, the hierarchically governed relationships based on gender and age, the violation of which spawns conflicts between women and men, young and old. In the realm of the family, the problem is attributed to the deviations of individuals from the all-important principles of gender hierarchy and roles that are the bedrock of family order but that have been undermined by the influence of modern individualism and egalitarianism.

The rhetoric of church leaders, however, suggests a more specific diagnosis of the problem: although the leaders generally attribute the problems of the family to deviations by both men *and* women from the proper principles of gender, men and women are not seen as being equally responsible for the problems. For them, the source of the current family crisis lies primarily in the actions of women and in female violations of the gender order, especially their attempt to rise above their proper positions and their "forgetting" of the importance of their family roles. According to one "family seminar" leader in a Presbyterian church:

> Many Korean women don't know why they have so many conflicts at home. They think they are doing all right, but after taking my seminar, one thing they realize that they all have in common is that they have all been too "smarty" in front of their husbands. They have tried to possess too much power, leadership in the family. Only when women change these things do husbands become truly family-oriented.... The purpose of my seminar is first of all to strengthen the basis of faith in the members, and to teach the women the position and duties of a wife, and how to raise children. Most Korean women these days just meet someone, get married, and just live. They don't really know how to maintain a family life. I try to teach them the importance of family

life, how important the role of the wife is to the husband and to the family. I try to instill in them the proper faith and Christian values through which they can influence the family as proper mothers and wives. The point is to transform their basic ways of thinking.[5]

At the most basic level, being "smarty" signifies women's violation of the fundamental principle of gender hierarchy and order by stepping out of their prescribed role and authority boundaries. In the Korean context, however, the application of such a term suggests a more encompassing critique of the fundamental deviations of contemporary women from all of the basic principles of "virtuous" Confucian femininity and womanhood, the decline of which are seen as the real causes of the modern family crisis and the unhappiness and suffering of women themselves. According to the church, such deviations are constituted by a number of major behavioral transgressions of contemporary women, the most central of which are the habits and attitudes of "egoism," "arrogance/haughtiness," and "impatience."

The term *egoism* denotes all forms of behavior deemed to reflect self-centeredness on the part of women, behaviors that directly violate the self-denying and submissive qualities of the ideal Korean female. Within the church discourse, all those actions considered to be egoistic refer in particular to women's assertions of their own desires and wants within the family, to "have one's way in everything." Although this term in the Korean context does not so much signify selfishness in terms of pursuing one's own personal desires as much as those regarding the welfare of the family (although the former does apply in some cases), the women are reminded that such an assertive orientation is responsible for the greater part of the domestic conflict. *Haughtiness* or arrogance, a trait closely related to egoism, refers to the attitude that a woman thinks she is better or knows more than others, especially her husband. Commonly, haughtiness denotes an attitude among women who are seen to behave without the restraint of proper feminine modesty and humility, another characteristic of the ideal "virtuous" woman. Finally, *impatience* refers to a lack of forbearance toward difficult situations and the shortcomings of others.

Despite its official view of women as essentially weak and dependent, such diagnoses makes clear what the church views as one of the main causes of contemporary domestic disorder—the unruly powers of women. That is to say, domestic order is threatened by the innate powerfulness and willfulness that reside deep in the Korean female psyche that have become increasingly unruly and undisciplined in the modern age. Indeed, as we will see, the narratives of women do not suggest images of "weak" women, but to the contrary, tough, aggressive women filled with an array of tremendous ambitions and desires that become sources of their frustrations because they cannot easily be fulfilled within the constraints of Korean society. These ambitions may not be for the purposes of personal self-fulfillment, but rather directed toward their families. However, women's single-minded pursuit of them nevertheless suggests a high degree of aggression rather than passivity, and their interactions with their family members often suggest concerted efforts at dominance rather than submission.

This observation reflects the reality that the image of Korean women has always been double and contradictory—submissive and subordinate on the one hand, but as "pillars" of the household, strong and "tough," even aggressive, on the other, especially in the realm of domestic affairs (see also Deuchler 1992). It also reveals the irony inherent in the gender ideology and structure of the Confucian family system: although the family provides a highly legitimate space for the expression and exercise of women's powers within the domestic sphere through its strict division between the "inside" and "outside" and the tremendous value it places on women's domestic roles, it must also address the constant danger posed by the possibility that these "powers" will break out of their bounds by vigilantly and relentlessly policing and containing them.

To achieve this goal and restore domestic harmony, the church's solution for women pivots around two key behavioral injunctions: docile obedience and endurance. For families threatened by women's willfulness, obedience is crucial because it is the essential behavioral principle necessary to helping reestablish gender hierarchy, especially as a means to discipline women's willful impulses. Although the churches do advise the husbands to love the wives in return, the emphasis is that the only way to attain real family harmony and reestablish family order is for the wife to begin to obey the husband in a heartfelt and unconditional manner that sincerely recognizes his superior position and authority. In addition to obedience, women must also arduously cultivate the virtue of endurance to avert family conflict since the reason for the instability in modern marriages is that Korean women have lost their traditional ability to endure marital suffering and difficulties.

These injunctions are, however, not easy to follow. Furthermore, many women often do not readily embrace these injunctions; indeed, despite the tremendous weight of the religious sanction behind the view on gender/family relations advocated by the churches, the initial reactions of most women are surprisingly ambivalent, even skeptical, questioning what appears to be the inherent injustices and unfairness of the call for absolute female obedience. One woman remarked, "Yes, well, in the beginning, I thought, gee, is she trying to turn us into slaves? How can she do that, with feminism and all nowadays? Why should we obey the husband only?" To foster appropriate and effective transformations of the consciousness and behavior of their female members, the churches then make use of a well-defined set of disciplinary strategies from which we can discern the workings of several key aspects of the "technologies of the self."

Disciplining Women: Technologies of Group Confession and Criticism

As Michel Foucault (1988) correctly observes, Christianity is not only a salvation religion but also a confessional religion. This means that Christianity does more than demand strict adherence to and acceptance of truth and dogma; it requires that one unceasingly demonstrate one's belief of these truths. But as Foucault also observes, Christianity demands yet another form of truth obligation from that of faith:

> [E]ach person has the duty to know who he is, that is, to try to know what is happening inside him, acknowledge faults, to recognize temptations, to locate desires; and everyone is obliged to disclose these things either to God or to others in the community and hence to bear public or private witness against oneself. The truth obligation of faith and the self are linked together. The link permits a purification of the soul impossible without self-knowledge. (p. 40)

One major disciplinary technique employed by the churches in my study to effect transformation of women's consciousness and behavior is that of group confession and criticism. In the churches, the primary venues in which these practices of confession and group criticisms take place are most often cell meetings—most of which are gender segregated—and other small-group gatherings like the family and marriage seminars. For women, the practices of group confession are regularized rituals of self-disclosure and intensive collective/self-critique that are designed ultimately to foster the members' receptivity to the church's views on gender and the family and help them arrive at a "proper" understanding of their roles and responsibilities in regard to their families. In addition to bringing about a group articulation of individual problems and orienting the members to the acceptance of and surrendering to the divine power and intervention for resolving these problems, a major part of these group meeting agendas consists of concerted efforts to engage the participants in the practices and rituals of intensive and repeated self-critique, which would pave the way for the acceptance of "correct" domestic solutions. This step signals the start of a self-breakdown process that prepares an individual for a more totalistic self-renunciation, then self-reconstitution as a model evangelical female.

Disclosure of Sins

The first step in this project of self-disclosure, of course, is to recognize and admit oneself as a sinner or a penitent. In evangelical conversion, it is only by first declaring oneself lost through sin that one surrenders oneself to salvation. Indeed, for all evangelicals in my study, this process of self-disclosure through admission of sins is the first critical stage in the self-transformative process. Although such self-disclosure can be arrived at privately, the means of accomplishing it are by definition collective, since the specific nature of "sins" is collectively defined and admission of these sins signifies aligning one's perspective with those of the group. It is important to note here that the specific technique the convert is expected to adopt in successfully moving through the process of self-disclosure is both an intellectual one (through critical reflection and self-examination) and a spiritual/ emotional one (through prayer and other forms of spiritual practice). In addition, the convert is expected to display evidence of knowledge of one's state of sinfulness through repeated participation in some variant of public testimony or witnessing.

For example, in several of the all-female cell group meetings I observed— informal, weekly Bible study/fellowship gatherings held in the homes of one of the cell group members—a major part of this process of self-disclosure for women consisted of correctly identifying the domestic sins outlined earlier. Once this state of sinfulness is embraced by the participant, the process of self-transformation is further advanced by the ritual of surrender, a relinquishment of one's will and control to God. In general discussions of evangelical conversion, surrendering is considered a step necessary to and constitutive of genuine commitment, a point at which a person, after admitting that she is a sinner, delivers herself up to God (Rambo 1992). Accepting sinfulness and surrendering, then, constitute key moments of self-breakdown, a beginning of a crucial break with one's past identity, a form of self-destruction. Such sacrifice of the self, of one's will, is one of the most important technologies of the self deployed within evangelical spiritual practice.

It is important to observe, on the other hand, that for these women, such acts of penitence and surrender simultaneously possess an empowering aspect since they serve as a central component of the healing process for many. For instance, in opening oneself up to God through the act of admission as a sinner, the believer undergoes an experience of profound release, which can become the first step in a healing process. For those weighed down by daily problems and conflicts that they feel helpless to solve or to control, the act of surrendering control to the divine, as well as to churchly authority, facilitates this healing process by enabling them to psychically "unburden" themselves of their problems and emotional pain, which is often experienced by women as liberating. Such emancipatory dimensions notwithstanding, it is important not to overlook the fact that these self-revelatory practices on the part of women *are* nonetheless a crucial part of the self-disciplining process that can undercut such liberatory potential. The rebirth that these women are expected to undergo denotes a specific form of gendered self-transformation aimed at enabling women to take up a specific set of subject positions in relation to the discourses and practices of Korean evangelical womanhood.

Rituals of Group: Self-Criticism

Along with identifying sins and embracing one's status as a sinner, another critical technology employed by the churches I have observed in my study to activate women's subjective transformations is that of group criticism, a strategy geared toward generating intensive self-examination and self-criticism within the group context for the purposes of helping bring about "rebirth," or reconstitution of identity.

One central way that the church works to help women recapture the proper feminine habitus from which they are seen to have strayed lies in persuading women to remember, and recommit to, their central role and responsibility as wives and mothers. These small-group venues, then, are spaces in which the women, through collective reflection and analysis, are expected to arrive at the realization of their various transgressions not just intellectually by way of sincere and heartfelt self-examination and self-criticism, which would lead to genuine repentance of domestic wrongdoings. Indeed, one of the most notable aspects about what occurs in these spaces is the intense level of self-critique that women engage in as they collectively struggle with and address their domestic dilemmas. A great deal of time and energy, whether through discussion or through tearful prayers, is devoted to confessing and atoning for their various domestic transgressions and misconduct, which the women are taught to believe are ultimately responsible for domestic conflicts.

This process of penitence and self-criticism—very similar to what Kanter (1972) has called a process of "mortification" in her studies of group commitment—begins with examining and then atoning for the variety of female domestic "sins" mentioned earlier. Women are repeatedly reminded, for instance, that the "sin" of egoism is one of the worst culprits of marital and familial discord. With respect to this, women are also told repeatedly that attempts to perpetually "have their way" in everything instead of deferring to the wishes of their husbands result not only in day-to-day marital discord but also in aberrant behavior of husbands, and eventually in their alienation. More specifically, serious domestic conflicts are seen to arise from the wives' attempts to assert their desires or wants toward their husbands such as those related to the husbands' general conduct or even earning capacity, because when wives are disappointed in these matters, which is often the case, resentments build with grave consequences for the husbands.

Furthermore, the inability of women to control their desires in this sphere results in such unproductive behaviors as constant "stir frying" or "nagging" of husbands, which not only anger but also ultimately emasculate them. For instance, one woman, speaking of her "greed" for money, admitted that she would not let her husband quit a job in which he was acutely miserable because she was afraid of financial implications for the family, subsequently driving her husband to drink and estrangement. Mothers also project their desires or wants upon their children as destructive ambitiousness. Confessions abound by women of their unbridled "greed" toward their children; one woman, for instance, admitted how pushing her children "to the limits" in school because she was so concerned about the "face" of her family to the outside world resulted in the children's permanent "mental paralysis." Another woman, reflecting upon her experiences of and lessons from participating in a family seminar, was led to confess the following:

> Before taking the family seminar, I was so self-centered. Got mad so often. When my husband said or did anything insensitive or hurtful, I couldn't endure it. I always had to say something confrontational, objecting. That is not in keeping with a life of faith. Even with the kids, it was centered on me, not on them. I drove them to do this or that and not to lose out to other kids because of my own desires and ambitions, not theirs. But I didn't realize how it hurt them, all the things I said, did. It killed their self-esteem.

This passage demonstrates how the charge of "egoism" is a critique not only of female assertiveness but also of something even more basic: the very existence of many and varied desires themselves, especially those that lead women to have "unreasonable" expectations of others, particularly of husbands and children. Such desires and the inability of women to keep them under control, then, become responsible for everyday disharmony and conflicts within the family.

The women are also reminded clearly that the "sin" of haughtiness—thinking oneself better or smarter than her husband—can be equally as destructive, and in one of the sessions, one woman said:

> I used to be so full of myself when I was in college. I used to not think much of boys. I used to think I was better than they were. So the thought of obeying men, that was very alien to me. So I caused a lot of trouble with my older brother, too. I wouldn't even bring him a glass of water when he asked. So when my husband and I first got married, he used to tell me to turn on the TV and stuff and I used to think, you do it, and I wouldn't. But then, this kind of thing just caused a lot of trouble and made me irritable and unhappy. I realized it would actually be easier just to do it for him, but I would still object all the time. So this caused so much trouble. But then I thought, if I really loved him, wouldn't I want to do everything for him? Do I really love him? But I still didn't think I should do it.

Another church member disclosed, "I really try to work on my personality, but it's hard to change. By nature, I'm quite hot-blooded you see. I have a lot of desire, greed. I have not been very good since my youth, I think. I was always really haughty. And you know, I had a good education too, so that made me even more arrogant, I guess. It's really hard to change these things."

Aside from being a major source of marital conflict, "bad" attitudes such as haughtiness and egoism lead to other negative consequences: for example, when things do not go their way, women are reminded that such attitudes lead to destructive emotions such as frustration, anger, and resentment that intensify family conflict. In cell meetings, members often seize upon violent outbursts of "ill- temper" and emotion as particularly "sinful" behaviors demanding correction because these are seen to have highly adverse effects on other family members. As one woman divulged:

> One of the things I'm trying so hard to change is my temper. I think I have the tendency to just act on my emotions. I am so irritable, get angry whenever things get bad, especially at my kids. If they don't do schoolwork or something, I'm always yelling at them. I know that this has a very bad influence on my kids but sometimes I just can't help it. So I repent about the same thing every week.

The groups also consider negative and critical attitudes toward others as being particularly detrimental to domestic relationships. Frustrated in a variety of ways at home, women are seen to develop all too often the nasty habit of criticizing and cutting others down, particularly their husbands. As one woman at a cell meeting disclosed, "What is my habitual sin? I find that my most egregious and habitual sin is toward my husband. I say things to hurt him all the time. I repent every week and pray that I may uphold him humbly and courteously, but this resolve doesn't last me a week."

Finally, in speaking of the "sin" of impatience, a cell leader noted that things may have gotten much easier for women in the modern age, but being a woman is still an extremely difficult matter in South Korean society, and women will not be able to keep their families together—and preserve their sanity—if they lose the ability to endure. After all, marriages stayed intact in previous generations despite the unspeakable difficulties of women because they were able to endure any kind of suffering. Nowadays, to the contrary, women have become weak, spoiled, and selfish with a sense of entitlement not conducive to enduring the difficulties of domestic life. The cell leader explained:

> These days, families are faced with unspeakable conflicts. High school kids beating up their fathers, couples beating each other up. We seem to have arrived at an age where people can't endure things. Until now,

we obeyed and submitted to our parents. But now, the attitude is that
people are born perfect so that they can do whatever they want. What
kind of principles are we using to raise our children? Things are this
way because of us [women]. We only focus on the negative things, the
bad times, can't endure them, and forget the good times. But what
kind of effects do these negative emotions have on our children?

Agreeing with the church's diagnosis, women affirm the belief that suffering
in marriage is inevitable, but that it is their inability to endure these trials
that is at the source of many domestic problems. The women reflect upon their
inability to forgive, in particular, as a central source of conflicts and are also
led to reflect harshly upon emotions of anger, resentment, and bitterness that
arise from feelings of pent-up hatred and frustrated desires, feelings that are
destructive not only to other family members but also, most of all, to themselves. As one cell member reflected, "I always had such a strong personality
that God had to work really hard to manage me. I had so much suffering in my
life, but my strong personality made it worse. I have always seen that those
women with gentle characters tend to lead relatively peaceful lives."

As the only way of restoring domestic harmony, women, then, are reminded
in one gathering after another that proper obedience and submission are the
only real solutions to their dilemmas, the bedrock principles of social order. As
I discuss later, a large part of these small-group activities consists not only of
enlightening women of these self-evident truths but also of instructing them
on the specific, practical techniques with which to achieve such proper obedience and acquire the capacity to better endure and forgive, techniques that are
simultaneously behavioral, psychological, and spiritual.

Self-Renunciation and Rebirth: Learning Obedience and Eradicating Unruly Desires

In my observation, one of the most interesting aspects of the churches' discourses regarding these matters is the oft-repeated declarations about how difficult it is to actually achieve *genuine* internal transformation, which attests
to the reality that these self-transformations are seen by the church as something that can only be realized through a regimen of intensive disciplinary
and learned techniques aimed at reshaping the women's identity, subjectivity,
and habitus. Indeed, according to this discourse, to recognize and to repent
for one's sins is one thing, but to truly reform one's behavior and thinking and
to live out the proper Christian life is quite another. Indeed, many of the committed women I talked to often stated that proper obedience is not something

that can be achieved without a sincere and deeply felt faith in God, especially without the experience of the Holy Spirit. As one woman put it:

> I don't think you can obey completely unless your heart is open with the Holy Spirit. The women who say they can't do this—well, I think it's because they haven't really been "awakened" properly yet. It's hard to go home and try to serve and wait on your husband totally. You must have faith to do this. But with faith, one can succeed in complete submission and obedience.

To help female members achieve these proper but difficult internal transformations, the churches, then, carry out programs of behavioral, psychic, spiritual, and bodily disciplining that are remarkable for their depth and intensity. One of the first important methods is composed of a set of techniques primarily aimed at behavioral transformation. For instance, asserting that obedience is something that requires much effort and practice, one of the things taught by the churches are specific methods and practical strategies for carrying out submission in a proper manner. According to the leaders of one family seminar, one important such method for helping women achieve "true" obedience is to pursue the practice of making the desires and happiness of the husband the center of the relationship, instead of the wife's. Some of the specific techniques for achieving this offered by the leaders included "studying up industriously on all the ways to make the husband happy" and "avoiding doing anything that the husband does not like." In being properly obedient, wives are exhorted to cease being aggressive and assertive, no matter how unjust the situation. According to one cell leader, "Wives, obey not only husbands who are good, but who are not so good, who can be evil to you. Husbands change when wives obey." Another specific behavioral technique offered by a marriage seminar to help women achieve this difficult goal of obedience is to imagine that they are talking to their husbands and then to say repeatedly to themselves, "Yes, you are right. Everything you say is correct. I'll do everything you say." The church also instructed the women to wash the feet of their husbands every night, as Jesus had done for his disciples. The seminar also taught that if possible, these kinds of obedience should extend to the bedroom.

In discussing the techniques for achieving patient endurance, another key to family harmony and women's long-term happiness, the women were told to cultivate a sincerely servantlike attitude. Speaking of the difficulties of enduring mothers-in-law, one seminar leader plainly asserted that love was the "ability to endure." Developing the capacity to forgive, after the example of Jesus, is of course necessary to cultivate endurance, as are pious self-sacrifice, unselfish love, and patient "waiting." One cell leader reminded her members of the rewards of spiritual authority and power that await those who patiently and without question "wait" under any circumstance, trusting in God's plan and power to take care of everything.

Finally, in developing the capacity to endure, the leaders stressed the important technique of cultivating positive attitudes toward life's situations, a strategy that requires both accepting any given structural situation and refraining from complaining about one's situation or other people. Reminding women that they are responsible for the "atmosphere" of the household—that is, the happiness of others—the leaders frequently focused on developing positive attitudes toward husbands in particular and encouraged the women of the various ways to make husbands happier, including improving their own general demeanor, appearance, and ways of relating to the husbands. This included efforts to be more "sexy" at night, pursuing studies to be better able to converse with husbands, and developing interest in the husbands' hobbies. Another seminar leader advised women to look into the mirror for at least half an hour every day and practice putting on varied facial expressions to make sure that their faces do not become "stiff" and ossified from perpetual resentment and unhappiness, as well as hugging their husbands when they got home to "convey love."

Going beyond such techniques of behavioral disciplining, however, one of the most striking tactics the church employs in helping women develop a habitus of submission includes techniques that aim to teach women to identify, root out, and renounce a range of deep-seated, inappropriate desires. For instance, in one of the cell meetings, the task of transforming the self in alignment with the virtuous feminine ideal involved attempts not only to change the members' beliefs and behaviors regarding gender relations but also to thoroughly discipline the internal subjectivities of women by helping them repress and, if possible, eradicate all of the underlying "negative" desires and emotions deemed responsible for their defiant or unruly behavior.

In this effort to discipline and normalize women's subjectivities, the group, for example, consistently employed the rhetoric of "dying" or "killing" of self. To "die" in sin is a classic metaphor in evangelical conversion that is considered a prelude to rebirth. In the context of Korean evangelical women, the "dying of self," while referring to the conversion process, also clearly carries another meaning—a process of eradicating the "sins" associated with gender violations such as arrogance, egoism, or impatience. Dying of self, however, has an even more specific meaning in the context of Korean evangelical women; it also refers to a process of more fundamental self-repression, which, involving the "death" of a person's "self" or "ego" (ja-ah), indicates the suppression of all the deep-down desires, emotions, and impulses considered responsible for generating the "sins" in the first place.[6]

Reflecting the influence of this discourse on church members, a number of women I talked to in both churches frequently used the related language of "killing of self" to refer to the repression of feminine desires and impulses, in particular, the desire to try to have things one's way, the impulse to assert these desires, and the desires or expectations regarding other people. As one cell leader who had a large plaque with the phrase "I die every day" prominently displayed in her living room repeatedly advised her members, "One of the things we have to do is to 'kill' (*juk-i-da*) ourselves every day. We keep coming back alive but that's no good. Everyday, we must die with Christ."[7]

One church member, talking about how she learned to handle her domestic situation, confessed, "The most important thing I had to do in my marriage was to learn to 'die.' I had to 'kill' myself. Before, I used to talk back to my husband, get mad or upset, but now, I don't do that any more. I always try to be happy even though I have difficult problems to contend with." The degree of self-repression and sacrifice often demanded by this process of feminine self-transformation is revealed especially vividly in the following narrative related by a former cell leader at a Methodist church:

> I'd say that I dealt with my marital difficulties by "dying." I am a learned woman. I have the ability to teach and lead others. And I have an intense and enthusiastic (*yeoljeong han*) personality. When I was a cell-leader, so many people would come to my meetings and listen to me. I became someone to whom people with difficulty would come for help. I have so much love, so much ability. But my husband disregarded me and this caused a lot of conflict. I like to study, I don't like to just gad about. And I think he didn't like that. And I also try to do every-thing best; I tend to be a perfectionist. And I think he couldn't stand this, so at a certain point, he put a stop to me. He blocked my way, kept me from developing, rising beyond. Like, at one point, I wanted to learn flower arrangement, for God's sake, and he didn't even like me to do this. When I'd be practicing at home, he would grab the flow-ers from me and fling them away. You know, whenever I tried to do something that would give me a sense of achievement or fulfillment, he tried his best to put a stop to it. Another example is that I wanted to take cooking classes once, so I asked him to give me money for the classes. But he said to me what did I need to do that for, all I needed to know was how to make *kkochujang* (hot pepper paste). See, whenever I tried to go beyond myself to be a little more professional in anything, he put a stop to it. So now, I just obey before God, and He helps me overcome, no matter how difficult things get. For me, "dying" means "killing" myself. Before, I used to talk back to my husband, but now, even when I'm upset, I pray and I get instantly turned around. Now, I am very happy even though I have difficult situations to contend with. And my husband has changed a lot in the last few years. He sees that

I've changed and this has softened him up considerably. I realize now that in the past, a big part of it was that he was very jealous that I was doing all this for God, that I was neglecting him.

Indeed, for many, it appears that killing one's ego in such a manner is seen as the only way to be able to obey "properly," and therefore to accomplish the task of transforming others. Another member attested, "I realized that only by totally 'getting rid' of myself and 'dying,' can I change the other person. If you try to do things by asserting your own temper and personality, it doesn't work. And that's how I deal with my husband, too."

Dying or killing of self, however, is not an easy thing to do. There is often much struggle and anger from the sense of injustice at having to submit to such a degree of self-denial and repression. As another cell member admitted, "Despite all my training in the church, the most difficult thing about the life of faith is not being able to apply everything properly in life, and especially, still having a strong ego/self (*ja-a*)." When it becomes very difficult, it is again to prayer, of course, that women turn to aid them in this inner struggle. One cell member explained, "When I lowered myself before my husband, he softened. But still, you know, there are many times when anger just rises up within me. But I know I have to press down my self/ego. When this starts to happen, I just pray a lot."

Prayer is, indeed, the primary vehicle, a key technique of spiritual discipline, through which women are expected to acquire the strength, inspiration, and submissive habitus needed to obey properly. Prayer, first of all, is the medium through which one can truly realize and experience repentance for one's sins. According to one leader, "Praying always helps you to realize that things are your own fault, and when you approach your husband and kids with such a humble attitude, admitting your fault, they will be moved to admit their fault and this will encourage love among you." But more important, just as prayer gives women the strength to transcend sufferings, prayer bestows the power to better endure, obey, and fulfill duties. Commanding women to pray ceaselessly, one leader observed, "Putting into practice God's wishes is so difficult because our faith is weak and our prayers are inadequate. Total obedience, for example, is so hard to do by one's own strength. We just have to entrust everything to God and find out all the ways to make Him happy through prayer."

Conclusion

In line with two of the four major "edges" within sociology of religion against which this volume is pressing, this chapter has attempted to illustrate the ways in which "critical engagements" with religion can be advanced through a rethinking of how power works within the context of religion, across varied cultural/religious contexts, and starting from within the congregational setting and extending beyond its boundaries (see Lichterman and Cadge, this volume). Seen from a nonbinary perspective, religious power necessarily embodies a dialogic tension between the forces of regulation/discipline and empowerment/liberation, the dynamics of which depend on specific contexts. For Korean evangelical women, evangelical faith is no doubt a source of empowerment, even subversion and resistance, especially in relation to the role it plays in women's efforts to cope with and transcend domestic suffering. This chapter, however, has focused on examining the disciplinary aspects of religious institutions and power and the ways that religion is implicated, both openly and subtly, in spiritual and psychological disciplining of women by generating a set of "technologies of the self." While opening up spaces of liberation for women from domestic distress, Korean evangelicalism, by helping to reconstruct women's gender consciousness through a process that goes beyond mere ideological reindoctrination to practical behavioral transformation and enforcing of intense internal, emotional/psychological self-discipline for "rebirth," is clearly an agent of discipline of women for the patriarchal system.

To be sure, the degree of success achieved by the churches in this regard is by no means uniform, and there are a number of ways that women deploy ideologies of submission and obedience consciously or subconsciously for their ends. One of these ways is for women to appropriate their beliefs and practices as an instrument or strategy of domestic negotiation or bargaining—by reforming husbands, for instance—and even as a weapon of internal resistance by placing God at the center of their lives and thereby gaining greater moral authority.[8] It would be remiss, however, to overlook the ways in which women's recommitment to religious patriarchy and the principles of submission that produce a deeply family-centered, traditionalist feminine subjectivity undercuts the liberationist possibilities and powers implied in the women's religious empowered selves as Christians, and the ways this countervails the full development and exercise of women's religious powers derived from their individual relationship with God and the potential to contest the status quo. I will briefly recount a few aspects of these contradictions.

To begin with, women's recommitment to the principles of obedience implies a creation of a gendered self that is fundamentally oriented toward authority, particularly male authority, which tends to deflect the potential for challenge contained in women's evangelical faith—for example, to critique male dominance or behavior. By the same token, such submissive orientation toward authority explains why the sense of newfound power, ability, and knowledge women gain through participation in church activities rarely seems to translate into a sense of individual authority or independence that can lead to the forging of new social power and boundaries by women. Instead, we find among many women not only a continued belief in their fundamental inferiority but also a belief that their powers, seen as "borrowed" from God, are not their own. Reflecting their firm belief in the necessity of submission, women disown these felt powers, exercising them only to serve others and God and to enable themselves to better obey, endure, and forgive. Furthermore, any felt powers or extraordinary abilities a woman may claim or experience are rationalized as an act of or reward for obedience to God or to church authority, effectively undercutting possibilities for contestation, although empowerment may be experienced subversively. It is no wonder, then, that many evangelical women feel a deeply conflicting sense of personal power and identity, a sense of an essentially powerless self existing alongside an image of an empowered self, mirroring their domestic self-conceptions as both weak and strong.

Finally, the church's call for the fulfillment of the qualities of self-sacrifice and endurance serves to limit the impetus toward the pursuit of new social power and change by fostering an attitude of forbearance toward difficult circumstances, discouraging active efforts to change the status quo. Indeed, the ideal of self-sacrifice effectively delegitimizes any goals or actions on the part of women that are interpreted as being oriented toward personal and individual gain and fulfillment, including those related to personal freedom and equality. The submissive attitude is also fostered through the nurturing of a highly dependent self that must rely on the will of God and others in authority to realize things in life, producing a contradictory sense of self that is, while empowered, also devoid of a sense of agency.

In closing, I would like to make a few remarks about the problem of religious power. Drawing inspiration from poststructuralist approaches to power, the notion of resistance to power seems to have been at the center of much theorizing about lived religion in America. Approaches that focus on celebrating powers "from below" and on religion as a domain of relative freedom against constraints of cultural discipline have, however, often given short shrift to or lost sight of the other important side of religious power: the fundamentally disciplinary and normative nature and effects of religious power. In addition to offering idioms and spaces for dissent and protest in particular times and places, there is no question that religious institutions, like other major institutions of society, have simultaneously functioned as disciplinary regimes par excellence. After all, in spite of his oft-quoted remark "where there is power, there is resistance" (Foucault 1990 [1978], 95) and his concern with illuminating the de-centered nature of power and its mechanisms, Foucault's intellectual project centered just as importantly on the identification and delineation of the repressive and productive operations of disciplinary power, especially through the ways in which human subjectivities were constituted "really and materially" through a "multiplicity of organisms, forces, energies, materials, desires, and thoughts, etc." (1990, 27). It is the workings of such disciplinary religious power that I have tried to trace in this paper. My approach and the investigation of the technologies of religious subject formation also dovetail with the observation of Manuel A. Vásquez in this volume that one of the reasons the sociology of religion continues to be blinded to the powerful "generativity" of religion in the contemporary age is its underlying epistemological assumptions regarding religion and selfhood, especially the continued reliance on the modernist, "unencumbered subject" (p. 40) and, relatedly, the inability to take seriously the "embodiment and the phenomenological-hermeneutic dimensions of religious practices, experiences, and institutions" (p. 36).

It is also important to keep in mind that although sites of resistance can be seen as representing possibilities for contingent progress insofar as they serve as possible points of transformation, it must not be assumed that resistance is necessarily successful or that it is even fundamentally subversive. If we accept the insight that the concept of resistance "...includes both conscious opposition and the mute automatic resistance of that which is in the process of being shaped" (Henriques et al. 1984, 115), we must be careful in our interpretations about what kind of liberatory or transgressive meanings and effects may be inscribed in a particular instance of what may look like "resistance." Indeed, while the disciplinary projects of the church are to be sure a complex, contested process, characterized by tensions between the church's aims and the efforts of women to appropriate and refashion religious meanings and practices in their own way, religion and religious institutions are not simply domains of autonomy and resistance against the disciplinary confines of culture, but where forces of discipline coexist with the impulses of resistance and subversion. "Just as faith does not eliminate pain or death, but renders them endurable, neither does religious practice obliterate social contradiction or liberate humans absolutely from their place in particular social, political, and domestic arrangements.... [J]ust as religious idioms are not stable bearers of power or unambiguous intentionality...so they are not completely reliable counterpoints to power either" (Orsi 1997, 16).

Although we must examine the ways in which religious power is shaped specifically by the particular settings in which it operates across different cultural or institutional (and noninstitutional) contexts, it is critical to examine, as numerous chapters in this volume have addressed, the processes by which such operation of power is transformed or maintained across transnational social spaces. For Korean evangelicalism in particular, such investigations have been pursued regarding first-generation immigrants and women in the US setting,[9] and they are robustly being pursued on works investigating second-generation religiosity, religiosity that simultaneously borrows from and transforms first-generation religiosity.[10] In the future, much more work needs to be done on the issue of the global circulation of religion and its transformations.

Notes

1. See McGuire (1983) and Beckford (1983) for an earlier discussion on the topic of religious power.

2. Foucault (1988) defines "technologies of the self" in the following way: that "which permit individuals to effect by their won means or with the help of others a certain number of operations on their own bodies and souls, thoughts, conduct, and way of being, so as to transform themselves in order to attain a certain state of happiness, purity, wisdom, perfection, or immortality" (p. 22).

3. Here, I use Pierre Bourdieu's concept of habitus, which can be roughly defined as a system of dispositions—lasting, acquired schemes of perception, thought, and action (Bourdieu 1977).

4. Presbyterianism is the largest Protestant denomination in South Korea, constituting about 73 percent of the Protestant population; Methodism is the second-largest denomination, claiming about 11 percent of church membership. The women whose narratives are presented in this chapter are those mostly of married female congregants between the ages of thirty-five and fifty-five. The interviewees for the research also included female church members of varying age groups, a number of men, church leaders, and experts on Korean Christianity.

5. In many of the larger evangelical churches, specialized seminars focusing around discussion of marital or gender issues/problems are frequently offered as a way of enhancing marital or family harmony, such as "family seminars," "marriage seminars," and "newlywed seminars." Although this quote represents the narrative of one person, I found that these kinds of views on gender and family relations were typical of most churches I have observed. It is worth noting that there is very little direct and public criticism of men in church discourses, at large, or within these meetings. In all-male group meetings that I have observed, by the same token, the participants spend far less time than women in agonized self-critique and self-reflection regarding family matters.

6. This theme of "dying" in conversion has been observed in studies of American evangelical conversion as well. For example, Gordon (1984), in his discussion of Jesus People groups, talks about "dying to self" in the process of surrender, which ultimately leads to rebirth and reconstitution of a more empowered self; "dying" of self is a form of surrender through which one becomes more empowered to accomplish one's goals by "letting go" of oneself and one's sins and allowing God in to direct one's life. Although the overall process appears similar in the case of Korean women, "dying" of self in the process of Korean women's reconstitution of domestic and gender identity seems to signify creating of a new self that, albeit spiritually and internally empowered, is a self reformed to better fulfill traditional gender roles through the negation or the submerging of one's desires and ego.

7. My findings regarding the rhetoric of "killing" of self in evangelical women's discourse is corroborated clearly by Ai Ra Kim's (1996) study of first-generation Korean evangelical immigrant women in America, suggesting that this rhetoric is a central part of Korean female evangelical discourse. In Kim's findings as well, the concept of the killing of self is understood by the women as a kind of extreme self-denial and self-repression (pp. 96, 121–123), an enactment of Jesus' sacrificial example and Christian virtue.

8. See Chong (2008) for a full discussion of this topic. Compare also with Bartkowski (2001), Brasher (1998), Brusco (1995), Burdick (1993), Gallagher (2003), Griffith (1997), Manning (1999), and Stacey (1990).

9. As an example, see Ai Ra Kim (1996).

10. There is extensive literature on this topic. See, for example, Chong (1998), Sharon Kim (2010), and Ecklund (2006).

References

Ammerman, Nancy, ed. 2007. *Everyday Religion: Observing Modern Religious Lives*. New York: Oxford University Press.

Bartkowski, John P. 2001. *Remaking the Godly Marriage: Gender Negotiation in Evangelical Churches*. New Brunswick, NJ: Rutgers University.

Beckford, James A. 1983. "The Restoration of 'Power' to the Sociology of Religion." *Sociological Analysis*. 44 (1): 11–32.

Bourdieu, Pierre. 1977. *Outline of a Theory of Practice*. Cambridge: Cambridge University Press.

Brasher, Brenda E. 1998. *Godly Women: Fundamentalism & Female Power*. New Brunswick, NJ: Rutgers University.

Brusco, Elizabeth E. 1995. *The Reformation of the Machismo: Evangelical Conversion and Gender in Colombia*. Austin: University of Texas.

Burdick, John. 1993. *Looking for God in Brazil: The Progressive Catholic Church in Urban Brazil's Religious Arena*. Berkeley: University of California.

Choi, Hyaeweol. 2009. *Gender and Mission Encounters in Korea: New Women, Old Ways*. Berkeley: University of California Press.

Clark, Donald N. 1986. *Christianity in Modern Korea*. Lanham, MD: University Press of America.

Chong, Kelly H. 1998. "What It Means to Be Christian: The Role of Religion in the Construction of Ethnic Identity and Boundary Among Second-Generation Korean-Americans." *Sociology of Religion* 59(3): 259–286.

———. 2008. *Deliverance and Submission: Evangelical Women and the Negotiation of Patriarchy in South Korea*. Cambridge, MA: Harvard University Press.

Deuchler, Martina. 1992. *The Confucian Transformation of Korea: A Study of Society and Ideology*. Cambridge, MA: Council on East Asian Studies, Harvard University.

Ecklund, Elaine. 2006. *Korean American Evangelicals: New Models for Civic Life*. New York: Oxford University Press.

Foucault, Michel. 1988. "Technologies of the Self." Pp. 20–49 in *Technologies of the Self: A Seminar with Michele Foucault,* edited by Luther H. Martin, Huck Gutman, and Patrick H. Hutton. Amherst: University of Massachusetts Press.

———. 1990 [1978]. *The History of Sexuality*. Vol. 1. New York: Vintage.

Gallagher, Sally K. 2003. *Evangelical Identity & Gendered Family Life*. New Brunswick, NJ: Rutgers University.

Gordon, David F. 1984. "Dying to Self: Self-Control through Self-Abandonment." *Sociological Analysis* 4(1): 41–56.

Griffith, R. Marie. 1997. *God's Daughters: Evangelical Women and the Power of Submission*. Berkeley: University of California.

Hall, David D., ed. 1997. *Lived Religion in America: Toward a History of Practice*. Princeton, NJ: Princeton University Press.

Henriques, Julian, Wendy Hollway, Cathy Urwin, Couze Venn, and Valerie Walkerdine, eds. 1984. *Changing the Subject: Psychology, Social Regulation and Subjectivity*. London: Methuen.

Kang, Nam-soon. 1996. "Christianity in Korea and Women." Pp. 50–59 in *Women of Korea: A History from Ancient Times to 1945*. Seoul: Asian Center for Women's Studies, Ewha Womans University.

Kanter, Rosabeth. 1972. *Commitment and Community: Communes and Utopias in Sociological Perspective*. Cambridge, MA: Harvard University Press.

Kim, Ai Ra. 1996. *Women Struggling for a New Life: On the Role of Religion in the Cultural Passage from Korea to America*. Albany: State University of New York Press.

Kim, Sharon. 2010. *A Faith of Our Own: Second-Generation Spirituality in Korean American Churches*. New Brunswick, NJ: Rutgers University Press.

Lee, Timothy. 2006. "Beleaguered Success: Korean Evangelicalism in the Last Decade of the 20th Century." Pp. 330–350 in *Christianity in Korea,* edited by Robert E. Buswell, Jr. and Timothy S. Lee. Honolulu: University of Hawaii Press.

Manning, Christel. 1999. *God Gave Us the Right: Conservative Catholic, Evangelical Protestant, and Orthodox Jewish Women Grapple with Feminism.* New Brunswick, NJ: Rutgers University.

Martin, David. 1990. *Tongues of Fire: The Explosion of Protestantism in Latin America.* New Haven, CT: Yale University.

McGuire, Meredith R. 1983. "Discovering Religious Power." *Sociological Analysis: A Journal in the Sociology of Religion* 44(1): 1–40.

———. 2008. *Lived Religion: Faith and Practice in Everyday Life.* New York: Oxford University Press.

Ortner, Sherry B. 1984. "Theory in Anthropology Since the Sixties." *Comparative Studies in Society and History* 26(1): 126–166.

Orsi, Robert. 1997. "Everyday Miracles: The Study of Lived Religion." In *Lived Religion in America: Toward a History of Practice,* edited by John D. Hall. Princeton, NJ: Princeton University.

Rambo, L. R. 1992. "The Psychology of Conversion." In *Handbook of Religious Conversion,* edited by H. N. Malony and S. Southard. Birmingham, AL: Religious Education Press.

Ro, Bong Rin, and Marlin L. Nelson, eds. 1995. *Korean Church Growth Explosion.* Seoul: World of Life Press.

Rubin, Jeffrey W. 1996. "Defining Resistance: Contested Interpretations of Everyday Acts." *Studies in Law, Politics and Society* 15: 237–260.

Stacey, Judith. 1990. *Brave New Families: Stories of Domestic Upheaval in Late 20th Century America.* New York: Basic Books.

Suh, David Kwang-Sun. 1985. "American Missionaries and a Hundred Years of Korean Protestantism." *International Review of Mission* 74 (January): 6–19.

Yi, Hyo-Jae. 1985. "Christian Mission and the Liberation of Korean Women." *International Review of Mission* 74 (January): 93–102.

12

Crossing Borders: Transnational Sanctuary, Social Justice, and the Church

JACQUELINE MARIA HAGAN

Introduction

Throughout the Christian era, the church has been recognized as an institution providing sanctuary to those in need. In the contemporary era, sanctuary for migrants in the United States has formally manifested itself twice: first in 1981 with the founding of the Central American Sanctuary Movement, and most recently in 2007 with the establishment of the New Sanctuary Movement. Both of these movements were motivated by faith and founded on political and religious principles to challenge US policies, educate Americans, and serve the needs of non-state-sanctioned refugees and undocumented migrants from Latin America who were either fleeing civil strife in their home countries and seeking refuge in the United State or fighting deportation orders from the US government. Both movements placed issues of responsibility, morality, and human dignity at the center of immigration debates in the United States. As faith-based movements for social justice, these sanctuary initiatives attest not only to the particular salience of religion and the church in the lives of immigrants from Latin America but also to the growing public role of religion in secular and political life in the United States today (Casanova 1994; Hagan 2006, 2008; Hondagneu-Sotelo 2008). In this chapter, I introduce a third important, but less known, sanctuary movement, the transnational religious network that has emerged since the mid-1990s to challenge and question the morality of state border policies and protect and serve migrants on the increasingly dangerous journey north from Central America and Mexico to the United States.

The genesis of the first US-based Sanctuary Movement was triggered by the Reagan administration's support of the repressive regimes of El Salvador that sent thousands of Central Americans fleeing to neighboring Mexico and then the United States, where they were denied political asylum and were in danger of deportation. By 1981, what became known as the Central American Sanctuary Movement was well under way. Originated in the border city of Tucson by Jim Corbett, a Quaker, and John Fife, a Presbyterian minister, the faith-based movement started small but grew rapidly during the 1980s as an increasing share of Americans were recruited after hearing or reading the dramatic personal testimonies of migrants fleeing the possibility of political persecution, rape, and murder at the hands of Central American governments (Nepstad 2004). The mechanisms and logistics of this sanctuary movement were complex; a network of clergy, faith workers, and advocates formed an underground railroad that funneled migrants across international borders to safe houses in cities throughout the United States and as far away as Canada (Coutin 1993).

To bring public attention to the repressive regimes in Central America and the corresponding immigration policies of the United States, US faith workers eventually shifted the movement from clandestine evasion of immigration officials to open defiance of the US government, which meant imprisonment for some, including the movement's two founders. Like liberation theology from which it was in part derived, sanctuary then and now emphasizes a movement from private to public action—namely, the taking in of strangers as a religious and moral imperative. During the original Sanctuary Movement, this reinterpretation of religion as a mechanism for achieving social justice was delivered from pulpits in churches throughout the United States, and parishioners responded by taking refugees into their own homes, despite the fact that they were committing acts of civil disobedience. In the minds and hearts of many Americans, the church trumped the state and sanctuary provided moral legitimacy for what the US government considered a criminal act. By the mid-1980s, a network of 185 churches and synagogues had declared sanctuary and the movement had gained support, funding, and other movement from eighteen national religious denominations.

Following the collapse of the Soviet Union and subsequent elections in Central America that ended a number of repressive dictatorships, this original Sanctuary Movement more or less folded. But ten years later a new sanctuary movement was founded by faith workers and, like its former counterpart, it combined faith, religious principles, and social activism to challenge unjust US immigration policies. In the spring of 2006, millions of people across the United States marched in what became the nation's largest immigrant rights mobilization. In large cities and small towns across the country, people flocked to the streets to protest a federal bill that would make it a felony to assist undocumented migrants. Some months later, in 2007, faith workers representing

Crossing Borders 265

twelve religious denominations and another seven faith-based organizations joined together in Los Angeles to listen to the personal testimonies of immigrant families fighting deportation. At that landmark meeting where the New Sanctuary Movement was founded, faith leaders conferred on developing strategies that would protect families separated by harsh and unjust immigration policies in the 1990s and 2000s and against ICE (Immigration and Customs Enforcement) raids in immigrant neighborhoods, homes, and workplaces.

The New Sanctuary Movement differs from its predecessor in important ways. First, the public thrust of the movement is to educate the American public about migration rather than to encourage civil disobedience (Chinchilla, Hamilton, and Loucky 2009). Faith workers across the country are relying on their moral authority to raise the awareness of Americans about our unjust and very complex immigration policies and their effects on immigrants who have established families and creditable work histories in the United States. Because the movement focuses primarily on undocumented immigrants living in the United States, it has redefined sanctuary as "prophetic hospitality," asking congregations to provide legal, social, and financial support for those fighting deportation (Hondagneu-Sotelo 2008).

Thus far, the story of sanctuary in the Americas has largely been a narrative of organized faith-based groups and congregations in the United States providing safety for Central American refugees fleeing political strife, as well as protecting from deportation both unauthorized Central Americans and Mexicans already in this country. The restricted US focus on sanctuary is not surprising when we consider that both initiatives were founded by US clergy who, by relying on their extensive national networks and institutional resources, have been very effective in drawing attention to the plight of immigrants, organizing events, and mobilizing congregational action. Yet, the role of religion and the church in protecting migrants and the public face of religion in challenging harsh and unjust federal immigration policies extend beyond formal religious institutions and US borders. As Peggy Levitt reminds us in her chapter, religious life is not contained to a particular site and all aspects of religious life are potentially mobile. Today, sanctuary is also practiced on the journey and encompasses the many churches, religious groups, faith-based organizations, and individual clergy that work the dangerous 2,000-mile migrant trail from Central America to the United States and advocate on behalf of those who are forced to travel this treacherous route.

Sanctuary today on the migrant trail differs both from the church-based Sanctuary Movement of the 1980s, which provided refuge to Central Americans fleeing political strife, and from the New Sanctuary Movement, which protects the rights of immigrant families living in the United States. Sanctuary along the migrant trail is largely about protecting migrants from danger and death on the northbound journey. It is about faith-inspired social action that challenges state policies that created the conditions of the dangerous journey. The movement is not bound by congregation, institution, or nation-state. It is an expanding and dynamic movement that changes according to the needs of migrants on the move. While some of its participants are reluctant to identify themselves as part of an organized initiative, the loosely defined movement does include transnational religious congregations, bilateral bishops' conferences and diocesan efforts, interfaith coalitions, and local religious workers. These groups and individuals share a similar theology of migration and regularly come together to organize social action to protect the rights of journeying migrants and change unjust state policies.

Motivated by a theology of migration to advocate for the right of migrants to cross borders in search of work, these religious workers and the transnational hierarchies in which they operate have emerged as important mechanisms for contesting nation-state activities and monitoring the regulatory practices of state institutions and policies. While not explicitly challenging the right of sovereign nations to control their borders, as was the case during the heyday of the original US Sanctuary Movement, these faith-inspired groups have become increasingly critical of current US and Mexico border and interior enforcement policies because they violate the human rights and human dignity of migrants.

This chapter, then, introduces the changing social and political context of sanctuary in the Americas and illustrates ways in which the movement has grown across borders to meet the needs of transit migrants and question the legitimacy of migration policy in the region. It is precisely the failure of governments in the region to protect journeying migrants from the consequences of failed polices that has motivated the development of a faith-based migration movement to assume that role. Indeed, to understand international migration from Latin America to the United States in the contemporary era requires a deep understanding of the central role of religion in the migration process. In my examination of what I call the Transnational Sanctuary Movement that spans multiple organizations from Guatemala to the US-Mexico border, I describe the factors that gave rise to the movement; who the movement's participants are; how the movement is organized; and what the functions of the Transnational Sanctuary Movement include, that is, how it meets the private and public needs of transit migrants and how it navigates and challenges state immigration policy.

The data for this chapter derive from field observations and interviews gathered from 2000 through 2005 for a larger project on religion and migration (Hagan 2008). The larger project explored how and why migrants turn to culture, faith, trusted clergy, and everyday religious practices for the spiritual and psychological strength to endure the hardships of the journey to the United States. To this end, I interviewed 150 undocumented migrants in the

United States who had traveled the dangerous journey from Central America and Mexico to the United States. To understand the private and public role of religious organizations in the dangerous migration journey, I traveled sacred places visited by the migrants during their trek north and interviewed over 100 religious leaders and faith workers who provide for journeying migrants and advocate on their behalf. Some of the interviews conducted with local clergy took place at shrines or places of worship that migrants visited before departing from their home communities. Other interviews with religious leaders took place along the migrant trail in the United States, Mexico, Guatemala, El Salvador, Costa Rica, and Honduras and included a cardinal, several bishops, and numerous church ministers, along with directors or staff of migrant shelters that provide religious counsel, humanitarian assistance, and legal assistance to journeying migrants. These programs, which are often referred to by the Catholic Church as "transit" as opposed to traditional "settlement" programs for migrants, have become increasingly visible in Mexico in recent years, as well as among other religious groups, such as the Presbyterian church along both sides of the US-Mexico border, the Maryknoll houses in Mexico, and, most notably, the Scalabrini in Mexico and Central America. In this chapter, I draw primarily from these interviews with religious leaders and faith-based coalitions to examine the institutional dimension of religion in the migration process. My concern is with describing the ways in which churches and faith workers—at local, national, and transnational levels—have become motivated into action and have responded to the private and public needs of undocumented migrants.

The story of sanctuary on the migrant trail is told in three sections. I begin with a description of the dangerous journey, demonstrating how state policies to fortify borders impose huge human costs for migrants journeying from Central America and Mexico to the United States. This overview section provides the context for understanding why migrants turn to religion for assistance and comfort, and why religious organizations feel morally compelled and motivated to advocate on their behalf. I then turn to my thematic findings: religion as mediator and religion as advocate, which respectively reflect the private and public roles of religion in the migratory process. I conclude with a discussion of the research implications.

The Dangerous Journey

In their attempts to reach the American Dream, unauthorized migrants journeying from Central America and Mexico must overcome a host of legal, social, and physical problems. They are forced to travel by foot and in poorly ventilated vehicles over thousands of miles across mountains, deserts, rivers, and several fortified international borders to reach the United States. Unauthorized entry from Mexico into the United States has long been dangerous, at times even fatal (Lee 2002, 2003). However, since the early to mid-1990s, migrants traversing Central America and Mexico have increasingly had to endure physical and psychological abuse and take ever-greater risks in their desperate attempts to reach the United States, in large part because of the border enforcement campaigns launched by the US and Mexican governments.

The US enforcement campaign, which is officially known as "Prevention Through Deterrence," was initiated in the early 1990s in response to the failure of the Immigration Reform and Control Act of 1986 to curtail undocumented migration (Massey, Durand, and Malone 2002). Under this campaign, resources devoted to the southwest border increased dramatically as agents and new technology were directed to the border area at a cost of roughly two billion dollars a year throughout the 1990s. The program included an influx of new technological equipment, including ground sensors, night vision cameras, and the construction of new physical barriers along the 2,000-mile border. The policy campaign also increased staffing along the border; the number of US Border Patrol agents working along the southwest border doubled between FY1993 and FY1999, from roughly 3,400 to 7,200. By 2006, less than three years later, it had almost doubled again to 12,300 (Andreas 2000, 2001; Lipton 2006). In 2009, the number of Border Patrol agents augmented once again, to 18,875, representing a 53 percent increase in roughly three years.

The Prevention Through Deterrence campaign deployed these new resources in historical urban crossing areas: Operation Blockade near El Paso in 1993, followed by Operation Gatekeeper in the San Diego area in 1994 and Operation Rio Grande in the Brownsville area in 1997. Collectively, these operations prevent migrants from crossing in well-established urban corridors where they have historically relied on familiar networks for assistance and deflect them to remote rural areas where they are then exposed to greater dangers and the risk of death, especially in the harsher environments of deserts and mountains. From the 1960s through the early 1990s, the majority of unauthorized migrants from Latin America entered through the urban crossing corridors of San Diego and El Paso. Since the mid-1990s, migrants have been increasingly squeezed into the Tucson Border Patrol sector, where apprehensions have increased by over 300 percent since 2000, and yearly migrant deaths in the southwest desert soar to the hundreds in the heat of the summer months (Eschbach, Hagan, and Rodríguez 2003; Jimenez 2009; Sapkota et al. 2005).

The rationale underlying the US border campaign is to move unauthorized migration to rural terrain where the Border Patrol believes it has the tactical advantage. During the early stages of the campaign, the US Immigration and Naturalization Service (since renamed the US Department of Citizenship and Immigration Services under the Department of Homeland Security) believed that the increased costs to migrants in terms of financial resources and personal safety would prevent many from crossing. But desperate for work, migrants have continued to come. Forced to circumvent well-established crossing areas, border crossers are exposed to the extreme elements of deserts and mountains, suffering dehydration, hypothermia, and drowning. In their quest to reach the United States, many die. Since Operation Gatekeeper went into effect in 1994, an estimated 5,600 migrants have died while attempting unauthorized border crossings (Jimenez 2009; Eschbach et al. 2003). Migrant deaths are now averaging more than 300 a year. In the first half of 2009 in the Tucson Arizona sector, more than 200 migrants died as they attempted to traverse the Sonora Desert in the scorching summer heat. More than 400 died in the same year along the entire border. Found in remote spots throughout the southwest, the bodies of these unidentified migrants are buried in pauper cemeteries along the border. Father Daniel Groody, a theologian and advocate for migrants, compares the journey to the Way of the Cross: "Migrants endure legal crucifixion by way of the state, social crucifixion by way of family separation, cultural crucifixion by way of discrimination, and actual crucifixion by way of their attempts to cross" (Groody 2004).

Central American migrants face even more dangers than Mexicans in their quest to reach the United States. They must navigate a migration industry that preys on transit migrants and cross thousands of miles and several international borders, some of which are more tightly regulated than others. Most Central Americans interviewed reported that the dangers begin when leaving Guatemala and crossing the thousand-mile length of Mexico. The first step in this dangerous journey involves crossing the notorious Mexico-Guatemala border towns of Tapachula, Tecún Umán, El Carmen, and La Mesilla, areas that in recent years have been characterized by criminal activities ranging from drug trafficking to human smuggling or corruption by border officials. After navigating the migration industry that dominates the economy of many of these border towns, migrants must then overcome the fortified border and interior enforcement efforts of the Mexican government.

By the late 1990s, control of its southern border had developed into a priority for the Mexican government. The Central American refugee crisis of the 1980s, which displaced many Guatemalans to the southern part of the country, is embedded deep in the memories of Mexicans. Additionally, as widespread poverty, market failure, civil strife, and natural disasters (Hurricane Mitch in 1998 and the 2001 Salvadoran earthquakes) continued to threaten the region, migration from Central America increased further in the 1990s (García 2006). Under the pressure of additional urging from the United States, in 2001 the Mexican government launched its US-backed border campaign "Plan Sur" to curtail undocumented transit migration through Mexico and to control drug trafficking. With US financing, two border enforcement operations were established at historic border crossing points. The first barrier was established along the jungle frontier with Belize and Guatemala, the other across the Isthmus of Tehuatepec. To police these barriers, thousands of troops were deployed to the southern states of Chiapas and Oaxaca to conduct border patrols and erect checkpoints along well-established crossing corridors (Flynn 2002). Following 9/11, the United States placed further pressure on Mexico to restrict transit migration from Central America, resulting in reinforced measures of detection, detention, and deportation. All of these measures are directed at restricting transit migration to the United States, and the human consequences, not surprisingly, parallel those on the US-Mexico border as the Mexican campaign is largely modeled on the US Prevention Through Deterrence program (Flynn 2002; Ackerman, Loughna, and Castles 2004).

In their attempts to evade Mexican border enforcement operations, migrants travel in the remote and harsh jungle areas of southern Mexico where they fall prey not only to natural physical dangers but also to members of numerous rival gangs, the most notorious of which is the *Mara Salvatrucha*,[1] which may rob, rape, or murder them. Once they reach more populated areas, the migrants then face shakedowns by border officials and local police who force them to pay *mordidas* (bribes) to pass further. The human toll from enforcement efforts and the resulting chaos along the Guatemala-Mexico border is staggering. In 2000, 120 migrants died at or near the 600-mile Guatemala-Mexico border. By 2001, less than a year later, this number had almost tripled, to 355. The most recent figures indicate another increase: in 2003, Mexican authorities reported 371 crossing deaths. As Father Flor María Rigoni, a Scalabrinian and director of the Albergue Belen in Tapachula, Chaipas, exclaimed to me, the border area has become a "cemetery without a cross."

Meeting the Private and Public Needs of Journeying Migrants: The Transnational Sanctuary Movement

Migration scholars have generally relied on social network theory to explain how unauthorized migrants from Central America and Mexico gain entry into the United States. According to this theory, personal networks consisting of family and friends and built on notions of trust and reciprocity provide journeying migrants with the companionship of seasoned travelers, contacts, and information about how to cross, sometimes including access to *coyotes*.[2] These networks are so strong and powerful that sometimes they overcome attempts by the state to regulate migration (Massey et al. 2002; Hagan 1998).

Yet as scholars increasingly recognize, migrant networks are neither fixed nor infallible. Like all human relationships, they can change over time, and in particular situations, such as poverty, marginalization, or isolation, they can weaken and even wear away.[3] The hardships of the present-day undocumented journey in the context of militarized borders provide circumstances that test the limits of migrants' networks. Because the crossing experience has become more dangerous and more costly, seasoned family and friends are unable to provide the necessary social and financial support to overcome the dangers. Migrants who possess the financial resources can rely on the crossing services of *coyotes*, but many other migrants, including young, unattached, and unseasoned migrants from Central America, do not have access to either personal networks or financial resources to hire *coyotes* to assist them on their journeys. Lacking the social protection and support that family, friends, and even trusted *coyotes* provide, migrants suffer at the hands of a for-profit migration industry composed of predatory coyotes, gangs, and corrupt officials that exploits the conditions of unauthorized transit migration.[4]

It is under these conditions and at this juncture in the migration journey that religion has donned its public face through the appearance of a transnational sanctuary movement. The changing conditions and social infrastructure of the undocumented journey—the disrupted personal networks, militarized borders, generally increased dangers, and the rise of a predatory migration industry—has resulted in the growth of religious and humanitarian organizations that provide for transit migrants and advocate on their behalf. In the absence of financial resources or personal networks to help them through the hardships of the journey, many migrants now turn to churches and their migrant programs, migrant shelters, and religious workers to perform network functions. These groups, which make up the local expression of the Transnational Sanctuary Movement, have become part and parcel of the social infrastructure that sustains transit migration in the region.

Movement Participants, Network Structure, and Mission

The organizations and institutions that provide and advocate for migrants journeying from Central America and Mexico to the United States can be sorted into three groups: international organizations, governmental organizations, and a collection of civil society organizations (CSOs) that mediate between the state and the migrants.[5] The CSOs include secular and faith-based nongovernmental organizations (NGOs), as well as other faith-based organizations, churches, congregations, and community groups, some of which are local while others are part of national, regional, and transnational organizations and advocacy networks. Motivated by common concerns about transit migration and state regulatory practices and connected across borders by exchanges of information, many also constitute their own advocacy network, the Transnational Sanctuary Movement.[6]

The movement's members cross borders and denominations and operate at different levels of hierarchy. Catholic bishops in Central America, Mexico, and the United States have reached across their common borders to express publicly their unified support of the rights of individuals and their families to migrate, as well as opposition to governmental policies that deny this right and border enforcement efforts that place journeying migrants in physical danger. In 2003, the Mexican Conference of Catholic Bishops and the US Conference of Catholic Bishops (2003) published the first-ever joint pastoral letter on migration, entitled "Strangers No Longer: Together on the Journey of Hope." The letter's message is that the current US immigration system is broken and in need of reform. The Tex-Mex bishops (as they refer to themselves) argue that the consequences of the US immigration system linking the two nations—family separation, increased danger for journeying migrants, and the exploitation of migrant labor—go against Catholic social teachings because they challenge the basic dignity and human rights of migrants. The title of the coauthored letter, "Strangers No Longer," reflects the migration theme of the alien in Christian theology that is repeated often in the Bible. Fundamental, then, to Catholic theology is the belief that migrants should be treated with the respect due to every human being, and the protection of this dignity for migrants, a communitarian position, is fundamental to the social and political message and agenda of the Catholic social doctrine of migration (Blume 2003). The links between social theology and the well-being of the migrant can be seen in multiple cross-border religious practices that directly challenge nation-state enforcement strategies. In this sense, many Catholic clergy and faith workers and missionaries are increasingly practicing a theology of migration that links church doctrine directly to social policy.

Members of the Transnational Sanctuary Movement's network also include front-line faith workers who run and coordinate programs and shelters situated along the dangerous corridor from Guatemala to the United States. These shelters and the programs they provide, which local, regional, national, binational, and international religious groups support and coordinate, can be sorted into three types: origin, transit, and destination. In contrast to Catholic settlement programs that provide education, legal services, and health care access to immigrant newcomers in the United States, the origin, transit, and destination programs were erected from the bilateral efforts of the Catholic Church in Mexico and the United States and provide a variety of humanitarian and social services specifically for the journeying, arriving, and returning migrant. While we don't really know exactly how many churches and shelters in the region have pastoral programs for migrants, I found that at the very least forty dioceses stretching the length of the migration journey from the dioceses of San Marcos in Guatemala to Tijuana, Mexico, house churches with migrant programs or shelters that serve departing and journeying migrants.[7]

Some dioceses are more involved than others in providing this support, reflecting the disproportionate impact of migration in particular dioceses (e.g., dioceses along the Mexico-Guatemala and Mexico-US borders), the viewpoint of a particular bishop, and the presence or absence of support provided by the country's Episcopal Conference of Bishops. The Diocese of San Marcos, Guatemala, for example, which straddles the Mexico border, has been affected heavily by emigration, return migration, and transit migration. Consequently, the diocese has worked hard over the years to establish "Human Mobility," a comprehensive program to address the migration issue. Working closely with local municipalities and twenty-nine parishes within the San Marcos Diocese, Human Mobility provides training and information workshops for displaced migrant groups (regional labor migrants, as well as transit migrants heading north), disseminates information about migration patterns and dangers through radio programs, organizes activities during the Week of the Migrants each September, documents cases of abuse of migrants, and facilitates institutional coordination among the participating parishes in the diocese (Ackerman et al. 2004).

In an effort to coordinate solidarity, hospitality, and advocacy activities along the migrant trail, the Mexican Episcopal Conference of Bishops (CEM) has organized an annual workshop on the pastoral care of migrants since 2000. During its annual meetings, representatives from Mexican dioceses and several US dioceses that straddle the northern border of Mexico convene to assess needs and coordinate resolutions to regional migration problems. As such, many refer to themselves as dioceses without borders and strive for a borderless church. One of the long-term goals of this annual workshop is to develop among local diocesan churches a network of shelters along the migrant journey.

Among the conference participants are the Scalabrinian Missionaries of Saint Charles, the sole transnational religious congregation with the mission of providing pastoral care to migrants. The Scalabrini congregation was originally founded in 1887 to minister to the needs of Italian immigrants in North and South America. To this end, the congregation established churches, hospitals, and other institutions to assist in the settlement of Italian migrants in the region. But by the 1930s, the congregation had undergone a process of internationalization, and by World War II, Scalabrinians were serving Italian migrant workers in Germany and France; by 1952, following the publication of the apostolic constitution *Exsul Familia* (*On the Spiritual Care for Migrants*), the Scalabrini presence was expanded to Latino Catholics in the Americas. In the *Exsul Familia*, the first modern Vatican document to acknowledge the right to migrate, Pope Pius XII authorized the Pontifical College to begin selecting priests to form Scalabrini congregations in Latin America. By 1966, the congregation's mission was redefined as one providing for all refugees, migrants, and seamen throughout the globe (D'Agostino 1997). In this expanded role, the missionaries were called on to work with local dioceses to develop pastoral plans for migrants, counsel the departing migrants, and if necessary direct them toward safe passage while monitoring those officials who regulate the process to ensure that they do not violate the law or exploit migrants. It is this pastoral challenge—the care of the journeying migrants—that largely constitutes the border ministry work of the Scalabrinians in Mexico and Central America today.

Beginning in 1987, the Scalabrini, with the cooperation of local parishes and dioceses, began to build their regional network of migrant shelters called *Red de Casas del Migrante* ("network of migrant homes or safe houses") that are situated adjacent to the most dangerous crossing corridors along the Guatemala-Mexico and Mexico-US borders. These shelters provide pastoral and humanitarian care for departing and journeying migrants, as well as resettlement and reintegration programs for the returned migrant who has been deported home. The shelters, which are more formally known under the acronym CAME (Centro de Attention al Migrant Exodus), are funded by the Scalabrinian congregation; by the Mexican, US, and Guatemalan Episcopal Conferences; by dioceses and local parishes with whom they partner; and by individual donations. Sometimes the shelters are erected and run solely by the Scalabrinian missionaries; in general, however, the Scalabrinian brothers erect or reorganize shelters according to their mission guidelines at the request of local dioceses and then hand them over to trained local clergy to run. Their legacy in the region will be a network of safe houses and institutionalized migrant programs in diocesan churches along the migrant trail.

The mediating role of the cases in buffering the hardships of the journey is multifaceted. The shelters provide humanitarian, educational, psychological, and spiritual support to hundreds of transit migrants each day. Because the Scalabrinian missionaries work closely with local parishes, most casas are located alongside parish churches where the Scalabrinian priests provide daily or weekly masses. If requested, services, religious counsel, and final blessings are provided to the departing migrant. From these parish pulpits the Scalabrini also inform parishioners about the migration phenomenon and present to them the human face of the migrants. As more than one brother has pointed out, "We try to challenge people to see the face of Jesus in the migrant." In their multiple roles of priest, provider, and advocate, they sometimes challenge their congregants to become more publicly involved in migration matters and more sensitive to the needs of the journeying migrants.

Collectively, the network of Scalabrinian shelters and the dioceses in which they are located provide true sanctuary for the contemporary journeying migrant. Because they are run by religious congregations and sanctioned by the parish and diocese in which they are located, the shelters operate as safe houses within the boundaries of the church and outside the reach of the state. Consequently, the migrants they attend are protected from apprehension and deportation, if only on a temporary basis.

Similar to other Christian groups who work with the poor in Latin America, Scalabrinian missionaries embrace communitarian social theologies that emphasize the quest for social justice, especially liberation theology, which focuses on engaging the world for the sake of transforming it from forms of oppression. Drawing on the words of the father of liberation theology Gustavo Gutiérrez, they believe that they "must be the voice of the voiceless. (Guitierrez 2004). For the Scalabrinian missionaries working the front lines in Mexico and Central America, being the voice of the voiceless involves speaking out for the hundreds of thousands of migrants who are at risk and vulnerable to exploitation. Consequently, many of the Scalabrini are more public than other Catholic orders in migration matters; different casas and their directors will join forces to challenge and protest state migration polices. Their activist orientation and identity also result largely from Scalabrini teachings, which emphasize the transformation and liberation of migrants. Each Christmas Father Rigoni, director of the *Casa de Migrante* in Tapachula, Mexico, and Father Eduardo Quintero, who is assistant director of the *Casa del Migrante* in Guatemala City, come together to express the theme of the stranger and guest and protest the injustice of Mexican border enforcement policies. On one of the days leading up to Christmas, each missionary travels with migrant followers to the Mexico-Guatemala border to celebrate the Catholic posada ritual, a procession that reenacts Joseph's and Mary's long and arduous search for shelter and refuge in Bethlehem. After traveling from house to house seeking shelter and eventually receiving it, the two groups meet halfway across the bridge connecting Guatemala and Mexico in a symbolic demonstration of unity across borders and welcoming of the stranger. Called the Posada of the Migrant, it is one of many posadas organized by cross-border and interfaith groups that have emerged along Mexico's borders in the past decade to illustrate Christian practices of support and solidarity and to protest border enforcement policies in the region (Hondagneu-Sotelo, Gaudinez, Lara, and Ortiz 2004). Further north, along the Mexico-US border, the Scalabrinian missionaries have also been active in linking faith to action and promoting peaceful social justice protests. In the border cities of Tijuana and Juarez, they have come together with sister churches and religious workers on the US side and organized cross-border posadas during Christmas week, services and educational activities and seminars during the Day of the Migrants in September, and numerous vigils on the Day of the Dead. Each November 1, the Day of the Dead, a memorial service is organized and crosses are placed along the border wall listing the names, ages, and origins of the thousands of migrants who have died while attempting to cross the border. Since 2001, the parishes of St. Anthony and St. Joseph in Holtville,

California, along with California Rural Legal Aid and the Scalabrinian mission-aries from Tijuana, have come together each year on November 1 at the Terrace Park Cemetery to remember the several hundred unidentified migrants who lie in what was once called a potter's field with numbered bricks to mark the graves. Many of these cross-border ecumenical commemorations—posadas at Christmas, vigils on the Day of the Dead, marches on the Day of the Migrant—are both commemorative and performative in that they are rituals to mourn the dead but also to bring public attention to the larger social and political circumstances under which poor migrants cross the border in their search for a better life (Santino 2006).

The Scalabrini have no fixed pastoral model. As one missionary explained to me, "We are part of a pilgrim church and we respond to the local pastoral needs of the populations we accompany." In this sense, the Scalabrini who work closely with the different levels of church hierarchy are always on the move and remain a crucial vehicle for disseminating transnational church migration policies and implementing migrant programs. Because they practice a theology of migration that extends beyond welcoming the stranger to encompass trans-forming and liberating migrants, the missionaries are also the public voice of the Catholic Church and its social justice work in the Americas.

The Catholic Church and its Scalabrinian emissaries are not alone in their opposition to the US southwest border enforcement. There are literally doz-ens upon dozens of shelters erected by faith-based groups to serve migrants; many are erected along the Central American and Mexican trail and far from any formal religious institutions. Rising migrant-crossing deaths in the Tucson area of the US-Mexico border have also mobilized a number of overlapping interfaith groups along the Arizona-Mexico border into action on two fronts: humanitarian services and sanctuary for migrants and social protest on their behalf. The goals and membership lists of these faith-based organizations have grown in range and size over the years, and some of the founders of these organizations, such as Rev. Fife, can trace their roots to the original US Sanctuary Movement. Initially founded and organized to provide humanitarian aid to migrants crossing the desert under the scorch-ing sun of the summer months, these present-day interfaith and civil efforts, along with their movement goals, have swelled in number, culminating in recent years in a collective, cross-border social movement with goals of pro-viding humanitarian assistance to crossing migrants, educating the public about the human costs of US border enforcement campaigns, and calling for reform in US immigration policy. Their Jewish, Catholic, Quaker, and main-line Protestant members share common meanings of protest. They embrace communitarian social theologies that stress the quest for social justice and civic and political action (Guth et al. 1997; Hagan 2006) and share a long and active history of social activism in the United States, ranging from public issues such as homelessness to social welfare to environmental efforts. Some of the present-day faith leaders and members are new to the immigration scene, while others, including Rev. Fife, have remained active in issues of poverty, migration, and social justice since the days of the original US Sanctuary Movement of the 1980s.

The first group to publically challenge current US border enforcement policy was a peace church that established its presence along the border in 1987 when the Quaker organization, the American Friends Service Committee, founded the Immigration Law Enforcement Monitoring Project (ILEMP), a program designed to monitor the civil and human rights consequences of US border enforcement. In 1999, as the California-based Operation Gatekeeper Campaign continued to push migration flows to the Arizona border, Quaker faith communities joined forces with Catholic and Presbyterian groups in the area to form Healing Our Borders, an international faith-based NGO located in Douglas, Arizona, a small border town separated from its sister city, Agua Prieta, in Sonora, Mexico, by a US government–erected wall. The coalition, which draws members from both sides of the border, was originally formed to provide humanitarian assistance to journeying migrants. In this capacity, they distribute blankets and provisions to apprehended migrants and since 2000 have been holding a weekly prayer vigil commemorating the dead. During the vigil, the group makes crosses for migrants who have died in Cochise County and places them against the curb along the vigil route. Like many interfaith groups who have witnessed a rise in human rights tragedies resulting from escalating enforcement activities along the border, Healing Our Borders has grown to involve advocacy and social protest.

Some of these humanitarian and social justice protests have attracted more public attention than others. In 2000, a year following a record number of migrant deaths in the Tucson area, Rev. Robin Hoover of Tucson's First Christian Church founded Humane Borders, Inc., a binational interfaith organization established to "create a just and more humane border environment." To this end, Humane Border volunteers began placing water tanks with thirty-foot flagpole markers along well-traveled migrant paths across the southern Arizona desert. By 2008, they had erected 120 flagpoles and tanks and were dispensing in private, public, and federal lands more than 500 gallons of water a week. By 2008, more than 15,000 people from all over the United States had volunteered for Humane Borders. Humane Borders' members are a diverse coalition of seventy Protestant and Catholic churches from Mexico and the United States and a number of secular NGOs including human rights organizations and legal advocacy groups. Like other coalitions involved in the Transnational Sanctuary Movement, Humane Borders was originally founded to provide temporary humanitarian relief to journeying migrants. With time, however, the Humane Borders mission statement has become increasingly public and political and has expanded, calling for a more equitable immigration policy that would provide legalization and temporary work opportunities for migrants living and working in the United States.

Although the humanitarian and protest activities of the various interfaith groups along the Arizona-Mexico border received considerable national and international media attention, their efforts did not lead to any changes in border policy, and the human consequences—increasing migrant fatalities—continued to escalate in the summer months as the scorching desert heat claimed lives. In escalated protest in 2003, an expanded coalition of interfaith groups from both sides of the border joined Rev. John Fife of the Southside Presbyterian Church in Tucson and one of the founders of the original US Sanctuary Movement and took things one step further by creating the Samaritans coalition of Quakers, Jews, Disciples of Christ, Methodists, Catholics, and Presbyterians that make regular trips to the desert in all-terrain vehicles equipped with water, food, a medical team, and first-aid supplies. According to Fife, the group was formed on the principle that it is the "right and responsibility" of civil organizations to aid victims of human rights violations in need of assistance. When migrants in the desert and in distress are found, the Samaritans either call on Border Patrol for helicopter assistance or transport them to a local hospital.

In the spring of 2004, with no indication of a slowdown in migrant deaths in the desert-crossing corridor and with summer approaching, religious-based protest activities began to challenge the law openly. A broader effort developed to work for justice along the border and provide sustained twenty-four/ seven humanitarian relief for journeying migrants. Entitled "No More Deaths" (NMD), its membership includes an expanded binational coalition of individuals, faith communities, religious leaders, NGOs, and human rights grassroots organizers. Its members refer to NMD as a "movement" and not as an organization. They engage in direct action to challenge and reform US immigration policy, limit crossing deaths, and raise public awareness. Its members share common principles regarding avenues to immigration reform. Central to the movement is the biblically inspired "Ark of the Covenant" effort, which involves placing moveable camps in the desert. The camps are named for a wooden Ark of the Covenant box in the Old Testament that symbolized the presence of God guiding the people of Israel when they were wandering in the desert. As Rev. Fife explains, "We took sanctuary of the church to the desert." In the summer months, volunteers work the desert camps twenty-four hours a day. The volunteers, many of whom are recruited from churches and universities throughout the United States, reach several hundred in number each summer. The desert camps provide water, food, clothing, and medical assistance. If a serious medical problem arises, volunteers are instructed to "evacuate" (transport) the distressed migrant to a hospital or to call the US Border Patrol's Search, Trauma and Rescue (BORSTAR) unit. In a less severe case of dehydration, exhaustion,

or minor injuries, volunteers arrange for the migrant to be transported to a
Tucson church or clinic. In the month of June 2005 alone, NMD volunteers res-
cued 175 migrants in distress in the Arizona desert. As Rev. Fife had explained
in 2004, "We have no choice now but to take Sanctuary out of the church into
the desert. State violation of human rights has been resurrected at the border and we have no recourse but to act out what Jim Corbett, the founder of
Sanctuary, called 'civil initiative,' which refers to peaceful protest within the
bounds of the law."

In summer 2004, a showdown between the state and church developed when
the US government challenged the sanctuary practices of two NMD volunteers,
Shanti Selz and Daniel Strauss. While transporting three dehydrated migrants
to a Tucson hospital, the two volunteers were arrested by US Border Patrol officials and charged with transporting and harboring illegal migrants, a felony
under US immigration law. The case gained national and international attention as supporters, religious groups, and human rights organizations joined
forces to protest the arrests of the two volunteers. In August of the same summer, the case was dismissed by US District Judge Raner Collins, who argued
that the volunteers "had made reasonable efforts to ensure that their actions
were not in violation of the law, and that further prosecution would violate the
defendants' due process right."[8] The Sanctuary Movement prevailed.

Conclusion

To truly understand international migration from Latin America to the United
States in the contemporary era requires an understanding of the expanding role
of religion in service provision and public policy. The changing conditions and
social contexts of the undocumented journey—militarized borders, increased
dangers, the rise of a migration industry that preys on migrants—have resulted
in the growth of religious and humanitarian organizations that provide for
migrants on the move. In recent years, these organizations have become part
of the social infrastructure that sustains transit migration. Indeed, it is only
through identifying and examining these religious actors that we can come to
understand how and why many migrants are able to overcome the hardships of
the journey and reach the United States.

Looking at international migration through the lens of religion also highlights the limits of migrants' personal networks in the contemporary era of
heightened border enforcement. Lacking the resources or personal networks
to assist them in their travels, many migrants now turn to churches, shelters,
and religious workers to perform network functions. These faith-based and
humanitarian migrant programs provide transit migrants with the social,

spiritual, and psychological capital to continue on their journeys. Shelters such as the *Casas del Migrantes* provide direct material assistance in the way of food, shelter, and clothing, while the clergy who care for these shelters offer services, blessings, and counsel to migrants to sanction their migration, help them endure the separation from family and community, and fortify them for the hardships of the remaining journey. From trusted faith workers and lay staff who run the shelters, migrants learn about the dangers of crossing international borders and are sometimes directed to alternative and safer routes than they would otherwise adopt. Shelters and programs along the route offer an alternative networking resource, the opportunity for migrants to connect with one another and exchange information about the journey. From deportees who are returned to the shelters by government officials, transit migrants learn the ropes of crossing the border while those who travel alone sometimes can link up with other migrants. These networks, built in the shelters, provide buffers against the disruption and isolation, offering solidarity and protection on the road.

Because of religion's particular moral and organizational resources, the church in multiple guises has become increasingly involved in the politics of immigration in the region. As such, religious organizations have become more than providers. They are also advocates of the rights of migrants and monitors of state policies. Through their mobilization efforts and transnational scope, the public face of these organizations has grown substantially in recent years as they have developed their own migrant programs and human rights offices all along the migrant trail, from Guatemala to the southwest United States. As advocates for the rights of migrants to cross borders to find work, these religious workers and the transnational hierarchies in which they operate have emerged as important vehicles for contesting and monitoring the regulatory practices of state institutions and policies. They challenge the migration state by documenting crossing risks and human rights abuses associated with current border enforcement policies. These organizations have become so effective that in some countries in the region, such as Mexico and Guatemala, governments now include them in discussions that formulate migration policies and programs. As such, faith-based actors have essentially become key players in policymaking. Along the US-Mexico border, binational interfaith coalitions challenge US immigration policy by providing humanitarian assistance to crossing migrants and encouraging political and social protest among followers. Collectively, the activities of these organizations represent a new Transnational Sanctuary Movement.

Unlike the 1980s Sanctuary Movement in the United States, which was largely limited to national efforts and geared toward providing refuge for Central Americans fleeing political strife, today's sanctuary efforts transcend national borders. They focus on the human rights of transit migrants and receive the sanction of multiple levels of church hierarchy, from the Vatican

to cardinals to transnational religious congregations, bilateral bishops conferences and diocesan efforts, and local faith workers throughout Central America,
Mexico, and the United States. In the absence of a retreat in state enforcement
policy, the Transnational Sanctuary Movement is unlikely to weaken or erode,
as it constitutes an important refuge from the expansive smuggling industry
and vast state military operations with which it shares the migratory route.

Notes

1. The *Salvatruchas* are often compared to their notorious northern counterparts in Los
    Angeles—the Crips and the Bloods. Considered a product of the civil war in El Salvador,
    many of the gang's members fled to Los Angeles during the crisis and were later deported
    from the United States. They have since established a visible presence along the El
    Salvador-US migrant trail where they prey on migrants as they hide in concealed train
    compartments or jump off the trains as they approach checkpoints.
2. See, for example, among many others, Taylor (1986); Massey et al. (1987); Hagan (1994);
    Singer and Massey (1998); and Menjívar (2000); Spener (2006;2009)
3. See, for example, Hagan (1998); Menjívar (2002); Portes and Sensenbrenner (1993);
    Hernández León (2008); Krissman (2005); Mahler (1995); Hondagneu-Sotelo (1994); and
    Gonzalez de la Rocha (1994).
4. Castles and Miller (2003) coined the term "migration industry" to describe the for-profit
    aggregate of recruitment organizations, lawyers, smugglers, and agents that facilitate
    international migration. Hernández León (2008) applies this concept to the case of
    Mexican-US migration and explores the conditions under which these for-profit actors
    complement or replace migrants' social networks.
5. See Ackerman, Loughna, and Castles (2004) and Orgen (2007) for more information on the
    numerous organizations, especially nonreligious groups that provide for transit migrants.
6. According to Keck and Sikkink (1998), it is precisely common values and concerns that
    often give rise to transnational advocacy networks.
7. The northern dioceses include Hermosilla, La Paz, Mexicali, Tijuana, Ciudad Juárez,
    Nuevo Casa Grandes, Matadoras, Nuevo Laredo, Satillo, and Piedras Negras. The cen-
    tral dioceses include Autlan, Cd. Guzmán, Guadalajara, San Juan de los Lagos, Tepic,
    Zacatecas, Morelia, León, San Luís Potosí, México, Cuernavaca, Texcoco, Tula, and
    Tulancingo. The southern dioceses include Coatzacoalcos, Papantla, San Andreas Tuxtla,
    Veracruz, Acapulco, Tabasco, San Cristóbal de las Casas, and Tapachula.
8. No More Deaths press release (http://www.nomoredeaths.org, accessed September
    2006).

References

Ackerman, Lisanne, Sean Loughna, and Stephen Castles. 2004. "Assessing the Human Rights
    of Migrants in Central America and Mexico." Report commissioned by Project Counseling
    Service (PCS), Lima, Peru.
Andreas, Peter. 2000. *Border Games: Policing the U.S.-Mexico Divide*. Ithaca, NY: Cornell
    University Press.
Andreas, Peter. 2001. "The Transformation of Migrant Smuggling Across the U.S.—Mexico
    Border." Pp. 108–125 in *Global Human Smuggling: Comparative Perspectives*, edited by
    D. Kyle and R. Koslowski. Baltimore: Johns Hopkins University Press.

Blume, Michael. 2003. "Migration and the Social Doctrine of the Church." Pp. 62–75 in *Migration, Religious Experience, and Globalization*, edited by Gioacchino Campese and Pietro Ciallell. Staten Island, NY: Center for Migration Studies.

Casanova, Jose. 1994. *Public Religions in the Modern World*. Chicago: University of Castles, Stephen, and Mark J. Miller. 2003. *The Age of Migration: International Population Movements in the Modern World*. 3rd ed. New York: Guilford Press.

Chinchilla, Norma, Nora Hamilton, and James Loucky. 2009. "The Sanctuary Movement and Central American Activism in Los Angeles." *Latin American Perspectives* 36: 101–126.

Coutin, Susan Bibler. 1993. *The Culture of Protest: Religious Activism and the U.S. Sanctuary Movement*. Boulder, CO: Westview Press.

D'Agostino, Peter R. 1997. "The Scalabrini Fathers, the Italian Emigrant/Church, and Ethnic Nationalism in America." *Religion and American Culture* 7(1): 121–159.

Dunn, Timothy J. 1996. *The Militarization of the U.S.-Mexico Border, 1978–1992*. Austin: Center for Mexican/American Studies, University of Texas Press.

Eschbach, Karl, Jacqueline Hagan, and Nestor Rodríguez. 2003. "Deaths During Undocumented Migration: Trends and Policy Implications in the New Era of Homeland Security." *In Defense of the Alien* 26. New York: Center for Migration Studies, pp.37–52

Eschbach, Karl, Stan Bailey, Jacqueline Hagan, Ruben Hernandez-Leon, and Nestor Rodriguez. 1999. "Death at the Border." *International Migration Review* 33: 430–454.

Flynn, Michael. 2002. "U.S. Anti-Migration Efforts Move South." Americas Program. Silver City, NM: Interhemispheric Resource Center.

García, Maria Christina. 2006. *Seeking Refuge: Central American Migration to Mexico, the United States, and Canada*. Los Angeles: University of California Press.

Gonzalez de la Rocha, Mercedes. 1994. *The Resources of Poverty*. Cambridge: Blackwell Publishers.

Groody, Daniel G. 2004. "A Theology of Migration." Paper presented at the International Conference on Migration and Theology, Notre Dame, IN, September 21.

Gutierrez, Gustavo. 2004. "Poverty, Migration, and OFP." Paper presented at the International Conference on Migration and Theology, Notre Dame, IN, September 21.

Guth, J.L., Green, J.C., Smidt, C.E., Kellstedt, L.A., & Poloma, M.M. 1997. *The Bully Pulpit: The Politics of Protestant Clergy*. Lawrence, KS: University Press of Kansas.

Hagan, Jacqueline. 1994. *Deciding to Be Legal: A Maya Community in Houston*. Philadelphia: Temple University Press,

Hagan, Jacqueline. 1998. "Social Networks, Gender, and Immigrant Incorporation: Resources and Constraints." *American Sociological Review* 63: 55–67.

Jacqueline Hagan. 2006. "Making Theological Sense of the Migration Journey from Latin America: Catholic, Protestant and Interfaith Perspectives." *American Behavioral Scientist* 49(11): 1154–1573.

Hagan, Jacqueline Maria. . 2008. *Migration Miracle: Faith, Hope, and Meaning on the Undocumented Journey*. Cambridge: Harvard University Press.

Hernandez-Leon, Ruben. 2008. Metropolitan Migrants: the Migration of Urban Mexicans to the United States, Berkeley: University of California Press.

Hondagneu-Sotelo, Pierette. 2008. *God Has No Borders: How Religious Activists Are Working for Immigrant Rights*. Berkeley: University of California Press.

Hondaganeu-Sotelo, Pierette, Genelle Gaudinez, Hector Lara, and Billie C. Ortiz. 2004. "There's a Spirit That Transcends the Border: Faith, Ritual, and Postnational Protest at the U.S.-Mexico Border." *Sociological Perspectives* 47(2): 133–159.

Humane Borders. 2005. Homepage. http://www.humaneborders.org

Jimenez, Maria. 2009. "Migrants Deaths at the US-Mexico Border" Retrieved from *www.aclu.org/files/pdfs/immigrants/humanitariancrisisreport.pdf*

Keck, Margaret E., and Katherine Sikkink. 1998. *Activists Across Borders: Advocacy Networks in International Politics*. Ithaca, NY: Cornell University Press.

Kerwin, Donald. 2006. "Immigration Reform and the Catholic Church." *Migration Information Source*. Washington, DC: Migration Policy Institute.

Lee, Erika. 2002. "Enforcing the Borders: Chinese Exclusion Along the U.S. Borders with Canada and Mexico, 1882 to 1924." *Journal of American History*, June.

Lee, Erika. 2003. *At America's Gate: Chinese Immigration during the Exclusion Era, 1882–1943* Chapel Hill: University of North Carolina Press.

Lipton, Eric. 2006. "Bush Turns to Giant Military Contractors." *New York Times*, May 18, section 1A.

Mahler, Sarah. 1995. *American Dreaming*. Princeton, NJ: Princeton University Press.

Massey, Douglas S., Rafael Alarcón, Jorge Durand, and Humberto González. *Return to Atzlan: The Social Process of International Migration from Western Mexico*. Berkeley: University of California Press, 1987.

Massey, Douglas S., Jorge Durand, and Nolan J. Malone. 2002. *Beyond Smoke and Mirrors: Mexican Immigration in an Era of Economic Integration*. New York: Russell Sage Foundation.

Menjívar, Cecilia. 2000. *Fragmented Ties. Salvadoran Immigrant Networks in America*. Berkeley: University of California Press.

Nepstad Erickson, Sharon. 2004. *Convictions of the Soul: Religion, Culture, and Agency in the Central America Solidarity Movement*. New York: Oxford University Press.

No More Deaths. 2005. Homepage. http://www.nomoredeaths.org

Ogren, Cassandra. 2007. "Migration and Human Rights on the Mexico-Guatemala Border." International Migration 45 (4): 203–243

Portes, Alejandro, and Julia Sensenbrenner. 1993. "Embeddedness and Immigration: Notes on the Social Determinants of Economic Action." *American Journal of Sociology* 98(6): 1320–1350.

Santino, Jack, ed. 2006. *Spontaneous Shrines and the Public Memorialization of Death*. New York: Palgrave Macmillan.

Sapkota, Sanjeeb, Harold W. Kohl III, Julie Gilchrist, Jay McAuliffe, Bruce Parks, Bob England, Tim Flood, C. Sewell, Dennis Perrotta, Miguel Escobedo, Corinne E. Stern, David Zane, and Kurt B. Nolte. 2005. "Unauthorized Border Crossings and Migrant Deaths: Arizona, New Mexico, and El Paso, Texas, 2002–2003." *American Journal of Public Health*, 96 (7): 1282–1287

Spener, David. 2009. *Clandestine Crossings: Mexicans and Coyotes on the Texas-Mexico Border*. Ithaca: Cornell University Press.

US Conference of Catholic Bishops. 2003. *Strangers No Longer: Together on the Journey of Hope*. Washington, DC: US Conference of Catholic Bishops, January 22.

US General Accounting Office. 2006. "Illegal Immigration: Border Crossing Deaths Have Doubled Since 1995; Border Patrol's Efforts to Prevent Deaths Have Not Been Fully Evaluated." Washington, DC: US Government Printing Office,

Conclusion: Working the Edges

COURTNEY BENDER, WENDY CADGE,
PEGGY LEVITT, AND DAVID SMILDE

If there is anything "new" in the study of religion, it is that interest in and questions about religion in social life are flourishing across the social sciences and humanities, in all kinds of ways—new and old, messy and not so messy. As sociologists studying religion begin new conversations with colleagues across the disciplines, and as sociologists working on health, politics, the economy, and the arts (to name a few) discover that religion affects their areas of interest, our dialogues deepen and broaden.

As we stated in our introduction, we do not aim to champion a new theory of religion or to offer yet another set of critiques. Rather, our goal is to highlight a new generation of scholarship on religion that carries older lines of critique forward and to showcase interests that have grown at the edges of the discipline. This scholarship allows us to articulate challenges to the traditional center of the sociological study of religion and bring to the fore the important new ways in which studies of religion are coalescing around a different set of questions and concerns. While our introduction maps out the critiques and challenges that working at the edges pose, our conclusion will briefly, and somewhat speculatively, propose the parameters and projects that it promotes—the intellectual moves that it implies.

Models *of* and Models *for* the Sociological Study of Religion

In his classic treatment of religion, Clifford Geertz provided a conceptualization of cultural symbols as "models of" and "models for." In the first sense, human beings put together symbolic structures so that they adequately represent some aspect of the external world, including physical but also social, emotional, and spiritual realities. These symbolic structures thereby provide a vehicle with which to apprehend these realities. Cultural symbols also can provide a model *for* reality. They can provide a map or reference guide for that which is to be done. Geertz finds models *for* everywhere in nature: genes, instincts, the habitual actions (and communication patterns) of animals that determine their behaviors. They do not need any added extra symbolic work to reproduce themselves. In contrast, the human cultural domain is made of things that have the character of both models *for* and models *of*—"linguistic, graphic, mechanical, natural, etc., processes which function not to provide sources of information in terms of which other processes can be patterned, but to represent those processes as such, to express their structure in an alternative medium" (Geertz 1973, 94). Our ability to create such models is uniquely human. This need to create "models of" comes from the underdetermined nature of human behavior. By creating models *of*, we create our own models *for*: "The intertransposability of models for and models of which symbolic formulation makes possible is the distinctive characteristic of our mentality" (Geertz 1973, 94).

We have found this conceptualization useful as we put this volume together. Through discussions with each other, the contributors of this book, and others, we have sought to put forward a "model of" contemporary sociology of religion. It is, of course, underdetermined by the facts. Some of the edges we point out in the introduction—for example, critical engagements of religion—clearly do represent majority trends within the subfield. Others—for example, diversification of research beyond Christianity and the United States—are important but minority trends. The contributions to this book, then, provide a model *of* the subfield with an eye toward putting forward a model *for* the subfield. In the pages that follow, we identify four intellectual moves that we see modeled in the work of our contributors. We highlight them as models *of* the sociological study of religion, hoping that, in the coming years, they will become models *for*.

We also find Geertz's formulation useful as a theoretical foil for developing nuances of our position. We agree with the many critics who claimed that he overemphasized the role of belief in religion. Geertz's base metaphor for culture is that of the cognitive code that is congruent with external realities and is assented to by people. However, beliefs are only part of the picture of culture, whether we are talking about religion or the sociology of religion. We see cultural models not just flowing through beliefs, but embedded in discourses, practices, and institutions in ways that function beyond whether anybody "believes" in them. We also take issue with the idea of "congruence" of symbols not only with external reality but also, most important, with each other. Whether we look at cultural models embedded in scholarship (where the noisy arguments over meaning and theory are ever more heated) or embedded in the religious world (where ambiguity and reinterpretation, doubt, and argument within religious communities challenge Geertz's concept that symbols imprint an order on the soul or the mind), there is little of the congruence or agreement that Geertz articulated. Rather, we see a messy set of claims and actions, wherein claims for congruence within a religious system are constantly reas-serted, but by a range of authorities positioned in multiple spaces and times. "Models of" are inherently open-ended, with varying powers to assert the kinds of effects and subjective stances that Geertz's definition asserts is part of the active work of symbols themselves. It is this open-endedness that makes "models of" a source of conflict and power.

One final way in which we distance ourselves from Geertz's formulation is with his tendency to reify the work of symbols as a one-way codification of non-symbolic reality. We will not try to resolve the complex philosophical issue of whether we can actually make sense of nonsymbolic reality. Rather, we focus on the fact that the cultural models we are studying here are all symbolizations of symbolizations. Sociological analyses of religion provide "models of" religious reality, ones that may have surprising power in the world. Our survey findings, ethnographic analyses and methods, and claims about "the religious" travel well beyond the confines of the academy and influence policy and politics. They also shape the dynamics of religious communities in multiple ways. Religious models and sociological models are less than discrete, with continual cross-fertilization that needs to be understood and incorporated into our analyses.

In sum, by continuing to embrace this "models of and models for" formula-tion, we call attention to the intersections of our own models of religion, those of religious communities, and those of a broader set of publics. We simultane-ously call attention to the dynamics of power, contention, interchange, and even cooperation that take shape as any cultural or theoretical "symbolic system" comes into view. Contra Geertz, the "noisiness" and messiness of the reproduction of models of any system highlight the ways that religions and theories about religions are reproduced in tandem. The reproduction of reli-gion—as a topic, a set of "traditions," a force in the world, a schema, a set of institutions—involves not just the people who work on the religious side of the story, the priests, leaders, and laypeople who "do religion," but also the scholars who pose questions in surveys, create ethnographic accounts, and so on.

Moving Forward

In this final section, we outline some of the shared intellectual moves that our contributors engage in and the path forward that they chart. The first pair is more substantive while the final pair is more methodological.

First Move: Deep Contextualization

The first substantive shift evident among many of our contributors is their commitment to approaching religions in the time period and contexts in which they were produced and to clearly specifying how those contexts influence what is considered religious. By doing so, authors show how deep historical and ideological templates continue to inform contemporary analyses and practices.

Building on Asad, several of our colleagues ask why, at specific moments, we are concerned with certain kinds of questions about religion rather than others, how those preoccupations change, and what the answer to these questions tells us about the history, institutions, and cultural contexts within which we work. They make clear how the ways in which religion has been understood are social and historical products. Vásquez models this contextualization by showing how, in their efforts to create an autonomous field of inquiry that differed from studies of the theological and the metaphysical, sociology's forefathers adopted an ambivalent, if not hostile, stance toward religion and its relationship to the modern. Sociology also emerged at about the same time Western modernity was defining itself as an enlightened civilization that contrasted sharply with the irrationality of the Dark Ages and with uncivilized, colonial other. Intellectual blind spots and silences ensued, the consequences of which are detailed throughout this volume. The kind of genealogical and archaeological inquiry Vásquez models might clear space in sociology for "the emergence of approaches that are simultaneously more humble and more robust."

David Smilde continues this "excavation" by showing how sociologists of religion have constantly been expected to explain the persistence of religion and therefore had a strong desire and need to define it as a clear, autonomous category of inquiry. Especially early on, he argues, this work of staking claim to religion as a distinct and legitimate field of knowledge reinforced the modern expectation of religion's disengagement with everyday realities. In other words, by putting themselves on the map, sociologists of religion ensured they would be pushed to its borders. More recent efforts to articulate a "strong program" vision of religion revive past wrongs by emphasizing religion as an autonomous, independent reality that can have causal impact but not be causally impacted.

Wendy Cadge and Geneviève Zubrzycki ask questions about how context affects what counts as religion and the ways actors negotiate diversity through specific empirical cases. They show how religious diversity is negotiated and explore what that reveals about the locations where it is produced. In Cadge's work, the shift from tradition-specific chapels in contemporary American hospitals to those in which chaplains and hospital administrators include multiple religious groups (often by including none) reveals how religious diversity is addressed by not being addressed—by basically being erased from particular areas of contemporary American life outside of congregations.

Geneviève Zubrzycki analyzes several incidents involving religious minorities that took place in Québec during the fall of 2006 and the winter of 2007 to show how Catholic cultural templates continue to pervade Québécois nationalism, despite the province's strong declarations of secularism. Although framed as a current-day contest between the nonreligious majority and religious minorities, the tensions were, Zubrzycki argues, largely about Québec's religious past and how to come to terms with the rejection of its religious roots. The debates, she says, were not "just" about "religion" or about "the religious and the secular." Rather, they were a collective reexamination of the way in which the secular emerged in Québécois society. Just as "Catholicism" means different things, locates itself in different spaces, and fulfills different political roles in different national contexts during different periods, so Zubrzycki shows that "the secular" takes shape in relation to specific religious and political backdrops.

Similarly, Courtney Bender shows how notions of religious autonomy in the United States grow directly out of American secular policy and doctrine and are shaped by secular norms, legal codes, and governmental regulations that privilege some religious actors over others. Ateş Altınordu focuses on contemporary Islamic politics in the Middle East, showing what it shares with earlier European and Christian experiences. Rather than seeing Islamic politics as produced directly by Islamic doctrines or as a unique feature of the political traditions of the Middle East, he urges scholars to focus on historical and contemporary patterns of religious activism and political interaction. Instead of analyzing Catholicism and Islam separately, he argues, we should examine them comparatively, using the same theoretical frame. Doing so generates a much-needed corrective to oversimplified, essentialist, and ahistorical analyses.

Finally, Kelly Chong's work drives home the need to examine discourse, institutions, and practice in context and foreshadows the second collective intellectual move that our authors make. The disciplinary aims of the Korean evangelical churches she studies, as well as the lived practices of members, she argues, are intimately tied to the discursive and structural transformations occurring in other social fields and institutional "regimes" of Korean society, such as the family, politics, and the economy.

Second Move: Pushing the Critique of Religion-as-Belief

The second substantive intellectual move evident in these chapters is their commitment to exploring the intellectual consequences of rethinking the relationship between religion and belief. Understanding religion as a matter of belief in a cosmic order and religion as deeply connected (morally, evolutionarily, and socially) to "belief" is problematic, as we have noted, for multiple reasons. It ignores myriad ways that "religion" works in the world and the multiple ways that religious activities and authorities are understood, experienced, and deployed. It reifies as universal a particular genealogy of religion based on a particular political history. Our contributors, like many others, have called for a move away from these approaches. But even more broadly, they identify multiple ways to reframe the question of religious experience and articulate strategies for taking on the sticky problem of belief in different registers.

Michal Pagis's work exemplifies these moves by arguing that content and "cultures" are constitutive elements of religious practices of self-formation. Based on the case of Vipassana Buddhist meditation—which takes place around the globe in a range of noncongregational contexts—she argues that both Buddhist and late modern concepts and ideologies "play a role in producing the motivation for practice and building expectations for certain outcomes." Studying beliefs, values, and worldviews cannot substitute for the more head-on study of the religious self or how it is constituted.

Paul Lichterman and Manuel Vásquez both take on the issue of belief in challenging sociological models that are "actor centered." Lichterman urges sociologists to focus theoretically and methodologically on "group styles in public settings" as an alternative to those approaches that focus on individuals and individuality. Likewise, Vásquez directs our focus to group action, writing, "Different group styles elicit different abilities, perspectives, even religious beliefs, that individuals may not exercise or express outside the group." A relational and cultural approach calls into question current popular understandings not only of what religion is but also of how religion promotes collective action or enables people to get along across religious divides. If scholars want to understand where religion is in *public* life, Vásquez argues, they must focus on social settings rather than actors. They must ask how different settings give rise to different religious identities, rather than assuming that people identify consistently and monovalently wherever they go.

Dawne Moon continues this broadening work through the case of reconciliation. While some people see the strong interpersonal connections engendered by reconciliation as central to most religious traditions, Moon argues that they also give rise to noninstitutional spirituality. The same people who see institutional religion as inherently flawed view reconciliation as bringing them into contact with something transcendent and universal. Participation is a "spiritual" rather than a "religious" act that transforms selves by bringing together people who would normally be institutionally segregated.

This critique of belief-centered studies of religion can be taken even further—to move from taking survey responses as indicators of what people "really believe" to understanding them as indicators of a certain kind of public speech. Focusing more on why, historically and today, Americans have been preoccupied with belief as a measure of religion can help us understand what people are really talking about when they talk about religious belief in surveys.

Third Move: Following Religion Where It Goes

The third intellectual move evident among chapter authors is a focus on move-ment and connection, circulation and change. Nearly all our contributors do not assume, a priori, the parameters or depth of the spaces they study but uncover them instead through empirical research. They are open to the ways in which what happens in allegedly contained spaces can be part and parcel of broader, deeper social processes. They are also listening to the ways in which the various levels of social interaction speak to and inform one another—how the local scales up and out and the global talks back, as well as to how these interactions sometimes unsettle the "natural" order.

The move to break open the boundaries of the spaces of the religious is, of course, explicit in the introduction and implicit in many places throughout this volume. But several contributors further this endeavor by modeling how to study words, meanings, or organizational forms in motion. Sometimes they track actual movement—how the work and content of migrating bodies and objects change as they move. Sometimes, they describe something that moves from the invisible to the visible. In other words, they show how the religious has been hiding in plain sight in secular spaces.

As anthropologists Anna Tsing and Carol Gluck (2009, 10) write, "Words stabilize our understanding. They allow us to insert ourselves into discourses, institutions, and social relations." Like the contributors to their book *Words in Motion*, who unfetter particular vocabularies from their traditional moor-ings and track how they change as they travel and elicit new understandings, our contributors do similar work for religion. Cadge's chapter, for example, shows the many ways that the religious circulates, and has always been pres-ent, within the halls of science. Lichterman's chapter looks at what happens when religious discourses are used in public spaces. Jacqueline Hagan's chapter addresses how bodies on the move are aided and abetted by the many churches, religious groups, faith-based organizations, and individual clergy that work the dangerous 2,000-mile migrant trail from Central America to the United States and advocate on their behalf. Peggy Levitt's chapter is a road map for studying religion in motion, which takes fluidity and movement as its starting point but also pays attention to what is rooted and blocked. She delineates several types of *vernacularization* to capture the encounter and subsequent reconfiguring that occurs when circulating materials come into contact with those already on the ground.

Following religion where it goes means that we are less concerned with identifying or explaining the boundaries of religion within a religiously dif-ferentiated "sphere" and that we are unsurprised by finding religion in so-called secular spaces. Sociological research on religion needs to abandon its assumptions about the places and processes where religion allegedly "lives" and empirically study where it rears its head. Whether the "religious" is identified institutionally, through somatic or discursive practices, experience, or identities of various sorts, or is connected to politics, social inequality, or economic processes, its intersections and interactions are present, challenging, and ongoing. Embracing a more empirically based, open stance to the places and textures of "religion" brings into sharper focus the definitional problems that have plagued the sociology of religion for so long. Its shared focus on belief, congregational/voluntary groups, and American and "Christian" definitions of religion seem ill equipped, without vigorous reevaluation, to adequately analyze the ongoing intersections of religious and nonreligious life, in the United States or elsewhere.

Fourth Move: Staying at the Edge

Our final methodological move is to make standard practice the gaze from the edge. This is the theme of the entire book. All of these chapters are connected by a stance that reconsiders key concepts and theories. But we are not simply pushing for an expansion of a clearly bounded sociology of religion. Indeed, many of the reifications of the religious versus the secular, religion as deeply held belief, and conflations of emic and etic are direct consequences of the Durkheimian/Parsonsian project of consolidating sociology by defining its boundaries. Nor do we want to simply reiterate the call for interdisciplinary research. That is only part of what it means to stay at the edge. Rather, we call on sociologists of religion to make interdisciplinarity and research on nontraditional religions, nontraditional religious spaces, and questions beyond their own national or cultural tradition their modus operandi.

Seeking unsettling perspectives and purposefully locating oneself on the edge of dominant empirical and analytic tendencies allows scholars to see how the frames, concepts, and theories they normally use change when seen from another direction or height. Such practices not only contribute to a revitalized, more provocative, and more nuanced sociology of religion but also give shape to a sociological study of religion permeated by and with other subdisciplines and disciplines that, similarly infused, are poised to pursue answers to the most pressing questions of a globalized world.

References

Geertz, Clifford. 1973. "Religion as a Cultural System." Pp. 87–125 in *The Interpretation of Cultures*. New York: Basic Books.

Gluck, Carol, and Anna Tsing. 2009. *Words in Motion*. Durham, NC: Duke University Press.

INDEX

Actor-Network Theory (ANT), 40n4
agency, 13, 49–50, 56, 61, 110
Alexander, Jeffrey, 45–7, 49, 51, 53–4
Altinordu, Ateş, 15, 79–83, 86, 288
ambiguity, 127–8
American civil religion, 118
American civil society, 144, 145
Ammerman, Nancy, 119, 144, 155n1, 201
anthropology, 26, 38–9
anti-semitism, 181, 184–5
Asad, Talal, 3–6, 29, 35, 47, 49–50, 69, 146, 287
asceticism, 73–4
Assemblage theory, 161
atheism, 147
autonomy. *See* cultural autonomy; religious autonomy
authority: obedience to, 72, 257, 258; political, 6, 73, 224; religious, 4, 8, 52, 70, 80, 83, 85–6, 138, 248, 253–4; secularization and, 23, 24, 28, 52, 139, 145

Bhaskar, Roy, 57
Belgian Catholic movement, the, 83, 85
belief, 59
Bellah, Robert, 155n2
belonging, 3, 131, 139, 140, 161, 195
Bender, Courtney, 15, 52, 54–5, 116–7, 201, 216, 288
Berger, Peter, 118, 131, 139
Bible, the, 95, 173
binaries, 51, 53
body, the, 103–4
borders, 128, 290, 291; national, 51, 159, 162, 280–1; religious, 10, 126, 160, 167–8
boundaries. *See* borders
bounded rationality, 168
Bourdieu, Pierre, 23–4, 30, 35–6, 37, 49, 260n3
Broad Program, the, 62–3
Buber, Martin, 182–196 passim

Buddhism: meditation and, 101–5, 112n2; research on, 7, 12–13, 37; and structure versus agency, 12–13

Cadge, Wendy, 9, 16, 118, 287, 290
Calvinism, *See* Protestant ethic
Canada, 215–234. *See also* Québec.
Caring Embrace of the Homeless and Poor (CE), 122–130
Casanova, Jose, 88
categorization, 161
Catholicism, 13, 102, 147, 159, 164, 169, 172; in Belgium, 83–6; in Germany, 79–83; in Mexico, 106; and migration, 153; and prayer, 106; organizational structure of, 85–6, 89n4. *See also* Christianity; Québec
causation, 50–1, 71, 120
Central American Sanctuary Movement, 263–4
Chakrabarty, Dipesh, 2–3, 48
Chaves, Mark, 50–1
Chong, Kelly H., 3, 16, 288
Christianity, 48, 71–2, 95, 119, 149, 263; research on, 7; Catholic/Protestant relations, 277. *See also* Catholicism; Protestant Christianity
Christo-centrism, 5–8, 29–33, 69–70, 92, 117, 131. *See also under* culture
Church-state relations, 72
civil religion, 155n2
civil society, 15, 137–8, 145, 148, 151–2. *See also under* Islam
collaboration, 124–130
collective action, 273, 276, 289
commitment, 128
community, 101, 120, 123–130, 195. *See also* imagined communities
comparative-historical analysis, 67–89; cross-regional, 74–86; cross-religious, 74–86; theory construction and, 86; Weber and, 88–9
competition. *See* religious pluralism